Political Ecology, Mountain Agriculture, and Knowledge in Honduras

Kees Jansen

THELA PUBLISHERS
AMSTERDAM 1998

Jansen, Kees

Political Ecology, Mountain Agriculture, and
Knowledge in Honduras / Kees Jansen. - Amsterdam :
Thela Publishers. - (Thela Latin America Series ; nr. 12)

ISBN 90-5538-030-X
NUGI 653/835

© Kees Jansen, 1998

Cover Design: Mirjam Bode

All rights reserved. Save exceptions stated by the law no part of this publication may be reproduced, stored in a
retrieval system of any nature, or transmitted in any form or by any means, electronic, mechanical, photocopying,
recording or otherwise, included a complete or partial transcription, without the prior written permission of the
publisher, application for which should be addressed to the publisher:
Thela Publishers, Prinseneiland 305, 1013 LP Amsterdam, the Netherlands.
Phone: +31 (0)20 625 54 29, Fax: +31 (0)20 620 33 95
E.mail: thesis@antenna.nl

Contents

List of Tables and Figures

Preface

Don Reducindo accompanied me on many walks to his fields or fields of other producers. He is a stocky, broad-shouldered man who enjoys talking with a particular vivid style, fond of using gestures as he speaks. I loved the beautiful mountain landscape, he did not. Hillsides are hard to work and yields are low. He took plenty of time to tell me about village life, agriculture, the past, and his personal feelings. Likewise, his wife Victoria was always ready to help or be interrogated. In their house maize, beans or tule on the mud floor were invariably put aside, and fowl, pigs, and children chased away to offer us their only chair or a bag of maize to sit on in order to carry on hours and hours of conversation. Victoria prepared the most tasty tortillas, tamales and home roasted coffee whenever we visited her. She was very keen on recalling family networks, household compositions, and historical facts. Both had strong opinions, they did not hesitate to relate their personal histories, were open for discussion and prepared to explore different explanations. They had a good feeling for gossip and the impulse to keep abreast of everything happening in the village, and they were optimistic about life and the future of humanity, although pessimistic about the principles of those in power. Victoria and Reducindo are natural storytellers and became very good friends. In contrast to many scientists they took a more open and critical attitude towards exploring the interweaving of personal perceptions of natural events, land struggles, agricultural practices, political power, crop choice, family ties, prices, and so on. It was normal for them to talk about the influence of the moon one minute, while the next recalling past conflicts about land. Combining such apparently different factors is often necessary to understand why producers do what they do. I hope that I do justice to their ideas and lives when I fit such talks in a single analysis which tries to unravel the socio-economic causes of environmental deterioration in mountain agriculture in Honduras.

Many other people of the village where we lived showed their hospitality and trust, and shared their life histories with us in similar ways. It is not possible to name them all but by thanking Reducindo and Victoria I hope to express my appreciation for all of them equally, each in a specific way. One person, however, needs to be mentioned by name; Hector Julio Dubón was not only a good friend but he also did an outstanding job as a self-trained research assistant. He was one of the people in the village who made me understand that analytical capacities have little to do with academic degrees.

I particularly wish to thank those who were there from the beginning, Esther Roquas and my friends from the CLS: Roland Brouwer, Jos Mooij, Peter Mollinga, and Marina Endeveld. Esther accompanied and guided me through the different places and stages and if I lost the route her intellectual support always brought me back to the right track. She put more love, care, and practical help into this project than I can ever return. Without the CLS team there would never have been a research proposal. Furthermore, organizing the Agrarian Questions congress with them was a good way to regularly distance myself from the particularities of rural Honduras in order to reflect on the subject with broader questions in mind.

The European Commission and the Netherlands Foundation for the Advancement of Tropical Studies (WOTRO) financed my work. The study was carried out as part of CERES (Research School for Resource Studies for Development). I thank my colleagues of the EU-project 'Farmer Strategies and Production Systems in Fragile Environments in Mountainous Areas of Latin America', especially David Preston for his confidence in me. I would also like to express my gratitude to David Gibbon and Norman Long, my research supervisors, who made it possible to develop and carry out my own research by creating an open academic environment and resisting the current tendency to revert to autocratically organized research groups.

I am deeply grateful to the directors and personnel of various institutions in Honduras who provided important support and sharing of their knowledge; first of all the Postgrado en Economía y Planificación del Desarrollo. People of the Secretaría de Recursos Naturales, INA, the Archivo Nacional, UNAH, Escuela Agrícola Panamericana (Zamorano), AHPROCAFE, BANADESA, and IHCAFE have also been very helpful. I owe much to the inspiring discussions with Rafael Del-Cid, Mario Posas, Hugo Noé Pino, the late Dario Montes, and Alcídez Hernández and hope that this ethnographic study may be useful for their work in the same way as I have benefited from their knowledge and help. Tatiana Lara is a great colleague, and her stay with Dagoberto Suazo in the Netherlands created a good ambience to write about and discuss Honduras, despite being far away from it. I look forward not only to continuing our friendship but also to accompanying each other on our intellectual journeys. Ana Lucia Restrepo's house is the best place to stay for an interchange of critical ideas and humorous reflection. I also give special thanks to Karla Lara, Orlando Lara, Josine van de Voort, and Erik Krikke for many reasons.

In the Netherlands I wish to thank my colleagues at the department of Sociology of Rural Development, Theo Jansen of the 'Sectorbureau', and Mark Sosef of the department of Plant Taxonomy. Gemma van der Haar, Mark Breusers, and Mary Omosa were considerate roommates and I hope our discussions will continue. I would like to express deep gratitude to all the people who have commented upon different drafts. Esther Roquas, David Gibbon, and Norman Long went through all the chapters. Bruno Benvenuti, Mark Breusers, Roland Brouwer, Gianluca Brunori, Andy Thorpe, and Sietze Vellema carefully read separate chapters. David Preston, Willemien Brooijmans, Tatiana Lara, Rafael Del-Cid, Sarah Howard, Jan de Groot, and Ted Benton provided useful comments on earlier papers, outlines, or short excerpts. Steve Coleman's 'Multiplicity of Approaches (The African Way of Knowing)' opened up my mind when I needed to generate new ideas. Fons Jansen, Samantha Punch, and Ann Long not only corrected my grammar and style but also made me write better English. Without all these people the book would have been different. Of course, all inaccuracies, logical errors, and stylistic confusions are faults of my own making.

Reducindo, Victoria, and Hector Julio will not read this book. Nevertheless, I hope that I have adequately realized their wish that this book should be written.

1

Environment and Agriculture in Honduras: the Study of Producer Strategies

Environmental Deterioration in Honduras: Uncertainty and Multiple Causes

The photograph shows a small landslide, no more than five metres wide with sharp cut edges. The photograph also shows signs of fire. A producer burnt the field in order to clear it. The phenomenon we see in this photograph is widespread in the mountains of Honduras. Similar photographs appear in booklets and newspaper articles which address the problem of environmental deterioration. Apparently it is considered as a good representation of the present environmental crisis in Honduran smallholder agriculture in mountainous areas.

The photograph does not show anybody working in this field. We only see materiality*.[1] Yet the picture is about humans and human relations. The field is a product of human action, of the men who worked in this field, who burnt it.[2] Hence, to improve our understanding of what we observe, we must make sense of the human behaviour behind agricultural practices. In spite of the increasing interest of social scientists in issues such as environmental management and natural resource use, there is little consensus about

1

the nature of the relations between humans and the materiality we see in this photograph. Likewise, rural people have diverse interpretations of what they observe and of the relations between land degradation and social context. A small selection of the opinions I recorded may reveal this.

· In the past the land here was fertile. Today the stones are born [appear on the surface], in the past there were no stones. The soils have been worked too much; nowadays our harvests are small.
· It is said on the radio that burning [to clear the field before sowing] washes the soil away. But the soil always washes away; even if one does not burn.
· We are ignorant because we continue to burn. We only use our head to put our hat on. We know that by not burning, the soil does not wash away. But we are lazy, we like to burn and to sow in clean soil.
· There is no forest-fallow any more, it is because there are too many people.
· This land will turn into a desert; we are too poor to put fertilizer into it, to give it strength.
· We are poor because we only have these mountains. In Holland they are rich because they have flat land.
· The soil washes into the river. The misery here prospers the wealth of the banana companies on the north coast [which possess land with alluvial soils].
· The people with cattle grabbed the land and converted the land into pastures; they put an end to the forest-fallows [guamiles]. They appropriated the valleys. We have to sow our maize on these rocky slopes.
· There is no longer ecology: the coffee producers like the money and when the coffee price raised to 1000 Lempira they started to fell the trees, even near the springs which give us drinking water. They say they have the title to the land, but land near springs cannot be titled. They spray [with biocides] and contaminate the water.
· Deforestation is forbidden. Today no-one respects the authorities any more, there is a lack of culture. The law exists only for the poor; the rich can do anything they want.
· The authorities do nothing. The military get permission to fell the trees. The poor cannot even fell one tree in their own fields. And those who are activists of a political party can burn the commons without repercussions. There is no authority any more.

In a nutshell these are several of the key issues that also appear in the public and academic debate about environmental deterioration. Crucial environmental issues mentioned are shortening fallow periods, burning, soil erosion, deforestation, and biocide use. In turn, symbols created in environmental debates filter through into peasant speech. Rural people, often illiterate, start using words such as 'ecology' and 'ecosystem' and give them their own interpretation.

These local views on environmental problems contain several types of explanation. The first two quotations show some disagreement about the direct causes. Is it agriculture (anthropogenic) or nature that causes soil erosion? Apparently there has been a landslide and this may be seen as a harmful form of soil erosion and bad for crop production. Is this landslide a result of agriculture, or would it have occurred even if the woodland had remained here? Do these types of landslide occur more frequently than in the past? Has soil erosion increased? What is the effect of soil erosion on productivity? These are questions about biophysical relations to which no answers exist (yet).

2

Several books and articles deal with environmental deterioration in Honduras, but despite large claims of environmental crisis little data is available about soil erosion and soil degradation (e.g. Leonard 1987, SECPLAN 1989a; Stonich 1993). Existing literature tends to generalize about the environmental crisis in mountain agriculture while using data taken from secondary sources (policy documents) which has in turn been taken from other sources.[3] In the existing literature, information about the biophysical processes at stake is generally fraught with uncertainty.[4] Nevertheless, the image of severe and dramatic land clearance and degradation in smallholder fields have enabled politicians, readers of newspapers, and journalists to draw the conclusion that bad land management is the central cause of environmental deterioration.[5] Proposals to prevent such malpractice focus on the education of the land manager in order to raise awareness of ecological responsibility, or they centre on restricting access of producers to forested land. Education proposals may go hand in hand with claims of ignorance and lack of education.

Several quotations challenge the idea of producers being irrational or uneducated. These argue that proper land use is limited because there are too many producers who are too poor. Demographic growth can be seen as the direct cause of environmental deterioration. But should such statements not be regarded as too deterministic? Does competition for land simply result from the growing amount of peasant producers or is this competition mediated by other socio-economic and cultural conditions (Turner & Meyer 1993)? Is it not competition between peasants and large landowners (Durham 1979)? Currently, poverty is replacing population growth as a more accepted candidate to stand as the main cause of resource degradation in smallholder agriculture, especially since this explanation was made popular by the Brundtland-report. It is this cause which links the environmental problem to development theory. 'Poverty reduces people's capacity to use resources in a sustainable matter; it intensifies pressure on the environment' (Brundtland 1987:49).[6] Unequal distribution is identified as a related phenomenon. Responses aim at stimulating economic growth with redistribution and fulfilling the basic needs of the poor.

The last four quotations refer to explanations which not only take into account the existence of poverty but also question the causes of poverty. Explanations are sought in the nature of the institutions related to property rights in land, type of technology, emerging commodity markets, systems of knowledge, and structures of authority and political clientelism. For each point, contrasting views exist in the public debate as well. Are the problems of access to land a result of unclear property rights, or is there a process of displacement whereby poor peasants are removed from their land and flee to the more erodible hillsides? Are the smallholders still producing with backward, traditional and harmful technologies, or have they adopted exogenous technologies which are detrimental to the local environment? Does the limited commercialization of smallholder products mean that profits are marginal and so no investment in resource conservation takes place, or is the capitalist penetration of the smallholder economy so great that traditional types of (environmental and social) reproduction cannot be sustained? Is the producers' knowledge of good land management inadequate (can one even label it as 'ignorance'?), or is farmer knowledge eroded by the introduction of a scientific rationality? Is environmental deterioration a result of actions of today's living individuals (which would imply that historical explanation is superfluous), or does the Honduran society have structural properties that stretch across time which explain present environmental deterioration (e.g. structures of authority, capitalist relations, cultural systems)?

This variety of explanations of environmental crisis is a problem. They may support very divergent and contradictory types of political projects. Some explanations of environmental crisis do not go further than correlating appearances, while others go deeper and point to underlying causes. To test the different explanations, they will be examined in this book within a case study. The case is a study of the social context and historical past of agriculture and environmental deterioration in the village of El Zapote.[7]

The main problem discussed in this book is how the social context and historical past of mountain agriculture in Honduras have shaped environmental deterioration. Is it possible to single out one main factor, one explanation, that determines land use and environmental change (the root cause), or do multiple factors shape environmental change? And if so, what type of analysis do we need to understand the interrelations between these factors?

This formulation of our main problem presents us with a second problem. Assessment of the different explanations is hampered by the uncertainty of the nature of the environmental crisis. Furthermore, different people perceive and define environmental deterioration in different ways; the varied interpretations listed above demonstrate this. These perceptions are not simply arbitrary constructions contesting each other in discursive struggles. I deliberately did not open with an eloquent citation but with an image of land degradation to indicate that perceptions are related to observations of materiality and human interaction with nature. This study intends to unravel some crucial aspects of the relations between knowledge and agricultural practices in mountain agriculture in Honduras.

Nature, population dynamics, and market development

The producer's quotations above include remarks about the state of the environment in the past, the number of people, and the expansion of pastures and coffee cultivation. To locate the case study within a process of historical change I shall provide some further information on these issues, before we turn to theory and methodology. The rugged landscape of El Zapote, a municipality in the Santa Bárbara district, is typical for most parts of Honduras. The mountainous areas alternate with small intermontane valley pockets. Several larger valleys near the north and south coast of Honduras provide fertile soils for mechanized and high-input agriculture, much of it in an entrepreneurial or cooperative form of organization. In the mountains we find mainly individual producers, most of whom are smallholders. Honduras remains, by and large, an agrarian country. Agriculture accounts for 28 per cent of the gross-domestic-product, 58 per cent of the population lives in rural areas, and 45 per cent of the economically active population is working in the agricultural sector.[8] Bananas and coffee alone made up 50 per cent of the total export value in 1992.[9]

Natural resources and population

When people from El Zapote recall oral histories of the occupation of the area by their ancestors they talk about the 'virgin' forest (*areas virgines*) which had to be cleared. Older villagers remark that in their youth one still felled large tracks of virgin forest to establish maize fields. Such histories have sometimes reinforced the idea that deforestation and consequently erosion is exclusively a product of man's recent activities and a result of the penetration of modern ideas about agriculture. There is some evidence, however, that this image of reclaiming 'virgin forest', of pristine nature gradually destroyed by the machetes of an increasing number of producers, needs reinterpretation.

The past has known periods of population growth and deforestation, and periods of abandonment and reafforestation. Archaeological research in the Copán region (Honduras) on the collapse of the Mayan culture provides one example. The collapse of the Mayan cultures in Guatemala and Honduras stemmed from problems of environmental degradation and population levels well above carrying capacity. Inappropriate agricultural production systems could not maintain the large populations that lived in the centres of these cultures (e.g. Paine & Freter 1996).[10]

After the Spaniards conquered Honduras, agriculture and the people themselves became a mixture, a hybridization of the old and the new continent.[11] The Spaniards searched for precious metals, but the mines did not meet expectations and the conquerors soon turned to cattle and agriculture in order to make a living. Newson (1992) studies the changes in the Indian population after the conquest, and concludes that this population declined from 800,000 people to 47,544 at the end of the seventeenth century. Besides factors such as military operations, slavery, diseases, malnutrition, and tribute, Newson outlines how changes in land distribution, cultivation patterns (new crops and cattle), trade, and hunting altered subsistence patterns, the Indian economy, and social and political structures. The disrupted social structures allied to the tendency of Spaniards to settle in Indian villages, notwithstanding royal prohibitions, stimulated the process of miscegenation. In most parts of Honduras this process was completed by the end of the eighteenth century. The number of 800,000 inhabitants was reached once more in the late 1920s (Molina 1975). With 800,000 people large parts of Honduras must have been changed as a result of swidden agriculture.

Cook (1909, 1921) argues that already at the beginning of this century, truly primary forests seemed not to exist in Central America. His studies of vegetation compositions show that most of them are secondary forests. Furthermore, in what are considered to be 'virgin forests' now (endangered by expansion of the agricultural frontier) Cook observes the presence of many relics of ancient agricultural occupations.[12] He suggests that in the past the Indians used large tracts of land for agriculture and collection of fuel wood. Cook maintains that processes of alternating denudations and reafforestations have evidently continued in Central America for long periods of time (1909:23).

It is difficult to assess whether deforestation and reafforestation also happened in El Zapote but it is not unlikely. The majority of the area is hillside, but some flat river terraces developed near the river Cárcamo and its junction with the river Malapa. The small valley pocket of Cárcamo probably had an open savanna vegetation at the time of conquest (cf. Johannessen 1959; see also Weeks and Black 1991). Here existed the location known as *Cálcamo* or *Cárcamo*.[13] Weeks et al. (1987) suggest that it was one of the focal settlements of the Care Lenca ethnic group. Populations of these focal settlements may have ranged between 1800 and 2900 people. In his effort to conquer Western Honduras Pedro de Alvarado passed through Cárcamo, and historical documents report that most of the 500 existing houses were destroyed, only 20 remaining (Chapman 1985).[14] If each house consisted of four to six people, the village could have had a total population of 2000-3000 people.[15] After this campaign of conquest Cárcamo was assigned as *repartimiento* to Juan de la Puebla by Pedro de Alvarado in 1539 (Alvarado 1908). The population must have fallen considerably in subsequent years as Contreras (1991:64) lists 15 tributaries assigned to the *encomendero* Alonso Polo in 1582, the Indians dispersing in order to escape Spanish control and the paying of tribute (Newson 1992). Tribute from the region of the Mercedarian mission of Tencoa, to which Cárcamo belonged, was maize and beans, cotton, wheat, chicken, honey, chile, liquidambar, fish, eggs, wax, handicrafts such as *petates** and labour services (*indios de servicios)* used to guard livestock (Black 1989:228). The Mercedarian friars did not succeed in accommodating the Indians into nucleated settlements in accordance with crown orders (Black 1989) and at the time of independence (1821), Cárcamo seems to have vanished as a village, since there is no reference made to it in later documents.[16] It took until the 1950s for the population in this area to grow again to 2500.

Villagers describe the vegetation of Cárcamo at the beginning of this century as 'virgin forests'. In that period the village took control of the land from a large landowner. The villagers cut the trees to cultivate maize. Part of the 'virgin forests' was old-growth secondary-forest as these *vegas* were cultivated several centuries earlier. However, it is very probable that part of it was much younger forest. The land belonged to the title of hacienda Maitúm and most of it has probably been used as pastures for its cattle. The presence of old tanks for processing indigo suggests that these plains were also used for agriculture. Other areas in the municipality must also have had uses in the past other than the 'virgin forests' encountered early this century. Villagers showed me the remains of cooking utensils of the past (a grindstone) in fields in the mountains. These higher areas had not been inhabited for as long as villagers could remember, and have recently been opened up for agriculture. Other areas in the village where one can still find forest vegetation, mostly because it is less suitable for agriculture, is also vegetation heavily influenced by human action. One hillside near the village had always been covered with pine according to villagers. Yet when a sawmill recently felled parts of this forest, the regrowth I observed was mainly oak and not pine, indicating that soil and rainfall may not be responsible for the former pure pine stand. It is possible that recurrent fires spreading uphill from the agricultural lands below this forest favoured the formation of forests of pine, being more resistant to fire (cf. Johannessen (1959) for other parts of Honduras).[17] Fires are more controlled in this area nowadays and regrowth of other species seems to get a chance. These indications support the supposition that the 'virgin forests' of modern history were not pristine nature but vegetation affected by former human action.

The lush secondary forest attracted people who were interested in opening up new 'frontier zones' in the nineteenth century. Most villagers are descendants of migrants who came from the south-east several generations ago.[18] They founded small hamlets in the area.[19] At present there is one dominant centre, the village with the municipal seat, six larger hamlets and several smaller hamlets.[20] El Zapote had 430 inhabitants in the census of 1887 (Vallejo 1888). The population of El Zapote then grew to 1228 in 1926, to 2465 in 1950, and to 5653 in 1988. The population growth was accompanied by increasing land pressure: the mean farm size reduced from 13.6 ha in 1952 to 8.2 ha in 1974, and to 4.0 ha in 1992 (DGECH 1954, 1978; SECPLAN 1994). This combination of population growth and pressure on the land is part of the context of degradation. No analysis, however, can consider them as single factors.

Economic development and state policy

Agricultural production in mountain areas include food grains, coffee, and cattle: three rather distinct forms of land use. A short review of economic policies may help to understand the different development paths. It took several decennia after independence from Spain before local *caudillos* transcended their rivalries and drew up programmes to enlarge linkages between the Honduran economy and the world market. The issuance of the first agro-export oriented modernization policies of the 1880s and the emergence of the banana enclaves are seen as crucial anchor points of modern agrarian change. The regime headed by Marco Aurelio Soto (1876-1883) developed a policy to promote agro-export production of coffee, sugar cane, chicle, indigo and cocoa. Export taxes were reduced, conditions were created for improving access to land for producers who initiated commercial plantations, tax exemptions on import of inputs were granted and, to improve labour availability, labourers of plantations were excluded from public work and military service obligations (Argueta 1975; Posas & Del-Cid 1981). As in the neighbouring countries, coffee was considered to become the main export product, but policies did not generate the intended effects. It is assumed that the topography, the difficult interregional communication, the scarcity of transport infrastructure, and the absence of sources of capital[21] and an active class of entrepreneurs made these policies fail (Posas & Del-Cid 1981; Williams 1994). Coffee did not gain the importance it achieved in the economies of El Salvador, Costa Rica and Guatemala (Williams 1994).[22] Soon afterwards, bananas captured all government attention.

Honduras is sometimes seen as the proto-type of a 'banana-republic'; by 1913 bananas accounted for 66 per cent of total exports (Lapper 1985). Subsequent Honduran governments were heavily influenced by the US-based enterprises United Fruit Company and the Standard Fruit Company who almost completely controlled banana production. Very favourable land concessions were provided to them in the northern plains. Notwithstanding resistance the banana companies succeeded in dominating Honduran politics at least until the 1970s (Argueta 1992; Barahona 1994; Brand 1972; Morris 1984; Murga Frassinetti

7

1978; Slutzky & Alonso 1980). During the land reform in the 1970s part of the land formerly in the hands of the companies was passed to cooperatives. Nevertheless, the banana companies retained control of all banana commercialization and soon started political and military intervention in the cooperatives (Posas 1992). Though Honduras certainly displayed features of a 'banana-republic', social life in the hinterlands was hardly defined by the bananas. In fact, coffee and cattle have been far more decisive for the local economies in the mountain areas. The dynamics of coffee, however, is much less researched than banana and cattle.

While the agro-export policies of the Soto administration did not immediately boost coffee production, it is evident that a steady expansion of coffee planting and exports was provided by small- and medium size producers during this century (Jansen 1993).[23] After World War II, coffee production continued to expand. In 1949 it was, after bananas, the most important export product.[24] Growth rates for coffee (8.6 per cent per year) were higher than for cattle for the period between 1945-1960 (Molina 1975:16-17). By 1993 92,528 producers (30 per cent of all Honduran producers) had coffee with a mean grove size of 1.9 hectare (calculated from SECPLAN 1994). Out of these coffee producers a class of rich peasants is emerging whose interests are represented by the producer organization AHPROCAFE*. These producers tend to dominate the local politics in many villages (Velasquez 1990, Jansen 1993).

Another important feature of agrarian change is the well researched expansion of cattle (Howard 1987, 1989; Kramer 1986; Williams 1986). Cattle and hides were a major product for Honduras during the nineteenth century (Guevara-Escudero 1983), being exported to Cuba, El Salvador and Guatemala. Cattle from Santa Bárbara also went to Belize and Yucatan (Squier 1856).[25] Booms and troughs in exports to Guatemala and El Salvador were related to the fluctuations in the indigo economy of these countries (Euraque 1992). In this century, loans from the World Bank, the United States Agency for International Development (USAID) and the Inter-American Development Bank (IADB) in the 1960s and 1970s made it possible to provide credit for pasture improvement, ranch building and breeding programmes.[26] Improved infrastructure saw the on-the-hoof trade replaced by motorized transport. The installation of packing plants provided access to the protected US market; demand for Honduran meat increased significantly and led to a 'beef bonanza' in the 1960s and 1970s (Williams 1986). The low value of land inspired the conversion of forest land into pastures (Howard 1987, 1989). The increase in cattle did not lead to more beef consumption by the rural poor (Kramer 1986:40).[27]

The changes in cattle and coffee are the most important for understanding the dynamics of villages such as El Zapote. The importance of other commercial crops, such as oil palm, pineapple, sugarcane, melon, and vegetables, is limited to specific regions. Coffee has been predominantly a smallholder crop up until now, but also a large part of the cattle was owned by smallholders in the nineteenth and first half of the twentieth century (Kramer 1986, Guevara-Escudero 1983) and sold to larger ranchers before exporting. Although some large cattle haciendas dominated certain regions (Southern Honduras, Olancho - see Wells (1857)- and Comayagua) many other hacienda owners were not rich and socio-

8

economically not very differentiated from the peasantry. Many of the cattle owning families in Santa Bárbara accumulated their property quite recently.

For a long time smallholder agriculture had to develop on its own. This does not mean that it remained dormant in a subsistence economy. The local economy has always been connected to (inter)national trade networks. El Zapote was on the *camino real* (royal path) from Santa Bárbara to Gracias, which was further connected to trade routes to Guatemala. Cattle was sold to traders as well as some other products (tobacco, pigs). In the first half of this century pig-fat (*manteca*), petates, coffee, beans, rice, legumes (potato) were important products that were exported from the village; coffee was the most important one. Besides these linkages to the wider economy there was also relative isolation of El Zapote. Famines passed without any outside help, for example in 1922 and 1954.[28] Most food consumed by villagers was produced locally. Little dynamic exchange of labour with the outside world took place. Modern transport infrastructure was lacking until 1968, when a dirt road was constructed.

The importance of villages such as El Zapote for the nation-state in the nineteenth and the first half of the twentieth century was due to revenues from taxes on spirits and tobacco, and from land sales, and to military conscription. The state hardly became directly involved with agricultural production, and producers were not heavily taxed. Sometimes the district governor tried to order the cultivation of certain crops, as in years of national food shortages, but such directives were in general defied.[29] Until well into this century state involvement in smallholder agriculture was limited to the issuance of agrarian laws regulating rights in land. After World War II, a developmentalist state evolved with new state agencies (with different degrees of autonomy) which had to modernize agriculture. The most important ones that had regional offices were, and still are, *Banco Nacional de Desarrollo Agrícola* (BANADESA*, formerly BANAFOM), the *Instituto Nacional Agraria* (INA*), the *Corporación Hondureña de Desarrollo Forestal* (COHDEFOR*), the *Instituto Hondureño del Café* (IHCAFE*), and the *Secretaría de Recursos Naturales* (SRN*).[30]

These agencies had to deal with conflicting objectives: promoting growth in production and productivity, meeting national demand for food grains, diversifying exports, incorporating the rural poor in economic development, and reconciling contradictory interests (e.g. with regard to access to land). BANADESA was important for channelling credit to cattle expansion; later it had to administer funds for the development of the cooperatives that emerged as a result of the land reform process. The peak of the land reform was in the 1970s when it dominated the agrarian as well as the political debate. INA's role in the land reform was complicated as it embodied legislative, executive and judicial powers into one process. COHDEFOR's role was not less complex or conflict generating. COHDEFOR had to manage all forestry resources in the country and had to exploit them in a profitable and sustainable way. Soon the population saw it as a repressive entity which, at the same time, was corrupted by sawmill capital, military economic power, and political clientelism.[31] IHCAFE was somewhat less involved in public conflicts as its main activity was a technical information service. In the 1980s the 'AID-IHCAFE project' was launched with credit and technical assistance for smallholders (mostly medium size producers) which to some extent contributed to coffee expansion. Assistance for food grains increased halfway through the 1980s and some activities (credit and technical assistance) with smallholders were developed by SRN within the integrated rural development programme PRODESBA*, but without much impact. All these undertakings reflect a strong belief in the possibilities of social management and planned intervention in a situation of complexity, conflict, uncertainty about the nature of social relations, lack of resources, failing control systems, political clientelism, and sharp inequality and social misery adding to fierce competition about resources. Most of them did not function as envisaged.[32]

This form of developmentalist state intervention confronted a deteriorating economic crisis in the 1980s and a changing international ideology on development which turned to neo-liberalism. Like many other Latin-American countries, Honduras contended with problems of foreign debt, stagnating economic growth, a deficit on the trade balance and fiscal deficits (Bulmer-Thomas 1987; Vinelli 1986). Various observers argue that there was very little alternative but to adjust, the main question being how (Noé Pino and Thorpe 1992; Thorpe 1995b; Walker et al. 1993). A major step in adjustment was taken by the Callejas administration (1990-1993) with the Agricultural Modernization Law (LMDSA*) as the legal framework for the agricultural sector passed in 1992. The basic thrust of this law is for the state to withdraw from direct intervention in production and commercialization only regulating it without disturbing the free flow of goods and capital (Honduras 1992). As a consequence of adjustment, input prices (fertilizers, pesticides) soared, while producer prices for grains also rose (Thorpe 1995b). In general agro-exports have been favoured. It is difficult to draw simple conclusions about the environmental effects of the LMDSA. An increase in input prices is welcomed by various authors because it would reduce environmentally unfriendly technologies (Farah 1994; Repetto 1989). Adjustment would also reverse the former anti-agrarian bias in policy, and thus favour rural economic development and limit migration to the cities as well as to frontier zones, which is seen as a positive environmental consequence (Walker et al. 1993). Others have taken an opposite position arguing that a further promotion to agro-export agriculture will have devastating environmental effects because of an increase in biocide use and the marginalization of smallholders (Murray & Hopping 1992; Stonich 1993).[33]

This short overview of economic development and state policy may help to rethink our approach. The opening picture refers to crop cultivation and land degradation on steep slopes. Subsequently, some crucial aspects of the natural environment, population and economic development have been outlined. The short survey of economic development and state policy has illustrated that producers' decisions about how to till the soil is not simply informed by agronomic features (slope, soil texture, crop characteristics), but is also shaped by economic processes, development of markets, and state intervention. Our basic task, however, is neither to describe the actions of the individual producer, nor to prove the existence of any form of macro-economic totality that determines producers' economic behaviour, but to explain social practices ordered across space and time. Producers do not respond simply, as individual actors, to their natural environment or to economic and

10

political imperatives. Instead, we need to explain institutionalized social practices. We will therefore have to answer questions such as how land distribution has taken place, thus not seeing land pressure as a natural outcome of population growth, but as a social process with various actors on the stage. The effects of different agrarian laws have to be understood. The specific participation of producers in coffee and/or cattle expansion and its influence on transforming the social relations of production have to be explored, and so on. In short, what I mean by the analysis of producer strategies for understanding the dynamics of land use and environmental deterioration is not a search for the individual motives of producers but a historical study of social institutions which structure producers' actions.

Perspectives on Agrarian Change and Environmental Deterioration

The problem of multiple causes of environmental deterioration may well be approached with a theoretical framework that locates land use in historically evolving political economic relations. This section will first discuss those theories which position the Latin American producer in structures of capital accumulation and related environmental consequences. These theories confront several shortcomings. Therefore, elements of (ecological) anthropology and recent advances in rural sociology will be discussed to refine these approaches.

The object of environmental social theory in Honduras

An analysis of environmental deterioration and agriculture in Honduras has to address the question whether the type of environmental problems are different from the environmental problems caused by industrial development which originally aroused world wide interest in the environment. Several authors (e.g. Martinez-Alier 1993; Redclift 1988) have emphasized that the environment plays a different role in different social systems. Environmental problems in industrialized Western society are rooted in an economy of abundant consumption and are problems of pollution and quality of life. In contrast, the problems of the poor in reproducing their resources for survival characterize environmental crisis in countries such as Honduras ('environmentalism of the poor'). A strict use of this distinction does not clarify environmental deterioration within Honduran agriculture. Some types of agriculture, especially the banana plantations and the cultivation of horticultural crops, are highly 'industrialized' and cause severe pollution problems through biocides, processing techniques, and exhaustion of soils (see Leonard 1987; Murray 1991). Such agriculture is generally not practised by the very poor and has been developed in fertile flood plains or mountain valleys. Industrialized agriculture is rare in the mountainous areas. This case study, nevertheless, captures both types of environmental problems: degradation of the resource base of the rural poor as well as 'industrialization' of agriculture (here meaning increased biocide use and other green revolution technologies) affecting the quality of people's life.

11

The distinction between the environmental consequences of industrialization and of environmentalism of the poor can be regarded as one element of another, more theoretical, discussion: whether it is industrialism or capitalism that lies at the root of the current environmental crisis (e.g. Goldblatt 1996). The extensive literature on agrarian structures in Latin America repeatedly shows that forms of land use are inextricably bound up with capital accumulation and capitalist relations of production.[34] The effects of industrialization on agriculture cannot be detached from the specific patterns of capitalist development.[35] Land use should be interpreted in the context of the distributional effects of the historical development of capitalism and the colonial and post-colonial state. This view is shared by recent studies on environmental deterioration in Latin America (e.g. Painter & Durham 1995; Redclift & Goodman 1991; Stonich 1993).

Painter associates the social causes of environmental destruction in Latin America with: (i) the impoverishment of smallholders, e.g. through loss of land; (ii) land degradation by wealthy and/or corporate interests whose activities treat land as a low-cost input instead of a costly resource that should be conserved; and (iii) policies which institutionalize unequal access to resources and result in the impoverishment of smallholders and the use of land on concessionary terms by the wealthy parties (Painter 1995:8-9). This points to a central issue for environmental social theory: the question of how producers are located in, and transform the relations of productions. This question links the ecological concerns about the eroding and degrading fields of Honduran smallholders to the theoretical field of peasant studies.

It is not sufficient to study the relations of production, the struggle about access to and use of natural resources and labour. *Agri-culture* entails the use of cultural frameworks: perceptions, knowledge, and interpretations.[36] Perceptions of environmental deterioration and what is considered to be 'good farming' and 'appropriate technology' are themselves contested. It seems important to identify how these perceptions are (not) related to the social organization of agricultural production.

Producers in the agrarian economy: subsumption and social differentiation

In literature on the social relations of production, the most simple theoretical conception of present day producers in Central America is based on a distinction between *campesino*, *agricultor*, and *plantation/hacienda*. The distinction between *agricultor* and *plantation* is mainly a question of scale. Both are modern enterprises based on wage labour, market oriented, and using industrially produced inputs such as machinery and biocides. In contrast, the *campesino* is a subsistence oriented smallholder whose main labour input is household labour and whose culture is shaped by this subsistence orientation. We have seen that change marks agrarian life in Honduras. Theoretically we need to come to grips with the way *campesinos* in villages like El Zapote become increasingly interconnected with markets that stretch larger distances, and how this is related to changes in the social relations of production and the environment. The concepts of subsumption and differentiation may be helpful to understand these changes.

12

Subsumption implies that the existing labour and production process ends up under the control of capital, although the process is not otherwise changed (Bennholdt-Thomsen 1980). Expanded subsumption can result from indebtedness, contract agriculture, or unequal exchange on the market. It includes the externalization of profitable parts of the production process, such as when these parts are no longer carried out by producers themselves, but by agro-industry (Ploeg 1990). Gudeman (1978) has described how the subsistence economy of *campesinos* in Panama becomes subsumed to the capitalist market whereby outsider control over rural production increases. This view suggests the existence of a pre-capitalist subsistence economy which articulates with a capitalist market economy. A problem of this distinction is that pre-capitalism may be interpreted as something static, traditional, and not affected by a market economy. It is a wrong model for the Honduran smallholders. Elements of their production process are a product of the extension of the world market via Spanish colonialism whereby people, agricultural technologies, crops, and animals were moved across the globe. Furthermore, peasants, even those who only cultivate maize and beans for household consumption, are currently part of a capitalist society: the society as a whole depends on commoditized labour and product markets, production depends on private property, state institutions separate economy and polity and are part of complex institutional alignments between activities of the state and those of private property.[37]

The environmental consequences of subsumption are assessed in different ways. The modernist view considers the incorporation of producers into the market as a way to get rid of the traditional *cultura de maíz* ('maize culture'), a swidden cultivation based on forest destruction and burning, which, because of the absence of a marketable product, cannot generate monetary resources to invest in soil conservation. A contrasting view considers subsumption as harmful to the environment. Producers end up in a treadmill of production: in order to survive they transform their former (potential) harmonic relation with nature, which evolved out of the need of a subsistence system to reproduce the resource base, into an exploitative relation against nature in order to make short term profits to survive in the market.

The subsumption thesis provides a one-sided representation at the level of exchange, thereby creating an image of superimposition of capitalist exchange relations on peasant forms of production. An alternative approach focuses on the different conditions of production and struggles about these conditions and uses therefore the concept of **social differentiation**. Social differentiation refers to the emergence of several classes out of a peasantry as different producer types develop with different relations to labour and capital. Social differentiation in Honduras is often seen as being more or less complete, that is that a middle size peasantry does not play an important role. The agrarian structure is mainly composed of two sectors: capitalist producers and semi-proletarian producers, the impoverished peasants (cf. Posas 1979; Stonich 1993).

In this two-sector model the agro-export economy and its particular mode of insertion in the world economy have been held responsible for a deepening of the ecological crisis in Central America (Brockett 1988; Carrière 1991; Faber 1992; Murray 1991; Williams 1986;

Weinberg 1991). The land question is given central importance in this body of literature. Due to commercial growers' encroachment on peasants' land, peasants have been pushed onto steeper hill sides which, once cultivated, are soon eroded by torrential rainfalls (Brockett 1988). The rapid conversion of forests and idle land into cotton fields in the Pacific lowlands of Central America since 1950 and the expansion of beef raising for export markets have contributed substantially to this expulsion process (Brockett 1988; DeWalt 1985a; Murray 1994; Weinberg 1991; Stonich 1989, 1992). This model builds upon the *latifundio-minifundio* distinction (dealt with in Chapter two) and is akin to the 'functional-dualism' model of the agrarian structure in Latin America which has been developed by de Janvry (1981) and which is still used as a major framework for explaining environmental deterioration.

In the functional dualism model, the coming into existence of a labour surplus in the countryside in Latin America after World War II reshaped social relations of production. A mass of semi-proletarianized peasantry appeared alongside a capitalist agricultural sector. A *functional dualism* has emerged between the latter, which produces commodities on the basis of hired semi-proletarian labour, and the peasant sector, which delivers that cheap labour. The sub-subsistence level of the wage is made possible by complementary subsistence production on the basis of family labour (de Janvry 1981:84, de Janvry et al. 1989). In exploring the contradictions of this functional dualism de Janvry points to the collapsing resource base controlled by peasants. Land accumulation by capitalist producers has relegated peasant agriculture to the least-fertile and most easily destroyed lands. The lack of adequate technological innovations results in low productivity (see Chapter three for comments on the underlying view of technology). The destruction of the few productive resources augments as poverty increases: the soil is mined and its fertility declines (de Janvry 1981:86-87).

Faber (1992, 1993) uses this model in order to explain environmental deterioration in Central America. According to Faber, the peasantry has responded to impoverishment by adopting survival strategies which result in widespread deterioration and the collapse of environmental conditions. His main argument is that 'disarticulated development in Central America not only *produced* severe ecological exploitation but *depended* on it for the subsidized reproduction of semiproletarian labor and generation of a larger mass of surplus value' (1992:27, italics by Faber). Exploitation of labour and exploitation of the environment are two different sides of the same coin, and reflect the class privileges and power of Central America's ruling oligarchies and agrarian bourgeoisie.

Rethinking Social Relations of Production

In Faber's approach environmental deterioration is functional for capital because it creates a cheap labour force. He implicitly excludes the possibility that environmental deterioration can be the *unintended* consequence of modernization, and not only of modernization induced by a ruling agrarian bourgeoisie but also by a wide range of other strata, amongst them being the middle peasantry.

14

In my view, this model has several weaknesses with regard (i) to explaining the more complex empirical diversity resulting from social differentiation; (ii) to the building of the model around one single root cause (one single structure) of environmental deterioration; and (iii) to the dynamics of technology development. I hope to elaborate this critique in Chapter seven after having presented the relevant data. Chapter five will present material that contradicts the empirical basis of a two sector model. Particularly a class of middle peasants with coffee is emerging. In general, there is more diversity in producer types than can be theorized with a functional dualism model. This suggests that we need a more sophisticated concept of social relations of production.

In order to rethink the concept of social relations of production, I shall draw on literature which investigates why the forms of production which do not rely on the typical capital-wage labour relation continue to exist. The literature on this theme is tremendously extensive and I shall only pick out some main points which are relevant for this book.[38] Firstly, agrarian production in Honduras cannot be analysed through the 'logic of the market' alone (cf. Friedmann 1980). This overlaps with a concern for the study of non-commodity relations in order to understand the dynamics of smallholder agriculture (Long et al. 1986). This means, for example, that I shall explore how producer strategies in El Zapote are shaped by patronage and kinship relations. Secondly, functionalist explanations of peasant production as 'cheap' labour power which 'subsidizes' capital accumulation have to be rejected (Bernstein 1988). This means, for example, that we have to investigate the political processes by which certain groups of producers become deprived of the means of production. Thirdly, peasant production, including the withdrawal from market production into production for household consumption, does not necessarily disappear in the course of capitalist development. A focus on subsistence production or farming with family labour only should not be explained in terms of a specific 'peasant mode of production' but through the particular conditions of insertion into a capitalist society (Gibbon & Neocosmos 1985). Fourthly, commoditization* or the deepening of commodity relations within the cycle of reproduction, for example of land, is crucial. A focus on the particular form in which commoditization takes place may help to explain, for example, the different effects of the expansion of cattle and the expansion of coffee (two processes which both are heavily influenced by external demand). Fifthly, the increased linkage between peasant producers and the market can be understood as specific combinations of subsumption and social differentiation. This study seeks to build upon these five points when exploring the case.

A remarkable feature of recent analysis is the attention given to *reproduction*. The organization of production is not simply functional to production. The concept of *reproduction* has gained central importance for investigating how land, labour and capital for household production and other forms of production become available for each new production cycle in processes of struggles and negotiations (e.g. Friedmann 1980, Lacroix 1981). Reproduction depends on wider economic and political processes as well as internal relations within the unit of production (e.g. gender division of labour, patterns of work organization). This double specification of the labour process opens up possibilities to

15

locate a critique of the 'politics of production' at the latter level (Burawoy 1985, van der Ploeg 1991, Thompson 1989). This observation has stimulated investigations into how knowledge, technology, and skills are subject to social struggles and thus highly political. The reproduction of the natural conditions of the labour process have been less specified in this body of literature. Benton (1989) has shown the deficiencies of social theory, in particular of Marxist theory, to incorporate conceptually the necessary reproduction of the natural conditions of production into a theory of the labour process.[39] This is reflected in the Marxist contributions to the peasant debate. For example, Bernstein (1979) recognizes that one of the pressures exerted on peasant households comes from the exhaustion of land and labour given the techniques of cultivation employed. But while the labour issue has received ample attention in many studies there has been little work done on the exhaustion of land. From Benton's critique one could conclude that more work is needed to study the 'politics of reproduction of the natural conditions of the labour process'.

I use in this book the concept of the relations of production to refer to the distribution of the means of production. The concept, however, also includes other aspects: how politics shapes this distribution, the struggles around technology (agricultural knowledge) and skills, and the relation between society and nature. This latter issue has been widely debated in ecological anthropology. Ecological anthropology studies the relations between population dynamics, social organization, culture of human populations and the environments in which they live (Orlove 1980:235). Concepts such as 'socionatural systems', 'ecological complex', 'social-ecological systems', 'co-evolution', 'human-use ecosystem' and 'techno-cultural complexes' are used to model relationships between biophysical environment, society (and individual), technology and culture.

Socionatural Systems and Nature-Society/Culture Dualism

The distinction made between nature and culture/society has led to a divide between natural and social sciences. Generally it is assumed that these sciences study different objects. At the same time the distinction is perceived as a problem. In understanding *agri-culture*, which consists of both the natural and the social, the call for an integrated approach has been reappearing time and again. Farming systems research (e.g. Shaner et al. 1982), human ecology and ecological anthropology (e.g. Bennett 1976) and philosophy of science (e.g. Latour 1987, Hengel 1987) all struggle with this issue. Recently, the issue has become an important topic in development theory dealing with environmental issues (e.g. Redclift 1987).

To summarize some of the most crucial issues I distinguish four ways of approaching the nature-society/culture distinction in theories on socionatural systems. For the sake of the argument I alternate between the terms society and culture and between environment and nature, although these abstractions refer to different matters.
· Nature and society, although different, are a same kind of entity, both are observable phenomena, and can be incorporated into one single model;
· Nature and society are essentially different; they need to be studied by very different sciences. Nature can by approached by positivist science, but for understanding society

and culture a hermeneutic approach is required in order to understand the specific human features of norms, values, meaning, cognitive abilities, and so on, which characterize human agency and the way agriculture is practised.

· Nature and society are both constructions of the human mind and in that sense not radically different; instead, thinking in dualisms is seen as a typical product of the Enlightment-philosophy and should be abandoned;

· Nature and society, although having things in common, have some definitive distinctive features. The way we think about both nature and society, however, always incorporates social elements as we use knowledge, models and metaphors.

Each of these views may lead to a specific way of studying agriculture and the factors causing environmental deterioration. The first view studies the various elements of socionatural systems with an identical positivist approach. This view is present in several recent system theories developed in agricultural science (e.g. Fresco and Westphal 1988) and linear programming models (e.g. Cárcamo et al. 1994; Valdés 1994). For example, the hierarchical system approach of Fresco and Westphal (1988; see also Fresco 1986 and Hart 1982a) takes the view that the difference between natural and social aspects of farm systems is an issue of defining sub-components of farm systems (cropping system, livestock system, farm household). The social is reduced to specific elements that are situated outside the physical and biological realm. All realms, however, are approached by the same kind of science. Primary determinants of farm systems are biophysical factors, although these systems can be substantially modified by socio-economic factors.

The second view can be regarded as a critique. Social systems are separated from natural systems and social processes cannot be explained by referring to non-social factors. For example, Spaargaren (1997:5) argues that sociologists should not rely on non-social factors for explaining the reproduction of social systems. Geertz (cited in Milton 1996:42) argues that it is difficult not to acknowledge the creative influence of environment on culture; 'the limiting influence of the environment is self-evident; agricultural activities *are* restricted by climate; technology *is* limited by whatever materials the environment provides'. But according to him environmental influences cannot account for cultural diversity 'in any but the most superficial sense'. The specific forms of agriculture are thus not shaped by environment but by people who construct their view of reality through social interaction (cf Berger and Luckmann 1967). Much of social science shares this view. Social science tends to rule out any non-human causality.[40]

There is a gradual shift from the second to the third view. Croll and Parkin (1992) consider environment-culture a false dichotomy and see persons and their changing environments as parts of each other. They argue that most peoples studied by anthropologists do ascribe agency to their environment and regard themselves as an inseparable part of it (what they call 'they are inscribed in each other'). Croll and Parkin tend to take over this analytical position. Subsequently, the non-human, the environment, becomes not more than a contested and negotiated entity between human beings (cf. p.35). In post-ecologist politics, the idea of a single nature which can be known is abolished (Blühdorn 1996). The proliferation of the metaphor 'Death of Nature' (Escobar 1996) stands for a deep disbelieve that we are able to understand (parts of) nature; we can only reinvent nature in discourse. This mode of thought is very influential at the moment; even Harvey (1993:15), who, I believe, voices the fourth view, slips into an ontological relativism at some points. In arguing that no values reside in nature (with which I agree) he states that what we see in the natural world comes to us via a 'framework of interpretation [which] is given in the metaphor rather than in the evidence'. The point here is that the metaphor seems to become *detached* entirely from any real world. In the third view knowledge of nature becomes impossible; it is a pure cultural product resulting from struggles around metaphors. If treated as discourses, the distinction between nature and society becomes blurred. Recent applications of theories on the social construction of the environment (Hannigan 1995) as well as actor-network theories sometimes tend to take a similar view (Latour 1994, Law 1992).

It is not very helpful for analytical reasons to regard it as unthinkable to distinguish between say the soil and the humans discussing how the soil should be worked. A bypass of the nature-culture dualism does not provide clues as to how existing forms of *agri-culture* should be explained and how natural science explanations could be incorporated into a theory of socionatural systems. With regard to current social science debates on the environmental crisis, the lack of serious integration of natural science explanations and the 'over-socialized' position of the second and third view is criticized (Benton 1994).[41] In developing a fourth view I rely on what is called 'critical realism' (Bhaskar 1989, Collier 1994, Sayer 1992). It takes on board some of the elements of each of the three other views but interprets them in a specific way.[42] In contrast to the first approach and similar to the second it attributes distinctive characteristics to society. 'Social structures, unlike natural structures, do not exist independently of the activities they govern' and 'they do not exist independently of the agents' conceptions of what they are doing in their activity' (Bhaskar 1989:79). Furthermore, social structures may be only relatively enduring. In contrast with the second and third view, it considers social structures as being real, existing independently from our knowledge about them. The properties of social structures differ from the properties of the individual. It shares with the third view the idea that our models and metaphors about nature (environmental deterioration) are social constructs which do not have a one-to-one relation to the 'real' world out there. These constructs are transitive objects which are subject to change, reversal, and contestation. Our study of nature and environmental deterioration produces transitive objects. Issues of knowledge struggles are therefore crucial for any analysis of environmental crisis. In contrast to the third view, however, it argues that rival theories have different transitive objects but they are not about different worlds (the intransitive object). In order to bridge the gap between 'nature' and 'societal' abstraction of agriculture we may investigate how specific social practices relate to their non-human condition. This approach does not limit itself to the analysis of perceptions and valuations.

The concepts environment and nature have been used above without making a distinction. Environment is something which *surrounds* a subject; in our case agricultural producers and villagers. The 'situatedness' of the producers and their needs have as much

18

to say about the definition of environment as the surrounding conditions themselves (Harvey 1993:2). Ingold (1992:44) states that 'nature is the reality *of* the physical world of neutral objects apparent only to the detached, indifferent observers, while environment is the reality *for* the world constituted in *relation* to the organism or person whose environment it is'. Environment is used, in this book, as something which is non-human and which may be both a product of human labour (e.g. secondary forest, tilled soil), an artifact, or something never touched before by humans (e.g. rain and wind) but which is a condition for practising agriculture. 'Nature' I shall use to refer to natural structures which may or may not be perceivable (e.g. gravity). Environment is always perceived by somebody, and more located at the level of appearances.

Causation of Change in Environment and Society

Contrasting views on causation and change complicate the discussion on society/culture - nature/environment relations. Two paramount issues of concern are whether environment determines culture or culture shapes environment, and whether individuals shape social structures or social structures shape individuals. The first question was addressed by ecological anthropology in the first half of this century; priority was given either to environment or culture and the type of causation was generally seen as unidirectional.[43] After World War II, systems theory, with its concept of feedback loops, and the concept of adaptation replaced unidirectional models. Concepts such as *succession, equilibrium,* and *dominance* were borrowed from ecological models of biology and cybernetics and applied to human societies without much revision. Cycles of energy and nutrients explained the performance of populations, and population pressure was emphasized as one of the principal mechanisms of change.[44] These approaches became criticized because of their functionalism.

Netting (1993) presents a latest view of functionalism (what he calls neo-functionalism). His analysis of environment-society relations is not at the level of society, but at the level of the individual producer. Netting considers the persistence of smallholder farming as a fine adaptation to ecology and demography. Smallholders have universal characteristics: they can mobilize labour at a relatively low cost, and in modern times of rising energy prices, smallholders are advantaged by their low level of energy use. Martinez-Alier (1995a) convincingly demonstrates that Netting regards the existence of smallholders as something natural, as effortless adaptation to ecology and demography. Against this, Martinez-Alier argues that the extensive debates on land reforms in Latin America have shown that the persistent existence of smallholders can only be understood in terms of social struggle.

This critique of Netting reflects the broader critique of functionalism in ecological anthropology. Notwithstanding the usefulness of identifying functional relations between environments and populations (and producing detailed descriptions of agricultural systems), ecological anthropology suffered from the 'functionalist fallacy': the observed functions do not explain the existence of the process, and may inhibit historical analysis of social structures and processes (cf. Barrett 1984:42). A functionalist analysis is unable to distinguish between functional alternatives because of its logical circularity and false attribution of purposiveness (Orlove 1980:244), and it cannot explain the conditions under which nature and human consciousness breaks out of the assumed homeostasis (Amanor 1994:19). Watts (1983:85-6) warns against taking society as an orderly adaptive structure, as a type of self-regulating, self-organizing living system isomorphic with nature itself, instead of being founded upon contradictory and conflicting relations.

In response to the limitations of structural-functionalism in ecological anthropology, Orlove (1980) observes the emergence of, what he calls, a 'processual ecological anthropology'. The various approaches falling under this umbrella are less preoccupied with the relation between whole cultures and environment but, instead, examine changes in individual and group activities. They focus on the mechanisms by which behaviour and external constraints influence each other. A focus on decision-making models, adaptive behaviour, actor strategies and human perception is thought to be useful to overcome nature-culture (Bennett 1976; Ingold 1986), ecology-economy (Mitchell 1991), and environment-culture (Croll & Parkin 1992) dualisms. Instead of treating populations as uniform, diversity and variability within them are examined (Orlove 1980:246).

Bennett's revision of ecological anthropology entails the development of a non-functionalist concept of adaptation to understand change in land use. Such a concept is not only about adaptation to the environment but includes adaptation to social relations as well as transitions of them; it enforces the important role of culture and choice; and also encompasses maladaptive behaviour. Adaptation, according to Bennett (1993:24-5), focuses on human actors who try to realize objectives, satisfy needs, or find peace while coping with present conditions.[45] Bennett seems to support to some extent the fourth view of nature-society distinction, but because of the centrality of adaptive strategies and the way he conceptualizes them I attribute the second view to him. He tends to underrate the importance of conditions imposed by social structures and overrate individual choice. Hence, although processual ecological anthropology has a dynamic concept of society-nature interaction, its explanatory power is limited because of the centrality of adaptation by individuals and individual choice. An unresolved issue in Bennett's work remains whether it is the adaptive behaviour of the individual or the social institutions that provoke change. This brings us to the relation between the individual and social structures.

The second point of debate can be formulated as follows: Is the way producers till the soil a consequence of their particular agency, a result of their knowledgeability and capability, or is it determined by economic and political structures, by the specific position of the producer in such structures? According to most current mainstream farm economics, the agricultural producer is a rational actor. This position can be seen as a response to the earlier view that the poor producer in the Third World is traditional and limited by the cultural framework in improving its agricultural methods. A basic tenet of much of the so-called 'Farming Systems Research' studies is that farmers operate *rationally* and work creatively with the context of culture, the availability of technologies, household needs, existing market relations, and biophysical production conditions.[46] Hence, farmers are not resistant to change, nor traditional, but just opting for the best choice under the given conditions. Farming systems research has a concept of rational choice wherein people want things and make the best choices. It can be questioned, however, whether it is useful to explain choices by referring to producers' rationality. To say that producers are rational does not explain *what* they do, but only at best (..) *how* they do it (cf. Bhaskar 1979:114-5). According to Bhaskar, 'rationality, purporting to explain everything, ends up explaining nothing. To explain a human action by reference to its rationality is like explaining some natural event by reference to its being caused'. He argues that such theories are incapable of explaining actual empirical episodes. Something similar occurs when actor-oriented approaches explain current events by *solely* referring to the fact that actors are capable and knowledgeable, missing the relational conception of actor, structure and transformation.

Bennett's theory of adaptation, and also Long and van der Ploeg's (1994) emphasis on knowledgeable and capable actors, can be interpreted in a way that it is not necessarily a defence of a 'farm logic' or 'rationalities of producer behaviour'. Bennet (1976) gives considerable attention to the structuring effects of institutions. His approach can be used to link present farm strategies to earlier processes that have caused multiple sets of (partly contradictory) relations, which could be termed structures.[47]

The problem is how to develop a concept of structure which evades the pitfalls of some structuralist schools of thought. Recently, it has been argued that many of the 1960s' and 1970s' models of underdevelopment cannot deal adequately with the variability of agricultural production because they lack a proper concept of human agency (see various contributions in Booth 1994, Schuurman 1996). It is put forward that many of these development theories pretend to uncover *the* determining structure and that this structure exists outside individual human action. One may question whether the critics of structuralism share to some extent the same view as their opponents, that is that structures are something exogenous, i.e. the outer world (system world) of politics, economics and the world market. The inner world (life world) of everyday experiences should then be understood separately from the outer world. In this view the idea of the existence of capitalism can be maintained as long as it is located in the outer world (up to the extent of a capitalism without capitalists) and not at the level of everyday life/actor/agency.[48]

If one, in contrast, starts from the idea of a stratified world, with multiple structures which operate in an open system, the explanation must necessarily refer to a multiplicity of causes (Collier 1994; Sayer 1992). This means that, for example, the structure of the soil, world market structures, kinship structures, and religious structures make it all possible that mechanisms may be triggered which lead to environmental degradation (or restoration) once a producer operates in these structures.[49] The multiplicity of causes are not just elements with which a producer has to cope, to which he or she develops adaptive strategies. It is not just the outer world. Producers operate in social structures, which means that every action, at the same time, reproduces and transforms these systems.

I have now defined how the concept of human agency will be used in this book: not as rational choice, simple adaptive behaviour, or rational farming, but as the inherent capacity to reproduce multiple social structures which offer resources as well as constraints to producers. This allows me to return to the issue of how the producer and groups of producers make use of, and are constrained by the environment. In working with the environment, the producer deals with natural structures: if a producer sows maize on a slope, gravity may cause soil runoff and gully erosion when it rains. These natural structures are not simple natural limits in my perspective. They are barriers that can be moved. Nevertheless, for any given organization of the agricultural production process only certain things can be altered. Others have to be taken as 'given' and adapted to as well as possible; there is for producers a relative non-manipulability of much of their environment (Benton 1992:61). By now, it must be clear that this does not mean that producers are simply the *object* of the laws of nature or the social structures, but active *subjects* transforming social structures, their selves, and nature, according to its typical powers (cf. Harvey 1993:28). Land use can be determined by a producer experimenting ingeniously with plants, soils, or with external technologies and generating alterations in agriculture. They can also be determined by the structuring effects of social structures, or by natural events and the powers of nature. In fact, determination will never be single.

Research methodology

It is increasingly recognized that land degradation is diverse in both form and impact on farming systems, suggesting that generalization is likely to be a problem (Biot et al. 1995:22). Nation-wide studies such as the environmental profiles (Campanella 1982, SECPLAN 1989a) present macro data plus summaries of local case studies. However, they do not integrate them nor provide a convincing account of how the observations in the cases relate to the presented macro data. Explanations of environmental change therefore tend to be cursory. Stonich (1993) has developed a methodological framework to overcome such shortcomings which coincides with the approach employed here. Following Blaikie and Brookfield (1987) she calls her approach 'Political Ecology'.[50] Stonich focuses on *interconnections* among the demographic, social, economic, and environmental aspects of development at different levels (from the individual to the international). She places rural people and the village at the convergence of local and world history. Like Blaikie (1985) she proposes a 'chain of explanation'. Such a framework starts with the producer (called land manager by Blaikie) and focuses upon the ways in which decisions over land use are taken. Subsequently the social relations between producers and other land users and others in the 'wider society' are traced (see also Schrader 1990). 'The state, and ultimately the world economy, are the last links in the chain' (Blaikie 1988:141). In this way Stonich is capable of demonstrating the close linkages between social processes and environmental deterioration in Southern Honduras.

Two issues within political ecology need clarification here: the role of the *locale* and of human agency. Only at a local level is it possible to understand thoroughly the ways in which humans, over a long period of time, in response to different social attitudes, changing economic aims, and evolving technical capacities reappraise the land about them, redefine its function and, by devising new ways to exploit it, restate the relationship with it (cf. Browning 1971:ix). A focus on a local or regional level does not necessarily lead to particularity; rather the approach of the *locale* constitutes an effort to identify how different constellations of class practices, production systems, farmer strategies, and political outcomes are produced and how, time and again, they shape agrarian change (Watts 1983, Giddens 1984). The premise of this work is that claims about macro level processes and macro theory can be tested through an in-depth study of socio-economic, technological and environmental change in one village. The development of coffee production in El Zapote, for example, reflects similar processes in large parts of Honduras. At several places I argue that the studies of agrarian structure and environmental change (e.g. Howard 1995, Stonich 1993, Williams 1986) have overlooked the importance of coffee for Honduras. Hence, the case study of El Zapote tries to tell not only the local history, but also what may happen elsewhere. With this example I do not intend to argue that generalization only refers to whether the phenomena observed are illustrative for larger scale processes. The specificities of El Zapote may be also as important.

One example of this is the *tule** and petate production which is accompanied by a whole set of local rules and resources peculiar to El Zapote. This does not make the case method less relevant: the study of tule production can be used to show how norms and actions with regard to land use, distribution of resources, the (effects of) technologies labour, etc., are manipulated. Therefore, tule production is seen as part of a 'series of connected events to show how individuals in a particular structure handle the choices with which they are faced' (cf. Velsen 1967). It places the actions of producers in their context. In a similar way, the specification of the particular historical context that shapes and shaped producer actions in El Zapote may provide a deeper understanding of change in agrarian Honduras. In line with Burawoy's approach it seeks generalization through reconstructing existing generalizations, that is, the reconstruction of existing theories on environmental degradation and agrarian change in Honduras. (Burawoy 1991:279).

The second issue is the focus on producer strategies. The methodological entry is to compare different producers and the way they manipulate the environment, interact with the technical-and-administrative-task-environment (TATE*), and develop, maintain, and alter social relations. I will look at how producers organize their production technically (use of technology; how they till the soil etc.) and socially (how they organize labour, how they get access to resources). This approach means that only those elements of cultural frameworks which are relevant to the actions under study will be discussed.

The focus on producer strategies incurs the risk of leaning towards a voluntarist interpretation of human agency. Stonich (1993) takes up the issue of human agency by examining the ways in which local actors mediate the impact of external forces. Although she intends to set aside the external-internal dualism of dependency theory, she does not succeed entirely. Human agency is mainly used for explaining individual responses and decision-making. As Long (1992a) has argued, effective agency requires organizing capacities and therefore a strategic generation and manipulation of networks of social actors. Agency is thus not a synonym for decision-making. 'Agency (..) is composed of social relations and can only become effective through them' (Long 1992a:23). Human agency in agriculture does not refer so much to producers who make decisions over how to work the land (to produce or to respond to external limitations), but to the capacity of an actor to process social experience and to devise alternative ways of work through manipulating and exploiting rules and resources (both part of social relations and of interaction with the environment). The issue of producer strategies is about making alliances with others to carry through tasks; it is about organization.

In my view, the foregoing implies a strong use of qualitative methods, not only in the study of social organization and perceptions, but also of technology. The following example illustrates that agronomy may benefit from an in-depth qualitative approach. During the research it was discovered that producers seem to underestimate the amount of land they have. The official *manzana** was much smaller (0.7 hectare) than what the producers in El Zapote call a *manzana*, which is considerably larger. I measured the *vara*, a stick which is stored in the village hall and used as reference for the local *vara*. A *manzana* consists of 100x100 *vara*. The different authorities assured me that a *vara* has to be 36 inches (*pulgada*) and indeed, the stick measured 36 inches. But a measurement of a *manzana* with this *vara* makes it 8361 m^2 instead of the official 0.7 hectare. Only after I read documents referring to English *pulgadas* as well as Spanish *pulgadas* I discovered that both were used in Honduras and probably some amalgam must have taken place in the past. The English *pulgada* is 2.5400 cm and the Spanish *pulgada* is 2.3194 cm. A *vara* of 36 Spanish *pulgadas* makes a *manzana* 6972 m^2. Hence the people maintain the rule of 36 *pulgadas* for one *vara*, although these 36 *pulgadas* are measured with modern tape measures using the international standard of English inches. Where census data of El Zapote are presented I have re-calculated them in order to give a better representation of the original situation.[51]

The combination of participant observation, oral history, and use of archives and secondary sources has generated the main body of data in this research. The many days I was in the field with producers were crucial for participant observation. Producers were eager for me to join them in their field and to tell me about their properties, work, life, struggles, and feelings.[52] In general conversations were unstructured in order to give the informant room to shape the conversation and define the themes. Furthermore, I visited all kinds of meetings such as elections of authorities or extension meetings with state officers, in order to study social gatherings, social interaction and interfaces with outsiders. The combination of the various methods requires the 'close acquaintance with individuals over a lengthy period of time and a knowledge of their personal histories and their networks of relationships' (Velsen 1967). My partner and I lived for two years in El Zapote over the period between August 1992 and January 1995.

Detailed life histories of five producers have been documented, with the history of access to land, use of technologies, labour, family networks, household formation, and patron-client relationships systematically mapped out. This material forms an integral part of some of the case studies presented in this book. These five producers are different in terms of their organization of production, wealth, literacy, record keeping, available time for interviewing, and intimacy in contact with the researcher. Consequently, different methods were adopted for each. For example, while only the accounting of one producer's farm inputs and outputs could be used, I developed a diary with another producer. He and his wife jointly filled in a daily record about the agricultural activities of the different household members.

Data from participant observation and oral histories have been combined with data collected from archival sources. Important sources have been the minutes of the municipality council (*actas municipales**) since the municipality was founded in 1917, recorded judgements of the authority in charge (*actuaciones de la policía*), the land titles (*títulos de tierra*) preserved in the municipality archive and in the National Archive of Honduras, tax records over several years, maps produced by the Cadastral Institute, and various documents found in different archives.

During the last phase of the field work, a survey was conducted. The rationale for this was that a survey would generate quantitative data on resource distribution, organization of production, use of technologies, linkages between activities, and household composition. The structured questionnaire was completed in a semi-structured, conversational, setting. The insights drawn from the first, more qualitative, phase, had made it clear that a conventional ('objectivist') approach of questionnaires would lead to a lower quality of information. The organization of production, aims, relationships, priorities, literacy, and confidence to contest hegemonic discourses varied so much that seemingly neutral formulation of questions were interpreted very differently by different producers. The conversational setting was used to obtain an answer as close to the intention of the question, e.g. by reformulation dependent on the context.[53] At the same time, this approach enabled me to understand *why* people tended to interpret the questions differently. The conversational setting meant that questions were not posed in a fixed order. In general, interviews took between thirty minutes and three hours, of which about thirty to forty-five minutes were devoted to the pre-selected questions and the rest of the time left for unstructured conversation. Answers were related to each other in the conversation and, thus checked, often readjusted. Quantitative data of eighty-three producers have been processed with a SPSS package. The sample was drawn with the help of a map of the village with all houses which had been made during the first part of the field work.

The methodology applied has several limitations. Firstly, the prime focus is not the household but the producer. A wide array of literature focuses on peasant household agricultural production (cf. Ellis 1993; Redclift and Whatmore 1990). The household is taken as a unit of analysis instead of the producer for explaining agricultural activity. This poses several problems. Producer behaviour is determined by household needs (such as food, shelter, and reproduction), but *not only* and *not necessarily* by them. Two producers of the same household or two producers of similar types of households may do very different things in the field, whereas two producers of very different types of households may practice agriculture in a similar way. The household can conceptually be separated from the production unit, as the household is principally interested in its consumption level and not the specific way in which production is undertaken. My focus on producer strategies does not deny the importance of household dynamics, but considers producer strategies as a more proper entrance for analysing land use.

One may object that a focus on producer strategies instead of household strategies makes the analysis less gender-sensitive. This study has not an a priori interest in household relations, but a study of producer strategies will encounter, as a matter of course, locally perceived gender differences in managing and working the land.[54] While taking the sample for the survey, it became clear that only in two of the eighty-three cases a woman feels she is a producer who takes the major decisions about how the land is worked. This pattern has also been found in other areas in a study by Stürzinger and Bustamante (1997). In those few cases that women manage the agricultural activities, they hire men to do the manual labour. Women rarely work in the field in El Zapote.[55] Many more women own pieces of land, which they see as a source of rent, a saving for the future, or a means to control children or husbands who may receive it later as an inheritance. Nevertheless, in most cases for them it is not an object of labour in a production process they control. When issues of land tenure (Chapter two) and labour (Chapter five) are discussed more attention will be paid to gender specific issues than in the chapters about technology, land use, and environmental knowledge.[56] When my choice of words refers to male individuals this is done deliberately, reflecting that such an individual will in general be a male, not excluding that in exceptional cases it may be a female. Land owners may be male or female, workers are predominantly male, poor producers are generally male, and labour employing producers may be male or female.

A second limitation is the focus on mountainous agriculture bypasses what happens in the more 'advanced' industrialized sectors of agriculture and agri-business located in the valleys. Hence, the conclusions of this study do not concern the entire Honduran agricultural sector.

Thirdly, the issue of frontier agriculture (and migration) is considered crucial in many studies on environmental degradation in Central America. El Zapote is no frontier area. The case study of El Zapote could nevertheless contribute to present research in frontier areas because it shows how frontier areas of a century ago have developed. Moreover, it considers the need for intervention in no-frontier regions facing a growing resource crisis.

Structure of the book

The central argument of this book is that land degradation through present agricultural practices is not simply an effect of poverty, inconsiderate acting or a direct consequence of a modernization process which is orchestrated and imposed upon the Honduran peasantry by external capitalist development. Instead, the social causation of environmental change in mountainous areas of Honduras should be understood in terms of a complex mixture of local patterns of access to resources, forms of state intervention, the heterogeneous paths of technological change and knowledge generation, divisions of labour, and the specific interactions of emerging commodity markets and the organization of production.

Chapter two focuses on issues of land tenure and property rights. It compares local histories of land distribution in El Zapote with widely used models of the *latifundio-minifundio* complex and the colonial legacy of the large landholding. Subsequently, it explores how local rules and cultural notions, local government and state laws, and state interventions through land reform and land titling projects, mediate the relation between people and the land. Conclusions deal with the multiple land histories which explain the complexity of conflicts, and with the many factors shaping the meaning villagers attribute to the value of land.

Chapter three explores technological changes in crop production and cattle husbandry and compares the findings in El Zapote with recent studies dealing with heterogeneity and diversity in agriculture, thus criticizing approaches which maintain a duality of traditional and modern agricultural technology. It stresses the recognition of the multiplicity of factors causing technological change.

This exploration of technological change serves as a starting point for the discussion of how different environmental problems are perceived by different actors. Chapter four identifies different perspectives on the fallow crisis, the use of fire to clear fields, vegetation and climatic change, and the use of new agro-chemicals. It deals with the paradox that agronomy cannot encompass the many factors involved in environmental deterioration, but that an alternative strategy of validating producers' environmental perceptions cannot provide a coherent theory of the causes of environmental deterioration as well.

In Chapters two, three, and four, it will be shown that environmental behaviour and perceptions about environmental change relate to access to, and distribution of, resources. Chapter five gives further consideration to the different aspects of the social relations of production in El Zapote, in order to understand the processes of social differentiation.

Chapter six broadens the issue of social differentiation with a discussion of local agricultural knowledge. The argument is put forward that we need an understanding of both the practical character of knowledge, (that local knowledge generation responds to environment and social context), and its discursive character. Knowledge is not only embedded in narratives on the epistemological level, but also in concrete natural environments and social relations. An important conclusion is that current 'local knowledge approaches' overestimate the potential of local knowledge for environmental conservation or restoration.

The concluding chapter starts by commenting on various explanations of environmental deterioration in Honduran mountain agriculture. Using the case study of El Zapote it presents an alternative explanation with the main argument that a linear relation between the distribution of the means of production and labour relations on the one hand, and use of the environment on the other, cannot be justified, but that, nevertheless, an inquiry into changing patterns of social differentiation may provide insight into important mechanisms of human interaction with nature. The final section challenges theoretical (epistemological and ontological) confusions about social and biophysical causation of environmental deterioration in environmental social science.

2

Fencing in Value: Land and Social Institutions

The latifundio-minifundio model in Honduras

Recent studies on environmental deterioration in Central America attribute a pivotal role to unequal access to land in explaining social processes behind degradation (Faber 1993; Painter 1995; Stonich 1993; Weinberg 1991). Many studies on Honduran land issues highlight the existence of a dual agrarian structure composed of a *latifundio* (large estate) and *minifundio*, in which there is historical continuity from the Spanish *encomienda* to the post-colonial land-based elite (see Benavides 1984; CONSUPLANE n.d.; Robleda 1982; Ruben 1989; SRN n.d.). According to this view, the control of state power makes the continuous reproduction of the latifundio possible. This control was exercised by a land-based elite, who promulgated laws in their favour (e.g. the liberal reforms of the nineteenth century, CONSUPLANE n.d.), or by the foreign banana multinationals (Barahona 1994; Del-Cid 1977; Posas & Del-Cid 1981). Others have pointed at the influence of agro-export producers in general (Brockett 1988; Williams 1986), or more specifically at the expansion of cattle (DeWalt 1985a, 1985b; Howard 1987). Stokes (1947), however, remarks that Honduras had rather progressive land laws which favoured peasant access to land. Boyer (1982:113) argues that access to land has never presented a problem to peasants until recently. Kramer observes that in Western Honduras few large estates existed before 1930 (1986:38). Nevertheless, large haciendas dominated certain regions: for example, large tracts of the Olancho district were controlled by the Zelaya family in the late nineteenth century (Wells 1982). These contrasting observations suggest that we have to identify more specific histories of different regions instead of *a priori* taking for granted the latifundio-minifundio model. The current inequality is not enough justification for this model. I shall show that even within one municipality the study of more specific histories may be useful to understand people's relation to the land and the concrete struggles about land.

The environmental debate mainly examines two elements of the latifundio. Firstly, the transformation process of the classical *hacienda* into more commercial estates which expelled tenants from hacienda lands and pushed them onto erodible hillsides (Williams 1986). Secondly, the appropriation of national and *ejido** land by expanding cattle ranchers, thereby reducing the amount of land available to smallholders (DeWalt 1983, 1985b). This chapter shows that the first process is not a phenomenon that characterizes agrarian transformation in entire Honduras. Furthermore, it argues that the second view may

28

describe what occurred in many parts of Honduras, including El Zapote, but it overlooks many other crucial processes. We need to explore more extensively the competition and differentiation among peasants, especially on lands not influenced by the large estate. We also need to analyse the precise role of social institutions, such as the changing forms of mediation by central and local government, the complex set of local rules about access to land, and inheritance patterns. Finally, we need to identify the meaning people give to land. In the literature, land is mostly discussed in terms of space. I shall argue that another concept of value should be developed: producers value land not only in terms of space but in terms of several other factors which will be explored below.

Early titling: liberal development or peasant production?

The earliest substantial data about access to land in El Zapote appear in the titles issued by the central state (Table 2.1 and Figure 2.1). Sale from state lands increased during the second half of the eighteenth century, probably as a result of expanding demand. The procedure to obtain a land title started with the application and the measurement of the land by an authorized land surveyor. A verification was carried out to control whether other owners had claims on the land. The measurement had to verify which parts were suited for agriculture or cattle, and the different parts were assigned a corresponding price (higher for agriculture, lower for cattle). Most titles mention whether extractable construction wood of high value was present. The survey had to be paid for by the applicants and this was a burden for poor people (cf. CONSUPLANE n.d.). Subsequently the sale of land was announced three times in a newspaper and the land was sold to the applicant if nobody made a higher bid. The whole procedure appears in the titles and it shows that the intricate titling process could take many years.

When land was adjudicated as *ejido*[*] it was gratis. Villages had the right to a certain amount of ejido land which their inhabitants could use for agriculture. The amount varied over time. In the nineteenth century municipalities applied for an ejido in response to opportunities offered by the then issued laws.[1] This shows that the ejido is not a remnant of the colonial period, nor of an indigenous communal system to organize land use. It is a mistake to view the ejido as communal land that is worked collectively. The municipality controlled the ejido land and gave individual villagers rights to use parts (concessions). From the point of view of the villagers the municipality had to defend the area against possible intruders from the outside and had to distribute the land according to individual needs. The central state sometimes issued regulations that concessions had to be distributed in such a way that efficient productive use would be promoted (e.g. taxes on idle land or obligations to plant coffee), but in El Zapote these were not implemented by the local government.

Table 2.1 Land titles of interest to the villagers of El Zapote.

name	area	year	price	status
A Nejapa	18 cab.	1865 (1863)	258.90	private (*comunero-municipality*)
B Teocintal	9 cab. + 176 cc	1887 (1884)	free as ejido (initially price was fixed at 270.625)	ejido
C Agua Caliente y Playada (Malapón)	726 ha	1898 (1889)	free as ejido (but 36.33 paid as tax)	ejido
D Juniapal	433.65 ha	1915 (1894)	800.48	private
E Cuchillo de los Yoreños	7 cab. + 199 cc	1887 (1883)	300 (by auction, initially price was fixed at 203.65)	private (*comuneros*)
F Cárcamo-Maitún	14.5 cab. (first 3.5 cab. issued in 1741)	1741-1803	unknown	private (only a part in El Zapote)

Sources: Titles in municipality archives, archives of INA and *Archivo Nacional de Honduras*.
Note: Area in cab.= *caballerías*[*] (1 cab. = 45 ha) and cc.=*cuerdas cuadradas* or in ha.= hectares. Prices in pesos.
Year = year of issuance (between brackets the year of first application). Cárcamo in the text refers to the part of Cárcamo-Maitún (F) which Figure 2.1 shows.[2]

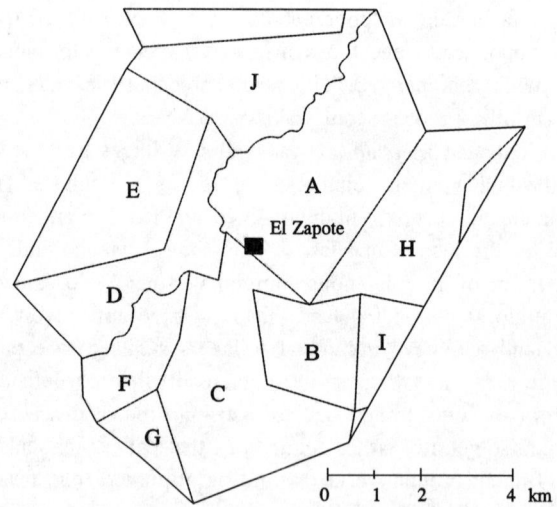

Figure 2.1 Map of land titles in El Zapote

30

The following histories of titles reveals how land histories can differ and how present struggles and modes of land use may be influenced by the social history of a particular piece of land.

Nejapa: private but communal

The land of Nejapa was claimed both by the villagers (*'vecinos de la reducción del Zapote'*) and an individual from outside in 1863. The villagers argued that if land was sold to this man they would have to migrate (*despoblando*) and 'leave the place destroyed losing all the houses and other possessions'. The villagers claimed that they and their ancestors had opened up the virgin forests to reclaim the land and thus legitimately had the land rights (*derecho*). Because of these rights, the villagers believed the president of Honduras should acknowledge them as the first beneficiaries to receive a title. They requested that the land to be donated to them as an ejido, or, if that was not possible, to sell them the land. After measurement in 1884, the villagers bought the land for 258.90 pesos. Notwithstanding their own classification of being poor *proletarios* (a legal category) they were unable to get the land as ejido. Half of the requested sum was paid in cash and half in tobacco. The title was issued in December 1865. A list names forty-nine villagers (including five women) who had paid their contribution and had thus obtained rights to use land in Nejapa.

This case illustrates that, in response to external processes (an outsider who intended to buy this large tract of land), the villagers had to redefine their concept of rights. Initially rights were given meaning in terms of *derecho*, which signified that previous labour invested in land cultivation determined the rights to the land and that labour to a certain extent was indistinguishable from land. Now land was given meaning with a concept of commodity (cf. Nugent 1993): the land had to be bought from the state. However, the buyers did not consider the land as private property (in the capitalist sense), but arranged for the municipality to control it in a way similar to that which would be applied to the ejidos decades later.

A century later, in the 1980s, the municipality lost control of Nejapa with the land titling project (see below). Although it was private property in the legal sense, the central state responded to the local interpretation of the relationship between villager and the land by considering it this time as ejidal. Thus, it was registered as a property of the state and fell under the land titling regime. The fact that the municipality had saved the title document and had provided concessions in Nejapa may have provoked the state's decision.[3]

Yoro: private but not clearly registered ownership

The title of 'El Cuchillo de los Yoreños' was bought from the state by four brothers and was thus also a 'communal' title from the beginning, that is a private title with various owners. At present, one century later, it is divided between a large group of heirs of the original title holders, most of them living in the hamlet 'Nueva York'.[4] Who owns what land is far from clear. Several people have a private document in which they are entitled with rights, but many of these documents indicate an amount of land (e.g. ¼ *caballería*) and do not specify the exact location of it. Others have inherited land but have no documents at all. The current situation is one of continuing conflicts, many with violence and very often between kin. These conflicting situations about land within large private titles remain outside the scope of the land titling project, which limits itself to national and ejidal lands. The conflicts on private land are certainly no less than on ejido land.

The ejidos Teocintal and Agua Caliente y Playada: complex measurements

Applications for ejido status could take a long time. As stated in the title documents of Teocintal, the villagers expressed in 1884 that they needed Teocintal for cattle and agriculture. Cadastral measurements began in July and the title could have been purchased in 1885. The villagers however did not pay and applied to receive it as ejidal land (free of any further costs). They finally received it as ejido in 1887.

The application for Agua Caliente y Playada to become an ejido was much more complicated. In 1889, the village applied for other ejidal land and measurements started in 1890 and after some problems were finished in 1891. There were confusions about the borders with 'Cárcamo' (privately owned) and with land south of the area, whose ejido owners (the village La Iguala) considered part of the land as theirs. Neither of these parties could, however, produce a title. Earlier measurements had been undertaken, but these had not resulted in the issuing of a title. A second survey was further complicated because some of the earlier border markers had been moved and new ones had been added. The survey team had to pass through dense forests and it took them three days to measure the land. When another surveyor checked the measurements, errors were discovered. But then the first land surveyor, who was supposed to correct his errors, had died in the meanwhile. Subsequently all the documentation was sent back to the Ministry of Finance. The villagers, however, kept insisting and argued that they only asked for half of the area measured. The other half was part of an ejido of the neighbouring village. A new surveyor came to draw the border between the two villages in 1896, and the costs of this were shared. The title was finally issued in 1898.

This case shows how earlier errors in measurement often generate problems years later. The amount of land and its inaccessibility because of dense vegetation on a rugged landscape added to many of these errors. Errors of the surveyors lead to new costs for the applicants who had to pay for the re-measurements. Small, seemingly negligible errors in the past (e.g. a border followed a meandering river while on the map in the title a straight line was drawn) could engender fierce disputes decades later.

Cárcamo and Juniapal: local government versus emerging landed elite

The associated history of Cárcamo (F) and Juniapal (G) illustrates the contest among the central state, private landowners, the municipality and villagers. People's memories often mingle the histories of both pieces of land, which is not strange if we consider their histories.

Various titles preserved in the National Archives (*Archivo Nacional de Honduras*) bear the name Cárcamo. Some had been issued in the seventeenth and eighteenth centuries and are contiguous titles within a much larger area. The many different measurements of Cárcamo and Juniapal (e.g. in 1803, 1898, 1905, 1953-4, 1955-6, 1965) express the battles between heirs of the original buyers and third persons (and their heirs) who had bought parcels. It is often not clear who is the legitimate heir of the different parts of land which were divided by former owners through sales and inheritance, practices which in many cases were badly registered, if at all.

In 1934, a certain Colonel Vicente Moreno offered Juniapal and a part of Cárcamo (two caballería) for sale. The municipality was very interested and tried, without success, to persuade President Carías to give them a loan of 5000 L. In December 1934 all villagers were obliged to pay a contribution to buy the Cárcamo part for 360 L, and the village received the *escritura pública** from Moreno. The land was never measured and the borders remained unclear. The *actas municipales** regulated its use as village common land. This means that it was forbidden to fence land permanently and to plant perennials. In contrast to the gist of the regulation, this land was divided and distributed by the authorities and considered as property by its owners within a couple of years. The only discussion that continued was whether it was allowed to sell parcels to people who were not living in El Zapote. Some villagers started to sell land.

The municipality also played an active role in getting hold of Juniapal. The first petition for Juniapal came from people of the hamlet of Cablotal, south of El Zapote, in 1894.[5] In 1898 they applied for an ejido. In their petition they argued that a land surveyor, in re-measuring Cárcamo, had located their hamlet within a private property, and that the 200 inhabitants of Cablotal feared they would have to leave their houses. During the ensuing procedure different surveyors disputed whether Juniapal was national land or not. Finally, in 1915, the villagers managed to obtain the title, paying half of it in cash and the other half with credit documents (*documentos de crédito*). What transpired afterwards is not documented, but oral histories of informants help to reconstruct what most likely happened. The inhabitants of Cablotal could not collect sufficient money to pay for the title and borrowed money from Vicente Moreno (or his father Claudio Moreno who may have passed his property on to Vicente Moreno afterwards). The villagers of Cablotal were not among the poorest, they had quite a lot of cattle, but nevertheless they could not pay for the title. Subsequently, Moreno claimed the land and forced the people to leave their hamlet of Cablotal, which was located within the title. Most of them moved to a newly founded hamlet four kilometres to the south. Several people were jailed during the conflict with Moreno. Moreno, who did not live in El Zapote, appointed a supervisor (*mayordomo)* who prohibited agriculture in Juniapal, though cattle could roam freely.

In 1934 or 1935 Juniapal was transferred to the central state, because Moreno, a state official at that time, had debts with the state which he cancelled by handing over the land title. In 1935 the municipality tried to obtain Juniapal as an ejido, and repeated efforts were made in subsequent years, but all without success. In 1945 the issue was raised again, but now the municipality wanted to buy the land; it borrowed 150 L from Alfredo Luna, a rich merchant living in the village, to send the mayor to Tegucigalpa in February 1946. Their argument that the population had grown and that therefore more land was needed, was used recurrently in order to convince the central state. Another argument was that their other lands were infertile (*esteril*). Nevertheless, the state did not respond. In 1949 a new mission returned from the capital Tegucigalpa: they had discovered that the land was leased by the state to Alfredo Luna.[6] Alfredo had occupied several key positions within the municipality (mayor and *síndico*) between 1932 and 1948, and had travelled as representative of the municipality to Tegucigalpa and Gracias in order to attain Juniapal for the village. He used those journeys to become designated personally as *arrendatario*, renter of state land, of Juniapal. Thus, with municipal funds and using his position as mayor he had established control over this land.[7]

To arouse opposition against this new competitor, the municipality objected to the measurements made by the land surveyor in favour of Alfredo Luna. In 1950, another surveyor came from Tegucigalpa to divide the land amongst the opponents, but he arrived without notifying the authorities. Hence the municipality protested against his division, and this time their protest was successful: the municipality was allowed to apply for an ejido of 471 hectares and regulations were formulated about land use. Finally in 1952 permission was obtained to cultivate the land in the northern part of Juniapal which was supposed to be allocated to the village, although a title had not yet been issued.[8] Since then this land, called 'El Salto' or the 'Zona', has been used as village common land.

Nevertheless, the division between the municipality and Alfredo Luna remained a source of dispute. In 1955 Alfredo Luna, who had not paid the state for his lease, claimed all the land of Juniapal, including the Zona. In turn the municipality tried again to obtain the whole of Juniapal including land which was controlled by Alfredo. Village authorities visited President Julio Lozano Díaz in 1955. In the same year Alfredo hired a surveyor who measured Cárcamo and included that part of Juniapal that was formerly leased to Alfredo in Alfredo's Cárcamo title. He did the same with a part of the ejido of Agua Caliente y Playada and with several parcels which he had bought from other land owners in Cárcamo. Alfredo's Cárcamo title unified all this land and totalled 794 hectares. This is an example of a practice for which land surveyors are more generally blamed (CONSU-PLANE n.d.:51-52): the inclusion of national land in private titles. According to the villagers Alfredo 'ended up keeping the best part of the land'.

Notwithstanding official measurements, struggles between Alfredo Luna and the authorities of the village continued. For example, in 1960 the assistance of two congress members was sought, and in 1963 the municipality again tried to receive Juniapal as an ejido. In the course of these struggles, the title documents that give the municipality rights to Juniapal and Cárcamo disappeared. There is some evidence that Alfredo manipulated the mayor between 1955 and 1957 and procured the title of Juniapal (it is suggested that he bribed the mayor with ninety pesos). When Eduardo Ramírez was mayor (1965-1967)

Alfredo got his hands on other documents, probably the *escritura pública* of Cárcamo.[9] It is not clear whether Alfredo received the title or whether it was burnt.

This brings us to the question of why land concentration, such as that undertaken by don Alfredo, was not opposed more fiercely by the villagers? When and why was the municipality effective in defending and increasing access to land for the villagers, and when were they not successful? To answer these questions it is helpful to recall an event that took place in the turbulent year of 1965. A conflict arose when a certain Pedro Iglesias from Gracias announced that he would come to El Zapote to enclose a part of Cárcamo (which in fact was Juniapal). His wife supposedly had documents which certified her ownership. People recall that many people left the village armed with machetes to bar (successfully) the surveyor, who was contracted by Iglesias, from carrying out his survey. Villagers had already been cultivating that land for some fifteen years.

Such a unified and violent opposition was never organized against Alfredo Luna. The villagers and Alfredo were not necessarily on opposite sides, and at one moment, when Pedro Iglesias made his claims, they even fought together against a common adversary. Different relationships linked Alfredo closely to the other villagers through a local network of personal relations. The most important authority in the battle with Alfredo Luna was Mayor Pedro Portillo. He extended the struggle up to the level of the central state authorities in Tegucigalpa, but in the village Alfredo and Pedro 'were friends, in fact they were *compadres* and brothers-in-law'. The municipality was also in many cases dependent on well-to-do inhabitants to cover the costs of defending the land, though sometimes the money-lenders were simultaneously opponents of the municipality.[10] Alfredo lent money on various occasions. For example, in 1963, when the municipality still sought to get hold of Juniapal, the mayor travelled to Tegucigalpa with money borrowed from Alfredo Luna.

Land grabbing took place on both sides and was mediated by the symbol of the fence. Several villagers individually invaded land that was legally part of Alfredo's title. Alfredo could never control this and only defended a section of his legal property with fences. Other fences were challenged and destroyed by villagers. It seems that Alfredo never insisted on clarifying the borders of his property and he concealed his efforts to obtain legal titles. In this way he evaded confrontations and until now many people wonder whether the Luna's have the documents of ownership or not. By giving in to some of the pressure Alfredo established a relationship of reasonable land occupation: no forced usurpation but claims based on accepted grounds of ownership.

This history illustrates that people such as Alfredo Luna, who would be characterized in the earlier mentioned latifundio-minifundio model with negative connotations such as large landowner (*terrateniente*) and land usurper (*acaparador de la tierra*), appear somewhat different in local popular ideology. Of course, many people say that he grabbed the land which formerly belonged to the village, and use concepts such as *terrateniente*. However, the man was also *vivo* (alive, shrewd) and *trabajador* (a hard worker), the latter carrying a positive connotation.[11] Many villagers reason that the village lost land in the past because the authorities ignored the issue. They were ordered to travel to Tegucigalpa, but they had no time or there was no money to cover the costs. Alfredo was in the right to act as he did. They say that people in general, and the authorities in particular, '*no se avivaron*' (did not protest vigorously) and thus gave in to his claims. In fact, with Alfredo's help the village secured access to at least a part of the land. Alfredo was able to use successfully family networks and his contacts with lawyers and bureaucratic institutions. Furthermore, it was said that 'Alfredo dominated the village' or that 'he was the axis of the village'. He was the only merchant in the village and the only person who could sell on credit and lend money: 'everybody was indebted to Alfredo'.[12] And he was the only person who could provide a substantial work to wage labourers (many orphans considered themselves adopted children of Alfredo who supplied them with food, housing and work). Hence, villagers developed mixed identities in their relationship with Alfredo. They saw him as friend, father, *compadre*, employer, money-lender, esteemed authority, and land grabber. These multiple identities towards Don Alfredo also influenced how villagers reacted towards the land occupation during the land reform which will be discussed below.

Local government and the defence of smallholdings

I have described the case of Juniapal at some length to substantiate the following conclusions about the role of the local government and about the relative nature of the notion of land scarcity and the diversity of land histories. The histories of how titles were issued demonstrate that, also in times with low population pressure, a lot of battles over titles were waged. Access to land had to be conquered. Land scarcity is a relative notion: with low population pressure people still perceive a need for more and better land. The conflicts took place between municipalities and between municipalities and individual absentee land-owners. Only after the 1950s did the authorities of the municipality have to struggle against landowners within the village. The local government served as a crucial defender of access to land for smallholders. The central state had indeed developed a legislation which made peasant access to land possible. The municipality was the political vehicle for realizing this access.[13] In a later phase the municipality became more corrupted from within, thus providing the opportunity for land grabbing. As a political entity, however, the municipality never became entirely dominated by a landed elite. It continued to mediate in favour of smallholders' access to land.

It is after the second World War that large estates really consolidate. These observations downplay the idea that the existence of large cattle estates was simply a colonial legacy.[14] The cases of Nejapa and Juniapal show that ejido applications were submitted when third persons jeopardized the livelihoods and access to land of villagers. In Nejapa the locals won, but they lost the land of Juniapal. Thus, the formation of a liberal state in the second half of the nineteenth century did not only promote the consolidation of larger estates and the commoditization of land, but also offered villagers the means to respond to threats to their livelihoods by providing space for ejidos and the so-called 'family plot' (*lotes de familia*) titles (see Honduras 1943). The large estate did not directly hinder the development of peasant agriculture through its land occupations.[15] The cases show that the various land titles have different histories which are relevant to understanding current conflicts. In the 'Cuchillo de los Yoreños' (among heirs), in Juniapal (heirs of Alfredo

36

Luna and people who have occupied parts decades ago), and in Teocintal (because of the land titling project to be discussed below) land is disputed, but these disputes cannot be understood in terms of the traditional latifundio-minifundio model.

It is difficult to classify the struggles over the original land titles using clearly defined, single and unambiguous, categories. In some instances it is not obvious what actually happened. What Cárcamo and Juniapal consist of is not clear: boundary markers were moved, pieces of land were sold, put together, divided and resold without precise descriptions, title documents disappeared, and so on. Land surveyors often did not clarify border conflicts and property claims but created new documents and with them new truths. Villagers (Juniapal) and the municipality (Cárcamo and Juniapal) borrowed money from adversaries in land conflicts: to fight the competitors, alliances were made with them. Sometimes the municipality even sold land in order to measure and divide other obtained land. However, although things do not seem very clear and history is 'misread' for several reasons, we know enough to understand the sort of processes that took place and the types of strategy pursued. The borders and other elements in land conflicts are contested but not fluid. The idea of borders does not change but rather the way in which actors define them as well as the location of border markings. Every title, and within titles every plot, has its own history which can be described. The description of such complex histories indicates that villagers do not think in terms of just two categories -*latifundios* and *minifundios*- nor do they identify themselves simply as *minifundios* or *terratenientes*.

Land Concessions and the Commons

Land within Nejapa, Teocintal and Agua Caliente y Playada was granted as concessions to villagers. They had to apply for concessions at the municipality but did not receive full ownership, only use rights (*dominio útil*). One authority, the *síndico*, measured the parcel and controlled possible claims of other people. The details of the measurements, including the types of crops already planted, appeared in the *actas municipales*. The process finished by issuing a concession.

Table 2.2 Recorded land concessions in El Zapote between 1917 and 1974.

Period	Concessions
1917-1920	7
1921-1930	101
1931-1940	189
1941-1950	46
1951-1960	28
1961-1974	3

Source: actas municipales

Table 2.2 shows that not more than a few concessions per year were requested during the first years of the existence of the municipality. The peak for granting concessions was between 1931 and 1935 (104 concessions), decades after the municipality had received the land titles from the state. It is not possible to specify the exact causes why the peak occurred in this period and not earlier (or later). The influential factors may have been increasing land pressure, a change in the perception of land scarcity, regulations in the Agrarian Law of 1924, and the notion of 'Family Plots' under this law.[16] The latter idea implied that the family constituted a fundamental unit in society and should be in a position to produce enough for its reproduction, for which it needed adequate access to land; this it was supposed would withhold rural strife (Honduras 1943). The number of producers in 1926 is estimated to have been 184. A substantial number of them received land in concession through the municipality.[17]

When the municipality rejected a concession application, the reasons appeared in the actas. The principal reasons were given as follows: when the rights about the particular parcel were disputed before a judge; when it was in use as commons for gathering firewood or for cultivating annual crops; when it enclosed water sources which one aimed to protect; when the parcel contained high value timber for construction purposes; when the applicants were under age; when the applicant already had another concession which he/she did not cultivate; when somebody else had a concession to the land or had planted perennial crops on it; when the petitioner had received concessions before, which he/she had sold.

From the mid-1940s onwards, most requests for concessions were for land that had been transferred in one way or another (sold to another villager, inherited, or when a concession of somebody else was annulled because the land was not used).[18] The number of concessions that mentioned that the land had not been cultivated before (*montaña virgen*) decreased sharply and, instead, crops (coffee, fruit trees, sugar cane) on the land were reported. Increasingly, the actas observed a diminishing availability of land for granting concessions. In several instances unused concessions were annulled. The mean area of concessions dropped from 9.9 hectares in the 1920s to 5.5 hectares in the 1940s.

New concessions were issued to heirs of people who had received land in the past. Conflicts between heirs were in many cases the reason to go to the municipality to renew a concession. Several of these concessions were probably never registered properly, because they could not be traced in the actas municipales and people quarrelled about whether they had been issued in the past.

In the actas municipales the terms 'concession' and 'property' (*propiedad*) are used. This, in fact, demonstrates how legal notions and local perceptions of these concessions intermingle. In interviews about the past respondents always talked in terms of property. Villagers generally believed that the concessions implied full property rights (use, administration and transfer, e.g. selling, renting, inheriting, and mortgaging).[19] Not all land was given in concession, some was simply 'occupied' by producers.[20]

Despite their local importance, few studies refer to the existence of commons in Honduran agrarian history. There has always existed land where the municipality of El Zapote could not issue concessions but only temporarily use rights for annual crops (predominantly maize and beans), and specific areas have been reserved for wood extraction.

After the purchase of Nejapa, the villagers dedicated an area close to the village to maize and bean production. Nobody could appropriate this land and when a particular plot was left fallow other people could use it after regeneration. However, in later periods authorities granted concessions on this land and these commons were gradually lost. In the first decades of this century concessions were requested when people had sown valuable fruit trees or coffee. It was important to clarify property rights to trees: rights in land were of secondary importance. Food grains (maize and beans) were mostly cultivated on the 'communal land' of Nejapa. Livestock did not graze on enclosed land but roamed freely outside the areas for food grain cultivation. This was not limited to common land, but also took place on private land (e.g. Juniapal) or in areas with concessions. In the course of this century, when gradually more land became enclosed with barbed wire, opportunities for free grazing dwindled to the extent that in the 1990s only the roadsides remained.

A new area for commons emerged with the acquisition of Cárcamo. To obtain a state loan to purchase Cárcamo and Juniapal the argument was put forward that all the ejido land had already been given in concession. The law (e.g. Honduras 1961) provided the opportunity to establish *Zonas Agrícolas* (cropping zones), *Zonas Ganaderas* (livestock zones), or *Zonas Mixtas* (mixed zones). The latter was the most standard, entailing that, after the cropping season (only annual crops), livestock could enter the fields to graze the crop residue during the dry season, a period of forage shortage. Two years after acquisition of Cárcamo, however, the first people started to fence land and plant perennial crops. In compliance with the enforcement of regulations several of these people received fines, but in the subsequent year the process of small enclosures continued in spite of recurrent discord and conflict.

With the acquisition of the northern part of Juniapal in the 1950s it became possible to reclaim new areas. Within a few years the dense forest was felled, as people moved rapidly to new plots in order to profit from the relatively high soil fertility after the first clearance. Soon a conflict emerged between cattle owners and maize cultivators. Several cattle owners wanted to graze their cattle in the Zona earlier in the year. Successive administrations approved changes in the dates for opening the Zona for cattle as well as in the designation of the area as a Zona Mixta or Zona Agrícola. Alfredo Luna, who did not make use of the Zona, acted as spokesman for the maize cultivators. In 1955 the municipality divided and distributed the remaining areas of Cárcamo and the southern part (with the best land) of Juniapal among villagers. I have no evidence that people were excluded against their will in this division. The most northern part with steep slopes and rocky soils became Zona Mixta.

Up to now this Zona remained a very important safety-valve for land-poor producers. Several administrations did not enforce the prohibition of fencing and the fencing in of the best land dates from these periods. Some of these fenced plots became paddocks for resource-rich producers. The majority of the Zona users, however, sows maize and is resource-poor.[21] The Zona users are not particularly young, suggesting that it is not a refuge for starters who later acquire their own land.[22] Maize plots are generally small (0.45 hectare). Several resource-poor producers indicate that the Zona is a great thing: those who cannot pay rent or cannot find a plot to rent can always work in the Zona.[23] Land pressure in the Zona has reduced the fallow periods to about three years. Several conflicts emerge around producers who have planted perennials. These planters complain that others do not respect their trees and pick the fruits or damage them. At the same time several producers use the planting of fruit trees as a sign that they claim a specific part of the Zona. Some people indicated that they do not like to work in the Zona because some people who claim specific parts threaten them. Other reasons why working in the Zona is not appreciated, despite the fact that producers consider the soil to be of reasonable quality, are the many rocks and stones in the Zona, the fast drying out of soils in the event of low rainfall, and the danger of falling rocks from a sheer cliff above the slopes. Recent attempts to fence off Zona land into paddocks have been curbed by destroying the fences and later by wounding livestock by cutting off tails.

Growing land scarcity

Several conclusions can be made at this point. An important feature of how access to land was regulated was the lack of direct intervention by the central state. Land transfers were not recorded. Instead, villagers were themselves responsible for mediating disputes and validating access to land, in short, for recognizing property rights. Sometimes, local authorities acted as brokers in the conflicts that might arise. Between the 1920s and 1940s, the municipality had a role in formalizing access rights through the concession system. Although political strife is often reported for that period (also locally) there is no evidence that the distribution of concessions was influenced systematically by party politics.[24] Due to the ejido laws, the local performance of the municipality, and the widespread distribution of concessions, access to land was not a major constraint for livelihood struggles, nor a determining element of social differentiation within the village. Land was in fact a far more mobile resource than labour and capital. Those with enough labour and capital available seem to have had no major problems in expanding their land base. Unavailability of labour and capital did not lead automatically to a small land base. One can thus support Stokes' reading of the land laws as being progressive: formerly national land was transferred to poor individual rural people (Stokes 1947) and access to land was not a major constraint for agricultural development in the first half of this century.[25] Hence, the minifundio was not functionally bound up with the latifundio in a long-term historical process based on unequal land distribution (e.g. Del-Cid 1977, CONSUPLANE n.d. who corroborate this view). Of course this should not imply that all people had equal amounts of land. Moreover, in the 1940s and 1950s, land as a constraining factor became more important and marginalization was increasingly determined by inadequate access to land. The emergence of cattle breeders and the expansion of pastures coincided with growing population pressure.

The local perceptions of scarcity have changed. 'In the past, we thought that there would always be enough land' is a popular saying. A number of people are angry that their parents did not request the municipality to give them concessions. They assume that their parents did not recognize the value of land and did not foresee the changes that would take place. People used to sell their land very cheaply, only enough 'to have a good drink', according the many commentators. Only some people were *vivos* (*los primeros viejos*) and appropriated and kept the land, while others got nothing, people say. The fact that these others were not excluded from access to land, but did not display sufficient interest in owning land, is the present judgment.

The commons, which were high quality areas for food grain production and grazing, have now been transformed into an escape area of marginal land for resource-poor producers. To guarantee continued access to land for them, the commons were defended at times by authorities or other spokesmen of the poor who had an interest in the existence of a safety-valve (e.g. Alfredo Luna). The dynamics in the Zona should not be understood as a remnant from the pre-capitalist past; instead it is a space politically created in the course of this century to allow for land concentration on other land without too much opposition.

Fences and Violence: laws and local rules

The focus in the literature on land reform, aggregated land distribution data and the dissolution of the large estate, has ignored the complexity of local rules about land rights. This section argues that, at the local level, people have differential access to a variety of rules of different sources that can lead to situations of security or insecurity in land rights.[26] Land distribution is not a static system where larger units are divided through the process of inheritance or where people stay during their lifetimes with a fixed set of plots. The following history of producer Excequiel, concerning his land acquisitions and losses, identifies crucial rules and resources in a dynamic system of land transfers.

Land transfers are in many cases regulated. The actas record concessions following specific procedures. The use rights obtained with a concession (*dominio útil*) can be transformed into a *dominio pleno* (full ownership rights) by a notarial act presided over by a lawyer (an escritura pública) and by registration of the land in the Property Register. Formalization of land sales among smallholders, however, generally involves only a deed of purchase (*papel de venta*), a private document between buyer and seller, drawn up in the presence of witnesses. The possession of a deed of purchase reduces the risk that others will claim the land. Local moneylenders generally accept a deed of purchase as collateral. The deed of purchase may be used to divide an inheritance: before the death of an owner, favoured heirs receive a document which states that they have bought the land, although they usually do not pay for it. Land transactions through deeds of purchase are legal: they follow the procedures stipulated in law and are recognized by state authorities and the judicial system. Because of the legal character of these transactions, this system cannot be labelled as 'informal' or 'customary' as, for example, Stanfield et al. (1990) do.[27]

Excequiel and the obstacles to obtain land

Excequiel (b. 1946) and his wife Rosa (b. 1956) have led a turbulent life with regard to their land. A series of events in the life history of Excequiel illustrates important relations in land transfers. At the age of seventeen he started to cultivate maize 'on his own'. While working as a day-labourer for don Rafael Luna, a son of Alfredo Luna, he could use some of his land (Table 2.3, plot A) without paying rent. This form of *patron-worker relationship* still exists today although its importance has lessened considerably. Excequiel left this land when Don Rafael sowed grass seeds, thus decreasing his maize yields. Excequiel fled to the Zona where he worked for four years (B). He left the Zona because of the exhausted soils, mentioning that at that time more and more people began to use the Zona. He settled with his new partner on a piece of his father's land.

Due to two cultural issues, Excequiel and Rosa both became excluded from the inheritance of their parents. The first related to local attitudes towards *gender*. When Excequiel wanted to marry Rosa (she was fourteen), he did not obtain her father's permission. They then agreed that he would 'steal' (*robar*) her; she walked away with him at night. The father became angry and decided they would never receive any help from him. In some way it is acceptable 'to steal' young girls, but repercussions are expected.[28] The local custom of 'wife stealing' led to the application of another local rule, namely that such a scandalous daughter should not be entitled to inherit.

Thus the father of Excequiel excluded them from inheritance when he decided to bequeath all his land to his youngest son. This practice of *ultimogeniture* in which the youngest son (sometimes another child) receives most, or all of, the parents' property is widespread. Excequiel did not receive anything, even though they had taken care of his infirm parents and had worked and lived on their land for several years (C). He cultivated his maize, beans and rice on this land and they had their house there as well. They moved. Excequiel is still embittered by this practice, and he keeps repeating how his youngest brother does not even need the land because he lives in San Pedro de Sula (the second largest city of Honduras). At the same time he lost access to another piece of land which he had leased without paying rent from a friend of his father. The man was a drunkard and had sold the land (D1).

After their displacement, Excequiel could lease land without paying rent for land from a close friend (D2). As we will see in several events, patrons, friends or family remain important channels for obtaining access to land for renting. He worked there for five years next to his friend, until the soil was exhausted and the owner said that he had decided to let it lie fallow. This time he had to lease land from non-relatives. He ended the first lease (E1) after two years because the owner stole his *elotes** and he did not want such problems; the second lease (E2) was terminated when the owner's brothers came back to the village and convinced the owner that they should have the land rather than a tenant.

This time Excequiel turned to a large landowner living in a neighbouring village, who owns a lot of land in El Zapote (title J in Figure 2.1). He became *arrendatario*, which here means that he would bring together a group of tenants and deliver the total rent to the owner (sometimes the arrendatario does not pay rent). When six of his colleague tenants did not want to pay the rent but instead made plans to invade the land, Excequiel told the owner he did not want to become involved in any problems and refused to be *arrendatario* any longer. The owner decided not to rent out any longer and so the land lay fallow at least until 1997.

Excequiel again turned to the Zona. In the Zona he moved once in response to neighbours who invaded part of the plot he had cleared the year before (B2). Since he accumulated some capital with coffee (see below) in the 1990s, he searched for a field of his own to cultivate maize. First he agreed with a woman to buy her nice piece of land near the village, but her brother, who owned the adjacent plot, warned Excequiel that he would *deny him the right of way*. Excequiel gave up the purchase and later the brother himself bought the land. In 1995 Excequiel could finally buy some land for maize from a close friend. His friend's wife had died and the man had started to drink. After he had drunk all his savings he sold his land in bits. In two stages Excequiel bought adjacent plots and he now owns one and a half manzana (G). The only problems are that the harvest of this plot is susceptible to theft by people from a hamlet nearby (it takes Excequiel many days and nights to guard the maize), and that a neighbour with livestock refuses to build a proper fence. Her livestock easily enters the field and destroys part of his maize for which she pays no compensation.

Table 2.3 Land use by Excequiel

	land use	form of acquisition	reason for giving up	period
A	maize	free lease from patron	owner started to sow grass seed	1962-66
B	maize	Zona	low yields, invading part by neighbour	1967-70; 1986-94
C	maize	free lease from father	youngest brother became owner	1971-72
D	maize	free lease from friends	1) owner sold land, 2) start fallow period	1971-72; 1973-77
E	maize	rent	1) owner stole maize, 2) loss of lease	1978-79; 1980-81
F	maize	rent as *arrendatario*	colleague tenants wanted to invade the land	1982-85
G	maize	purchase from friend	in possession (problem of theft of product)	1995-96
H	tule	purchase	removal by state	1972-80
I	tule/banana	indemnification	sale due to threat by PLAN group	1980-87
J	tule	purchase (later extended)	in possession, but river may carry away the land, already one tule crop destroyed	1991-
K	coffee	purchase	sale due to threat of a neighbour	1973-1985
L	coffee	purchase	sale due to threat by father of former owner	1985
M	coffee	purchase	in possession: neighbour who moves fences	1986-
N	beans	rent; via networks	-	-

Excequiel confronted even more problems in establishing his own tule field. In the 1970s he bought a plot in Cárcamo (H) with money saved by raising pigs. However, his satisfaction with the good soil and the beautiful tule he harvested, was short-lived. The state claimed this land (which was supposed to be national land because nobody could show an escritura pública) in order to build a dam and a power plant in the 1980s. The electricity company displaced 178 producers involving almost the entire tule production of El Zapote. Initially the company did not compensate for the loss of land, but after joint protests it paid for the *mejoras* ('improvements' such as tule or fruit trees) made on the land and bought land from a large landowner in order to distribute small parcels for planting new tule. Nevertheless, many producers felt deceived because they considered themselves owners of the land and not only users. The distinction between different types of rights defined by the state was not clear to them. This was the first time they became aware that mejoras could be disentangled from property rights. Up until then, they perceived improvements as a manifestation of the property rights in land. The occupation and use of land result in a certain claim. According to these local norms, one cannot remove a producer from the land once it has been worked and labour has been invested. The actions of the company, however, transformed land and (the product of) labour into two different commodities. The people accepted the compensation for the mejoras and the relocation when they understood their limited room for protest. Excequiel suffered an extra blow when it turned out that he received only one quarter of his original area. One local informant hired by the company opposed Excequiel's *political activism* for a specific party at that time, and provided incorrect data to the company when measuring the plots. The new land (I) proved to be unsuitable for tule cultivation and so he decided to plant banana trees on it, though he would never harvest the bananas. Producers organized in a Foster Parents Plan (PLAN) group - the owners of a neighbouring plot - had deliberately opened the fences so that their cattle could forage on the Excequiel's land. It was the dry season and their cattle were in crying need of forage. The group leader responded to Excequiel's grievance by saying that he should stay quiet because they were many and they had 'PLAN' on their side. In the face of this threat, Excequiel complained to the PLAN authorities and received some money by way of compensation. Since he was convinced that it would happen again, he sold the land to an intimate friend who was at the same time a relative of the participants of this PLAN group. Again in 1991, Excequiel bought land for tule from a man who had occupied it after the meandering river had deposited good quality clay-loam on this place (J). The river remains a threat: in 1994 it flowed into the plot and destroyed part of the planted tule, and in 1996 it streamed for three months through the plot, depositing one metre of clay and destroying all the tule. At the present moment Excequiel is looking to buy another plot for his tule.

With his coffee plots he experienced similar moments of hope and despair. In the 1970s, he and Rosa bought their first coffee plot (K). About a decade later he replanted half of the plot and cultivated it for three years, when, in sight of the first harvest, the owner of an adjacent plot ordered him to leave because the plot was hers. This woman was not very rich, but she was related to powerful families in the village. Therefore Excequiel perceived her as 'rich' and decided not to await problems but to sell his land to another buyer for exactly the same sum for which he had bought the land, thus throwing away the last three years of hard work in cultivating new coffee trees.

In 1985, he purchased another plot for coffee (L). However, the father of the seller, the former owner of this plot, alleged that he did not accept that Excequiel would get the land because he belonged to the opposing *political party*. This man still possessed an adjacent plot and he had moved his fences to enclose three quarters of Excequiel's land. Excequiel asked the mayor to intervene in the conflict. The mayor argued that to sell land it must be free of problems and he arranged that Excequiel would get his money back. In 1986, for the third time, Excequiel bought a plot for coffee (M), which he still owns. Here he has some problems with a neighbour who has moved the fences in order to grab some of Excequiel's land. Another problem is that the father of the former owner still retained a document from the land titling project (see below). This man did not want to hand it over to the individuals who had bought different parcels of the area that were described in the document. These people had bought the land from his son, to whom he had transferred the land.

The history of his first coffee plot illustrates why conflicts regarding property rights are generally not solved in courts. The fear of becoming involved in a court case operates as a threat. Poor people rather tend to enlist the help of political leaders instead of turning to the juridical system to claim their rights. They can manipulate the clientele system better than the juridical system. Local political leaders or municipality officials may act as intermediaries.[29] Villagers perceive lawyers and judges as severely politicized and corrupt, and only accessible to the rich. At the same time this activates their involvement in political connections. Furthermore, the trips and stays in town and the stamps and official documents are expensive. People recall how various people have become bankrupt because of these expenditures. The history of Excequiel's coffee plots shows how the political clientele system restricts or gives opportunities to obtain land.

For bean cultivation Excequiel has to rent land. The practice of renting land is not an impersonal market transaction but involves personal relations (social capital) or the use of other means which gives the tenant status (cultural capital) as the following example exemplifies. Above it was indicated that labour relations may be another factor that influences land rent. It becomes increasingly difficult to rent land. In 1994 one producer approached seven landowners who had available land, and asked them to rent him a parcel, but all of them refused. Family, patronage, or friendship relations are a condition for obtaining land, and sometimes only a combination is effective. Rosa, the wife of Excequiel, had asked her uncle Tino for a piece of land to sow beans but he refused. Later, Excequiel invited me to visit Tino, whose coffee fields I had visited just a week before. During our visit Tino and I talked for a long time, whereas Excequiel, in contrast to his normal talkative behaviour, sat quietly and nervously in a corner. To help him I introduced the theme of how difficult it was to find land to plant beans, but Excequiel remained silent. Later I asked about Tino's yields, and he then asked for the yields of Excequiel. At last Excequiel could say that he lacked land to safeguard his *raza* (preferred cultivar*). Tino offered him some land for rent (N), adding that many people had come to him to request a piece of land but that he could not provide any. Excequiel was more successful because he could deploy a double set of personal relationships. While Rosa did not succeed in convincing her uncle, the special status of a white outsider-researcher was effectively used by Excequiel, in addition to the family relationship through his wife, to clinch the land. Personal relations are crucial to get access to land for renting as well as for buying land. Excequiel could rent various seasons from his uncle until he moved to a plot of one of his brothers.

The importance of non-commodity relations does not mean that the situation is less violent than under market conditions. The loss or sale of Excequiel's land was a response to a *variety of threats*. Many people prefer selling land rather than waiting the consequences of a possible threat; they do not want 'to get into trouble'. They 'prefer to lose their property instead of walking through the village with problems'. Excequiel lost (or almost lost) his land because of: (i) the eradication of his banana crop and the concern that it would happen again; (ii) the intended occupation of his coffee field by a neighbour who had the resources for confrontations involving lawyers or courts; (iii) differences in political party affiliation which motivated and glossed over land grabbing; (iv) the sustained unwillingness of a former owner to pass him the necessary documents; and (v) the denial of the right of way by a neighbour. Such threats demonstrate forms of insecurity present in local rule systems. Another important element, but not yet illustrated, is the fear of violence. Violence may not only mean physical threats with or without weapons (machete, guns, stones). It also includes threatening practices as for example moving fences, destroying plantations, or the poisoning of horses, mules, pigs or dogs of the other party.

At present, boundaries of a property are determined by *fencing in* the land. This has not always been so. According to Browning (1971:41), fields were fenceless in pre-Columbian times in this part of Central America, which facilitated free grazing of the crops of the Indians by the cattle of Spanish colonists. This may have given origin to the later legal regulations that crops should be protected with fences (instead of the cattle). The opposite of 'free land' is 'fenced land'. Fences are the symbol of a claim. Property holders are obliged to fence in their plot of land.[30] Barbed wire, which is nowadays used for fencing, can only be fastened with the permission of the municipal council, which is only granted if one can submit the receipt of purchase of the barbed wire. One has to prove that both the barbed wire and the land is really one's property and that it is not taken from somebody else.

The prohibition of fencing in some situations illustrates the power to exercise rights with the fence. It is strictly forbidden to fence in land on the village commons. Nevertheless, several villagers have fenced in parts of the commons and have even sold plots or have rented them to others afterwards. Everybody respects the property claim to this land, although everybody also knows that the 'owners' do not hold a legal title. Once the fence is accepted the property claim is accepted too.

Fences are important instruments in struggles over land. Moving fences is a common strategy for grabbing some land of a neighbour (see Excequiel's case). In most of the literature the fence, as an artefact, is equated with land grabbing. The fence is considered the material metaphor of omnipotent large landowners who fence in land at the expense of poor peasants. Recent conflicts are explained by referring to the fences who 'walk at night', the enclosures with fences of other's land by large landowners (e.g. DeWalt 1985a). But the production of the meaning of the fence, or *el cerco*, is broader and more complex. The fence not only refers to a material construction, but also has a normative connotation, a juridical meaning, and it can be a category for structuring social relations about rights. In daily life the fence is given at least as much value as a legal document. Fencing land expresses a claim which is sustained in law and in local norms but which at the same time can be challenged by the actions of others. The destruction of a fence by cutting through the barbed wire is therefore a very symbolic and threatening action to which people often refer. For example, a producer named Constantino Herrera and his brother had arranged through legal authorities that some occupants of their land be removed. However, Constantino still does not want to plant coffee in his field. The former occupants cut the barbed wire each time. This destruction is taken not only as revenge (the material losses are relatively small) but as threatening behaviour which symbolizes that more actions may follow. Another example, which shows that the symbol cannot easily be negated, is the case of Eduardo Sagastume who had fenced a part of the commons. Other villagers did not accept this and destroyed his barbed wire and the entrance to the paddock. Eduardo, however, negated this sign and repaired the fence. Later on, he found his animals with chopped off tails and had to confine his claims.

These examples and the story of Excequiel show that local regulation of property rights in land does not guarantee security for property holders: although Excequiel had to confront a unique record of obstacles, his case reflects the experiences of many other people. Normative notions of the fence, improvements, gender, ultimogeniture, patron-worker relations, party-politicking, threats, and use of norms about rights of way are elements, besides price, supply, and demand, which structure access to land.

Managing inequality: an aborted land reform

Despite the many concessions and wide availability of land in the 1920s and 1930s, land was unequally distributed a few decades later. Figure 2.2 shows the land distribution in 1974.[31] These data reflect the pattern of land concentration repeatedly documented for many other areas in Latin America (Barraclough 1973). In 1974, 48.3 per cent of producers had access to 6.9 percent of the land (including rented land); 7.0 per cent of landowners controlled 52.0 per cent of the land area. 72.2 per cent of the farms had a farm size smaller than five hectares and are thus defined as *minifundio* according to the Agrarian Reform Law of 1974 (Honduras 1975). Parallel to this representation, which focuses on the opposition between producers with a small amount of land and producers with a lot of land, one should stress the role of the intermediate category: 20.8 per cent of the producers have farms of five to twenty hectares and occupy 29.7 per cent of the land. Hence, almost one third of the land is cultivated by producers with medium size farms.

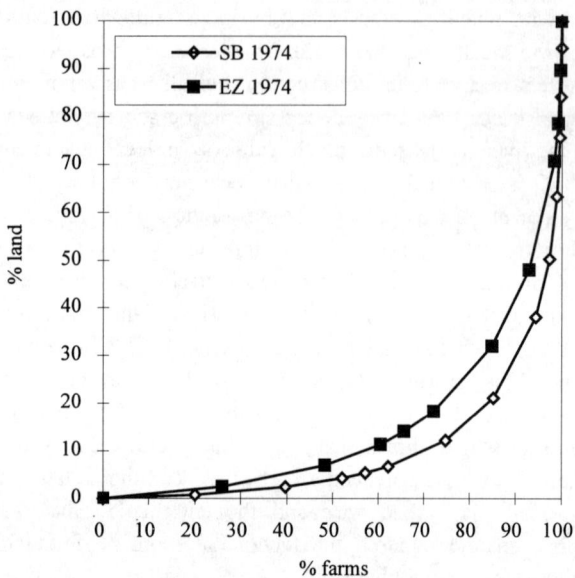

Figure 2.2 Land distribution in El Zapote and Santa Bárbara in 1974
Source: calculated from DGECH (1978).
Note: Gini-coefficient for land distribution in Santa Bárbara district is 0.80 and in El Zapote is 0.70.

Land shortage for poor producers motivated the emergence of land reform politics from the 1960s onwards. The Honduran land reform has received much attention by national and international scholars. Sometimes one is left with the impression that besides the capitalist estates (e.g. the banana companies) the remainder of Honduran agriculture consists of not more than the land reform sector. Even the recent debates on structural adjustment and liberalization often limit their scope to the land reform sector (e.g. Honduras 1992; Noé Pino and Thorpe 1992).

Studies of the origins and evolution of the Honduran land reform have mostly focused upon the different political forces and struggles (e.g. Kincaid 1985; Ooyens 1988; Posas 1979, 1981, and 1996; Ruhl 1985; Sieder 1995; Stone 1990), the unequal distribution of land and the diversity of forms of production (e.g. IHDER 1981, Thorpe 1991), or the problems of its planning and implementation (e.g. Noé Pino et al. 1992; World Bank 1983). Several studies have investigated transformations in the organization of production (e.g. Brockett 1987; Del-Cid 1977; Williams 1986). Much has been written about the rise and fall of the cooperatives in the process of land reform (e.g. Goud 1986, Posas 1992, Ruben & Fúnez 1993; Santos de Morais n.d.). Less attention has been paid to what happened in the margins of the land reform and to initiatives which never came to maturation, but history may increase our insights into the land reform process.

The political gulf of land reform also reached El Zapote. A land reform group planned to obtain parts of Cárcamo and Juniapal which Alfredo Luna had in his possession.

Land accumulation by Alfredo Luna

The prototypical large landowners in this story are members of the Luna family. When I first met the old Alfredo Luna there was nothing which indicated that he had been the richest man in the region. He greeted me barefooted and stripped to the waist in old trousers decorated with holes which were held up with a simple piece of rope. His house had no other furniture than a pair of the cheapest, locally made, chairs and a pile of bad quality corn was drying in a corner of the central room. During our conversations he always stared at my eyes with a look which is talked about, and feared by some, in the village. He says he is 90 years old but still rides horses: 'I have a son who looks much older'. He arrived in the village as a pedlar in the late 1920s, fell in love and married a *Zapoteña*. He established himself as a retailer of consumer goods, but soon became involved in agricultural production and the merchandising of agricultural products. In his old age he likes to talk about his forty children, of which twelve have already died.[32] He comments on having spent a lot on his children and their education: 'I have an engineer, two are in the USA, there are secretaries, nurses, accountants, and my grandchildren are lawyers, engineers and doctors'. This list is quite different from what most villagers can produce and it illustrates how the landed elite typically invested in educating their children for urban jobs, often state jobs. The backbone of his fortune formed his shop, the first one in the village, where many people bought and drank on credit.[33] With the profits he started to accumulate land and cattle, and he invested in a coffee *finca*. The period between 1960 and 1965 was probably the height of his career as an accumulator of land.

Most of the land listed in Table 2.4 was reserved for grazing. The plots near the village were permanent pastures for the many mules he had for transporting his merchandise. The land of Cárcamo was in use under a rotation of maize, pasture and bush fallow. Many villagers could make use of this fertile flat land to cultivate maize. They could pay rent in kind or in labour, and, regularly, no rent was paid at all. In 1967, Alfredo Luna sold all his land in Cárcamo to his son Pedro, who subsequently sold parts to his brothers Jesus and Rafael.[34]

Two slightly different views interpret why Alfredo passed the land to his son. Some villagers suppose that it was because the municipality continued its attempts to get hold of this land: 'His children received it because Alfredo saw that the people continued their struggle to seize it from him; he thought it better to distribute it among his children'. Rafael gives the following explanation.

[P]resident Ramon Villeda Morales (1957-1963) gave the people some years to arrange the documents of their land before it would be affected by the land reform programme. (..) My father had bought a thousand manzana and part of this land was situated in the title of Cárcamo but was never well measured. That's why he had it surveyed. His thousand manzana had to be split off from the fourteen and a half *caballerías* of the [original] Cárcamo title. He had contracted engineer Streber from Tegucigalpa and became friends with him. Therefore, that man demarcated the borders in favour of my father. In fact, his land had been scattered but then his land came to be situated within one contiguous parcel in one title.[35]

Alfredo Luna was much better informed about the laws and national politics than other villagers. There was not only pressure from people to recover Cárcamo-Juniapal but he also anticipated and responded to political changes in Tegucigalpa by starting the procedure to obtain a legal title.

Table 2.4 Land properties of Alfredo Luna in 1965

	name	area	value
1	Potrero de las cuevas	15 mz	1000
2	Potrero de Antonio Nejapa	12 mz	400
3	Potrero de la Camapusa	14 mz	550
4	Malapita	55 mz	3000
5	Terreno Malapita	12.5 mz	680
6	Potrero de Malapon	50 mz	1500
7	La Garroba Zacatal	7 mz	500
8	Finca Lagunetas	25 mz	20000
9	Cafetal Daniel Alvarado	20 mz	4606
10	Finca la Bragina	7 mz	5000
11	La Yarrabal	?	450
12	Cárcamo	108 ha	25000
13	Nejapa	20 mz	1000
14	El Portillo	12 mz	600
15	Malapita y Retiro	60 ha	4000
16	Malapita y Playada	?	800
17	Esquinal de Beto	40 ha	100

Source: inventory of Alfredo in his administration books.
Note: Value in Lempira in 1965 as estimated by Alfredo. Note that he only included a small part of Cárcamo as his property.

The land occupation

Some inhabitants of the municipality became inspired by the land reform discourse, and a plan was developed to occupy land from the Luna's in the beginning of the 1970s.[36] After a presentation of the history as told by the key occupiers, I shall report on how the Lunas perceived the occupation. One of the crucial political leaders of the group was Juan Martínez.[37] He says:

The people appointed me as president of the group. The group had thirty-nine members. The land of Cárcamo was from the municipality in the past. I knew a lawyer in Santa Bárbara and I also visited Tencoa [a successful land reform group nearby]. That's how I started to learn to think. The lawyer told me that I should also set up a group. The UNC [the Social-Christian peasant union] came to talk and to explain things. I think that the group existed for four years. I went to San Pedro sixteen times to visit INA. We received a *título de garantía* (provisional title) from INA.

50

We have not worked the land for very long; we only cleared the fallow, we have never sown. I left for Santa Bárbara because they wanted to kill me, and the group disintegrated. One of us died when he fell under a tree and the people became disillusioned.

While I lived in Santa Bárbara the group did not preserve the title with care. A man from another village went to our hamlet and convinced my compañeros that he needed the title to remodel something in it. They gave it to him and so lost it. That man sold the title to the large landowners for 300 L [150 US$ at that time]. I have talked with the director of INA and he said that only one title could be issued. If you lose that one you have nothing.

In the village Don Hugo Portillo is generally considered as the leader of this occupation, although he was no more than an advisor and he kept the account of the member's financial contributions. 'We never thought about the consequences', he said. His son was also involved and said:

We first received a lot of talks in Santa Bárbara, from a lawyer, from other people, until the approval of INA was brought, three days before the operation. One o'clock in the morning we left from here, with all the peasants, to the *'recuperación'*. We had already cleared about half a *manzana* at seven o'clock in the morning. The next day two of the Lunas arrived armed, with five armed body-guards. I was there with a few other people. I had a problem because at that time the people had a bad concept of me and they put me and my father down as a communist, even though I do not know what communism means. They shot at me with a hand-gun, some shot into the air. Later dynamite was put in our house. I happened to sleep in the other corner, otherwise I would have been dead. The desire to work was lost, because of the persecution. Soldiers came to the house of my father, who had already fled into the bush. They said that he had to present himself at INA. INA had given the authorization to till the land but the same INA sent the military to evict us. That has always been the politics of INA. First they say they want to favour the peasantry, and when they give the land the large landowner goes to INA, saying that one needs the military to evict us. This has caused many deaths in Honduras.

Although the land was occupied for not more than eight days the impact on the minds of the larger landowners was notable. Pedro Luna points out that because of the land 'invasion' he sold much of his land to his brothers.[38] He places the event in a wider context of a longer struggle about the land between villagers and their family.

The official title of my father mentions 1138 *manzanas* but Alfredo never occupied more than 600 *manzanas*. The rest was in the hands of other people. The lawyer who had arranged the title of my father told him he could have the people removed but advised him not to, because it could be dangerous, because they could kill him.

Alfredo's appropriation was obstructed by the threat of violence by people less endowed with resources. The case shows how the state supported, or at least permitted, violence as a means of settling disagreements about access to land in small village such as El Zapote, far away from the political centre or the great confrontations of peasant organizations and large landowners in the South and in the Northern valleys. A better understanding of such local conflict may modify the approaches of social scientists who try to explain the relative political stability of Honduras in the 1970s and 1980s as compared with the neighbouring countries (Ruhl 1984, Stringer 1989, Sieder 1995). The main causes identified in these explanations are (i) the broader-access-to land hypothesis (a lower pressure on land in

Honduras), (ii) the less repressive character of the Honduran political and military elites and the political access of peasant organizations (sometimes described as them being coopted), and (iii) the poor socio-economic conditions of the rural poor which gave them low expectations and no demand for radical change (Stringer 1989:378). The way people's actions and decision-making were influenced by an operating violent and repressive environment has so far hardly been analysed.

This case of an untimely unsuccessful land reform shows the significance of the political environment of the 1970s in stimulating peasants to form groups and to organize land occupations. It illustrates the double position of INA favouring the peasantry as well as the landed elite. The combination of the political environment and the specific history of the land in dispute motivated the occupation. Occupation of the other land of Alfredo or of land of other large landowners had not been planned. It was not large landownership that was contested but the specific appropriation of this land by the Lunas. At the time this appropriation took place, in the 1950s, there was no political discourse on land reform.

Furthermore what is revealed in this history is that villagers reacted in different ways to the process of land grabbing and the political opportunities opened up by land reform discourse. Many people condemned the land occupation stating that one should not enter into others' property (*meterse en lo ajeno*).[39] Despite the fact that nobody knew whether the Lunas had legal title to the land, and that Alfredo had probably manipulated the authorities to get access to the land, a certain legitimacy was granted to the reaction of his sons to the occupation. The village had already acknowledged that Alfredo had obtained the rights at a time when people did not react (*el pueblo dormido; no se avivaron*) and what his sons had bought the land. Two local norms - being owner of something you buy (even if it is from family) and having rights because you have fenced off the land with approval of the villagers - were violated by the land occupation.

The economic power and access to state-supported violence were key resources for the Lunas to counter land reform. But not less important was their relatively better access to information and juridical titling procedures. When we consider how people in the village look back upon this event, it becomes clear that their information about whether the Lunas had titles or not, is extremely scant. The description of land titles (section 2.2) and of what happened could only be made after a laborious process of data collection and reconstruction. Most villagers can only reconstruct small pieces or little at all of this history. Those who relate more details mostly suggest that they do not know whether Alfredo or his sons really had a title, nor how they 'arranged' to get it. Sometimes they knew that the Lunas travelled to Copán, Gracias and Tegucigalpa 'to arrange something'. The Lunas told me they had intensive contacts with lawyers, people who were knowledgeable about titling procedures, and other large landowners who were afraid of land occupations and land reform laws. The Lunas anticipated (and still anticipate) laws which other villagers do not know. The particular title of Cárcamo, now in the hands of Rafael Luna, is still not fully legalized. Rafael is currently completing procedures to prove that it is his land, but to this end he again has to contest claims of producers with land within his title.[40] These people, however, have little information about procedures and existing titles (and their histories). In

52

the land reform process the organization of people was very local and centralized, but not embedded in links at a regional level. An illustration of this is that even politically active villagers hardly have coherent information about two land reform initiatives in other hamlets of the municipality. The exchange of information about details of the struggle is scanty and incomplete. Knowledge about what happened in neighbouring municipalities is limited to cases of murder and extreme violence. Information exchange took place only between official representatives of the peasant organization and the land reform group.

In general, one can say that the land reform discourse survives more in the memory of the large landowners than among the villagers. Typically, villagers interpret the distribution of the land among Alfredo's children in terms of pressure by the village, while his sons refer to the threat of the land reform, the political development of peasant organizations and the changes in the legal framework. Both the large landowners and the peasants point to the inconsistent role of INA which, it is argued, enlarged the functional use of violence or threat of violence. This contradiction of INA in terms of its objective of establishing peace in the countryside and its forms of operation resulting in more conflicts and violence appears again in the 1980s with the land titling project.

Land Titling: new institutionalized insecurities

The Land Titling Project

At the beginning of the 1980s, in a context of violence, political struggle and an inert land reform institute (INA), the state accepted USAID suggestions for modifying the land reform process by combining the slogans 'land rights for the poor' and 'peaceful rural development' in a land titling programme (PTT*). A central concept in land titling is that of capitalizing family farms (Stanfield 1989) through modernization. Land titling entails collecting and registering data about property rights and the distribution of land. Plot boundaries are combined with the name of property holders in a register of land holdings, thus providing possibilities to levy taxes.[41]

The official objectives of PTT are to convert small and medium size producers into legitimate landowners; to provide rural people with security and 'peacefulness' in order to increase their investments; and 'to attain that coffee farmers, and small and medium size producers, can obtain technical assistance and credit to increase the production of food, work and family income' (INA 1990). Hence, increased rural peace and modernization of the production of smallholders are central. Credit facilities were supposed to improve because having titles could serve as collateral for bank loans, and tenure-security would encourage greater on-farm investment, soil conservation measures, and adoption of new technology (Atwood 1990). In addition, the property holder who has a land title would be less willing to migrate (Salgado et al. 1994). Land titling supposedly improves the land market, thus moving the land into the hands of the most efficient and productive users (Melmed-Sanjak 1993, Salgado et al. 1994). One general assumption is that before the implementation of a land titling programme, the land market is 'imperfect' due to a lack of clarity regarding the division of the different elements in the bundle of property rights (rights of use, sale, trade, rent, and division).

Evaluations conclude that PTT did not attain its objectives. It did not lead to the expected development of a complete cadastral and **registration system** (Jansen & Roquas 1998). Many parcels will not form part of the system because they are not eligible for titling, and many people have not applied for a title. Most importantly, practically all transactions and parcel divisions that have taken place in El Zapote after 1984 (when the land was measured) have not been registered which means that the actual register is a very distorted representation of the locally and legally accepted distribution of land rights.

With regard to **productivity improvements**, PTT has not given the projected stimulus to investment and productivity and PTT titles have not substantially improved access to credit (e.g. Fandino 1993; Montaner Larson 1995; Wachter 1992). For 91.4 per cent of the beneficiaries the title has not served as a collateral for credit (Salgado 1987).[42] Stanfield et al. (1990) write that the improvement of the supply of credit 'is not dramatically impressive' (and 75-80 per cent of the title holders do not receive any credit at all). Nesman et al. (1989) suggest that a credit and technical assistance programme should accompany the titling project, but this, in fact, undermines the assumption that titling automatically generates an improved credit supply. These evaluations do not question whether a credit programme really needs a new system of land registration. The same applies to recent studies which have analysed the effect of PTT on improved soil conservation. Sustainability issues have recently emerged as an added justification for land titling and land taxes (e.g. Strasma et al. 1992). Wachter (1992, 1995) concludes that PTT did not have a significant impact on the extent of investments in conservation, but, nevertheless, he underwrites the case for more development assistance for land titling, in order to establish the complex cadastral and land administration, and to deliver credit and applicable technologies (Wachter 1994).

The conclusions about a free **land market** are more ambivalent; many scholars assume the need to improve land markets (Salgado et al. 1994; Stanfield 1992; Thorpe 1995a). They seem to apply a rather legalistic definition of the land market in which a market only exists if it concerns transfers of registered land titles. Following this definition, one could conclude that PTT has not improved the land market in El Zapote because very few transactions take place in that way (Jansen & Roquas 1998). An expectation of PTT was that land prices would rise (Stanfield 1992:199). One can question why a rise in land prices would benefit the target group of resource-poor farmers, but, even if one finds this necessary, two other shortcomings of this abstraction remain. The *a priori* definition of land market is methodologically blind as to why and how resources are transferred among smallholders. Secondly, it conceals the possibility that prices can rise because PTT functions as a hindrance to sales. Jansen & Roquas (1998) conclude that PTT has added additional costs that did not exist in the earlier rule system.

Most evaluations of PTT concentrate on its limited impact on the modernization of smallholder agriculture. These evaluations, although in my view devastating for PTT because they show that crucial objectives were not fulfilled, generally conclude with recommendations for adjustment (e.g. in the line of more credit programmes). The starting point of these evaluations is the measurement of the modernization impact. Another approach is followed by Esther Roquas and myself. We start from the views of the people of El Zapote who are almost unanimously negative about the land titling project.[43] In our discussion of why PTT leaves this negative imprint on the villagers we conclude that PTT has increased insecurity in land rights in El Zapote, instead of attaining its first objective of creating more security and rural peace (Jansen & Roquas 1998). The following section summarizes our investigation.

Land Titling in Practice

Land titling started with the mapping of parcels by the National Cadastral Directorate in 1983-1984. The titling brigades of INA registered the users. According to the titling decree all parcels between five and fifty hectares on national or ejidal land could be titled. Parcels smaller than five hectares but with coffee could also be titled. Parcels less than seventeen hectares could not receive full ownership rights but only a title called *Unidad Agrícola Familiar* (agricultural family unit) which the law prohibited from being divided or sold without consent of INA.[44] PTT issued full titles (*dominio pleno*) without restrictions on larger parcels. The majority of the titled parcels is small, 79 per cent is smaller than the official five hectares (see Table 2.5). In many titles, parcels used for maize were combined with parcels with coffee to allow for the grouping of parcels smaller than five hectares. The title could be paid in quota; one could pay at once, although this was rarely done. The state remained owner of the land until all payments were made.

Table 2.5 Delineated area and issued titles in El Zapote.

Delineated parcels	962
Total of titles issued	477 (consisting of 668 parcels)
Titles with more than one parcel	112 (23% of 477)
Delineated area	4113 ha
Titled area	2175 ha (53%)
Parcels < 5 ha	760 (79%)
Titles < 5 ha	342 (72%)
Titles > 18 ha	16 (3.4%)

Source: adapted from Jansen & Roquas (1998); calculated from Dirección Ejecutiva del Catastro (30 May 1984) 'Listado de Propietarios Proyecto Titulación de Tierras', and INA: 'lists of PTT titles'.

One of the main problems faced by villagers with PTT is the idea that it imposes 'new taxes'. Property holders had to pay for a part of the value of the land, which was fixed at 60 L (30 US$) per hectare for the *Unidad Agrícola Familiar*, at that time about one third of the market value of the land in the case of land for maize. From the project's perspective, producers received national land from the state for a very low price (Stanfield et al. 1986). However, for the villagers this was a substantial amount considering the fact

55

that, according to their legal conception, they already owned the land. In most cases they had purchased it and they did not want to 'pay twice'. Several people felt severely misled arguing that they were told that their applications implied payment only after they had signed the form.

A second problem was the rule that one person could only receive one title, which could contain a maximum of two or three parcels despite the highly fragmented distribution of parcels. It is unclear why the project imposed this constraint.[45] The titling brigade advised people to register parcels in the name of relatives. Many people put these in the names of their wife, son, brother or *compadre*. Subsequently, INA considered this third person as the legal owner, while the actual property holder usually retained the documents and the control of the parcel. This practice led to many intra-family conflicts, for example when the official title holder sold the land without the consent of the locally recognized 'owner'. Women property holders form another case: many of their parcels were titled in the name of their husbands, thus denying them their legal claims and sharpening intra-household conflicts.[46]

A third problem was that INA did not accept joint owners, e.g. brothers with an inherited parcel on one title, and forced people to title the parcel in one name. This led to problems when this person sold the land without consent of the other heirs, an act he or she was legally allowed to do.

These three problems were built into the system of titling, but there were also a number of problems with regard to errors in implementation, for example: names wrongly written, lists of property holders which were lost, parcels that were combined with the wrong name, INA who accepted the wrong people as 'owners', INA personnel who collected the quota while the payment should have been made at the bank, and wrong measurements such as including one's parcel in the parcel of others. This offered opportunities for some to enrich themselves at the expense of others. Or in the villagers' words: 'the titling opened up space for those who are avaricious'. Hence the titling project could be manoeuvred by some to grab the land of others.

Jansen and Roquas (1998) describe several cases of how people exploited the new resources PTT offered. The strategy they followed was to have INA officials put the document in their name and to pay it directly afterwards. Thus, payment of the title is not a means to evade future conflicts (PTT objective), but one action in an ongoing conflict. Unintentionally, INA acts as a defender of one party, which in many cases turns out to be already the most powerful one. INA brigades have to reach their targets and have no time to investigate land conflicts and complex situations, which are more the rule than the exception.

Villagers were cheated and put under pressure in order to have them collaborate with project implementation, as the following cases of enforced payments illustrate. Payments of the titles resulted in being low and INA developed a 'campaign' in 1994 to collect outstanding debts. At that time, 21 per cent of the titles in El Zapote had been fully paid.[47] A conditionality of international funding agencies for new loans was that INA would collect overdue debts. The official story propagated on posters and pamphlets, and in radio spots, was that new titling would take place which would solve people's problems. We were told repeatedly by INA officials that people are very happy when their land is titled. Landholders, however, were very unhappy with INA's new campaign. Producers were put under heavy pressure to pay. We observed that the campaign did not develop any action to solve ongoing land conflicts but instead threatened people with the fact that they would come into conflicts with others if they did not pay the title (Jansen & Roquas 1998).

People who showed an *escritura pública* to explain the conflicts they had, were told that 'such a document has no value', which is untrue in a legal sense. People were told that they had to pay within fifteen days, or INA would confiscate and sell the land.[48] This never happened, thus emphasizing that INA only intended to threaten people. Another threat used was that producers would not receive their *bonus*, a subsidy, for their coffee harvest, when the *bonus* had no relation to the titling issue at all.[49] Producers were also told that they would have to pay because only then the state would help them in case of others invading their land. The fear of land invasion, which had been absent for more than two decades, once more became discussed in the village, introduced by INA. Besides the fact that INA's working style is not very elegant, the threats do not contain more than some invented stories.

During this campaign the brigades did not correct earlier errors made by INA in the 1980s which had provoked conflicts. Despite its propaganda, interest was only in recuperating outstanding debts. For example, people whose parcels were measured incorrectly did not receive any help. INA brigade told the people that they themselves had to sort it out with the other partners in the conflict or with a lawyer, always adding that any conflict could only be solved after the title had been paid, no matter by whom.

The campaign of 1994 again offered new resources in land struggles. Responding to the propaganda of INA, several people paid the title of land measured in 1984 and sold it afterwards to other people with a private deed of purchase. They had not handed over the PTT document to the buyer (in general without any further intentions). After the campaign they started to claim the land and several conflicts emerged in the village. However, despite INA's propaganda the old system of deeds of purchase has not been replaced by the new PTT titles and the deeds of purchase have not (yet) lost their legal significance. It is impossible to disregard them because most of the land does not have a registered title.

Villagers suggest that the titles will not cause many changes in the transaction practice, but that the land will become more expensive because people want to recover what they spent. They also feared more violence within families. And they are sure that the bank will not give loans with this INA title ('they even prefer the old *escritura pública*').

Mistaken assumptions: the capitalizing family farm and the power of the state

It can be concluded that many people of El Zapote feel deceived by being forced to participate in a project which obliged them to buy the land which they already perceived as theirs. The titling practice, either its legal and illegal elements, intensified existing problems and resulted in new conflict. Some people lost their property rights over land, others were given the opportunity to use PTT as a resource in order to gain rights over land at the expense of others.

A complete official registration of land property in a land register and dynamic cadastre will not result from PTT. PTT has neither increased security of land, nor induced a modernization of agriculture. It will probably not replace the old rule systems. People continue to divide, bequeath, and sell their land without taking the trouble (and the capital) to register the transactions and modify the PTT title.

The failures of PTT are not only an effect of the organizational incapacity of INA, USAID and the Honduran state. A more basic problem is its foundation on mistaken assumptions about social relations with respect to land transfers. Titling advocates make universalistic assumptions. The notion of a 'capitalizing family farm' entails a theoretically homogeneous peasant farmer; it disregards social differentiation and it does not assess the social consequences of development programmes for marginalized sectors. The notion obscures the possibility of diversity and contradictions, of a delicate situation of security and insecurity, in Honduran rural society. Typically, PTT overlooks local conflicts and differences in power (and striking differences in access to legal defence). PTT, further-more, does not recognize the strength of the existing rule system regarding land rights, and up to now, despite its rhetoric, does not replace it. Other riddles for PTT are how poor its 'target group' is, and also how producers' economic calculus (encompassing the social relations) can differ from that of the 'small farmer' or the 'rural entrepreneur', which lives in the minds of the project designers.

Producers evaluate the opportunities offered by the ecological and economic environ-ment very differently and probably more realistically. Most people do not presume that credit can be obtained with a PTT title. People do not consider their 'minifundios' to be unproductive and judge that very small farm sizes should be considered as their legal property. They also do not understand why properties smaller than seventeen hectares (the *Unidad Agrícola Familiar*) should not be divided and sold in parts; notwithstanding legal restrictions they continue to do so.

The second conclusion deals with the role of the state in PTT. The implementation of PTT has reinforced local perceptions of state agencies as populated by incapable personnel and regulated through party politics. Jansen and Roquas (1998) argue that a critique of PTT should not stop by pointing to the weakness of the Honduran state apparatus. The issue is that land titling implies a transformation of the relation between property holders and the central state. In earlier systems property holders arrange land transactions among themselves. The PTT title, in contrast, establishes a direct relationship between the state and the property holder. It is the fundamental character of this proposed change in crucial state-peasant relations that makes titling in Honduras so complex. In fact, the state never developed a substantial interest and apparatus, nor created the necessary trust, to maintain this relationship, but instead has been driven by short term pressures.[50] PTT could not escape from the neo-liberal paradox. The transformation of the social management of land tenure through the land reform process into ownership regulation through land titling did not lessen the need for a strong state with a high capacity to intervene. Moreover, the weak

Honduran state apparatus became even further dismantled with the structural adjustment policies of the 1990s. With the neo-liberal assumption of a homogeneous rural entrepreneur and its utopia of a free, non-disturbed, land market, any prospects for a land titling process that reduces rural conflict and provides instruments to the rural poor to improve their livelihood are obstructed.

Space, mediating institutions and the meaning of land value

Agrarian social relations in Honduras have often been represented in terms of the concept '*latifundio-minifundio* complex' (e.g. Murga Frassinetti 1977). This complex is defined by Del-Cid (1977:81-2) not only by reference to the existence of large estates with specific forms of production organization (e.g. plantation, ranch), but by pointing to the enclosure in this complex of small properties, the *minifundios*. Smallholders will continue to exist as long as large estates are dependent on the supply of cheap labour and cheap food by smallholder households. This theoretical view developed by Latin American scholars has later been reworked by de Janvry (1981) into the concept of 'functional dualism'. Although the latifundio-minifundio complex reveals important structuring relations between large estates and small properties, the presented material suggests that it conceals crucial elements of the agrarian structure: the importance of parallel land histories, the distorted focus on labour relations defined through space, the Janus-faced character of mediating institutions (personal relations, market, state), and the different meanings given to value and scarcity.

Land histories and space

The land histories given above demonstrate that the latifundio-minifundio complex as a social structure does not exist as such in El Zapote, nor did it in the past, even though the inequality of land distribution is quite similar to the disparities on a national scale.[51] The histories lead to the conclusion that unequal distribution has not been inherited from colonial *hacienda* structures. There are several arguments to substantiate this conclusion. Firstly, large estates emerged in a process of capitalist development in the course of this century. Primitive accumulation, illustrated in the histories of land grabbing, and social differentiation were more important than the take-over of production by monopoly capital from the capitalist centre. In the research region internal inequality is not simply a response to the development of the large banana plantations in the North of Honduras. Although they have been, to some extent, a pull for migrant labour, they do not constitute a logic that can explain local inequalities in land distribution.

Secondly, it was not predominantly cheap labour or cheap food that sustained the expansion of the large estate in times of increased demand for its products, but the 'availability' of cheap land (cf. Howard 1987). The labour-extensive cattle ranching did not depend on cheap labour. The way it developed can hardly be explained in terms of functionality of labour relations. There is no evidence that large estates stimulated regulations and intervention resulting in semi-proletarianization of the peasantry in this region. Instead, smallholders synchronically appropriated land and sustained independent forms of agriculture.

A third argument underlining the non-applicability of the latifundio-minifundio model deals with the reification of labour relations in a spatial concept (latifundio-minifundio). This is, for example, reflected in the widespread use of tables which summarize and reinterpret census reports on land distribution and which subsequently deduce whether a certain farm size class represents a sub-family-farm, a family farm, a multi-family farm, and so on. Social relations of production, however, are not only defined by space. In El Zapote it can be observed that producers with one hectare of land suitable for coffee and with a highly productive plantation have a very different socio-economic position from those producers who have ten hectares available for low-productive maize. Inequality is thus not only a difference in access to land, but also in the way in which land is embedded in a specific organization of production.[52]

A fourth argument is that in a dualistic model the middle categories remain undertheorized. Land was never distributed in two categories. About one third of the producers can be considered to have middle-size farms.[53] On which end of the binary opposition do they have to be placed: latifundio or minifundio? Diversity of farm sizes has always been much larger than can be captured with this dualistic concept.[54] Once inequality exists statistics can always be interpreted in such a way in order to prove a dual structure. The problem is that meaningful changes are often not explained.[55] Medium-size producers increasingly play a role in the shaping of the local rural labour market.

Mediating social institutions

Three main types of institutions that structure land distribution are developing commodity markets, non-commodity relations, and the state. Development of markets is important with respect to the demand for cattle, coffee and petates, for which different forms of marketing infrastructure have evolved. The growth of these markets was accompanied by the specific development of animal, coffee and tule production and the demand for land and capital to obtain this land.

The influence of non-commodity relations on land distribution has been discussed throughout the text. For example, kinship and friendship, violence, inheritance patterns and gender ideology shape access to land for each individual or family.

This chapter also leads to some preliminary conclusions about the state. The role of the state with regard to access to land has been rather ambivalent in Honduran history and displays a Janus-faced character. In each historical period the central state supported the development of large estates (especially with regard to export agriculture), but it also undertook actions to secure the reproduction of an economy of simple commodity production (e.g. the ejido elements in agrarian laws). A more recent example of its Janus-faced character has been the role of the state in the land reform process, especially through INA. The case of the land occupation in El Zapote illustrates INA's contradictory role in stimulating land occupations but without giving full support and, instead, acceding to the

pressure of holders of large estates.[56] The land titling project, which intended to modernize smallholder agriculture and provide rural peace, was likewise a poorly implemented
intervention. PTT increased conflicts without improving agricultural production or
generating a more 'just' distribution of land rights.

Although the Janus-faced character of the state has remained a constant feature
throughout history, the means of intervention have been changing. Contrary to the
dominant view that state support for poor people in improving access to land has increased
recently, through reformist policies such as the land reform and the land titling project, this
chapter shows that in the past the poor could receive as much, and probably even more,
help from the state in arranging access to land. The municipalities have been for a long
time an important instrument for resource-poor producers to gain access to land and to
defend them, to a certain extent, against land usurpation. This role gradually was eroded
not only because of the reduced amount of land available for distribution, but also because
of the centralizing tendency of state power in the second half of this century. This is
exemplified with the land reform in which the state developed an autonomous bureaucratic
apparatus (INA) that took over the control of ejidos from the municipalities. The state
developed projects (land reform, PTT) which were unmanageable and clashed with the
realities of rural economies and social relations.

Meanings of land value

A prime notion of the latifundio-minifundio concept is space.[57] The notion of productive
quality of land remains confined to a simple, fixed, agronomic category: the different
production capacities of fertile river terraces versus hillsides. A feature of land quality,
however, is that its valuation is never fixed.[58] The 'quality' of specific land as perceived
by producers changes historically. To value land quality producers do not only take into
account soil properties, fertility, and suitability for a certain crop, but also a whole range of
other properties: for example, judgments by a producer about house-plot distance, whether
a plot can be reached with animals, the type of improvements already made (the stored
value of past labour), water availability, the history of local conflicts around the plot, type
of neighbours (see the case of Excequiel), conflicts with the state (PTT), and issues of
right of way. It includes both an assessment of the production possibilities of the natural
environment as well as of the economic environment and the mediating institutions. This
observation is difficult to fit in with approaches that theorize unequal access in terms of
size of area only; producer's definitions of land and the access to it are different from
those meanings attributed by officials in land reform, PTT, and in development project
discourse, and different from intellectual constructions of a latifundio-minifundio complex.

Land quality is for producers not only *buena tierra*, that is whether the soil can produce
a good yield, but it also refers to the production process, the labour process, and the
historical relations between villagers (and sometimes with the state) which may be different
for each plot. In this way, land quality is on the one hand located in what producers

experience as their engagement in livelihood struggles, production for households needs, and the opportunities of the local market. On the other, it is the way in which they perceive relations to others (villagers), to the rule systems, and to the productive potential of the land.

3

Land Use Dynamics: Heterogeneity and Diversity

Change, Standardization and Diversity

Once producers have obtained access to land they can use it in different ways. Most policy approaches in Honduras still advance a dualist view of 'traditional' versus 'modern' agriculture. The 'traditional' refers to the cultivation of subsistence crops with simple tools, the use of a mixture of local cultivars*, and a low external input level. 'Modern' agriculture is based on wage labour relations, mechanization where possible, monocropping, high energy use, high external input, direct links to input and output markets, and the use of high–yielding cultivars. Agriculture as practised in El Zapote falls then into the category of traditional hillside agriculture which hardly ever changes. A typical example of this view is advocated in the first environmental profile of Honduras: '(..) migrant agriculture (*sic*) [is] practised by thousands of peasants, perhaps in a form more primitive than two-thousand years ago' (Campanella 1982:6). Such approaches aim at transforming the 'traditional' without considering the internal dynamics and processes of change. This chapter provides evidence that the variety of production systems in mountainous areas is much wider than a dualist view can conceive.[1]

In disagreement with this mainstream view, several approaches within agronomy and rural sociology deconstruct the dualist view and, instead, investigate diversity in whatever form of agriculture (see Table 3.1). A revalorization of diversity and dynamic change in so-called 'traditional agriculture' does not necessarily imply the attribution of an inherent positive value to diversity and traditionality.[2] Farming systems research (FSR) investigates variation in production systems by discerning agro–ecological zones (areas with similar soil conditions, vegetation, climate and population density). The variation in production conditions explains the absence of one optimal farm size and technology level (Shaner et al. 1982). Studies of styles of farming criticize not only the idea of a dichotomy between 'traditional' and 'modern' but also the idea of a linear relation between levels of technology and output (Ploeg, 1990). Producers do not react uniformly to similar environments but, instead, evoke different responses. Van der Ploeg argues convincingly that most agro-economic models of farming do not conceptualize diversity (mainly discussed as variability of output per hectare); they treat empirical diversity only as a residual factor. Van der Ploeg (1990:259) demonstrates that diversity is neither accidental nor a secondary characteristic of agricultural systems, but a 'structural result of the fact that farm labour, as a goal-oriented and conscious activity, takes place under increasingly diverse relations of production'.

Table 3.1 Views on diversity in agricultural systems

approach	difference and similarity in past and present agriculture	source of differences
main stream policy view in Honduras	change from subsistence agriculture into complex modern agriculture leads to diversification in the modern sector, which develops along a static subsistence agriculture	modernization leads to increased opportunities in production activity and choice of technology
FSR	all forms of agriculture show signs of high complexity which classical commodity-oriented research ignores	heterogeneity in production conditions
styles of farming	all forms of agriculture show signs of a diversity in styles which policy makers do not acknowledge	individual actor strategies
critique of capitalist development	past agriculture was diverse, modernization leads to standardization in crop choice and technology	modernization causes differences of past and present agriculture; other differences not explained

The various critiques of capitalist modernization stress that a *commoditization** of peasant economies entails the standardization of the technical conditions of production systems (e.g. Bernstein 1990; Kloppenburg 1988; Shiva 1988). They point to structural determinants that provoke standardization, acknowledging the possibility of some eventual empirical diversity.[3]

Hence, if the Honduran mountain agriculture displays patterns of complex and dynamic changes (see Jansen 1996), which the dualist policy view ignores, one still has to identify whether this complexity is caused by heterogenous environmental conditions, or whether it is entirely a result of diversifying actor strategies. Furthermore, commoditization processes may increase diversity or lead to standardization. This chapter explores the various arguments of these views in the context of agriculture in El Zapote. The next section deals with producer responses to biophysical production conditions. Then a discussion follows as to how emerging commodity markets change land use by reorienting cattle, coffee and tule production. Subsequently, I will analyse the dynamics of production activities which market development does not affect directly (maize, beans and other crops) but only indirectly. Before drawing conclusions, a presentation follows of the agrarian life of José and Excequiel, in order to explore the importance of actor strategies and structures in these processes.

Environmental Heterogeneity in El Zapote

The villagers feel that the environment of El Zapote is *feo* (ugly), because of the hideous mountainous landscape. They regard flat land as beautiful. Soil conditions in El Zapote vary considerably although most soils have developed on limestone sediments.[4] The zones north and north-east of the village (see Figure 3.1) used for maize, beans, and grassland, show deficiencies in potassium and sometimes of phosphorus. Producers like to work there because the fields are free from stones. 'The mountains' to the south–east rise to 1865 m.a.s.l. Coffee is cultivated up to 1500 m.a.s.l. The rainy seasons opens earlier than in the village and even during the dry seasons precipitation occurs regularly. Due to the high annual rainfall and lixiviation soils are more acid than at lower altitudes. The soils in the mountains are extremely or very strongly acid (pH range 3.4–6.3; mean 4.3, values below 4.0 are associated with high levels of aluminium). Nevertheless, coffee thrives well on these soils, although different problems with micro-nutrients have been observed. In contrast to the mountain zone, soils in the east and north-east are less acid (mean pH of 5.7) and have high levels of calcium and magnesium. The village commons to the west are used for maize cultivation; beans do not form pods according to the producers. Stones and rocks pose the main problems. Two rivers have formed river terraces with alluvial soils to the south-west. Livestock rearing is the most dominant form of use, but with practically all tule fields in between the different pasture areas. This summary illustrates that soil conditions vary over short distances. For instance, while the village commons are not suited for beans, the main bean area is not further than 500 metres away. In this mountain environment soil texture can vary from heavy clay to sand within one field. Furthermore heterogeneity causes some to 'dry out' very rapidly, entailing a high risk of losing harvests in dry years, while nearby soils may remain humid for very long periods.

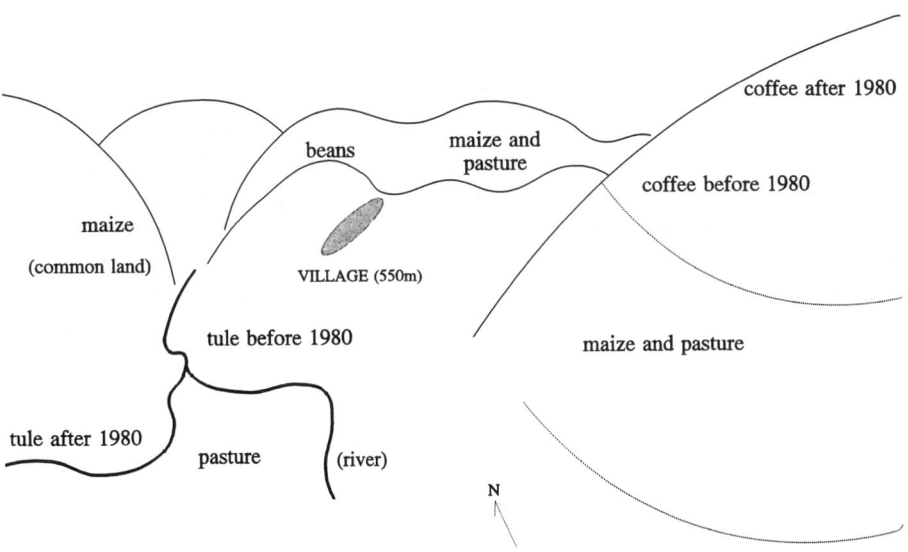

Figure 3.1 Sketch of the locations of the fields in the surroundings of El Zapote

As suggested above, the climatological conditions differ according to altitude. In the village location the mean annual temperature is 24.4 °C and the rainy season lasts from May to December. Rainfall distribution shows two major peaks in June and September (annual mean is 1615 mm), while both drought and excessive rain occur regularly. The drier period between mid–July and mid–August (the *canícula*) is less prominent than in some other parts of Honduras (Zúniga 1990), but drought stress may occur. The rainy season is long enough for two maize cropping seasons, but there is a considerable probability that the second crop (sown in October-November) faces water shortages at the end when the dry season starts. Its success depends to a large extent on the water–holding capacity of the soil. A long dry season may cause problems for grassland management, especially on steep slopes with shallow soils with low water retaining capacity, and for coffee. In the mountains, however, the rainy season tends to start earlier and precipitation is much higher (probably around 2200 mm).

It is not possible to produce a general cropping calendar as, for example, sowing and planting dates vary to a great extent. People sow maize or beans in different places in the municipality at very different times in the year, depending on altitude, humidity, and soil characteristics. Planning of tasks such as harvesting tule depend more on scheduling of labour time than on calendar time (rain). In a following section, I shall present a specific cropping calendar for one producer (Figure 3.5). Two examples may illustrate how variation in production systems relates to producers' responses to this heterogenous biophysical environment. Firstly, producers try to get access to fields with different environmental conditions for different objectives: in the mountains for coffee, near the rivers for tule, land with water sources for grasslands, plots with the right soil for beans, and so on.

A second response is the phasing of planting in time and space in order to enlarge the number of crops and to augment yields. For example, producers sow vegetables and beans during the dry season months (December–February) in the river terraces, on soils with a large water–holding capacity and enough water for the growth period of the crop. In this season less fungal infestation occurs. These fields, and the fields sown in the mountains between February and April, provide good quality seed for the two main bean seasons (June–August and September–October). Although less pronounced, the same strategy can be observed in maize cultivation. Maize can be sown on some river terraces until late December.[5]

The environmental factors that condition agriculture are not 'outer limits', that is they are not immutable natural circumstances. Winds have always blown, but wind becomes increasingly damaging when the surrounding forest is cut and loses its function as a wind break. Sowing *Planta Baja**, a new maize cultivar with short stalks, is the producers' response to this problem. Micro-climates change due to extensive vegetation clearance. Agriculture continuously interferes with nature and alters its own conditions. The next two sections deal with the various agricultural practices.

Production for the market: cattle, coffee, and tule

Emerging commodity markets in the course of this century have heavily influenced agriculture. Table 3.2 presents the most important cash-making productive activities in the 1950s. This section discusses the land use activities which predominate today: livestock rearing, coffee and tule cultivation.

Table 3.2 Registered sales of local products to national trade networks in 1950

	Value		
coffee	13061	454.3	qq
petate	10016	1378	dozen
pig-fat	5703	439	tin
cattle	3195	107	piece
pigs	1775	71	piece
rice	714	80	qq
beans	60	10	qq
potato	135	27	qq
others	42		
TOTAL	34701		

Source: composed of data from administration books of the municipality: '*Movimiento de extracciones y exportación de productos*'.
Note: Value in Lempira*: one Lempira is 0.50 US $ in 1950; qq is quintal*.

Cattle Republic or Short-lived Revolts?

The best developed theories to explain recent land use changes in Honduras focus on class analysis: that is the competition over the means of production between groups with different relations to systems of surplus appropriation. The key process is the increase in land under pasture and the expansion of cattle herds by a landholding class, causing marginalization of subsistence producers and maize production (Brocket 1988, Howard 1989; Stonich 1991a; Williams 1986). Many studies on Central America link pasture expansion to deforestation (e.g. DeWalt 1985b, Nations & Komer 1987). Based on an analysis of census data Stonich (1991a) concludes that land in the South of Honduras was reallocated from forest, fallow, and food crops to the production of export crops and livestock. Both Howard and Stonich conclude that the expansion of cattle ranching displaced small producers to marginal highlands, with environmental destruction as a consequence.[6] Howard considers the expansion of the cattle sector and the political strengthening of a class of ranchers as the central feature of recent changes in the agrarian structure: she argues that Honduras has become a Cattle Republic (Howard 1987). This section deals with the question whether El Zapote can be fully characterized as a part of that Republic.

The data on deforestation, and pasture and cattle expansion in El Zapote reflect the empirical trends observed by Howard very well. Cattle ranching is extensive because of a low productivity and low labour inputs per hectare. Furthermore, milk production is low and does not exceed a few 'bottles' (of 0.75 litre) per day per cow. The dry season is an important constraint for dairy farming as it causes a shortage of quality forage. Under these adverse conditions most cattle is of the resistant *Criollo* type. Only a few larger cattle producers with somewhat improved pastures have crossed *Criollo* cattle with *Brahman* and *Holstein*. Figure 3.2 illustrates the trend of a reduction of forest and fallow area and an increase in pasture between 1952 and 1974 (see also Table 3.3).[7]

Table 3.2 shows that the number of cattle increased by 52.1 per cent between 1952 and 1974, the golden period for cattle in Honduras, although cattle ownership became further concentrated.[8] The local expansion of pasture area also coincides with data at a national level (Howard 1989). The share of agricultural land under pasture rose from 24 per cent in 1952 to 40 percent in 1992. Figure 3.2 seems to confirm Howard's argument that the bulk of the conversion of primary and secondary forest to pasture took place before 1965. Thus by using a similar method the history of land use in El Zapote seems to confirm the Cattle Republic thesis.

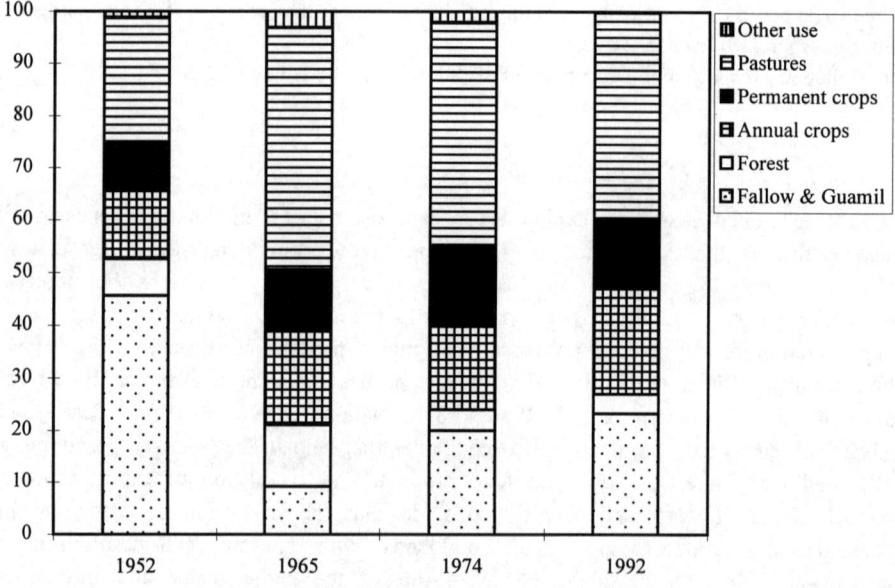

Figure 3.2 Land use in El Zapote as a percentage of the enumerated area.
Sources: DGECH (1954, 1968, 1978) and SECPLAN (1994). Total enumerated area is 3741 hectares in 1952, 3519 hectares in 1965, 3157 hectares in 1974, and 3151 hectares in 1992.

A closer look at several empirical features, however, reveals the limited scope of this thesis. The focus on cattle never allowed a clear appreciation of pack animal expansion.[9] Horses and mules bring the harvest of maize, beans, coffee and tule from the fields to the house. Producers say that they felt less need for pack animals in the past as maize and tule fields lay closer to the village. Furthermore, the people did not transport maize to the house after the harvest but stored the cobs in huts in the field. Every so often a bag of maize found its way to the house on the producers' back. Bringing the harvests to the house in one go with pack animals has become a common practice more recently.[10] The rise in coffee production boosted demand for pack animals even more and generated the revenues to buy and to feed them.[11] The displacement of coffee fields to higher up in the mountains further increased the need for pack animals.[12] Table 3.3 shows the substantial increase in pack animals, especially since 1974.[13] In fact the increase in pasture area lagged behind the growth in the number of animals, thus increasing the pressure on grassland (animals per unit area).[14]

Table 3.3 Livestock and pasture expansion in El Zapote

	% pasture	area pasture	cattle	pack a.	Increase in % of: area	pack a.	cattle
1952	24	899	726	249			
1974	43	1357	1104	333	50.9	33.7	52.1
1992-3	40	1256	1131	569	-7.4	70.9	2.4

Source: Jansen (1997); calculations based on census data (DGECH 1954, 1978; SECPLAN 1994).
Note: '% pasture' refers to the percentage of agricultural land in pasture; 'Area' is in hectares; 'pack a.' refers to the number of pack animals.

The fact that, in El Zapote, about one-third of all livestock are pack animals places the expansion of pasture in another setting and relates it partly to the growth of coffee production. Coffee has been crucial for the creation of a class of relatively rich petty commodity producers in El Zapote (see below). Hence, pasture expansion cannot simply be related to the development of monopoly capitalism (Howard), through the Junker road of capitalist development, because at the same time it is related to a process of internal differentiation of the peasantry.

Although the Cattle Republic thesis investigates land use changes, the more complex interlinkages between sub-systems remain under-explored. Figure 3.2 illustrates that the shares of land allocated to specific uses did not change very much between 1965 and 1992. Pasture expansion between 1952 and 1965 may be a result of a reduction of land under fallow, and not so much of a reduction of food grain production or forests as is suggested in Howard (1989). Much of this fallow land pertained to a forest fallow–maize–pasture system, in which a medium-long period of fallow was alternated with a few seasons of maize cultivation (often by tenants) and pastures afterwards, until the fallow-regrowth suppressed the grasses.[15] Furthermore, fields in fallow were relatively more important for grazing than at present. Thus, land enumerated as fallow also served to maintain a cattle population. In fact, maize and forage production became separated in more recent censuses. The tremendous shifts observed in census data by Howard and Stonich, which indicates an increase in the area dedicated to cattle raising, are less tremendous on the ground.

Another complicating factor is that, until a few decades ago, many livestock grazed not on pastures, but on land in fallow or with coffee, and on the unfenced 'free lands'. 'Free lands' disappeared gradually and with it the livestock owned by the poor. Roadsides and a few other pieces of land form the last resort, although local authorities increasingly forbid its use for grazing too.[16] The somewhat richer people moved their livestock to paddocks (owned or rented). For those without the resources to purchase or rent pastures stubble remains the only opportunity left for grazing. This second comment thus argues that the amount of pasture expansion does not indicate that all this land became used by livestock for the first time. Furthermore, land pressure and fencing reduced the access of the poor to livestock due to forage shortage.

A third comment is that the Cattle Republic thesis suggests a total take-over of the land, of the opportunities for capital accumulation, and of the political power by large cattleholders. It is undeniable that with a further expansion of the agricultural frontier the absolute amount of pastures grew further in the period between 1965 and 1993, but the relative share of the land under pasture remained practically the same (in fact declined somewhat).[17] Recently more insight is gained into the temporal character of the cattle boom. Since the 1980s external demand, an important initial stimulus for the cattle boom, has been in decline and beef prices have dropped. A further growth of domestic demand has partly compensated for this (see for example Edelman 1995). Furthermore, the institutional support for the cattle sector has diminished considerably since the sixties, when cheap credits were easily available for herd expansion. In the land's economy cattle is just one of the many businesses.[18] The subsidy of nature, i.e. the surplus extraction based on a low land value (Howard 1989), has already been cashed and it has to be seen whether extensive cattle ranching under the current conditions makes the big profits that are necessary to support a Republic.[19]

A final comment is that the cattle economy is more differentiated than assumed by the researchers who have investigated the link between foreign demand and beef production for export. Kaimowitz (1996b) illustrates the important contribution to the national herd by small and medium size cattle holdings. This sector owns a substantial part of El Zapote's cattle.

The cattle-thesis as formulated by authors such as Howard (1989), Williams (1986), and Stonich (1993) has enlarged our understanding of how the expanding cattle economy has restructured land use in Honduras. The four comments, however, suggest the need for rethinking the Cattle Republic thesis in terms of exploring the diverse ways in which cattle is part of complex production systems of smallholders and medium size farms. The case of El Zapote shows that the link between pasture and cattle is complicated by pack animals, which may have become more important in mountainous areas during the last decades of coffee expansion.[20] Pasture expansion is a less uniform process than sometimes suggested. More insight into the dynamics and diversity of cattle keeping and the interlinkages with other forms of land use, soil types, and land histories may be helpful to counter the tendency to reify agrarian class relations by conceptualizing them in terms of the dominance of cattle and pasture. A shift from interpretations of aggregated data to practices on the ground would also improve our understanding of the complexities behind deforestation.

Coffee

The cattle-thesis contends that the expansion of cattle displaced poor peasants from the more fertile lands to the hillsides. Baumeister (1990) takes over this argument and adds that this process explains the rapid expansion of coffee cultivation in Honduras in the last few decades. As a large share of the Honduran coffee comes from small fields on hillsides, Baumeister concludes that resource-poor producers substituted coffee for food grain production due to its higher economic returns per hectare on these slopes. In an earlier publication (Jansen 1993), I have argued that Baumeister (1990) perceives coffee as an 'escape crop' for marginalized hillside producers. Coffee, however, is produced by a wide range of different types of producers, but, notwithstanding the differences, it always requires some initial land, capital and labour resources.[21] Therefore, because they are too poor, half of the producers in El Zapote are unable to start a *finca**, although they would be very willing to do so.

The coffee boom of the last decades is a result of many different factors, but the roots of the recent expansion developed a long time ago. The list of '*agricultores*' (producers who could profit from the mentioned regulations) of 1914 reports three producers in El Zapote with fincas of nine, ten, and twelve *manzanas** (Honduras 1914). These were only the largest fincas. The publication of official books and manuals illustrate the interest in coffee cultivation in the course of this century (e.g. Montes 1928; Ortega 1951; Reyes 1927). Table 3.1 shows that coffee was already the most important export product in El Zapote in the 1950s, long before cattle expansion could have generated the effects described in Baumeister (1990). The expansion of coffee started before the construction of the road to El Zapote and before any institutional development in the coffee sector had taken place. Table 3.4 illustrates the expansion process in El Zapote in recent times.[22]

Productivity increased considerably between 1952 and 1974, and an even more substantial rise in productivity took place in the 1980s. This rise in productivity does not take place in all fincas, instead there is high variation in productivity (see Table 3.5). This variation is somewhat lower on fertilized fields but still remarkable. This variation cannot be explained by differentiating by farm size. Figure 3.1 expresses that producers with larger fincas do not necessarily obtain higher yields than producers with small fincas.

Table 3.4 Expansion of coffee production in El Zapote

Year	% producers	Area coffee	Productivity	% of area
1952	57	236	0.19	6
1965	50	331	0.31	9
1974	47	397	0.26	13
1992	46	375	0.86	12

Sources: calculated by author from DGECH (1954, 1968, 1978) and SECPLAN (1994).
Note: '% producers' is the percentage of producers that cultivate coffee; 'Area coffee' is in hectares and includes fields with young trees which do not yet produce; 'productivity' is in metric tons per hectare producing coffee; '% of area' is the percentage of enumerated area that is planted with coffee.[23]

Table 3.5 Variations in coffee yields

	Harvest 1993-1994
Mean of all plots (N=45)	754
CV (SD)	76 (571)
Mean of plots without fertilizers (N=25)	559
CV (SD)	76 (427)
Mean of plots with fertilizer (N=17)	984
CV (SD)	65 (641)

Source: producer survey of producer estimates of their yields.
Note: All means and standard deviations (SD) are in kg/ha. CV is the coefficient of variance and calculated as the standard deviation divided by the mean and presented as a percentage of the mean yield. T-value for differences between means for plots with fertilizer and plots without fertilizer is 2.58 (two-tailed observed significance level is 0.014).

The variation relates to diverse practices of coffee cultivation, with differences, for example, in the amount of fertilizer, weeding, age of plantings, spraying of biocides, shade tree density and shade tree composition, pruning, and fields with different soil characteristics and micro-climates. Numerous factors influence the final outcome of coffee cultivation. A producer can choose among various alternatives for some factors, but many of them are just given consequences of an earlier action. I shall outline only a few of them.

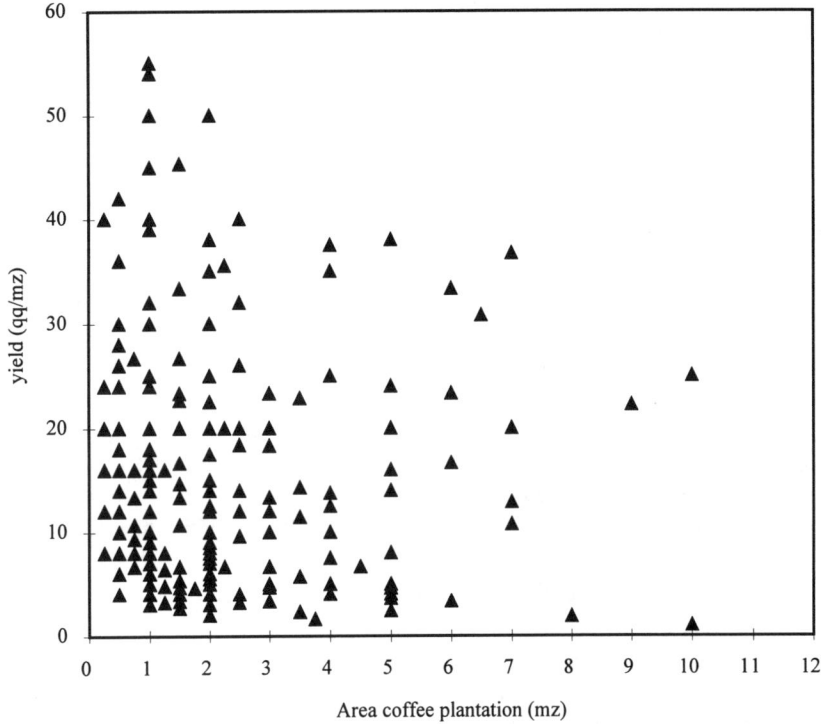

Figure 3.3 Variations in coffee yields in relation to finca size in El Zapote (1992-1993)
Source: IHCAFE census 1992-1993.

The location where a finca is started is crucial, of course. Soil quality varies, for example, in relation to soil depth, structure, amount of rocks and stones, acidity, aluminium content, and so on. Does the plot lie on a south slope or a north slope (influencing light intensity)? Is water available to process coffee, to spray with biocides, or to irrigate a nursery? Resource-rich producers, often in groups, have developed networks of hosepipes to take water from sources. Then the form of clearing the (mostly secondary) forest and sowing is important. Are rows of undergrowth slashed with axes and machetes and coffee seedlings directly planted with a dibble stick, or does one use a nursery system? The latter technology generally means that all the vegetation is cleared (sometimes burnt) and that seedlings are transplanted from a nursery into bigger holes. Spacing varies as well. The form of clearing may influence the type of shade vegetation (originally coffee could not grow under direct sunlight, only the modern varieties under high levels of fertilization can). Some producers leave tall original trees in the field and occasionally plant fruit trees. Others select desired shade trees (*Inga* spp.) by not weeding them from the sprouting vegetation. Only a few producers plant preferred shade trees (*Inga* spp. or Madriado, *Gliricidia sepium*) in a pre-designed spacing.

Producers have to choose between different varieties. They rarely sow the classic *Arábigo* (other local names are *Indio*, *Café del País*, and *Fantasía*) any more. *Bourbon*, which arrived in the 1950s, and the shorter, high–yielding cultivars *Caturra*, *Catuai* and *Paca*, distributed in the 1980s and planted in higher densities, are more popular nowadays. The initial phase of field preparation and planting influences the production of the coming twenty to forty years, the local lifetime of a coffee field. In fact, a sort of structure, with specific properties of which only some elements can be altered, results from the initial phase. Standing coffee cannot be shaped in whatever form (or the field must be totally renewed). The amount of labour invested in the preparation and planting phase is therefore crucial.

Two important practices during the further development of the coffee are fertilization and weeding. Fertilization rates vary according to available capital, and relate, therefore, to the farm gate coffee price in the foregoing year: higher prices provide money to buy fertilizers and offer an incentive to do so.[24] It may also be dependent upon the producer's willingness to enter into contracts with local coffee merchants who provide advances in fertilizers (making profits on fertilizer sales, rent on capital, and coffee commercialization). These producers with a low production, use most or all the income from coffee for household consumption (including larger investments such as the construction of a house), leaving little to re-invest in coffee fertilization.

Producers apply various forms of weeding. Some practice weeding in the same way that it used to be carried out half a century ago: clearing the fields of weeds and bushes with a machete or *machete vuelta** just before the harvest. Most producers, however, weed with the *pando** two or three times a year. Crop growth and weeding interact very much: a well grown crop with closed canopy suppress most of the weed growth. Local disagreement exists whether the practice to spray herbicides (*gramoxone**), as applied by some producers, is good for coffee. On the one hand, people see the sprayings as harmful for coffee, but on the other hand, weeding with the *pando* may damage the roots of the coffee. Producers who spray argue that they prefer not to hire day labourers for weeding, or that grass invades their field which cannot be eradicated with the *pando* alone.

Field location and technology choices interact with fungal diseases. In fields with much shade vegetation or on northern slopes, coffee may suffer from 'ojo de gallo' (*Mycena citricolor*), especially in rainy and cloudy years. Before the 1980s, Coffee Leaf Rust (*Hemileia vastatrix*) was unknown, but when it arrived it devastated practically all the fields at lower altitudes. Producers turned to the higher altitudes for planting new coffee (see Figure 3.1) and used new methods of making nurseries and lower densities of shade vegetation. This provoked other diseases: 'Damping–off' (*Rhizoctonia solani*) in nurseries and 'Mancha de hierro' (*Cercospora coffeicola*) in spots with much direct sunlight; also 'Derrite' (*Phoma costarricensis*) became more important. The emergence of Coffee Leaf Rust was followed by the first use of fungicides, mainly copper sprays and later Benlate. The arrival of Coffee Leaf Rust encouraged the purchase of rucksack sprayers which in turn stimulated herbicide spraying and the use of endosulfan to decimate the Coffee Berry Borer (*Hypothenemus hampei*).[25] Whether producers spray or not does not only depend on the progress of Coffee Leaf Rust (climate dependent, location dependent, shade dependent, cultivar dependent, and so on) but also on water availability (distance to water), availability of a rucksack sprayer, labour and capital availability, and willingness to spray. Several producers do not want to do the spraying themselves because of the health risks, but do not have the capital to hire day-labourers.

When coffee producers substituted groves with a few shade trees for forest vegetation at higher altitudes, Coffee Leaf Rust and the Coffee Berry Borer spread to higher altitudes, probably because of the micro-climatic changes such as the rise of temperature at higher altitudes. As an unintended consequence of their massive relocation the Coffee Leaf Rust followed the producers who tried to escape it. Producers, however, have learned to live with this disease, and some again establish coffee fields at lower altitudes making use of more copper spraying per year.

Practically all producers in El Zapote process coffee wet with a hand pulper to remove the beans from the berry. After washing, they sell it either as 'wet parchment' or 'dry parchment', the latter providing higher returns. To sell it dry one needs a drying floor near the house (only a few dry coffee in their finca). During the picking-season there is normally enough sunshine in the village to dry the coffee.

This short review of some of the many factors that influence the production process may help to understand the high variation in output. To carry out many of the described practices an adequate amount of labour has to be available, be it family labour or hired labour. For poor producers, even if they have some land, this is an important bottle-neck. The expansion of coffee, also in a situation of petty commodity production, is conditioned by a growing and cheap labour force, especially for picking. Most labour in El Zapote is recruited locally and many producers use family networks and debt bondage on a small scale to secure sufficient labour in harvest time. Today's amount of coffee could probably never have been produced fifty years ago when the current labour pool did not exist. Under the current conditions the expansion of coffee production increasingly defines processes of accumulation and surplus appropriation in mountainous areas (instead of being an escape crop or a 'last resort'). One possible result is an internal differentiation of the peasantry in which coffee plays a pivotal role for accumulating wealth and capital.

Tule

Tule (*Cyperus canus*, fam. Cyperaceae) is only commercialized in the village, but the sleeping mats (*petates**), woven by women from the dried leaf stems, are sold to traders.[26] The price of petates and tule is thus related to external demand. El Zapote is one of the main centres of petate production and supplies a large share of the national market; villagers consider tule their cultural patrimony and its production for the market dates back at least to the nineteenth century (cf. Rosa 1929). The different censuses of the nineteenth century registered people who made panama hats (sombreros) and petates.[27] The state recurrently showed interest in handicraft production in the region. For example, in 1918 the district governor ordered that the women of El Zapote should improve the quality of their petates.[28] However, it seems that the petate has remained the same product up to now, woven daily, on the floor of their house, by most of the women.

Tule plots are small (about 0.05-0.1 hectare) and require year round humidity. Hence, river-sides and sites near streams lend themselves to tule cultivation. Stands can produce for twenty years or more. Tule is a perennial, hardly needs weeding thus leaving the soil undisturbed, and the closed canopy guarantees that rain never splashes on the ground. Practically no biocides are applied.[29] Many would consider it an ideal crop for 'sustainable' farming systems. Variation in tule production depends on its location (guarantee of year-round humidity and soil quality), how often it is harvested and by whom. The tule harvest consists of cutting the 'ripe' (sazón) stems out of the bundle of unripe stems with a sharp knife just above the ground. Some producers go each cycle of the moon to cut tule, while others only go a few times per year. Regular cutting is generally considered to be better for the plant as ripe stems delay the growth of sprouting stems. Labour use varies as many producers swear by their own labour and consider day labourers as unsuited to do the delicate job, as their careless cutting damages the plants and reduces production in the long run. Children may only help in cutting the leaf from the stem and bundling up the tule.

External actors have never improved nor regulated tule cultivation but nevertheless tule production cannot be described as 'traditional' and outside capitalist market relations. The growth of a national market for sleeping mats turned tule into a major cash crop during the course of this century. Oral histories suggest that its importance to secure livelihood has grown gradually. The number of women in the villages has increased with population growth. Moreover, it seems that the production per woman per week has increased, although the evidence is not conclusive. In the past women spent much more time on washing cloths (they no longer go to the river but have tap water at home) and maize grinding (the daily trip to the maize mill replaced maize grinding on a stone). This time can now be used to make more petates. More and more traders became involved in buying petates and transporting them to other parts of Honduras.

The expansion of tule cultivation has not much direct effect on other forms of land use, as it uses little space. Nevertheless, it may fulfil an important economic role and, in that way, impact on other productive activities. Tule profits sometimes support intensification in coffee cultivation; producers may buy land or fertilizers with tule profits.[30] Tule and petate revenues subsidize the hiring of labour for coffee and maize cultivation. Conversely, there are many examples that producers use coffee revenues to establish tule fields. In contrast to this positive feed-back linkage there may also exist negative feed-back linkages. Several producers drop tule production because it diverts them from their principal activity: coffee. After the displacement of tule fields (see Chapter two and Figure 3.1) most tule fields are far away (two hours' walk) and people without pack animals experience difficulties in transporting the crop. While tule cultivation is a complementary activity for the lower-middle strata of producers, it has become inaccessible to the very poor and undesired by the richer coffee producers.

Tule, coffee, and cattle have all expanded and changed the outlook of agriculture in El Zapote. Market expansion has not led to standardized production systems, however. The next section discusses the changes in agricultural production activities which are not directly oriented to the market.

The dynamics of non-market productive activities

Maize

The poverty of poor producers in Honduras cannot be attributed to the fact that producers fail in breaking out of the traditional 'maize culture'. Instead, current forms of maize and beans cultivation for subsistence consumption seem to be a product of recent processes. One of them is the 'locking in' of resource-poor producers into low-yielding forms of maize cultivation, away from the more diverse cropping systems of the past.

The people in El Zapote distinguish between the milpa* (the first maize crop), and the postrera* (the second maize crop). These differ in cultivation practices and yield expectations. Table 3.6 shows the different yields and variation for three seasons.[31] Fertilizer use leads to higher yields and explains a part of the variation. But even within the group of fertilized plots the variance is very high. Steenhuijsen Piters (1995) makes a similar, but more quantitative, analysis of the different variables that explain variation in yields and he confirms the existence of many different sources that cause variation. The countless number of possible combinations of techniques (burning, fertilizing, spacing, and so on) and the heterogeneity of field conditions lay behind this variation in yields. Furthermore, these techniques are not fixed things among which producers can choose, but entities shaped under the influence of their experimentation. Relatively important changes take place currently with regard to burning (or not burning), the disappearance or reintroduction of a fallow period, use of fertilizers and biocides, cultivar choice, plant spacing, and storage.

Apart from the remarkable variation, Table 3.6 displays the difference between milpa and postrera. Producers in El Zapote expect postrera yields to be half those of the milpa. Table 3.6 confirms this general expectation. Oral histories suggest that the importance of the postrera for people's livelihood has increased during the course of this century. In the 1920s and 1930s most people only prepared a milpa, except for years with a poor first harvest. In the face of climatic adversity a postrera could provide a second chance. It is quite well possible that, with the reduction of fallow periods and the combined problems of low soil fertility and weed invasion (see Chapter four), an expansion of the postrera was a Boserup (1965) type of intensification: despite the lower yields and lower returns to labour the land use was further intensified. Besides changes in the postrera other elements altered.

The mean cultivated area of milpa per producer dropped from 1.78 hectare in 1952 to 1.25 hectare in 1974, and to 0.71 hectare in 1992, according to census data.[32] The mean productivity has not increased in spite of increased input use after 1974.[33] The producer survey reveals that yield expectations for milpa and postrera result in fewer producers sowing postrera than milpa (80 per cent versus 96 per cent), and in the area sown to milpa per producer being larger (0.86 hectare) than that sown to postrera (0.56 hectare).[34] The postrera receives less attention than the milpa, for example: fewer producers apply fertilizers to their postrera, which indicates that producers take less investment risks for the postrera.[35] The expansion of the postrera does not seem totally successful, however. Several producers suggest that they have considered not sowing postrera because of increasing drought stress. Others are experimenting with an earlier second sowing, in August instead of in November, the so-called *postrera de agosto*.

Table 3.6 Variations in maize yields in El Zapote in three different seasons

	Milpa 1994	Postrera 1993	Milpa 1993
Mean of all plots	826 (N=117)	428 (N=74)	890 (N=85)
CV (SD)	76 (626)	77 (329)	63 (565)
Mean of plots without fertilizers	634 (N=69)	357 (N=55)	696 (N=51)
CV (SD)	82 (519)	87 (312)	62 (430)
Mean of plots with fertilizer	1101 (N=48)	632 (N=18)	1199 (N=29)
CV (SD)	61 (668)	48 (305)	55 (661)

Source: producer survey
Note: All means and standard deviations (SD) are in kg/ha. CV is the coefficient of variance and calculated as the standard deviation divided by the mean and presented as a percentage of the mean yield. T-values for differences between means of plots with fertilizer and plots without fertilizer are 4.25 for milpa 1994, 3.26 for postrera 1993, and 4.12 for milpa 1993; for all seasons there is a significant difference in yields of fertilized and non-fertilized plots.

Besides the difference between the milpa and postrera many other important sources of variation exist. A first source is the heterogeneity of locations for cultivating maize with differences in soil, temperature and precipitation, thus influencing sowing dates, growth period, and yields. Maize cultivation at low altitude can be combined with maize cultivation at higher altitudes, to guarantee maize production in dry years when milpas in lower areas do not yield. Since the higher altitudes are sown with coffee nowadays, not more than a few producers continue to practise this combination. The majority only sow maize at lower altitudes. Another factor is the length of the preceding fallow period or number of years of continuous cultivation. Chapter four discusses the existing differences of fallow periods in more detail.

Different forms of clearing are the machete and burning; the axe to fell trees is no longer a very important tool as, practically, no forest-fallow exists nowadays. The machete and the *pando** (for weeding) have replaced the axe. Burning, however, has not disappeared with the axe. Chapter four will explore the many reasons for burning.

After field preparation people use a dibble stick (*pujaguante, chuzo,* or *huisute*) to sow maize, without any soil tillage. They soak the maize in water the day before sowing. This speeds up the uniform germination and reduces the time that animals may damage the seed.

It is not useful to separate the cultivars in traditional land races and modern high-yielding cultivars. The majority of the cultivars are, as far as I could trace, those introduced in the course of this century and a lot of mixing of genes has taken place. Producers who returned after temporary migration to the north coast often brought seed of new cultivars with them. The 'famine year' of 1954 forced people to eat their own maize seed, and afterwards they obtained seed from elsewhere, often seed of new cultivars (*Maizón*, *Tusa Rosada* and *Capulín de Estica*). During the 1980s development programmes introduced high–yielding cultivars such as *Planta Baja*, *Guayape* and *Híbrida*.

A change in space was another modification. The classical way of sowing maize is *en cuadro*, a square pattern of holes, with three to five seeds put in each hole. Many producers apply other spacing patterns; a newer pattern is in rows (*en surco*) with the holes in a line, mostly along contour lines, two or three seeds per hole and more holes per unit area.[36] Producers adapt spacing according to field considerations (fertility, humidity, possible damage by birds) and the cultivar.[37] Fields vary according to other crops, such as *frijol de milpa* (*Phaseolus* sp.) and squash (*Cucurbita* sp.), intercropped with maize.[38]

Fertilizer use started after 1985.[39] Fertilizer application may express itself in higher yields, but may also lead to no more than a stabilization of yields by masking decreasing soil fertility. In general fertilizers are not bought with the proceeds from maize sales, but with money obtained from other activities, for example coffee, tule, or off-farm income (day-labourers, petty merchants). This often determines whether fertilizers are applied or not. This also counts for the use of biocides, predominantly herbicides.

Fungal diseases are the most important threat to maize apart from drought[40]. Pest damage is less critical.[41] Theft may cause a producer to prefer not to sow his field. In El Zapote no biocides are used against diseases and pest, except for the Gorgojo during storage of maize. The first use of chemicals started in the 1950s, with small quantities of the insecticide *Clordano** being applied to maize storage in the house. Pills with insecticides (PH_3), to kill the Gorgojos in maize stored in *silos** and drums, replaced *Clordano*. Herbicides, especially paraquat, became popular in the 1980s and were distributed via local traders, in a period when weed infestation became a pressing problem for producers as an effect of shortened fallow periods and frequent burning. An intensification in the use of biocides and fertilizers in maize was conditioned by opportunities offered by an emerging coffee–based agricultural system. The use of biocides started in maize (*Clordano*) but the extension of herbicide use took place after coffee producers purchased rucksack sprayers to spray against Coffee Leaf Rust.

Weeding in maize varies according to whether a producer uses herbicides or the pando, and whether he does the work alone (a long period of weeding per manzana) or whether it is done with a group of day labourers (short period of weeding). Weeding is a very labour intensive task and producers often judge others by referring to whether a field is weeded well or not.[42] The 'lazybones' can be recognized by the amount of weeds in their maize field. People may start too late with weeding because of illness, off-farm work or other urgent tasks; this has a substantial impact on the final yield. Weeding may also be problematic when one sows on rented land that afterwards will be used for grazing. Owners may prohibit the use of herbicides that affect the grass growth.

In the ripening phase the plant is snapped and doubled below the lowest cob, probably to provoke a disease free ripening. Only a few producers who follow the official advice, carry out this practice as early as possible in order to reduce the affliction of Maíz Muerto. Most wait until all the leaves are shrivelling. The maize is harvested when the seed is dry, but sometimes it remains stored on the dry, snapped, plants in the field for several months. A few producers still store the maize cobs in small huts in the fields as was a common practice in the past. Most, however, take it to their house where, in general, the kernels are stripped from the cob and dried in the sun before storage. Bags, old oil drums or special silos containing just under 1000 kg grain, serve to store the maize. Most producers in El Zapote cultivate maize for household consumption only.

Rent for land to sow maize is paid in cash before the season. I know of only one special case where a sharecropping arrangement existed. The old practice of paying rent in kind of one and a half to two loads of corn cobs per manzana, is practically non-existent.[43] Some owners ask for such a rent but tenants consider it too high and prefer the relatively lower cash rent.

Even without the use of elaborate quantitative measurements it may be presumed that this enormous heterogeneity of conditions for maize production and the diversity and timing of cultural practices will lead to a considerable variation in maize yields.

Beans

Bean cultivation takes place in a variety of ways and at several times throughout the year. People prefer to sow beans (*Phaseolus* sp.) as a sole crop (*frijol de palito*) on small plots (mean area 0.15 hectare).[44] Some producers of El Zapote intercrop climbing beans with maize but producers do not include this so-called *frijol de milpa* in the category of 'beans', which only refers to the beans sown in single stand.[45] People prefer the taste of frijol de palito above frijol de milpa which has a taste of soil according to them, and the soup of frijol de palito is much better, less watery. Producers also indicate that frijol de milpa suffers more from diseases and climatic adversities than frijol de palito.

Whether producers sow frijol de milpa depends on the soil: many areas in the village are not suitable for this (for example de *Zona* where many resource-poor producers sow maize). In one hamlet people sow frijol de palito intercropped with maize, because they have good quality land to do that, while in another hamlet (Yoro) nobody sows frijol de palito and only frijol de milpa is known. People say that the frijol de milpa they use is better suited for higher altitudes. We see within one small municipality a wide variation in the conditions for bean cultivation.

Deterioration of environmental conditions is probably the cause of a change in spacing towards a higher plant density. The current higher density of holes is somewhat compensated for by putting fewer seeds (one or two, sometimes three) in each hole; producers report that in the past they used up to five beans per hole.[46] Producers explain the

80

necessity for a different spacing in terms of the diminished soil fertility and the less vigorous plant growth.

Producers generally sow beans for household consumption but nevertheless a lively trade in locally produced beans exists among villagers. The uncertainty of bean production means that producers may sow much more than needed in a good year. If their crop succeeds they have a surplus to sell. But it is not uncommon for villagers who have sown a few days earlier or later to suffer a period of drought, heavy rain, or cloudiness and to ask friends, relatives and patrons to sell them some beans. Households may consume all their beans if yields are low and can lose their own seed stock when there are adverse circumstances. They therefore do not sow beans in the next season or they buy new seed from others or from a local store. Many of these beans come from the productive valleys elsewhere in Honduras and are modern varieties which originate from the national bean programme. Hunger may lead to the consumption of bean seed and sometimes becomes the driving force for the introduction of new cultivars.

Shifts in other activities

Shifts in agricultural production not only entailed changing practices in maize cultivation, livestock, and coffee but also the disappearance or drastic reduction of certain activities. Indigo, cotton and tobacco have vanished. Guatemalan traders bought balls of spun cotton during the first decades of this century. Cigars made from tobacco were sold in the village. The cultivation of rice (rainfed), onions (and other vegetables), potatoes, sesame, and sugar cane has diminished. Cheap imported rice, sugar and cigarettes have replaced locally produced rice, *dulce* (brown sugar cake) and cigars. Producers also consider the declining yields and increased weed problems as an important reason to stop rice cultivation. The few rice fields which one can find nowadays produce solely rice for household consumption, and not for sale as was the case in the past. The change in sugar cane cultivation is even more impressive. Sugar cane provided cash for producers with oxen and a sugar mill. These oxen, also used for the transport of wood and other materials, have disappeared since the 1950s.

The reduction of pig fattening is an important change in the agricultural system. Table 3.2 shows the importance of pig-fat sales in the 1950s. In the 1950s and 1960s passing Salvadorean traders bought large numbers of pigs. Pig-fat sales have disappeared totally and pigs no longer leave the village. The reduction of pig raising is associated with a reduction of areas sown with maize per producer (see above). Pig fattening with maize and squash was a source for the poor to begin to accumulate wealth: to construct their first house or to plant a small coffee grove. Pigs were a form of saving, of putting the harvested maize in an account near the house and in a form which could be capitalized through an international trade network. This strategy has been curtailed.

The relation between maize and pigs illustrates how subsystems have feedback relations. On the one hand, productivity in maize cultivation decreased (return to labour) according to producers, thus increasing the costs of pig fattening according to producers. On the other hand, the war with El Salvador in 1969 disturbed the existing demand of pigs. Later, in the

1980s, the prohibition by the municipality of free–ranging pigs further jeopardized pig keeping, thus reducing the need for maize cultivation. A related effect was that intercropping of squash with maize has become less important. Squash, which in the past served as pig feed, is now only used as young squash in small amounts for human consumption.

It can be concluded that the diversity in crops and other production activities has diminished. Some activities have disappeared or become rare. The number of different crops sown by a single producer has declined. Furthermore, production objectives have changed: maize and rice production no longer generate cash or savings (maize via pig fattening). Nowadays only production for consumption remains. Opportunities for the poor to generate cash with agricultural products have diminished: they do not continue with a traditional subsistence agriculture but are 'locked' into maize production for their own consumption. Those who want to generate cash, and succeed in doing so, cultivate coffee and tule besides maize cultivation. This does not mean that food grain production for household consumption is a simple, uniform activity. A great variation exists in ways to carry out the many practices.

Land use and farm technology of José and Excequiel

The previous sections discussed the variation in production activities but did not reach a conclusion about why individual producers carry out activities in different ways. Some differences are obvious. The children of Alfredo Luna with their cattle herds and large coffee plantations have developed other maize cropping systems (ploughing, fertilizers etc.) different from, for example, the maize systems employed by their day labourers. Such differences can easily be conceptualized as structured by differential access to means of production. This section compares the agricultural life of two producers whose production circumstances are not that different. In the wealth-ranking of the eighty-three producers in the survey, José Delgado took position fourteen and Excequiel position twenty-seven.[47] Both would be labelled as poor small farmers in marginal areas in most official classifications.

José: making agriculture profitable
Although born in El Zapote, José (b. 1951) grew up with his grandmother near the border with El Salvador. She was keen for him to complete his primary school. At the age of twenty José visited his parents in El Zapote for the first time and he decided to stay because he considered that the conditions for agriculture were better than in the South: more land, much cheaper rent, and a better climate which allowed for two maize harvests per year. Life appeared to be much easier in El Zapote.

His father's main agricultural activities were maize cultivation and pig raising; he used to sow two manzanas of maize in the lower zones and two manzanas in the mountains, and he used to fatten ten to fifteen pigs. He also had some cows. José made his first milpas on his father's land. When I met José in 1992 he had a small amount of land: a little more than one manzana to cultivate maize. He had bought the field in the early 1980s. In 1993 he bought one manzana next to his first field for maize and in 1994 he bought six manzanas of land for pasture, for future maize cultivation, and for fuel and construction wood. He was also negotiating with his brother to transfer a piece of land to him where he had planted his coffee in the late 1980s. It is interesting to see how José arrived at this situation of accumulation.

In contrast to his father he only sows about one manzana of milpa and postrera. He sold his few pigs in the 1980s when free wandering pigs were no longer allowed in the village. Most of his maize harvests are for household consumption. Eventual surpluses do not enter an anonymous market as he sells them to neighbours and family who worked for him as day labourers in maize cultivation and coffee picking. Typically, richer coffee producers may use maize and beans to bind labour; labourers buy the grains somewhat cheaper than in the shops or receive them as a pre-payment. José says that day labourers never earn enough to save for making investments in their agriculture. For most of his field tasks he hires day labourers. José only carries out light work in the field because with his 'flat feet' he cannot work on the hillsides. He prefers to carry out cultivation tasks with a large group of day labourers in a short time, for example weeding his seventeen tareas* maize in two days with five to six day labourers. Similarly, sowing and harvesting of maize and beans takes not more than one or two days of work.

José is very able to keep the costs of different activities in his mind or he writes them down (see Table 3.7 for the milpa of 1993). He considers the yield of 1993 (1431 kg/ha) as a 'good' yield (cf. Table 3.6). Of the twenty-eight bags he directly sold four bags for forty-five Lempira each, because he had 'no place to store all the maize'. Using this price the monetary value of his maize harvest was about 505 L or 78 US$.[48] Not much for this very good year, especially if one takes into consideration that the labour of José himself and his family, and the use of his mules are not included.[49] His sons help with drying the maize and picking up and bringing the mules to the paddock. José perceives that he has to harvest at least twenty quintal 'to get his money out of it'. Each year he makes a postrera as well. The postrera requires less labour input (less weeding), but yields are much lower and the risks of losing a crop are higher. To my question whether it is not more convenient to have a fallow with green manure instead of a postrera he answered that 'the next milpa can fail, and if you have no postrera you will have hunger'. Besides, 'at present [1993] the coffee prices are very low. but we in El Zapote have no problems because we have maize while the people in San Rafael [a village nearby] are in trouble, because they live from coffee and do not sow maize'.

José ceased burning for milpa shortly after he had bought his own plot for maize. He has already been cultivating it for twelve years consecutively, without burning or a fallow period. Without burning, he says, 'there are less weeds and the earth remains more humid'. Since he joined a PRODESBA group in 1986 to receive training and credit to 'technify' his maize cultivation, he uses *gramoxone* and fertilizer, and succeeds in maintaining his yields at a constant level. The lectures of PRODESBA agronomists made him feel more assured about the usefulness of not-burning, for which other producers ridiculed him. On one field visit he showed me his neighbour's maize of about fifteen to twenty centimetres high, the same as in his own field. The maize of his neighbour, who had burnt, is clearly much greener than his own yellow maize and he says: 'the people see this, once burnt one views the milpa more beautiful'. But he thinks that yields 'are the same'. He understands the people who burn and is not pleased with spraying *gramoxone* either, which is the alternative he uses, as he thinks it increases the amount of grasses and the earth 'turns into powder and erodes'. The agronomists he has confronted with this problem denied that *gramoxone* causes this effect. Despite his objections he continues to use *gramoxone* because 'at present one cannot weed the maize when one does not use *gramoxone*', thereby referring to the time he worked with his father when weeding was easy and required little labour. He weighs up the advantages and disadvantages of burning and *gramoxone* and does not carry out one particular practice because of conviction or clearly visible better results, but by considering what may be better in the long term.

Table 3.7 Variable costs of maize production (milpa) in 1993, made by José Delgado

Task	Inputs and cost per unit	Total costs
clearing field	5 day labourers á 9	45
Gramoxone (herbicide)	1 litre á 35	35
spray Gramoxone	2 day labourers á 9	18
sowing	4 day labourers á 9	36
first weeding	11 day labourers á 9	99
fertilizer, 12-24-12	2 bags á 73.50	147
applying fertilizer	2 day labourers á 10	20
second weeding	13 day labourers á 10	130
fertilizer, urea	1 bag á 64.50	64.50
applying fertilizer	2 day labourers á 10	20
snapping the maize	2 day labourers á 10	20
harvesting the cobs (three days)	9 day labourers á 10	90
separate grains from cob, paid per bin	child labour	25.50
insecticide pills for storage	1 tube á 4.80	4.80
TOTAL (A)		754.80
HARVEST (B)	28 quintal á 45	1260
Calculated 'profit' (B-A)		505.20

Note: All costs in Lempira. The daily wage increased from nine to ten Lempira during the season. The plot is seventeen tareas* (about 0.9 hectare).

His style of planning through a sort of cost-benefit analysis becomes even clearer if we look at how he built up his finca. His youngest brother allowed him to make a small finca on a quarter manzana of his land. He used some wages from the construction company of the hydro-electric power plant where he worked around 1980. He does not like to talk about this finca as it never became very productive because he 'gave no love' (*no le daba amor*) to it. He did not invest in it and the low production level could not generate his interest. Things changed when PRODESBA started with coffee groups. First PRODESBA did not allow him to participate because he owned no land. He put pressure on his brother to give him an extra manzana of land and subsequently could convince PRODESBA that the land was his, becoming eligible as a group member.[50] PRODESBA supplied training and credit for equipment, labour, fertilizers and biocides.[51]

His finca is now well established. The coffee has been planted with a high density and he applies fertilizers (once or twice a year) and two sprayings with copper. He has two rucksack sprayers and he can borrow an extra one from the local council of AHPROCAFE. The main problem in his finca is the lack of water (to spray biocides and to wash the coffee) in the dry season. To solve it he has gathered a group of neighbours together to install a network of hosepipes to get water from a natural source. In the 1990s he produces about fifty quintals a year and his goal is to keep production at a constant level (about 1582 kg/ha).

In his view 'PRODESBA helped the middle size producer'. He is convinced that his way of coffee production is profitable but that without capital (from PRODESBA) it would have been impossible to establish such a fine finca. When he took credit people told him that with such a loan PRODESBA would take away his house, but he was convinced that without taking risks he 'never would get anything'. After the establishment of the first manzana with PRODESBA he could extend his finca with another half manzana of high-productive coffee. After each harvest, he first buys the fertilizer and biocides for the coming year. Then he puts money away for the wages of day labourers for a whole year and a specific amount for household expenditures. When there is still some left he spends it on new investments (e.g. land, house improvement), luxury goods or puts it in a bank account.

He likes to recall how he uses his income in a planned way. He writes down his expenses in a notebook. He has calculated that the harvest of 1993-94 gave him 19.000 L income and 5000 L expenditure, leaving a profit of 14.000 L (about 1986 US$). With the profits from coffee he could carry out the above mentioned investments. He wanted to have more land for maize cultivation in order to reintroduce a fallow period and to rotate fallow and maize between the two fields. He wanted to become less dependent on his mother and her land for grazing his two pack animals. A key concept which often recurs in our conversations is that his agriculture has to be 'profitable' (*rentable*). He always reflects upon his undertakings in terms of a type of cost-benefit analysis. He does this not only with regard to his current activities but also with regard to activities he has discontinued. José has ceased to cultivate rice since 1990 because it requires too much effort, the 'earth is tired' and you have to spend a lot of labour on weeding: 'it is not profitable' (*no es rentable*). Likewise, onion cultivation is no longer profitable for him. The use of such calculations, however, do not turn José into a flat *homo-economicus* who only sees himself as an individual operating on anonymous markets and optimizing factor costs.

When I asked José how his finca has changed his life he says that the success of his finca means that he 'can work less'. He no longer has to sweat so much in the field. Most labour on his farm is hired labour. The two eldest sons (of his five children) attend the primary school. They and his wife do some agricultural processing activities around the house (drying coffee, beans and maize, bringing the pack animals to the pasture). The sons carry out much less farm work than many of their peers. He does not want his sons to become important workers in his fields but instead aspires to offer them the opportunity for secondary (and, so he hopes, higher) education. Financial prosperity should lead, according to him, to his wife at home 'working less'. He has never had tule. He mentions playfully that he is 'not even able to cut tule'. Tule cultivation is not an esteemed profitable economic activity in his particular view. Some men do not work; 'they only cut tule and have the woman in the house making the sleeping mats and earning the money while the man is lying in the hammock'. His wife is an exception in the village as she is one of the few women not to make sleeping mats. This is the advantage of coffee, he says, that his wife 'does not need to work any more'.[52]

Because of health problems he only does light work and he restricts himself to vital tasks, such as de-pulping coffee and packing the maize and coffee loads on his animals (many day labourers lack this knowledge, according to him, because they do not own pack animals). Most day labourers are close kin (father-in-law, brother-in-law, brother, first son from a first wife) or people of his neighbourhood in the village.[53] He is well aware that he makes his money by hiring labourers. This is not to say that he considers that money makes the world go round. 'Only money is nothing, you also need people. The day labourer serves the patron and the patron serves the day labourer'.

The way he organizes tasks and the allocation of labour gives him time for his passion for political and community activism. He is an activist for a main political party which occupies much of his time during the election period. He does not reject the idea of becoming a candidate in the near future for the office of mayor. He is secretary of the local committee of AHPROCAFE for a second time, he is member of the committee for the construction of a new drinking water system, and he is a member of the parents' council of the primary school. He was treasurer of the committee which collected funds to establish a secondary school in El Zapote. He was also a member of the *Centroamericano* church council.[54] In many of these activities he operates as an administrator: the man of the books or the auditor of labour and funds. He figures in positions where he can assess the value of new opportunities. His style of working is calculating, and less jovial than some other authorities, causing other people to regard him as too strict and inflexible. This calculating style was present in the way he judged whether to come back to El Zapote, to take up a job with the company which constructed the power plant, to ameliorate his maize production and to become incorporated in a PRODESBA coffee group.

Excequiel: if I don't work I don't eat

Excequiel (b. 1945) is only a few years older than José.[55] His father produced some coffee, *dulce* (brown sugar cake) for which he maintained a pair of oxen, and normally prepared three manzanas of milpa to provide maize for household consumption and for fattening five to seven pigs. In the first week of his second school year, at the age of seven, Excequiel had to leave school after a conflict with the school director who had ordered him to buy some booze, which he refused. During the following years he worked with his father and eldest brother in the field. He always deplored their squandering of the profits from pigs, dulce and coffee, on booze. He first earned his own money during the price boom in coffee in the mid-1950s. As a small boy he gathered fallen berries and spent the earnings on his first pair of trousers, to have an alternative to the distasteful trousers his parents bought for him. Some years later, at the age of fourteen, he decided not to work any longer with his alcoholic relatives; he made his own first milpa and contributed the harvested maize to the household. Looking around for a way to earn some money he became a day labourer for Rafael Luna at the age of seventeen. Rafael soon turned him into his main muleteer who had to bring provisions for the coffee pickers to the finca and to return with the coffee.

Excequiel remained muleteer for seven years until he married Rosa. They jointly decided that they would try to work for themselves: 'To be a day labourer is serious, only the rich go up'. Day wages only covered daily necessities but never allowed for savings and larger expenditures. He followed the accumulation strategy of the poor of those days, which is based on high labour inputs: he made a lot of milpa, without having the resources to hire external labour, in order to fatten pigs. This meant several years of very hard field work. After some lucky sales he was able to buy his first finca and start with coffee. Each new activity of Excequiel is centred upon achieving farm improvements through intensifying the labour efforts of the family. Rosa had to work harder too when they decided to work for themselves, that is to produce more sleeping mats in order to generate the necessary monetary income until the farm would produce surplus. Chapter two described several of the adversities experienced by Excequiel and Rosa. When I first met them in 1992 Excequiel owned about one and a half manzana of unproductive coffee, one tarea of new tule which was just starting to produce, and he sowed his maize in the Zona and beans on rented land. All their hard work had not yet resulted in a significant accumulation of assets. Halfway through the 1990s he produced less for the market than his father did forty years ago. Criticizing those who participate in party-politics in order to get small jobs he says: 'if I do not work I do not eat', which implies that he cannot spend his time on party-politics. This motto illustrates his reasoning for his farm: that only with hard physical labour of the family one can build up a farm and improves one's living conditions.

His style of maize cultivation does not cling to a technical optimum but is a continuous adaptation to changing conditions, including the availability of family labour. Although he had once a good result with spreading fertilizer and herbicide in the beginning of the 1980s he did not try fertilizer again until the 1990s. One main reason was that he generally produced enough maize for the household, also because he needed less maize as pig fattening had become less important. In the 1990s, however, maize yields were no longer sufficient and Rosa's petates supplied the money to buy a bag of fertilizer. In 1992 Excequiel put aside his belief that weeding with the pando is better because 'the roots stay alive and serve as manure'; *gramoxone* replaced hand weeding when it was not possible to weed on time with the pando (unavailability of labour). The money for *gramoxone* did not come from profits earned from maize, but again originated in Rosa's petates. In 1993 he started to sow in rows, a technique he had learned two decades earlier when working for Don Rafael, but which he had never practised on his own field. In 1994, he also wanted to change his mode of maize cultivation by ceasing to burn. But when he saw the debris he 'felt a desire to burn', and ultimately he did not act as he had planned to do. Excequiel is continuously in doubt as to what to do: sowing early or late (waiting for the rains or not, and trying to figure out which rains are really 'rains'), spreading fertilizer or not, which cultivar to sow, etc. I often found him worried and with a headache, and not having slept a night because of not knowing what to do. The problem is that a producer never knows beforehand which combination of technologies is best in his or her situation.

The following example elucidates that doubt dominates in crop production instead of a mechanistic rationality of optimalization. In 1994 Excequiel had two maize cropping systems in one field, more or less an accidental result of earlier choices. When I visited the field the appearance of the crop in both parts was rather different. On the lower part of the field the maize had remained short and had turned yellow, with some indications of deficiency in phosphorus. Many plants were flattened or showed signs of leaf rust infestation (a fungal disease). The cultivars *Maíz Negrito* (black maize) and *Maíz Amarillo* (yellow maize) had been sown here and this part of the field had not been burnt. They had weeded it twice with the pando, but weed infestation was clearly visible. Initially the crop had developed well with two stalks out of each hole. Excequiel had applied fertilizer (urea) after forty-five days, when he saw signs of coming rain in the sky. It did not rain for eight days, however, and the urea did not work according to him: the plants remained yellow. The upper part of the field with the cultivars Maíz Amarillo and *Planta Baja*, a high-yielding cultivar, was remarkably different. The drought had damaged this part: many plants had not survived and only a few scattered plants remained. These had developed well and were much greener and contained good cobs. This part looked 'clean', even though they had not weeded it intensively because of low infestation: only once with herbicide and a *chapea* (light weeding with the *machete vuelta*). Few weeds had proliferated under the trees of the *guamil* they had burnt on this part. As Planta Baja does not resist drought Excequiel did not want to sow it in the 'drying earth' of the Zona. His son, however, had argued that Planta Baja was better as it does not grow high and resists heavy winds. The result was that in both these parts the chosen technology combination was unsuccessful in producing a good yield although the outcomes were nevertheless very different: one part with many yellow plants invaded by weeds and another part with very few but beautiful green maize plants.

The comparison of these two parts shows how difficult it is for the producer to choose between the many technological options: burn or not burn; application of fertilizer; cultivar choice; and how, how often and how much to weed. Different combinations were made on different parts with different results. It appears that Excequiel's choices are not simply an outcome of finetuned cognitive adaptation to the environment, nor of a functionalist evolutionary process in which activities that produce unwanted results lose their appeal automatically and will not be repeated. His actions cannot be captured with a mechanistic concept of rationality either. Which was a more rational cropping system: the upper part or the lower part? The basis of the differences was how rainfall in this particular year interacted with weeds and maize development, and the producer and worker (sons) reactions to this. The soil was the same in the two parts, rainfall too, as well as the psychology of the producer and his approach to agriculture and environment. This case shows that an over-emphasis on producers' individual agency as the cause of differences is not appropriate as it suggests that differences are solely a result of purposeful, planned, actions. Excequiel finds it difficult to plan his actions; he is often distressed by the problems of what to do, when, and how. Recurrently he scorns his own past decisions in crop production.

One objective that keeps him busy is how to produce a cash crop. Maize is for the household and he has sold maize only once, when a son was ill. Coffee and tule are his cash crops. Excequiel made his present finca in a twenty year old forest fallow, at the end of the 1980s. In subsequent years he made nurseries to enlarge his plantation little by little. 'I have set up my finca by my own efforts', he used to say, thereby referring to others in a PRODESBA group, such as José, who did it with a bank loan and could establish at once a field of one manzana. Participants in this PRODESBA group, on the other hand, do not consider Excequiel's finca and nurseries to be good agricultural practices. The nursery is not well maintained, plants are sown too late, fertilizers are not applied and production is low. In 1993-94 Excequiel harvested fourteen quintals on his one manzana finca (760 kg/ha), his biggest harvest until then. But parts of his finca show signs of 'die-back' (exhaustion of plants, mostly due to relatively heavy fruit-bearing) and the crop is in a bad condition with high rates of leaf fall. Signs of soil erosion in his field, located on a steep slope, are clearly visible. A part of the finca is located so that sunlight does not enter very well; this increases the incidence of the fungal disease '*ojo de gallo*' (*Mycena citrocolor*). Excequiel dislikes the high-yielding cultivar *Catuai* (introduced by PRODESBA), 'because you have to apply fertilizer three times a year'. This cultivar does not respond to his labour efforts. He does not reinvest any profits in fertilizing the field.

Excequiel always worries about whether he can contract enough supplementary labour to pick coffee as family labour alone is not sufficient and the berries may fall. The finca is far away, a two and a half hour walk, and day labourers do not want to go there, or they demand day wages instead of payment per bin ('*galon'*). When paid in day wages they come late and leave early, because of the distance, and they resist working hard to pick a substantial amount of coffee, according to Excequiel. In 1992 he held the opinion that only adults could pick coffee well without destroying plants, but in 1994 he was more in favour of children. His youngest son had lured a few friends who liked the idea of staying some nights in the finca (partly to prove they were not afraid to sleep outdoors in the dark forests); they formed the largest part of the hired labour. The adults he had payed in advance did not appear. This reinforced his view that the amount of hired labour should be reduced as much as possible.

Excequiel and Rosa have a close affinity with tule and petate production. Excequiel talks with much pride about the beautiful tular he had lost with the construction of the power plant. Since then, Rosa buys her tule. In 1992 he planted new tule on a recently bought plot near the river. The land is of good quality but there is a high risk that the river will change its course and take over the land. In 1994, for example, the river invaded his land during heavy rains, destroyed a corner with maize and deposited a thirty centimetre layer of clay. The field is still appropriate for tule, but it may be lost completely next time. Excequiel experimented in 1994 with some fertilizers and the results seemed promising; Rosa now wants to make extra sleeping mats to buy fertilizer for the tular. She pays other women who make sleeping mats with her tule.[56] She wants Excequiel to harvest tule in months with a high demand for tule. In June, July and August, the months of scarcity, hungry poor women ask for her tule to make petates for her. Many producers 'only cut enough for their wife' due to a lack of time in these months as they are weeding the maize and other crops. Again during the coffee harvests, producers do not want to spend time on cutting tule. The labour calendars of other crops define dates for tule harvests and influence the negotiations in the contractual arrangements between women with tule and those without tule. Excequiel and his family appear to have work all year round with the four main crops: maize, beans, tule and coffee. Figure 3.4 represents the labour input in Excequiel's farm and Figure 3.5 relates it to the cropping calendar. Figure 3.6 shows who is involved in different activities.[57]

A main conclusion emerging from these figures is the heavy work load of all family members and the absence of any slack periods. Excequiel works forty-nine hours a week (on average), his sons forty-five to forty-seven hours. This does not include even their work and the work of Rosa at home. This calculation refers to weeks in which he is not ill and normally works six days. Apart from most Sundays he did not work on seventeen days spread over the year, mostly after a few days of hard physical work (e.g. clearing a field). In ten weeks Excequiel worked more than fifty-five hours. The three lowest values in Figure 3.4 are periods with many days of illness which caused a substantial reduction in working hours. Excequiel suffers a lot of illness and in 1994 he stayed at home for sixty-five days; these days his sons worked less hard and sometimes they also stayed at home. Despite these sixty-five days of illness he still worked more than 2000 hours, while his sons worked more than 2300 hours in the field. Figure 3.6 confirms the observation that women carry out few fields tasks. In 1994, Rosa worked in the fields for eight days (one day coffee picking, three days tule cutting and four days harvesting beans); it was the first year since her youth that she had worked in the field.

Figure 3.6 depicts how subsistence activities (maize, beans, other tasks) utilize the major part of the labour input (53 per cent). Excequiel employs less labour in commercial crops (tule, coffee) which supply most of the monetary income. He does not shift labour employment from food grains to cash crops despite the monetary profits. From Figure 3.4 it follows that Excequiel uses mainly family labour, not only for maize but also for coffee. Nevertheless, in coffee picking the hiring of wage labour is inevitable. He plans activities in such a way that first all available family labour can be employed before he turns to contracting day labourers.

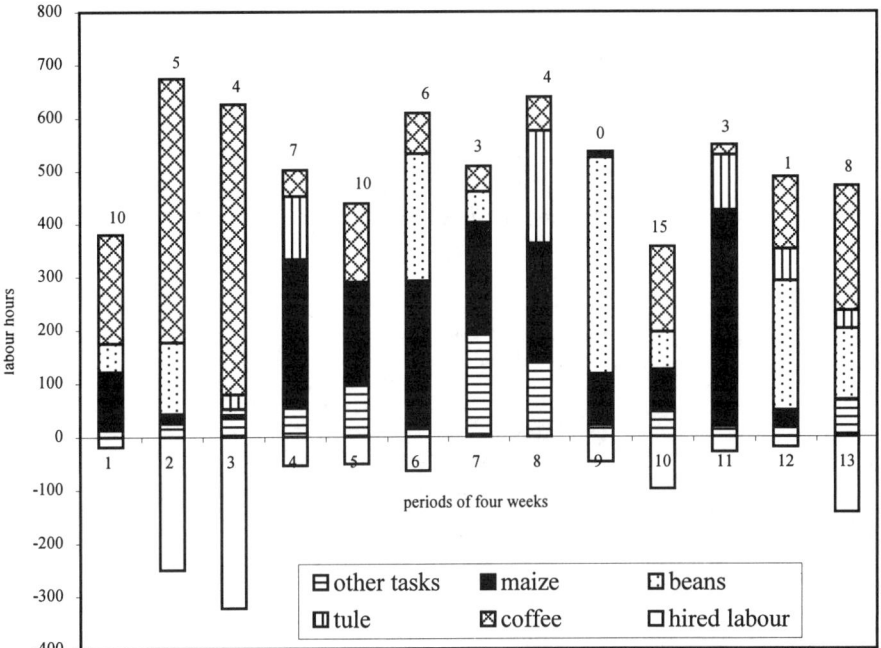

Figure 3.4 Distribution of labour over different field activities in time on Excequiel's farm in 1994
Notes: X-axis represents periods of four weeks. Labour hours include the time to walk to the fields. The numbers above the bars refer to the days of illness of family workers per period. The negative numbers represent the hours of hired labour. The category 'Other' includes collecting fire wood and fodder for the animals as the most important other activities. The figure does not include the small tasks carried out after arrival at home (such as feeding pigs, sharpening tools, drying coffee).

In fact for most of the tasks he prefers to work without day labourers at all. He regularly expresses his doubt about the willingness of other people to work and he considers it difficult to find day labourers for a particular day. In most cases he has to give them payments in advance (in the range from one to four day wages). Especially before the weekends they visit him when they know that he is searching for help. Several people who still owe him money have left the village. But although Excequiel does not like it, advanced payments are often the only way to assure labour. A short example of an encounter between Excequiel and day labourers on a sunny Saturday afternoon may illustrate this. It was the time that he needed labour to clear the field. Two young men in an inebriated condition came to Excequiel's house and talked stealthily with his youngest son. He called his father who accepted the idea of advancing money. His son was delighted because this meant less hard clearing work for him. Excequiel seemed less happy with the arrangement and to me he recalled his aversion to drunkards and complained that the village authorities did nothing about the many (illegal) cantinas. Groaning and moaning he had to admit that his advancements maintained the drunkards over the weekends but he argued that whether they drank or not was their own business. Rosa often plays a role in deciding whether to hire labour for maize cultivation because in many cases her money is essential for payment. Excequiel sells the first coffee, harvested with family labour, in order to contract day labourers for the following bigger harvests. Non-household labour is primarily used for coffee.[58] The sons of Excequiel sometimes work for other people but the number of days is approximately three times lower than the number of days that day labourers are hired (30:107 in 1994).

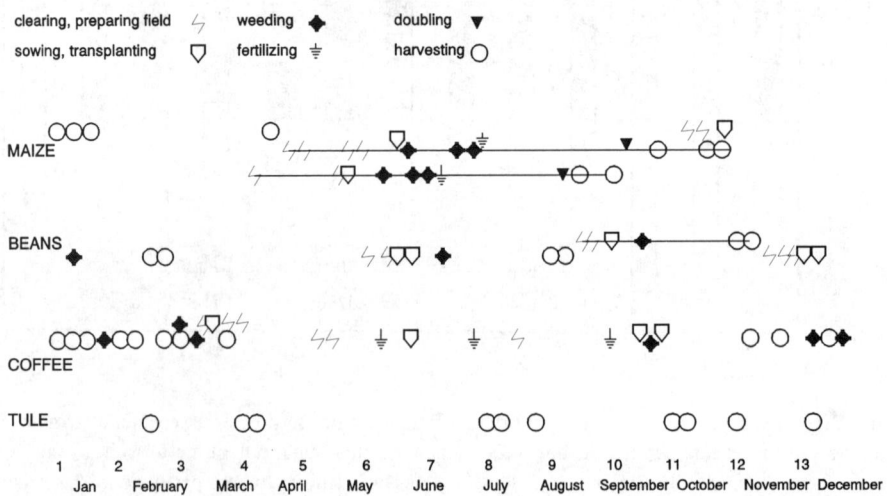

Figure 3.5 Cropping calendar of Excequiel in 1994

Notes: The numbers refer to the same periods of four weeks as in Figure 3.4. There are two main maize crops, a milpa and a postrera in the Zona, and a small plot of milpa sown on a small river terrace plot, next to the tular (sown in May). Besides the two main bean crops (sown in June and September) he also sows beans on the river terrace plot in December. Activities in coffee include the preparation of an extension of his field and the transplanting of coffee; application of fertilizer is in the nursery only. For weeding maize he used herbicides on two occasions. This figure does not mention 'Other tasks' (see Figure 3.4) as these are carried out in many of the weeks (thirty-eight of the fifty-two) throughout the year.

Despite the casual hiring of day labourers, Excequiel continuously worries about finishing tasks on time. The absence of slack seasons means that every change in technology needs to take into account the present situation of maximal use of family labour. The returns on labour are not high. I cannot precisely relate the labour in 1994 to the returns because some harvests took place after my field work period. The harvests in other years however, may be indicative. In the 1994 milpa he harvested thirteen quintals of

92

maize and the 1993 postrera provided four quintals.[59] His two bean harvests were three quintals each in 1994 while he harvested 1.7 quintal on the small plot next to the tular.[60] His coffee yielded fifteen quintals in the 1993/94 season. During 1994 he harvested a little more than twenty-four loads of tule. An estimation of the market value of these harvests is: maize (total) 2352 L, tule 1080 L, beans (total) 2695 L, and coffee 4650 L. A comparison with the labour investment displayed in Figure 3.6 shows that in this year of high bean prices and relatively very low coffee prices the return on labour was roughly similar for all crops. In years with high coffee prices (such as the 1996/97 season), however, coffee gives a much higher return. Excequiel, nevertheless, claims that he will never reduce the area sown with maize.

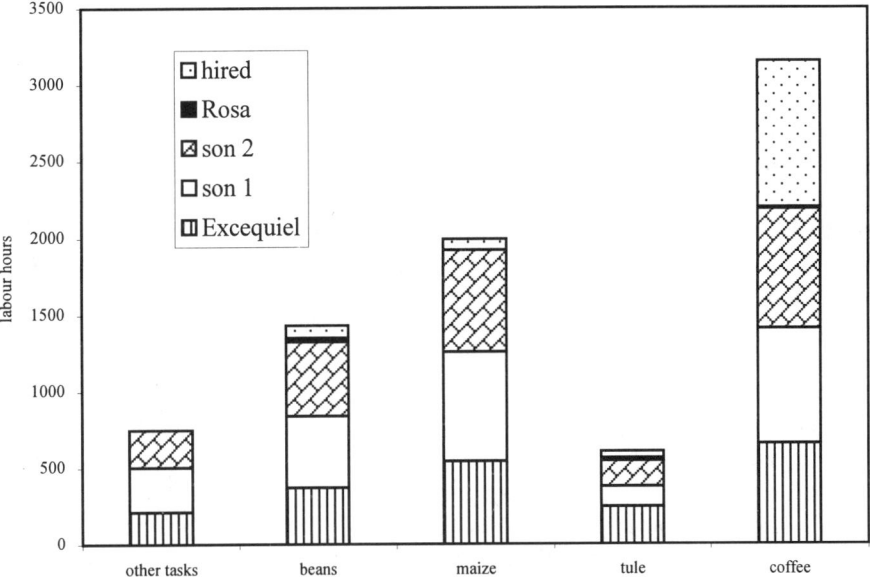

Figure 3.6 Amount of labour hours in the field used for various activities
Note: See note of Figure 3.4. Labour use in hours in 1994.

Comparing José and Excequiel: time and investment in agriculture

The above descriptions of selected farming practices of José and Excequiel exemplify how producers respond differently to external circumstances. In the following comparison I try to go beyond listing the differences of assets and levels of production, and instead try to understand some of the differences in strategies.

The most crucial differences can be observed in how they use labour and invest savings. José depends completely on day labourers and uses his resources to establish long-term relationships with some of them, partly through the supply of food grains in times of scarcity. Excequiel decides how much land can be sown and how to cultivate maize according to the availability of family labour. He has no long-term relationships with day labourers and his access to them is limited, sometimes he even has to borrow money or his wife does a long working day to finish a sleeping mat to give a day labourer a payment in advance. Excequiel has to accept unwanted visits to his house from drunkards despite his aversion to them. With one friend he maintains long-term labour relationships, sometimes paid, sometimes unpaid and mostly reciprocal, but these exchanges of labour only take place a few days a year. José sells all his coffee in one go after the final harvest, and saves money for next year's wages, including for the coffee harvest. Excequiel starts to pick the *requema* (the first grains that ripen) with his sons and he sells this coffee wet (depulped but not dried) to cover the labour costs of the following harvests.

Divergent forms of labour use and investment coincide with different responses to intervention, technological experimentation, and adversities. Their current situation results from the way they have dealt with past interventions. The difference in education of José and Excequiel had not much influence on their lives until the end of the 1970s when both worked for the company that constructed the hydro-electric plant. José could work as an administrator in the company store and earned a lot of money and was able to construct his house and buy a piece of land for maize cultivation. Excequiel could not read or write and worked as a manual labourer in the construction. He earned much less than José, and he spent all of his money to start building a house. As a result José obtained good quality land to cultivate his maize while Excequiel had to settle for the village commons where yields of maize are much lower. When PRODESBA started its activities José, who initially could not join the programme, created a situation so that he could participate in the credit and extension programme. Excequiel was asked on various occasions by PRODESBA personnel to join a group but he refused every time, referring to the limitations of his own farm which did not generate enough monetary profits for taking the risks related to participation in credit based development programmes. Excequiel certainly did not have less contact with the technical personnel of PRODESBA. He became very good friends with them, was part of the social network, and is now one of the few villagers who can tell a lot about the specificities of the different technical officers of PRODESBA.

Although working in a similar context and without differences in access to external technological knowledge their farming systems show crucial differences at characteristic moments. Interestingly technological differences encompass the use of fertilizers and biocides, burning, organization of weeding and harvesting, crop choice, and responses to external conditions. José belongs to the first group of producers who apply fertilizer and herbicides to maize each season. Excequiel is one of the latest, not because he was unfamiliar with its use (he did it once a long time ago), but because he considered it unnecessary until recently. When maize comes up poorly, José applies extra fertilizer while Excequiel decides to withhold the fertilizer he had planned to apply and which he had already bought. José had already stopped burning fifteen years ago, Excequiel has only recently been considering the possibility. José plans tasks such as weeding and harvesting in one or two days, with large work groups, while Excequiel prefers to carry out such tasks with family labour and, thus, spreads the task over more days.[61]

A striking difference with regard to crop choice is the very distinctive way they value tule production. Excequiel builds up both a finca and a tular, while José concentrates on coffee. Local quotations represent the different interpretations of the profitability of coffee versus tule: 'tule produces every month and coffee only once a year' and 'coffee is once a year but pays better'. For José tule competes too much with coffee and is not very profitable; for Excequiel it is a crop with guaranteed production and profit and with a labour demand that can be adjusted to labour availability in the household and coordinated with other tasks on the farm.

Under changing external conditions both may respond in different ways. José sold his pigs in the year that local authorities prohibited free pig wandering; he considered pig fattening to be no longer profitable and turned his pigs directly, and for the last time, into money. Excequiel, in contrast, slaughtered his pigs one by one and continues to raise one or two pigs, challenging thus the criticism of some neighbours and authorities when his pigs wander around the house. He likes pig raising although he wonders whether he really earns any profits.

Besides these different strategies towards technology choice, José and Excequiel also experiment in different ways. Trough 'experiments' new technologies are tried, tested, discussed, adapted and sometimes rejected. There is no technological treadmill which forces the producers in a specific path of technological change even though one may observe that many producers prefer a specific technology and pursue its application, like having one's own depulper to process coffee to produce a high quality coffee. We see that José and Excequiel do not take up a new technology as a simple compulsive consequence of the technologies they already use. Instead there is room for experimentation and choice. In this process, however, they differ typically in line with their specific farming systems. The following example may illustrate this.

One day I gave them both a bag with velvet bean seed, a green manure receiving widespread attention from NGOs for its possible role in a more sustainable agriculture (*Mucuna pruriens*, locally known as *frijol de abono*, see CIDICCO 1991, Hesse-Rodríguez 1994, Post n.d.). Beforehand both were convinced about the useful qualities of this bean they had never utilized before. José hired some day labourers who carefully sowed the bean between the maize in a much lower density than I had suggested. This meant more weeding and not using the weed-reducing capacity of this green manure crop. He had distributed the seed over his field and thus could not meaningfully compare an area with velvet bean and an area without it. He first wanted to reproduce the bean to have seeds in large quantities and to have enough to incorporate it in higher plant density in his crop and in his fallow in the following years. Excequiel acted differently; he threw the beans in a corner of his maize field to see what would happen. The structure of the experiment in both cases is very different; José started with making costs for hiring labour, while Excequiel invested not more than a few minutes. José makes an investment and can wait a longer period to see what the results of this new way of working will be. Excequiel does not spend efforts and time on a new technology; nevertheless if it produces a positive result on the small 'test plot' it can be considered as being adapted to his style of farming. The new technology is then in line with his inability to employ more labour.

Not only do they experiment differently with a new opportunity, they also respond differently to a similar hardship. Both suffer from chronic disorders and have physical problems when doing manual field work. However, the effect on their working styles is different. José is glad that he has coffee because now he can work less and has money to hire day labourers. He uses his coffee profits to hire labourers for maize cultivation and he diminishes the pressure on his body as much as possible. When Excequiel is very ill his two sons do all the manual labour. When Excequiel recovers from his worst complaints he forces himself to go to the field to work, often coming back with more of a headache and pain in his eyes and stomach. He continues to put the maximum pressure on his body. Any profits from the farm are not employed to relieve him of this burden. He spends most of the coffee profits on remodelling their house.

The above differences in strategy towards labour employment, intervention, technological changes, experimentation, and illness cannot be separated from individual differences, capacities, preferences, psychologies etc. The cases here, however, serve to illustrate how these differences are also embedded in social structures and relations.

It would be unjustified to interpret these differences between José and Excequiel in terms of dichotomies such as market-oriented and subsistence-oriented, or modern and traditional, or industrial rationality versus indigenous knowledge. Both try to increase yields of their export crop and both cultivate maize in the first place for household consumption and for securing their livelihood. Both use combinations of new external knowledge and historically generated local knowledge. Sustainable low input farming for subsistence is for both no option for the future, but at best a limited option for the maize cropping system.[62] Hence we need another interpretation of these differences.

The interpretation of such differences between these producers in terms of 'cultural repertoire' to indicate their specific relations to labour, markets, technology, and so on (Ploeg 1994) improves our comprehension of different types but also has its limitations. The cultural repertoires of José and Excequiel may be summarized as follows. José views his way of cost-benefit analysis in monetary terms and employment of hired labour as the distinguishing elements of his own style. He evaluates experiments and makes projections into the future on these terms. He perceives people who are in a more unfortunate position sometimes as lazybones or unlucky in access to the means of production, but he mostly describes them as people who cannot think and cannot calculate. Excequiel's strategy, in contrast, is to combine family labour, hard work, and non-commodity relations through friendship in an optimal way: 'if I don't work I don't eat'. His plans about what and how to cultivate change continuously during the season, but are always adapted to use all available labour time. Improvements depend, in his view, on hard work and gradual technological changes which fit in his style of labour employment. This may improve their life, but will never lead to wealth: 'I am poor; the other producers want to be more than they are (*crecer más que son*); that is difficult today'. He classifies people in a more unfortunate position according to their laziness and the days that they do not work and stay at home.

One limitation of the concept of cultural repertoire, however, is that it can mistakenly be appraised as the origin of differences among producers who operate in a similar context, under the same structural conditions.[63] When I arrived in the village José and Excequiel did not seem to manage their farms so very differently. They both produced an export crop, had access to pack animals, cultivated maize and beans, and owned little land. During the field work José's property increased considerably, he bought much land and invested in his finca, which seems much in line with his type of calculation and mode of accumulation. Comparing more closely the situation of José and Excequiel there is only an apparent homogeneity at the start of our analysis. Initial disparities may seem insignificant but can make a big difference later in processes of change. One example above is the role of education. Literacy did not influence their farming until job opportunities appeared in the construction company. José got a well paid job and saved more money for investment in agriculture, while Excequiel came off badly. It is these types of small structural differences (e.g. education, labour availability, access to means of production, support from religious networks, or successful patronage and clientelism relations) which may remain unimportant for a long time but which may produce an emergent differentiation under certain conditions of change. Small differences can be amplified or have amplifying consequences.[64]

Diversity and the reproduction of multiple structuring principles

This chapter's task was to reflect on the discrepancy between the observed diversity of agriculture in mountainous Honduras and the mainstream modernization view which labels this agriculture as archaic, pre-modern, and a way of perpetuating poverty. This concluding section comments on the three views, summarized in Table 3.1, which contest the mainstream policy view. Our empirical exploration reveals that not only is 'modern' agriculture dynamic and diverse but so also are forms of agriculture that have been classified as 'subsistence' or 'peasant' agriculture. Production activities in this 'category' are changing continuously. These changes have been conceptualized as passive or active adaptations.

Netting's study (1993) is, in my view, an example of an emphasis on passive adaptation. Technological change appears as a logical and gradual response to population growth and land pressure in order to maintain yields in spite of shorter fallow periods and soil degradation. Netting (1993) fails, in this adapted version of the Boserup model, to interpret the social struggles and negotiations behind processes of change. For example, land tenure is not an effect of land use systems, as Netting argues, but is subject to intense social struggles and social differentiation (see Chapter two). A notion of differential access to resources is important. Furthermore, technological change is not merely a passive adaptation to increasing land pressure and environmental crisis.

Instead of portraying producers' responses as passive adaptations by producers with a universal form of rational (passive) response to the environment and socio-economic context, producers are active (knowledgeable and capable) strategists. Environment, new technologies and markets are mediated through producers' agency: 'different farmers (or categories of farmers) define and operationalize their objectives and farm management practices on the basis of different criteria, interests, experiences and perspectives. That is, farmers develop, through time, specific projects and practices on how their farming is to be organized' (Long & Ploeg 1994). The cases of Excequiel and José can be approached and understood in this way. Once having acknowledged such agency, however, it is important to understand under which conditions operationalization of producers' objectives take place.

The study of land use in El Zapote reveals the limited potential of this 'activeness' of agency. Environmental heterogeneity and climatic uncertainties condition individual actor strategies, and variability of yields is a logical outcome of this heterogeneity. Producers cannot control many crucial characteristics of the environment according to their will. The location of the fields for different crops reflects this (see Figure 3.1). Small differences in rainfall, temperature and in soil conditions generate big differences in production conditions for different producers. Hence, Netting and FSR are correct in this sense. Actual diversity in agricultural production cannot be solely explained by referring to the social, be it exploitation/labour relations or producers calculi. The biophysical/technical also possess causal powers which can generate diversity.

From the discussion of farming in El Zapote it follows, furthermore, that active adaptation cannot be conceptualized independently from how it is conditioned by structural socio-economic relations. The process of commoditization has affected land use in El Zapote. Land use is a result of responses to the specific developments within the national economy and trade networks. For example, tule production expanded after the demand for sleeping mats increased. Cattle and coffee expanded in El Zapote in line with the development of market structures for these commodities at a national level. Market development not only stimulated crop production but also constrained it, for example, a decline of sugar and rice cultivation (although one should not overlook that the diminishing rice cultivation is also related to soil degradation). There is some empirical evidence that a process of standardization occurred as conceptualized in the critiques of capitalist modernization: for example, less crop diversity, increased regulation of soil fertility through fertilizers, and increasing the use of seed originating from official breeding programmes. Changes in market structures have affected whole production systems as market and non-market activities are closely connected. Production system dynamics involves the coordination of activities associated with different crops, cattle, fields to manage, and products to harvest (labour). Interconnections between, for example, maize and pigs, tule and coffee, biocide use in maize and its use in coffee, have been discussed above.

The simultaneous occurrence of diversity and shaping of farming within structural relations has consequences for the interpretation of the so-called room for manoeuvre as source of diversity (as, for example, conceptualized by Long and van der Ploeg, 1994). By

98

now it must be clear that producers have not an unlimited room for manoeuvre to transform their agricultural practices. Competition over resources (land, markets, surplus, labour) structures production and circulation. Room for manoeuvre by producers to shape their style of farming should therefore be interpreted in the context of local processes of social differentiation. For example, the poorest sector has completely fallen back on small plots of maize, supplemented with a few banana trees. They claim to have increasing difficulties in sowing beans, planting tule, sowing secondary crops and so on (owing to decreasing access to or availability of land, seed, and labour). The richest sector concentrates on coffee, while the middle sector continues, more than the others, to cultivate a wider variety of crops. The above discussions on cattle and coffee shows that relating land use to modes of surplus creation and appropriation increases our understanding of the dynamics of land use. However, a shortcoming of current approaches is that the dynamics of cattle at a local level seem to disappear from sight because cattle and pasture have become the simple synonyms for exploiting classes and marginalization of the peasantry. The discussion also shows that it is possible to discuss issues of political economy at a local level and that such an exercise can contribute to studies which until now remain restricted by the use of highly aggregated data only. To understand local forms of diversity one has to investigate local sets of structures. In my view the idea that one macro-structure exists within which producers develop different calculi (as Ploeg 1990 and Steenhuijsen Piters 1995 in fact suggest), is a theoretical construction which contrasts with the conditions of farming in El Zapote, where a wide variety of different mechanisms, rooted in structured relations, shape different production circumstances for each producer. It cannot be assumed that producers are located within similar structural circumstances. Furthermore, if one takes the wide variety in biophysical production circumstances and more contingent factors, such as household composition, into consideration then a more complete picture of the origins of diversity comes into view. A theory of diversity should accept the idea that each producer can be entangled differently in a set of relations and production circumstances. This contrasts with a theory of diversity which assumes the possibility that producers may be situated in exactly the same structural circumstances whereby diversity is constructed afterwards by agency. It also puts more emphasis on historical processes; for example, of social differentiation.

The cases of Excequiel and José illustrate that producer practices build upon previously developed production systems, technology patterns and production goals shaped by household dynamics. Producers interpret external changes and recombine them with the already existing (organization of) production systems (what Ploeg 1990:12 sees as the result of 'antecedent practices and decisions'). New practices (e.g. changes in spacing, not-burning, new cultivars, and reduction of fallow), have to be reshaped in line with existing patterns of production systems' dynamics and household reproduction. Individual producers in fact link many different structural relations and contingent factors, thus shaping diversified concrete forms of farming and reproducing structural relations. These cases elucidate that the coordination of different elements of a farm (sub-systems or domains if you wish) is highly complex, whereby small changes or differences may lead to important differences later on.

Both FSR, which points to the biophysical production conditions as the causal factor, and Styles of Farming studies, which focus on variation in actor strategies, tend to under–theorize how biophysical heterogeneity, actor strategies *and* structural socio–economic relations shape and transform production systems in an interacting process over time. In the following chapters I will elaborate more fully on several of the local socio-economic structures.

4

Spotting environmental change: beyond conventional agronomy and local discourse

Problems of understanding environmental change

The latest environmental profile of Honduras summarizes quite well the conventional agronomic approach to land degradation in Honduras (SECPLAN 1989a).[1] Smallholders cultivate food grains on hillside slopes. It is taken as self-evident that their use of hillsides and their cultivation practices, such as burning, sowing along the slope, and having their cattle grazing the stubble, lead to high levels of soil erosion and degradation (SECPLAN 1989a:122). Little if any evidence exists, however, about the rates of land degradation on different soils in Honduras, let alone any information about possible effects on yields. Since scientific research on such processes in Honduras has not yet produced detailed substantive studies, general agronomic wisdom prevails as the only tool to guess at the effects of existing forms of resource use. Policy recommendations follow directly from such generalizations made about the causes of land degradation.

Over the last decades contrasting perspectives which depart from generalizing agronomy have gained influence. They stress that land users may have perspectives on environmental problems which are equally explanatory, but very different from those in science or policy. Accordingly, land users may opt for other paths of action than those prescribed by science-based policy. For example they may not implement proposed alternatives such as the construction of terraces. The first critique of conventional agronomy is that it fails to understand producers' perceptions, which may correspond better with local practices and relations between natural resources, cultivation and yield than classical 'solutions' to 'proper' land use. A second critique refers to the technological optimism of the official approach. It assumes that a stock of available conservation techniques exists from which techniques can be selected. A ban on burning, soil conservation through terracing and structures such as diversion channels, and, more recently, contour cropping, minimal tillage, and green manuring with velvet bean, are the techniques generally proposed in Honduras. Explanations for the non-adoption of proposed techniques are mainly attributed to 'lack of education'. Conventional agronomy pays less attention to the many cases of technical failures through inadequate or misapplied research and extension or due to a lack of fit between techniques and local farming systems and livelihood strategies (cf. Ardón 1992; Biot et al. 1995; Mejía 1993).

One response to conventional research is Farming Systems Research (FSR) as it developed in the late 1970s and 1980s. FSR focuses on the rationality of producers and aims at surpassing agronomic research which limits itself to biophysical factors of agricultural production and land degradation. Farming systems research includes an analysis of constraints at the farm level, assuming that the producer is a rational decision maker (for FSR examples in Honduras see: Bravo 1989; CATIE 1984, 1986; DeWalt and DeWalt 1984; Hart 1982b; Puerta 1990). An understanding of his/her decisions may help to surmount the limitations of constricted commodity (crop) oriented research.

A second school defending the rationality of producers in managing natural resources consists of various 'agro-ecology' approaches (cf. Altieri 1987; Conway 1985). These approaches have shifted the research focus to local farmers' knowledge and issues of organic farming and sustainability (for Honduras see: Bentley 1989a; Bunch 1982; Bunch and López 1995; Smith 1994). In contrast to FSR, these approaches take a more overtly populist stance and intend to give voice to the peasant. Local knowledge informs this type of research. One of its central research questions is how producers can participate in technology development on a reciprocal basis. Environmental issues such as burning remain primarily appraised in technical terms (nutrients, erosion, soil structure, organic material, effects on weeds etc.).

Both FSR and agro-ecological approaches define environmental constraints in 'objective' systems terms and in this respect resemble conventional agronomy. Recent efforts to understand environmental deterioration in terms of the various social forces that are at work have tackled the underlying assumption of the possibility of obtaining an objective description of systems and processes. One group of studies (Blaikie 1993; Peets and Watts 1993; Zimmerer 1993a) combines political economy and discourse analysis. Thompson and Warburton (1985) use an applied systems analysis for developing a similar argument. Zimmerer (1993a) makes a strong case for analysing how environmental deterioration is differently perceived by different social groups in Bolivia: the government and development agencies, the older peasants, and the younger generation. Blaikie (1993) develops a similar framework in which more or less coherent groups with specific interests and aims share views on environmental management which differ from the views of other groups. These recent critiques of conventional approaches conclude that the whole field of resource degradation is riddled with uncertainties, which throws doubt on the assumption that science is superior to local knowledge as a basis for action: there cannot be one 'right' analysis of problem and solution.[2] Hence environmental deterioration cannot simply be read off from nature by agronomy and its definition always involves conflicting perspectives.

The question now emerges as to how we can develop a sound account of environmental change: using conventional agronomy, using producers' knowledge, or taking them as two valuable independent discourses? This chapter approaches this question empirically by investigating different perceptions on environmental deterioration in El Zapote. The chapter

102

is structured around four main themes of environmental deterioration: the fallow crisis, burning, change in vegetation and climate, and biocides. These emerge as crucial themes both in official discourse on environmental deterioration and in producer narratives.

Perceptions and responses to the fallow crisis

A fallow period which is long enough reproduces the conditions for new cultivation cycles of annual crops. In the Honduran literature the function of a fallow period in food grain cultivation is generally conceived as follows: the fallow period allows for the restoration of nutrients and organic material depleted by crops and it can improve soil structure.[3] Disagreement exists whether in the long run fallow systems will lead to degradation. Cook (1921) assumes that a maize-fallow rotation system 'carries with it the agency of its own destruction'. After each clearing and cultivation cycle, renewal of the bush will take more time and in the end the system will produce only grasslands instead of bush and forest fallow. Others argue that little erosion or impoverishment of the soil occurs in a rotation with a long fallow period. They envisage nevertheless that it is more economical to replace fallow agriculture by more productive methods such as continuous cultivation with a moderate use of fertilizers and legumes (Semple, 1963).

The fallow system is regularly misinterpreted. Firstly, it is quite common for it to be labelled as 'migratory agriculture' (e.g. Campanella et al. 1982).[4] This persistent misunderstanding portrays producers as nomads (Cochet 1993). This image of 'wandering peasants' might correspond to some producers in some areas of Honduras, but it certainly contrasts with the situation of the majority of Honduran producers who cannot go one step beyond the edges of their small plots. Another misinterpretation is the view that land in fallow is under-used land, or even waste land (e.g. SECPLAN 1989a). This representation means that land lain in fallow appears in censuses and surveys as 'not in use'. This inability to see it as an essential part of production systems, contributes to the low priority fallow improvement has received in agricultural policy.

Producers perceive land in fallow as part of the production system and central to their way of cultivation. They use the words *descanso* and *inculta* to indicate an important difference: *tierra en descanso* is land in fallow, and *tierra inculta* is land that is not used. Tierra inculta is a rarity in the village. What producers call a 'good fallow' is a field that will lead to a high output per labour unit when cultivated. On the other hand, the concept *tierra trabajada* (worked land) refers to soils which have been cultivated too long and which are therefore exhausted. These fields should lie in fallow in order to 'rest' (*para descansar*).[5]

Producers interpret the increasing absence of 'good fallow' as negative and express a nostalgic longing for the *'guamiles de hacha'* (the guamil* that had to be felled with an axe) with long fallow periods. They use phrases such as: 'in the past it was all guamil' (*antes era puro guamil*), 'now one doesn't need the axe any more' (*ya no se ocupa la hacha*), 'all places have been sown with grasses' (*enzacataron todo*), and 'now all the land has been worked, there are no *guamiles* as in the past' (*ahora todas las tierras están trabajadas, ya no hay guamiles como antes*).[6] They claim that yields in general have declined and that actual yields are much lower than in the past. It is not clear, however, how much yields have, in fact, declined. The decline in absolute numbers is probably not very large.[7] Despite a reduction of fallow land since the 1950s (see note six) producers have succeeded in keeping the amount of fallow land at a constant level. Table 4.2 shows that about one third of the rotations with maize start not in a fallow but on an already cultivated plot (cultivated by other producers or used for other purposes, such as cattle, beans or coffee). Less than a quarter of the rotations start after a long fallow period of more than six years.

Table 4.2 Frequency of different fallow lengths in maize rotations in El Zapote

	% (number of plots)
no fallow period	31.5 (34)
short fallow period (2-3 year)	25.9 (28)
medium long fallow period (4-5 year)	21.3 (23)
long fallow period (6-10 year)	13.9 (15)
secondary forest (11-50 year)	7.4 (8)

Source: survey of producer estimations of the length of the latest fallow period before the most recent series of maize crops was sown (N=108 plots). For those plots which have been fallow (N=74), the median length of the fallow period was 4.25 year.

Producers perceive the effects of shortened fallow periods not only as a reduction in yields, but also in terms of erosion. 'The earth disappears; one does sow in pure *laja*[*] now', is a popular saying. The widely used concept for soil run-off is 'to wash' (*lavar*). Older informants conceive that the river Cárcamo is now full with sediment (*lodo*) while its water used to be clear in the past. Some producers point to rills, gullies, and small land slides in the fields. This awareness of producers of the effects of shortened fallow periods and their observation of forms of soil erosion invalidates the findings of Tracy (1988) that Honduran farmers 'rarely understand the cause-and-effect relationships involved'.

In general, producers mention a second effect of the shortening of fallow periods: an increase in weeds and the necessity of more weeding. 'Today weeding cannot be done without using herbicides'. The problem of weeding receives a more central place from producers than in the literature which often regards it as only a secondary problem. Only some authors (e.g. Watters 1971) consider that the possibility of yield decline is caused by increased weed competition. The termination of a cropping period in a rotation may be a consequence of increased labour demands for weeding instead of decreased soil fertility. Watters comments that the reasons why producers apply a fallow in their production cycles are location specific.

One can conclude that producers have an encompassing view on the fallow crisis and take into account factors such as soil fertility, erosion, weeds and labour. The official view based on agronomic research (e.g. SECPLAN 1989a) is often much simpler, is obsessed with the problem of soil fertility thus disregarding the problem of weed reduction, and mostly assumes that the same process is taking place everywhere. Producers and conventional agronomy differ, albeit not substantially, in the perception of the effects of the shortening of fallow periods. The shortening of fallow periods generates a complicated set of problems. The concept of 'fallow crisis' will be used here as a generic term for the constraints in a maize-fallow system which are a combination of soil erosion, degrading soil fertility, and increasing weed infestation and labour demand for weeding. Although both producers and official discourse perceive a fallow crisis they differ in their responses. The common reaction of conventional agronomy and state interventionism is a plea for better land use planning and soil conservation projects.

Official responses: Land use planning and soil conservation projects

Many studies that outline the problems associated with the fallow crisis recommend land use classifications as a tool for planners to qualify biophysical production conditions and constraints (e.g. Campanella et al. 1982). Two favoured types of qualification in Honduras are the 'life zone' concept, as formulated by Holdridge, and 'capability classifications' as promoted by FAO.

Studies that use the life zone concept of Holdridge classify El Zapote as Subtropical Humid Forest (FHIA 1989; OEA 1962). Characteristic of this life zone is its location between 10 m and 1600 m altitude, a precipitation between 1000 and 2200 mm per year, and a mean annual temperature between 18 and 24°C (Agudelo 1988). Most areas in El Zapote fall within this category. Subsequently, several authors conclude that vegetation in El Zapote is predominantly pine. This life zone concept leads to strange descriptions such as: '..almost all the vegetation in Santa Bárbara [district] is pine forest...(..). Nowadays, almost all of this resource has been felled' (FHIA 1989:28). Indeed, some pine trees embellish El Zapote and some parts, which villagers consider not to be suited for crops or pastures, still have pine groves. However, if regrowth of forest were allowed on fields now used for agriculture, most of the land in El Zapote would turn into broadleaf forest. Historical documents and narratives of older villagers reveal that in the past most forests were broadleaf forests.

The life zone concept is a deductive classification, mainly based on three criteria: mean annual biotemperature (the yearly mean of mean daily temperatures), precipitation, and evapotranspiration. It is incorrect to suppose that such criteria could predict which type of vegetation will exist. Soil characteristics are left out of the concept. More importantly, still, is the fact that human influence in plant distribution does not form part of the concept. Bennett already criticized such a life zone concept some three decades ago (Bennett 1967:7): 'For who dares to suggest that ecology has advanced so far that a few temperature and rainfall data are sufficient to predict what lies on the other side of the hill?' The use of the life zone concept results in maps which show the vegetation predicted by Holdridge and followers for a given region, rather than what in fact lies there. Bennett (p.8) asks: 'Of what current ecological use are such maps when they do not show what is extant? Is it erroneous to characterize such efforts as *a priori* ecology?' Nevertheless, the concept of life zone seems so attractive that three decades later many researchers still apply it (Agudelo 1988; Campanella et al. 1982; FHIA 1989), notwithstanding the serious critique and valid arguments of Bennett. The latest environmental profile again recommends continuing with the refinement of the original map of Holdridge for Honduras (SECPLAN 1989a).

Another way to classify land use in Honduras is what is called 'capability classification'. In contrast to the life zone concept this approach takes soil conditions into account. Soil mapping units are grouped primarily on the basis of their capability to sustain specific types of agricultural production without deterioration over a long period of time (Euroconsult 1989:139; Vargas 1992). Although one may consider climatic, economic (e.g. expected value of crops) and social variables, the most important variables are soil type and slope. Areas on maps are assigned to a capability class, in Honduran research from I to X, in which only I to III are suitable for annual crops. Most soils in El Zapote would fall into class VIII or higher: only suitable for forest (e.g. Chávez et al. 1987; FHIA 1989).

In the same way as for the life zone concept, one can question whether capability classifications can contribute to identifying and solving the fallow crisis in Honduras. A problem is that classification criteria in Honduras are based on US classification systems which exclude land steeper than 10-15 per cent from any cultivation. Hudson (1988) calls the research focus and the development of conservation practices on gentle slopes only, a 'mental hurdle'. The 10-15 per cent ceiling diverts attention of researchers away from the problems which hill farmers confront on steep slopes (Blaikie 1985:23). It is on such slopes that a lot of farming is taking place in Honduras. Although such theoretical classifications are rooted in technological science, they presuppose far reaching authoritarian development schemes in order to remove cultivation, and thus producers, from hillside plots. If these theoretical constructs would really inform practice this would result in an undermining of existing ways of survival and a complete change of production systems. Capability classifications in general do not offer very much insight into the dynamics of existing production systems. Why and how producers operate on these slopes, and the nature of fallow systems remains invisible. Chávez et al. (1987) applied a capability classification in the region of El Zapote and recommended to displace producers from precipitous slopes and to reforest these slopes. Typically this capability classification had few consequences. Producers effectively contested imposed land use systems and reallocations. The weak state institutions were not able to implement the proposed measures. Producers successfully argued in public meetings with officials that they need to sow maize on these slopes for their survival and that they have no other place to go to.

A second type of official response is the implementation of soil conservation projects. In the 1980s PRODESBA*, an integrated rural development project, became active in El Zapote. In contrast to land use planning, this project followed a more participatory approach to transforming fallow systems. PRODESBA promoted physical conservation structures combined with new maize varieties and new inputs. Producers have taken up several of these PRODESBA initiatives: (i) herbicides, in order to reduce labour input in maize cultivation (which had increased because of the demand for weeding due to the fallow crisis); (ii) fertilizers, because these increase or stabilize yields and compensate for the declined soil fertility; and (iii) short stalk cultivars of maize because these are better at withstanding heavy storms. However, producers have rejected the proposals of PRO-DESBA to increase labour input in the construction of physical conservation structures or the application of compost. Producers time and again provide a simple socio-economic account of their reluctance: they say that such activities 'cuestan demasiado' (cost too much), which means that it takes too much labour effort to apply these techniques.[8]

Producer responses and strategies

Official approaches to the fallow crisis neglect the fact that producers already pursue a set of strategies to cope with it. Most of these strategies seem to reduce the effect of the fallow crisis on an individual basis and are not necessarily a solution to the crisis in the long term. Although some strategies imply an increase in labour demand, it may be much less than the amount of labour required for PRODESBA's conservation structures. I discerned eight important strategies.

A first strategy of producers is to maintain at least several years of fallow on one's own plot. Intensification of land use (in terms of increasing cropping years and reducing fallow years in a rotation) is displaced to the fields of others. Producers rent land, so that their own land can lie fallow. They generally have to capitalize on personal relationships to obtain such land. Many producers complain that landowners do not want to rent out land any longer.

A second strategy is to enlarge the amount of land in the maize cultivation system. A producer can buy extra land or stop renting out land, and keep it in fallow to recuperate fertility. In order to follow this strategy producers have to resist 'claims' on their land made through personal relationships. Some producers are in a contradictory position, because they have to rely on personal relationships to hire or buy land but simultaneously have to resist them to keep their own land in fallow. They are in a better position when they can resist such claims by overruling them with claims of other personal relationships, for example by arguing that they have sons who will need a particular fallow soon.

A third strategy is to sow less milpa to reduce the demand for labour in the weeding period; the area of maize per producer has reduced over the last decades. Lower yields and a labour crisis (lower return to invested labour) due to increased weed infestation have also resulted in less maize being used for pig fattening. Not all producers are reconciled to the reduced area of their milpa. A new practice emerges as a reaction to the reduction of milpa area. For a few years now a handful of poor producers have sown a third maize crop in August: the *postrera de agosto*. In the past a few maize plants were sometimes sown in August to produce fresh corn cobs for making *tamales* (a favourite dish) on Christmas eve. But at present producers experiment in the village commons with sowing whole plots for mature maize sown in August.[9]

A fourth strategy entails a change of plant spacing. People recall that they sowed four, five, or even six maize seeds per hole in the past, and that one used a spacing of 40x40 inches. Now people use two or three (some two, some three, and some alternate between two and three) seeds per hole and use a much shorter planting distance. Those who do not sow in a square pattern but in rows along the contour sow closer and generally use two seeds per hole. Plants are now better distributed in space, which probably has led to a more efficient use of available nutrients, which in part could have off-set the lower total availability of nutrients. This practice, however, has also led to an increase in labour demand for sowing, since those who sow have to make many more holes per area. A similar process has taken place in bean cultivation.[10] In the past, producers sowed three to four beans per hole, while now they use two or three beans per hole. The density (of holes) is somewhat higher now (8x8 inches).[11]

A fifth strategy is the use of new inputs. Weed infestation and increased labour demand is countered with herbicides and declining soil fertility with fertilizers. The intention is not so much to intensify maize production (in terms of increased yields per area under equal conditions) but to keep labour demands and yields at acceptable levels. The input side becomes more market-oriented while the output (maize) is predominantly kept outside commodity circuits and mainly used for household consumption. It would be inaccurate to interpret the increased use of these inputs as a modernization strategy to transform agriculture; it is not a 'production enhancing' but a 'production maintenance' technology.

A sixth strategy is the proliferation of the postrera in the course of this century. As one increased the use of one field for successive seasons, it became more opportunistic to use the field also for the season in between two milpas. Accounts of old respondents and documents in the municipal archives reveal that there was not widespread practice of the postrera in the past. It was only sown when they expected a complete failure of the milpa.

A seventh strategy is to concentrate on major crops and leave more demanding crops out of the rotation. For example, sowing rice or vegetables as cash crops was widespread in the past. Producers insist that without good guamil it is not possible to sow rice, especially because of the increased grass infestation on exhausted soils.

The last strategy which provokes much discussion among producers is to stop burning. This strategy (which also relates to the issue of mulching) is the subject of a separate section.

The different strategies for responding to the fallow crisis involve 'technical' judgements about effects of changes in certain practices (for example spacing) as well as social action, for example manipulating personal relationships in the game of land renting. This implies that an analysis of the fallow crisis needs more than agronomy's classifications and material interventions in nature. It needs a social science inquiry ass well. The different strategies of producers and their views of the fallow crisis illustrate that an understanding of natural resource crises must go beyond the perception of it to investigate the interlocking of perceptions and practice.

The fallow crisis and unequal distribution of resources

Producers do not perceive the fallow crisis in an equal manner. A fallow period was mainly an obstacle for the landowner in the classical systems of grassland management — with a sequential alternation of fallow periods, maize cultivation and natural pastures.

108

Although tenants and landowners 'needed' each other, their perspectives on the fallow differed (Cochet 1993). While the objective of the cattle owner was to keep the land under grass as long as possible, the interest of the tenant was to have a regrown secondary forest as early as possible, so that maize cultivation could start again. With rising meat prices and a growing labour availability (needed to clear pasture from bushes) the fallow and maize cultivation disappeared from the cattle system. The reduction of fallow periods constrained food grain cultivation but provided opportunities for the extension of cattle areas. Poor producers say the rich have caused the fallow crisis by having destroyed the guamiles; the cattle breeders have sown 'the best lands with grasses'. 'Those who still have some guamil do not want to rent it out, since others sowed all the land with grasses. They get all the people after them.' A son of a cattle breeder, in turn, argues that poor producers are the source of erosion and degradation, because they work on steep lands and 'continue with burning'.

The fallow crisis is more than a contentious issue between the rich cattle breeders and the poor, however. Access to land in fallow is differentiated among all producers. Figure 4.1 demonstrates that larger farms have more land in fallow which is kept available for maize production.[12] Land in fallow as a percentage of the total area increases as farm size enlarges, which is especially important for the lower farm size classes.[13] Independent of soil conditions and the use of inputs, larger farms may have better production conditions to cultivate maize because of access to land which benefits from longer fallow periods.

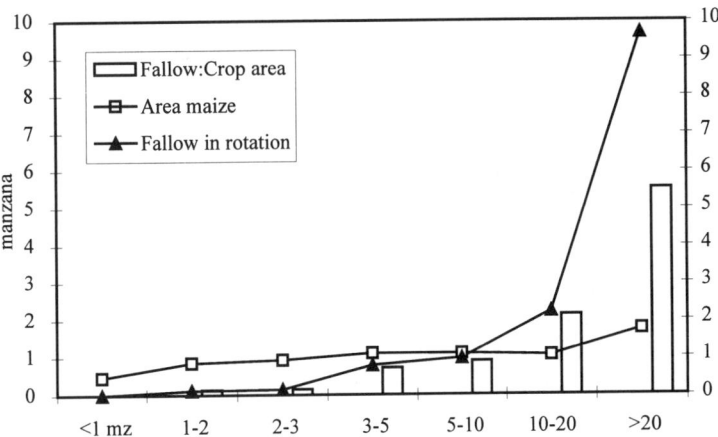

Figure 4.1 Land in fallow available for food grain production per farm size class in El Zapote
Note: Left Y-axis: area in fallow per farm which is available for grain production, and area per farm with maize. Right Y-axis: ratio of land in fallow available for maize to actual area with maize for different farm size classes in El Zapote in 1994 milpa.
Source: producer survey, N=82. Area in local manzanas.[14]

Several producer strategies to overcome the fallow crisis relate to this distributional pattern. For example, only those producers with sufficient land can afford to have part of their land in fallow without falling back on renting land. Producers with less land sow less maize, the third strategy for riding out a fallow crisis. Although the absolute difference in area with maize seems rather small in Figure 4.1, it is statistically significant.[15] Producers seem to prefer a reduction of the area sown with maize rather than having land in fallow for a shorter period. Another strategy entails the incorporation of extra land into the farm instead of intensifying the rotation, but this requires opportunities to rent land or to obtain common land in order to accommodate having fallow.[16]

An analysis which stresses the unequal distribution of the consequences of the fallow crisis has implications for development intervention. Most calls for solving the fallow crisis propose the development of more intensive systems of *permanent* land use without fallow periods. Discourses on agricultural modernization in Honduras tend to reject fallow periods for being a characterization of traditional inefficient practices, and downplay the advantages of fallow periods, despite international research on improved fallow management and agro-forestry (see Amanor 1994). More emphasis on the improvement of fallow vegetation rather than abolishing the fallow period could be rewarding but it will have to confront contradictions. Agricultural modernization has chiefly been targeted on the local rich and middle peasants. Middle peasants prefer not to replace their fallow for permanent food grain cultivation, but, instead, try to strengthen the fallow period, or even to reintroduce a fallow period in their rotation if they obtain the resources (e.g. with coffee). The reintroduction of fallow periods, however, could limit the amount of land available for renting to land-poor producers. A serious approach to improving fallow practices and reassessing the fallow period could be worthwhile agronomically but may mean that landowners will reduce access to land in fallow for tenants.

Burning: multiple interpretations of a practice and its effects

Producers practice burning to prepare fields before sowing maize and beans. Up until a decade ago producers also burnt before planting coffee. After a short exposition of the practice of burning in El Zapote, this section reviews anti-burning views of outsiders and diverse arguments of producers for or against burning. New perceptions on burning have emerged recently, but producer practices still differ substantially from general agronomic prescriptions. I will argue that changing producer views on burning are related more to changes in production systems than to the rejection of burning by external actors.

Burning in El Zapote

Research into slash-and-burn agriculture reveals common patterns as well as remarkable diversity in both the use of fire in cultivation and its environmental impact (e.g. Bartlett 1957; Peters & Neuenschwander 1988; Steensberg 1993). In El Zapote burning for maize takes place between April and June, and for beans in June and September. Producers burn before the *milpa**, but not before the *postrera**, when the incidence of drought is much higher. A mulch layer of weeds and crop remnants are considered to be crucial 'to retain humidity' during the postrera.

In the dry season, from March onwards, men clear the vegetation with machetes and *pandos**. Men work with a *machete vuelta** in their left hand and the large machete in their right hand when they have to clear spiniferous vegetation. Clearing is a very arduous job: it is carried out during the hottest months of the year and many people can relate horrifying experiences of accidents that can occur when one is tired and loses concentration and control over the machete. When vegetation is sparse the dried bushes, grasses and herbs are piled up and set alight. Producers normally make a firebreak. From a two to four metre wide corridor they remove by hand all trees, branches, and bushes, and they sweep the remaining litter with a broom made on the site. After this work the much enjoyed lighting of the fire follows.

A 'good burn' is a local generic concept for various aspects of fire quality. It can be an indication of a fallow with a large biomass and a high soil fertility which will probably result in secure and high yields. It can also refer to a complete burn where no debris remains and a re-burn is not needed. It can furthermore indicate that the fire was hot and sufficiently slow to burn 'into the earth'. According to some, the fire must not go 'over the earth' but 'into the earth' to kill pests, diseases and weed seeds. The earth has to be heated up. A 'good burn' also refers to a pleasant activity.

Ignition techniques are a popular topic for conversation. A qualified farmer should not 'let the fire pass' to adjacent fields or forest. Boys are very proud when they are allowed to kindle a cleared field without their father being present. Those men who let the fire pass are called 'lazybones' *(haraganes)*. They do not make the firebreak sufficiently wide, or they ignite the fire and go home without controlling the fire. Many men, however, admit that they themselves have let a fire pass in the past. While admitting their faults they seem generally very amused as they express that, although their actions caused problems, it was also a lot of fun. They explain how they worked whole nights with friends to smother the fire in order to prevent damage to coffee fields or houses and hamlets located uphill.

To have a secure burning the quality of the firebreak is important. It must be wide enough and be cleaned very well. On the top side of the field it should be wider, while it can be smaller at the bottom of the hill. The fire sensitivity of the vegetation must be known, especially those of neighbouring fields. Some grasses 'burn like paraffin'.[17] Also knowledge about winds and the possibility of sudden gusts changing wind direction at the locality of the field is imperative. For a safe burning you need many people, which is often problematic for poor farmers. The ignition device used is a bundle of dried grasses and twigs. First the *contrafuego* is set alight: the backfire lit at the top and allowed to burn downhill. A headfire lit at the bottom of the hill would rage to the top and pass the firebreak. The second *contrafuego* is set on the sides towards which the wind blows. After these *contrafuegos* have advanced, the other sides can be kindled. A secure burning ends somewhere in the middle of the field. After the burning, any litter which remains is re-burnt in a pile.

Burning is not only an instrument of clearing a field for sowing. It is also done by villagers as a *picardía* or prank, i.e. burning to harm others who have yet to complete their firebreak. Other people light fires to have fun by witnessing a large (forest) fire.

Cultivators express their positive feelings about burning in aesthetic terms, a 'good burn'. A good burn gives a 'clean field' and a soil 'with strength' (*fuerza*). Under such conditions 'the maize will germinate beautifully'. Sowing without burning is called 'sowing in dead earth'. As I have illustrated above, the beauty of burning and the visibility of its strength can induce people to continue burning. Burning requires skills, knowledge of the locality, and the materials. You need to control the destructive power of fire. 'Fire is a good servant but a bad master' (Moore 1969:52).

Outsiders opposed to burning

In Honduras, most intellectuals share the idea that burning means destroying the soil. Burning is for them synonymous with deforestation and erosion. There is a long-standing tradition condemning burning. For example, in 1910 Campos argued fiercely against burning: 'If there is a reform necessary, urgent, in our agriculture, it is the abolition of the barbarian method of burning, because burning in agriculture begins to be the ruin of the earth and concludes being the barrier which impedes the development of our villages and agricultural populations'(p.602). In his instruction book of 1939, Pinel states that: 'Burning the fields for sowing has been an ancestral practice for our people. Nothing is more fatal, nothing is more detrimental for the fertility of a field'. His argument is that the humus, which is important for vegetation growth, is burnt. 'This [burning] is not a way to cultivate the earth. It is a destructive practice which we should ban from our agriculture' (Pinel 1939:29). Pinel considers burning to be antithetical to cultivation. Burgos (1941) likewise argues that burning is not necessary at all for maize cultivation. It only results in forest fires. 'The fire-raiser ignores that destroying a tree or a forest of trees is committing a crime. The laws impose sanctions for these actions; but ignorance and being uncultured (*incultura*) do not take into consideration the punishment, and the act is realized by natural tendency' (p.73). Burgos' notion conveys the uncontrollable nature of 'uncivilized' peasants. Burning, in this view, is antithetical to civilization. This is illustrated by capturing burning within the concept of 'ignorance'.

The idea of 'ignorance' of peasants who burn can be found in many articles and letters of readers in Honduran newspapers. Many of these contributions arise out of a recently awakened environmental interest in which forest protection has become the central issue for urban-based environmental groups. The fear of fire is part of what Redclift and Goodman (1991) have called the 'urban adventure' in Latin America which started with colonialism, and Goudsblom (1992) has argued that the conception of fire changes according to the material relationship one has with fire. City dwellers can loose all their property in a simple fire. At the same time, the management of fires is a skill that many city dwellers have lost, especially the middle and upper classes with electric cooking apparatuses and employees. According to this urban thinking, burning is 'uncivilized', a 'natural tendency', and characterizes pure 'ignorance'.[18] Moreover, burning in agriculture is consequently equated with being 'traditional', and thus is the opposite of all that is 'modern'.

The anti-burning view is less rooted in scientific thinking than it might first appear. The assumption that burning leads to a crucial loss of all nitrogen, other nutrients, and valuable organic matter is not correct. Recent studies explain how burning makes nutrients available and changes soil conditions without which crops would hardly grow. After burning, pH rises, which is important for crop production on acid soils such as in the mountains of El Zapote. It can reduce the regrowth of weeds. It can release important nutrients such as calcium, magnesium and phosphate. The idea that nitrogen is lost is not correct in all cases and the content of useful organic matter is not always lowered (e.g. Ewel cited in Loker 1986; Peters & Neuenschwander 1988). Burning is an intelligent part of swidden cultivation systems under conditions of low population density (e.g. Boserup 1965; Conklin 1957; Webster and Wilson 1980). These studies view burning as a rational and adapted technique which leads to adequate yields at low labour expenditure. This is not to say that burning never provokes problems; the literature generally concludes that growing land pressure and reduced fallow cannot sustain a system based on clearing by intensive burning (e.g. Bandy et al. 1993; Peters & Neuenschwander 1988). The point here is that outsiders' views do not generate a single definitive evaluation of burning and cannot formulate a universal judgment on it. Even agronomic advice in Honduras contradicts itself concerning the role of fire. While peasants are advised not to use burning, one can read in leaflets from the Ministry of Agriculture written for producers in high-input agriculture, that maize stalks in fields that suffer from heavy fungus attack should be burnt. Recent literature re-assesses burning practices and new uses of controlled burning are becoming prominent.[19] The use of fire, then, should not be seen as a product of tradition, stupidity and ignorance.

Arguments of producers in favour of burning

Producers cite the prevention of *maíz muerto**, a disease, as the main reason for burning. The main reason given for not burning is that the earth 'washes away' as a result of burning. But there are many other arguments. I have ordered them in groups, being aware that such an ordering may obfuscate many of the relations between them. I distinguish the arguments of producers in favour of burning from those against. A third group encompasses arguments which can work both ways: for and against burning. Some repetition is unavoidable because it is impossible to place the various arguments into exclusive categories. I start by listing the arguments in favour of burning.

Labour efforts to sow on a recently slashed fallow are high because of the huge amount of debris. It gives one the feeling that sowing is nearly impossible. Producers argue that they 'like to sow in a clean field' and that therefore they burn. Furthermore, they find 'it hard work to weed with the pando in the debris'. Characteristically trash and debris are often called *estorbo*, or hindrance. Sowing after burning requires less labour.

Diseases and Pest evasion is the main argument producers use to defend the need for burning, with maíz muerto as the prime originator.[20] Popular explanations are: 'Without burning the maize will die', and 'Burning kills many *polillos*'. The term *polilla* or *polillos* covers many pests and diseases which leave signs of filth and sticky remains of animals. Producers do not always differentiate between pests and diseases. The effectiveness of burning for pest management is related to the quality of the fire. Producers argue that 'in a *guatal** with little debris the fire goes over the earth. With a *guamil grueso** it goes slowly and inwards. Only then, will the small animals in the earth be killed. But burning is always important against insects'. Many producers, especially those who do not burn, argue that it is not so much the burning that determines the occurrence of maíz muerto but the season. I will return to this later. On a minor scale fire is said to be used against some other creatures, such as wasps and birds.[21] The *cuijin* (a reptile like a lizard), who pulls out young maize sprouts, disappears from a burnt field.

Producers hold opposite views when they argue that burning causes maíz muerto or that burning has no influence on this disease. A lively discussion continues among producers about how burning does or does not influence the occurrence of maíz muerto and harmful insects. This indeed, as Thurston (1992:77) observes, makes it remarkable that so few studies on slash and burn deal substantively with the importance of burning as a disease management measure. But it contradicts Thurston's suggestion that farmers are less conscious about the effects of burning on plant diseases and pests and that they primarily burn for other reasons.

Crop characteristics determine decisions about burning the field in which a particular crop will be sown. Producers can, for example, burn in a specific field before sowing beans or rice, but do not burn if they intend to sow maize in it. Many producers who do not burn for maize, state that you need a clean field without debris for planting tule, beans, rice, or vegetables, because moving the debris during weeding can damage crops, for example by breaking the bean stalks. Producers who do not burn but find clean fields necessary for such crops, use two alternatives. Some remove all debris from the plot to the borders. Others choose for a 'bad burn'. They pile the debris and wait for the rains before setting the piles on fire, so that the fire only goes 'over the earth'.

Stones in a field, so argue producers, make burning necessary. If not, the layer of debris on a rocky soil will prevent one from seeing the soil and one will not know where to sow and where to remove the debris. A second problem with stones is that clearing and weeding is more arduous and that 'you ruin your nails' if you have not burnt.

A **'warm'** soil is considered by some to be essential for maize cultivation. High temperature does not only kill the *polilla* but also stimulates maize growth. Especially when the rainy season starts with a drizzle, one should burn to heat up the soil. 'More warmth enters, and the maize grows well. Without burning you have more chance that the maize remains small and yellow'.[22]

Arguments of producers in favour of not burning

Labour efforts, diseases and pests, crop characteristics, stones, and warmth are the main arguments in defence of burning practices. The range of arguments for not burning is similarly rich and includes 'washing', weeds, future or past use, and field surroundings.

114

'**Washing**' refers to soil run-off and washing down of debris and ash. Some producers argue that without burning, you do not see stones, '*canales*' (rills), and 'roots of peeled trees'. Producers observe that a non-burnt field 'consumes water' (good infiltration of water). The second run-off problem mentioned is that *abono*** (substances such as ash, manure, fertilizers, or debris) washes away on burnt fields.[23] Some argue that burning does not matter: if you burn, the ashes wash away, if you do not burn, the abono (in unburnt form) washes away.

Weeds and weeding are a minor problem in a slash-and-burn system with long fallow. A fallow period suppresses weeds. Repetitive burning of 'worked fields', however, is considered to increase weed and grass invasion. Some producers maintain a mulch layer in cropping systems as a new method against grasses. Not burning and leaving the debris is considered to result not only in less weeds sprouting, but also to cause weeds to be easier to eliminate. Without burning 'the earth is looser' and easy to enter with a pando, and sprouting grasses are 'feeble and easy to weed'.

Future or past use of fields influence decisions about burning. For example, maize fields in the mountains will not be burnt when coffee is to planted afterwards.[24] The alternate use of fields for maize and cattle can also be decisive. For example, one producer, who strongly argued that burning improves maize production, said: 'I do not burn since I have cows. I always clean [a field in fallow] for the postrera [which producers never burn]. After the harvest, the cows go into the field. By the time it is necessary to prepare the field for the milpa there is little debris left. There is nothing to burn.'

Field surroundings can make a producer decide not to burn even when he or she perceives that burning would improve maize production. Many producers mention that they stopped burning because of fruit trees in their fields or adjacent pastures with valuable forage for their cattle. They also fear the transfer of the fire to others' properties. Producers say that, in the past, one often did not make firebreaks in the mountains: 'It was from nobody and one would just light it'. But now it is the area where people are most afraid to burn because the land has been planted almost entirely with coffee.

Other arguments of producers for or against burning

All the above arguments are subject to discussion among producers. In general each of these arguments leads into a clear direction, in favour of or against burning. Several other arguments relate to mechanisms which can induce burning as well as not burning. For example, tenure relations can both encourage and discourage a producer from burning. A closer look at these arguments further enlarges our insight into the complexities of burning.

Yields will decline in the long run because of burning, according to many agronomists. Very few producers, however, mention that not burning improves yields.[25] Instead, they point to higher yields on burnt plots, compared with non-burnt plots. This observation is in line with the literature cited above which mentions the important release of phosphate and other nutrients as an effect of burning. Producers describe incidents when they did not burn a cleared guamil and had low yields. Hence, the yield argument can work in both directions; high yields now or more stable (but not guaranteed) yields in the long run. This means, for example, that several producers do not burn any more on their own land but burn when they have plots on other's land.

Vegetation in a field is another decisive argument. Many producers burn in guamil but feel that in guatal it is better not to burn. These producers are not against all burning. After all, according to them one should burn in guamil. But after this first burn, there is not enough debris to burn. Not only the quantity of vegetation, but also the type, motivates decisions about burning. Thorny debris demands burning. And many producers find the skin irritation caused by the *pica pica* plant insupportable.[26] They try to eliminate the pica pica from their field by burning. But the presence of pica pica is not automatically an argument for not burning: 'We sow each year in guamil. We clear for the postrera because it is a '*gran pical*' (big field with pica pica). You cannot clear this before the milpa'. In the dry season, when most guamiles are cleared, the pica pica pods are ripening and each touch will free the irritating hairs. Producers do not burn for the postrera season and at the start of the milpa season debris has already been decomposed so much that burning is no longer necessary.

Location of the field provides arguments for burning or not burning. It is common to hear arguments such as: 'We do not burn the river terraces, it ruins the earth. In the Zona we do burn'. Burning or not burning is related to specific areas in the municipality. The mountains of El Zapote are considered to be a region where one has to burn, because of more problems with maíz muerto, and because maize will not grow and will turn yellow without burning.[27] Producers mostly refer to the lower temperatures in the mountains. However, higher humidity is probably a more important factor that stimulates maíz muerto in the mountains. Another factor could be that on the acid soils in the mountains it is more necessary to burn to make nutrients (such as calcium, magnesium, potassium and phosphate) available for young plants. Location, in fact, refers here to those biophysical production conditions not yet discussed. Apart from, for example, soil characteristics and climate, slope can be important: 'one can burn on flat land, but not on slopes'.

Ownership and control over land influence decisions on burning: 'When the land is mine I do not burn. I only burn on other's'. That can be on common land or on rented land. However, several landowners who rent out land prohibit burning.[28] Other landowners do not bother, and in several cases a landowner may even stimulate or demand burning by tenants. Owners can hope for a good maize growth which, after the tenants have harvested their maize cobs, will serve as good forage for the owner's cattle. Other owners want to scatter grass seed after the harvest. Whether owners can forbid burning and enforce these prohibitions is actually a matter of dispute. Several producers argue that: 'When one rents, the land is at ones disposal'. They want to set the norm that renters can decide whether or not they want to burn. Indeed, some owners agree that choosing to burn is a matter for the tenant. Family relations and personal labour relations can counteract the prohibition of burning. I met producers who absolutely do not burn on their own maize fields but permit a brother or their 'permanent' day labourers to burn on land they have freely lent to them.

116

Humidity is 'saved' (conserved) by the debris according to most producers. Nobody burns in the postrera because of the dry season which follows immediately. For the milpa the necessity of debris in the field, and of saving humidity, is in dispute. Intensified burning can consume organic material and reduce moisture retention. To prevent droughts producers increasingly want to maintain the debris to 'save humidity'. But a high humidity may lead to maíz muerto and thus to crop failure. The reaction of those who choose not to burn is twofold. Some deny that not burning results in too much humidity and thus in maíz muerto: in their view one gets 'humidity' because of close spacing which means that 'the sun cannot reach the plants'. Others agree but consider more humidity as beneficial, especially when the debris causes an improved infiltration of water. They use the argument that with burning 'the earth dries out'.

Burning: a practice in transition

The agronomic approach to burning has mainly focused on soil fertility and, to a lesser extent, on weed invasion. Producers refer to biophysical elements as well as social relations, and any serious study of the reasons why producers burn cannot limit itself to only one of those fields. Several arguments fit well into agronomic discourse: yield, soil temperature, erosion, weeds, and humidity. Then there are the more location specific arguments such as crop type, stones, location, type of vegetation, etc., and the social and economic arguments: labour efforts, ownership, expectation of punishment, and future or past use. Although the list of arguments might not be totally exhaustive it is not an accidental list. Instead, it can be perceived as the local 'discursive consciousness' (Giddens 1984) about burning. It is the cognitive map to which producers connect their practices. A quantification of the value of the different arguments would be onerous. Producers will not construct a quantitative model before taking a decision. Producers value the factors qualitatively, of course with expectations of actual and future yields and required labour input. But they will also qualify the expected pain to their nails, the beads of sweat on their backs, the sensation of pica pica and the effects of ignoring the orders of a landowner. The approach explored here also tries to validate such arguments. Taking this list as a cognitive map does not imply, however, that it proves the existence of a shared body of knowledge.

From the discussion of the arguments it follows that, for example, differences in control over resources or labour availability shape opinions about burning. For the 1994 milpa 61 per cent of the producers burnt on one of their milpas (although 24 per cent did not burn all their milpa plots), and 39 per cent refrained from burning (source: producer survey). Producers of the last category might have burnt in recent years, since only 23 per cent of the producers (N=83) did not burn their milpas at all during the last five years. From the interviews it can be reconstructed that, until a decade ago, burning was applied by almost all producers on most of the milpa plots. Nowadays, attitudes towards burning are changing and more and more producers experiment with not burning. The question emerges as to which factors influence the change in burning practices.

Two new conditions for agricultural production are the increasing availability of inputs and the increasing land pressure coupled with changes in land tenure. Herbicides and fertilizers have influenced decisions about burning since the 1980s. Poor producers explain that they continue burning because they cannot pay for fertilizers and herbicides, while those who can afford them may stop burning. Nevertheless, in contrast to what I expected, the change to not burning could not be associated significantly with the use of new inputs (see Table 4.3).

Table 4.3 Association between burning and the use of inputs

	no inputs	herb.	fert.	herb.& fert.	total
burnt	11	12	7	9	39
	(52.4)	(54.5)	(38.9)	(52.9)	(50.0)
not burnt	10	10	11	8	39
	(47.6)	(45.5)	(61.1)	(47.1)	(50.0)
total	21	22	18	17	78

Source: survey of burning practices in the *main* milpa of each producer in 1994.
Note: herb. is one or more applications of herbicides; fert. is application of more than 20 kg/ha fertilizer; column percentages between brackets. None of the associations was significant.

This absence of statistically significant associations does not imply that causal relations between input use and burning do not exist. Producers often relate decisions about (not) burning and recent changes in burning practices to the use of one of these inputs. Producers argue that those who do not burn need the 'strength' (*fuerza*) of fertilizers to compensate for the loss of the 'strength' of burning. The use of fertilizer may replace burning. But, on the other hand, application of fertilizers may mask the soil degradation which may result from burning. Fertilizers can thus support a continuation of the practice of burning.

Something similar can be remarked about the relation between herbicides and burning. Producers take the paraquat-based herbicide *gramoxone** as a substitute for fire: 'I will go burning with *gramoxone*. Maize requires warmth, therefore you have to burn'.[29] Paraquat makes it possible to stop burning since it is an alternative method for cleaning fields. On the other hand, several producers mention that they can continue burning just because of *gramoxone*: with this herbicide they can counter the grass invasion which results from continuous burning and reduction of the fallow period. Producers describe how in the past they had the long fallow to reduce weeds, now they have *gramoxone*.[30]

Another factor is access to land. The survey data do not prove a significant association between the use of burning and quantity of land owned, nor with the amount of land that one has in fallow. The data, nevertheless, indicate a tendency that producers with more land or more land in fallow burn less. However, such producers in general do not work in the Zona, the village common, and depend less on rented land. Land tenure seems to be a more important factor than the amount of land which is 'owned' by the producer. Table

4.4 shows that land owned by the producer or close family (e.g. spouse or father) is burnt less than rented land or communal land.

Table 4.4 Association between burning and tenure type

	own	rented	Zona	total
burnt	16	7	15	38
	(34.8)	(50.0)	(93.8)	(50.0)
not burnt	30	7	1	38
	(65.2)	(50.0)	(6.3)	(50.0)
total	46	14	16	76

Source: survey of burning practice in the main milpa of each producer in 1994.
Note: 'own' is land from producer, spouse or close family (e.g. father or son); Zona is the village common; column percentages between brackets; significant association.

Producers' views on burning develop in relation to broader shifts in land use. More and more land was fenced in the 1940s and 1950s due to the expansion of cattle and coffee. After the 1960s, a rotation of guamil-maize-pasture-guamil was transformed into pure pastures. Burning became more important for clearing pastures of thorny shrub infestation than for clearing guamil for maize cultivation. Two new grass species, Calinguero and Jaraguá, had been introduced for grasslands and established well on annually burnt land used for maize cultivation. The emergence of permanent pastures pushed maize cultivation back to a smaller part of the municipality. Coffee expansion in the mountains did the same because land was taken out of a long fallow-maize rotation. This provoked reduction of burning in the mountains and increased control of burning by coffee producers because of the increased value of their intensified coffee stands. Fire control at lower elevations where maize is cultivated did not improve. The Zona is particularly famous for poorly controlled burnings. The intensity of cultivation in the Zona has increased, also because of the lack of available land elsewhere. The shortening of the fallow has increased grass invasion especially for the Calinguero and Jaraguá species. Calinguero increases the risk that fires spread and that young fallow vegetation catch fire, which further reduces the recovery of soil fertility. These processes seem to have concentrated the fires from a large area to one small area. Changes in burning practices are thus unevenly distributed over different spaces. This observation may help us to draw an initial conclusion about views on burning.

It is possible to distinguish different approaches towards burning: why do people never burn, always burn, or burn under certain circumstances but not in other situations. A discrepancy between outsider views and views of some producers exists. State officials locate the difference between their view on burning and the reasons of producers to burn in terms of a confrontation of modernity and traditionality. They consider burning as a custom, a system inherited from the past, which is neither 'technological' nor 'modern', but a cultural tradition. This view is not really attacked by agronomists who have discovered that burning was a rational method under *past* conditions of low land pressure. However, many producers can articulate well why one should burn in the *present* context.

119

It has been argued above that arguments of producers are quite 'sound' and relate to a pragmatic view of agricultural production. As one producer clearly stated: '*Logically* one should not burn, that is not good, but *in practice* it is very convenient'. Producers have a lot of experience on how to survive and produce under marginal conditions, and burning is one of their techniques. But it is a technique in transition. Producers explain that they are not sure whether one should burn or not. The different arguments are contradictory. Producers not only shift between different arguments for different crops or plots, but also in time. The fallow crisis, changes in land use and production systems, and the availability of new inputs have caused many producers to rethink the practice of burning. As a result of changing conditions and practices some producers have refrained from burning while others continue. Although producers tend to practice less burning, this decrease is not once and for all. Producers who strongly argue against burning can, surprisingly, burn under certain conditions, for example, only in guamil, or only in the mountains, or they can change the form of burning, for example producing a burn which only goes 'over the earth' instead of 'into the earth'.

Vegetation, climatic change and water

The public discourse in Honduras which tries to understand why producers deforest offers two explanations: that rural people ignore the importance of forests or that they are forced to fell forests to plant crops for their survival. Both views disregard the local struggles over preserving some forests for village use. This section discusses how rural people perceive changes in vegetation and the consequences for water and the climate.

The first issue is to what extent rural people recognize possible functions of forest vegetation. The point made below is that it is a misconception to suppose that ecological awareness has only been raised in modern times after publication of environmental profiles and proliferation of environmental education programmes. The following history exemplifies how villagers can have profound ideas about forest conservation and how these protect vital water sources, but also how such ideas may clash with the need to use the land for agriculture.

Concern about the drying up of water sources due to deforestation around the springs was publicly discussed directly after the formation of the municipality in 1917.[31] Discussion in subsequent years focused on the issues of expansion of production and the securing of water sources by forest conservation. Agriculture in the areas surrounding the village started to expand. Therefore, in November 1917 a proposal was launched at the municipality to prohibit the straying of goats. A month later voices to prohibit the straying of pigs were raised, because these animals also caused damage to crops. But pig raising was considered too important and after protests pigs were allowed to stray within a distance of two kilometres from the village. Two weeks later this discussion was broadened and went beyond the limits of the theme of agricultural production; it was observed that the destruction of forests produced the reduction of public water sources. The village council decreed that no one was allowed to destroy the forest to sow grains or make grasslands within a distance of one kilometre of the village.[32] The ideal of forest conservation was combined with animal production at the expense of crop production. In the following years this decree regularly led to strife, for example when some producers received a permit 'by mistake' to clear and sow maize. In 1919 the radius of forest conservation was reduced to 500 yards 'to foster agriculture'. The use of water sources near the village was limited to 'domestic use'; the laundry had to be washed further on in the mountain streams and people had to bath in the river. In 1927 the decree was reiterated and was extended with the obligation to make fences around this area with forest conservation to protect the fields against pigs. Copies of the minutes were sent to the District Governor for approval, 'to heighten its effects'. In the 1920s and 1930s disputes stirred the village council when several producers fenced in land with water sources, a prohibited practice, and deforested around water sources. Again in 1935 some villagers went to the council and asked to revoke the agreement of 1917. This resulted in the lifting of the ban on forest clearance near the village because of 'the unavailability of uncultivated land and the justice to protect agriculture'.

This history of the ban between 1917 and 1935 illustrates that villagers perceived well that the destruction of forests led to the drying up of water sources. Nevertheless, the ban was continuously contested, which finally led to the opening up of the area for agriculture.[33] This clash between perceptions on conservation and the pressure of producers to clear forest and the related inability of local authorities to administer in favour of conservation is also a contemporary issue. Hence history shows that deforestation is not exclusively caused by an absence of consciousness about possible environmental effects of deforestation.[34]

A second issue concerns is how state intervention to protect forest lots has been perceived. From 1974 onwards, the Honduran Forestry Development Corporation (COHDEFOR), a state institution installed by a reformist military regime, controlled by law every forest in the country.[35] Local authorities were not allowed to give one single pine tree to an inhabitant. This prohibition was, of course, widely evaded, but some villagers were fined for cutting trees in their field. What these villagers feel as an injustice is that small producers were fined while COHDEFOR officials earned money, as locally believed, by granting licences to big saw mills.[36] As in many other places, COHDEFOR issued permits to a sawmill from outside the village to exploit (formerly communal) forests in El Zapote. All revenues left the village. This bred bad blood among the villagers. Such experiences from the past remain the point of reference for producers. They joke with COHDEFOR's name by saying that it is the Corporation for Forest Destruction (*destrucción*), instead of Development (*desarrollo*). The Honduran Forestry Services and the Ministry of Agriculture time and again reject that they protect particular interests and, instead, develop slogans to locate forest conservation under the patriotic banner.[37] Notwithstanding recent campaigns to rebuild the conservation image of COHDEFOR, villagers still consider COHDEFOR as the greatest extractor of trees and they are not very willing to consider COHDEFOR as the protector of the environment.

A third issue is whether rural people can understand variations in climate and relations between climatic and vegetational change. The way people deal with climate has been of interest to ecological anthropologists. Richards (1985) illustrates how producers in West Africa have advanced techniques to cope with seasonality and master weather forecasting techniques on which to base crucial decisions relating to cultivation. Such forecasting techniques are also known in El Zapote. Most techniques refer to the coming of rains. Producers say it will start to rain when 'the *chachas* chant', when 'large quantities of those small insects appear' (it endures raining when *mostacilla* insects jump from bean pods), when 'the *guaco* bird sits on a green tree (when it sits on a dry tree drought will continue)', when 'a colony of ants is moving' (some also refer to the specific sound ants make), when 'the moon becomes full', or 'fifteen days after a certain *Sapote* tree near the river sprouts'. Others add that rains come when 'humidity sprouts from the earth, then it is very hot, and then it will last eight to fifteen days before the rains start'. Rain can also be expected when 'the cocks crow in the afternoon' or when the 'sky is *petateado*' (a sky with sun and specific cloud features).[38]

The most elaborated system of forecasting is the '*cabañuelas*'.[39] In El Zapote this is described as follows: the weather on the first days of January coincides with the weather in the different months during a year. The *cabañuelas* have different phases. The first is from the first to the twelfth of January; each day is one month, the weather on the first of January parallels the weather during the whole month of January, the second of January for February and so on. On the thirteenth of January the *chiquitas* start (also called *pequeñitas*, the small ones); for example on January the fourteenth the morning equates with March and the afternoon with April, etc. For most people the *cabañuelas* are finished then, but some recognize the 'days of San Sebastian', after the *chiquitas*. The weather of one of the days of San Sebastian stands for the weather in four months; in three days the weather of one whole year is forecasted. The *chiquitas* are taken as the most reliable days of the *cabañuelas* for weather forecasting. If it rains in the morning, it will rain a lot in the corresponding month; when it is dry and hot in the afternoon the corresponding month will be dry and hot; when it drizzles it will do so in the coinciding month. People exhibit a lot of fun in talking about the use of signs to forecast, such as the *guaco* or the *cabañuelas*, but this talk seems more of a ritual than a knowledge framework that guides practices such as sowing. The ideas are repeated regularly while underlying meaning and practical utility have apparently little or nothing to do with each other.[40]

Richards (1985) stresses the importance of similar techniques. He suggests that they are a useful tool for planning agricultural activities and that they are not sufficiently recognized by climatologists. In his description producers use these techniques to determine exactly the optimal moment to burn fields. The suggestion is made in these types of descriptions of ecological awareness that producers act in line with expressed knowledge. But when people say 'We focus on the cabañuelas' it does not mean that they really take the cabañuelas into account. Most people do not remember at all how the weather was like at the matching part of the day in January. I did not meet many people who acted in accordance with the phenomena forecasted with the techniques discussed above (for example, to define the sowing date). Instead when people are confronted with the question as to how they use forecasting techniques they say: 'we sow when it starts to rain, but you never know whether summer returns after the first rains'. Doubt dominates. Those who burn in El Zapote continuously show hesitations and a feeling of uncertainty about the coming of the rains. Similar expressions appear during the time of sowing. The *cabañuelas* do not seem to be of any help at such moments. Not all knowledge about climate is practical in planning the agricultural cycle and taking producers' knowledge seriously does not automatically provide the clue for action or knowledge which is better adapted to the local context.

As far as the relationship between vegetational change resulting from agriculture and climatic change is concerned, only farmer knowledge exists and there is no agronomic knowledge about the specific relationship in Honduras. Practically all producers assume that the climate has changed and that the rains start later nowadays than they used to do in their childhoods. The consequence is that producers sow and burn later. No weather data over longer periods exist which could sustain this farmer observation. The observation is nevertheless so generalized and put forward unanimously that one can suppose that real changes have occurred. All the people tell you that in earlier times, one started to sow maize on the first of May. Sowing starts about the fifteenth of June now. I came across a letter sent by a son in the army to his father. In this letter, dated 4 April 1921, he writes: 'I think that at least the milpa has already been burnt'. In those days, apparently, it was normal to have already burnt the milpa in March or at the beginning of April, much earlier than nowadays.[41]

Producers not only perceive changes in rainfall but also in temperature. Temperature has risen at all altitudes. It remains to be seen whether the perceived changes have anything to do with macro-climatic changes or only with micro-climatic changes. It can be reasoned that the enormous removal of vegetation has increased temperatures. Many villagers point to the relationship between a reduction of forest vegetation and higher temperatures. Vegetation loss could have provoked more winds which have increased evaporation. At the same time soil erosion and lower content of organic material may have caused a lower water holding capacity of soils. Light rains in May could have been sufficient to secure maize growth in the past but may be insufficient nowadays. The fear of early rains, which may hamper the burning of a cleared fallow, has been replaced by a fear that the rains will come too late or irregularly.

From the discussion of the three issues it follows that rural people have historically given importance to forest conservation. The need to expand agriculture and the way COHDEFOR operates are seen as activators of deforestation. Deforestation by other villagers was contested repeatedly and disputes were brought before village authorities. But it was regarded as impossible to fight legally the deforestation that was supported by COHDEFOR. The consequences of deforestation for local water sources are well known. Producers' knowledge about climate varies from ritual conversations (*cabañuelas*) to precise indications of cause-effect relations such as between deforestation and temperature rise. It is quite clear that people acknowledge climatic effects and changes in hydrology as a result of deforestation.

Agro-chemicals and the limits of escape

Environmental consequences of overuse generally count as the central problem of biocides. Subject to the view of the reviewer, overuse results from producers' ignorance or the structural conditions of production which victimizes producers (an example of the former position is SECPLAN 1989a:123, and of the latter Faber 1993). Although one could conclude from a conventional agronomic perspective that 'overuse' is not an issue in El Zapote (producers generally use lower quantities than recommended), the discussion is still relevant since producers perceive biocide use as problematic. I shall argue that villagers have gained knowledge about biocides without any formal education; and that we have to draw on local perceptions to obtain an understanding of environmental problems of pesticides because formal studies are practically absent. This local knowledge is to a certain extent differentiated and knowledge struggles take place between, for example, producers and day labourers.

The development of spraying practices

*Clordano** was probably the first synthetic agro-chemical used in El Zapote. Producers spread this insecticide on stored maize against storage insects or they mixed it with maize seed before sowing to keep off ants. Its special smell also repelled larger animals and birds. Hence, producers employed only small quantities on very specific places and did not need further equipment. Its use started around 1950, and Alfredo Luna, the main local merchant, had it on his stock list in 1954. Its use seems to have ceased since the end of the 1980s simply because the supply has stopped. Producers still appraise it as a wonderful product. FHIA (1989) describes the contamination of one water source in El Zapote with Chlordane.[42]

A second step in the propagation of biocide use was the introduction of herbicides. Most references to its first use in maize cultivation date back to the beginning of the 1970s, when a few producers had obtained rucksack sprayers. Paraquat-based herbicides, *gramoxone**, became the most important (source: own survey).[43] Initially, users of *gramoxone* were denominated as 'lazybones' because it seemed that they did not want to work. Nowadays many producers consider that 'without *gramoxone* one does not work', i.e. without *gramoxone* it will be impossible to clean the field.[44] The use of *gramoxone* increased gradually, but an extra impetus was given by PRODESBA.[45]

In the 1980s a third group of biocides came into use: fungicides entered the local agricultural system to counter the emergence of Coffee Leaf Rust. *Copper* (synonym for copper-based fungicides) became the main response to this disease. En passant other fungus diseases were suppressed and other fungicides were introduced.[46] Furthermore, soil treatment in nurseries and seedbeds started to become a normal practice.[47] AHPROCAFE (with international development aid funds) made rucksack sprayers available for reduced prices. The proliferation of these sprayers encouraged herbicide use in the village.

This short description challenges empirically some prevailing notions about the introduction of biocides in Central America. Firstly, the use of agro-chemicals did not start in export crops. In El Zapote agro-chemicals were used in maize (for household consumption) long before they were employed in the export-crop coffee. Secondly, producers did not start to use agro-chemicals because of intensified campaigns by product sellers or extensionists. The expansion of its use was a gradual process from *Clordano* via herbicides to copper. Farmer experimentation and farmer-to-farmer knowledge transfer - the processes worshipped by agro-ecologists - stood at the roots of this chemical expansion. Only later was PRODESBA an extra stimulus to the distribution of biocides. Thirdly, although the chemicals used are not very selective, producers use them to tackle specific problems and not to kill diseases and pests in general. *Clordano* was not sprayed on crops but only used on stored maize and to treat maize seed. Paraquat became one of the answers to the increasing weed problem in food grain production but is normally not applied to coffee. Fourthly, the use of chemicals has not led automatically to the so-called 'pesticide treadmill': the unavoidable increasing demand for pesticides due to pests becoming resistant to a product so that increased quantities of the product or new products are needed. *Clordano* use in older forms of maize storage has not been replaced with other pesticides. Only if maize is stored in silos or drums, is a relatively low dosage of another insecticide used.[48] Producers who started with the recommended two or three copper sprayings per year tend to reduce it, or even abstain from spraying, when they see little evidence of leaf rust. 'The coffee has become resistant to rust', is what many producers say.

These comments should not be interpreted to mean that I disagree with the notions of the 'suppliers push of pesticides', the 'pesticide treadmill', or the 'triggering role of export crops in pesticide use'. But they should be comprehended as indications of important mechanisms and not as empirical generalizations which explain what has happened or will happen in all places, with all producers, in all crops, and with all types of agro-chemicals.

Perceptions of risk and displacement of hazards

The use of biocides is not so widespread in El Zapote as in some other areas and crops in Honduras and there are no signs of strong overuse. Why is it then that many producers show interest in possibilities of reducing biocide use even though its use generates economic profit? Up to now no organization has disseminated ideas systematically about the potential dangers of biocides in the village.[49] Only incidentally have extensionists made comments to producers about the possible effects of biocides. Nonetheless, producers handle an extensive set of local perceptions concerning environmental and health risks. This set seems to be an outcome of producers' experiences and observations, a process of trial and error.

A principal concern of several producers is the effects of certain biocides on their crops or soil. For example, the effects of *gramoxone* on coffee and soil are questioned. Unlike in maize, the use of *gramoxone* in coffee is regarded as a 'bad practice'. Producers ignore the recommendations in the IHCAFE leaflets and disagree with extensionists. They assume that *gramoxone* 'dries out the roots' and some argue it 'dries out the soil'.

A second concern is that biocides may have wider environmental effects, beyond the place of application. Frequently worried villagers asked me about whether the spraying of *gramoxone* and insecticides against the Coffee Berry Borer could result in contamination of the drinking water that was taken from mountain streams. They posed such questions before I raised the topic. In contrast to what, for example, Guivant (n.d.) suggests for farmers in Brazil, I would say that health considerations with regard to biocide use are a concrete category for villagers. They perceive the possibility of health threats even if they do not observe any contamination or any immediate health effects. They only know that producers near water sources spray biocides.

A third concern is the danger for the person who applies biocides. Biocide users, for example, recall their negative and grave experiences with endosulfan and *gramoxone*.[50] Referring to endosulfan Paco Ramirez explains: 'I once got problems with Thiodan and everything went black, the smell turned out badly for me, I almost tumbled headfirst. I could walk to the stream and wash my face to get better. It appeared as if I was drunk, like in the bar'. And many others report problems with *gramoxone*: 'with *gramoxone* my lips sleep'; 'I have sprayed with *gramoxone*, but I will not do it any more, it is nasty, pure chilli'; 'look at Paco Ramirez who savours *gramoxone* but whose arm is now bloated'; 'many people have been taken to the hospital, they had got *gramoxone* over their body, I always get a headache, and I feel my nails'; 'once I had an accident when I bent over to cut weed, the liquid flowed out of the cap and the skin of my back was peeled. I could alleviate it with lemon, but later I got a rash on my legs.' It is well known that such accidents may happen with biocides, especially when labour is cheap and body protection expensive and troublesome. It is clear that the experiences of accidents (including various attempts to commit suicide) have taught people to be careful with biocides.

Systematic information about health risks does not exist and is difficult to obtain (cf. Castillo et al. 1989; SECPLAN 1989a). The short summary above of producer views on biocides suggest that, contrary to official wisdom, producers perceive environmental and health risks of biocides, even though they lack any formal education. That producers perceive risks does not mean that they use biocides safely, as Whitaker (1989) assumes. Whitaker surveyed 120 small producers about their perceptions of health risks with Gramoxone and concludes that small producers are well aware of the possible harmful effects of Gramoxone and that they take much care in using it. He concludes that therefore serious health problems do not exist. My data confirm that producers are, to a certain extent, aware of health risks. However, contrary to what Whitaker assumes, awareness about possible risks does not imply that no accidents and health problems will occur - an issue which is pushed to the background when one focuses exclusively on perceptions.

We should also investigate why people differ in their views about biocide risks. Besides clear supporters of biocides, I also met producers who intended to abstain from biocide spraying. For example, one producer explicitly preferred to lose his tular, his main source of income, instead of spraying against a fungal disease. Also the many day labourers refrain from biocide spraying even when they are paid a somewhat higher wage when spraying. In El Zapote we find a situation in which some are reluctant to spray while others are known to be willing to spray, even as day labourers. As Guivant (n.d.) observes in Brazil, people can be well informed about the risks of pesticides but at the same time may hold the opinion that only a few people are susceptible to such hazards. It is said that the people who suffer from spraying, fail to use biocides properly (the victim is blamed) or they are 'non-resistant'. Non-spraying labourers told me that they had 'feeble blood' (the same words as in Guivant's case). Sprayers, on the other hand, say that they are strong, and like the smell of *gramoxone*; they tend to express this with a large smile. This presentation of strength is embedded in a discourse of 'being macho': those who are able to spray are 'bien macho'. Such mechanisms to accommodate the psychological pressure of running risks is considered to give a 'sense of subjective immunity' (Douglas in Guivant, n.d.): because of the sprayer's personal properties, risks are ruled out (the remaining chance to have an accident is not more than the will of God). This concept of a 'sense of subjective immunity', however, is only one aspect of ideological constructs about biocide spraying. Non-sprayers undermine the macho element by asserting that those who spray need the money to get drunk (the archetypical examples of sprayers are people famous for their drinking habits).[51] Sprayers who ward off risks in the described way can stress in one and the same conversation that they have to take the risk of spraying in order to survive: 'I do it only because of poverty'.

Differences in representation do not simply result from loosely-floating cultural notions: resistant macho bodies and drunken losers. Knowledge struggles about biocides interconnect up with social inequality. The creation of a sense of subjective immunity can be found among producers who themselves spray in their own fields. Nevertheless, many of these (relatively) resource-rich producers prefer to displace the possibility of hazards on other people. They search for day labourers to do the spraying jobs. Regularly one observes producers who borrow money or go to work as labourers elsewhere in order to pay somebody else to do the spraying in their own fields.

Producers who employ labourers (*patrones)* were among those villagers who in eloquent terms could explain the risks of biocides. Several patrons, however, tended to maintain double standards: one front stage (for example with the researcher-outsider) and one back stage (with the labourers). For example, Carlos Salgado, an 83 year old *patron*, always studies carefully the leaflets he receives and the labels on the inputs he buys; and Paco Ramirez, his most contracted day labourer, complains that Carlos does not care for him.

'I like the smell of *copper*, but at home I feel it in my stomach and below it; the same with Thiodan. Don Carlos says it is nothing. He says the product is not dangerous. He says that I only have to undress and wash myself. But only the rich can read what is written on the label.' Paco asks me to explain about the effects of these biocides and reacts: 'A poor person does not know that. And the *patron* does not acknowledge what you feel; and that man is rich.'

Carlos knows that biocide use entails occupational health risks but tries to disguise this from his workers. Other employers, however, warn their labourers. Rafael Luna claims that he takes care of his labourers.

> About seven times I have had problems of labourers with symptoms of poisoning. We always could treat it at home by provoking vomiting. I require that the labourers undress completely and wash themselves after work. They have to work in pairs and are not allowed to spray too long.

Not long after this conversation I passed nearby one of his fincas and met a labourer who was mixing endosulfan in a rucksack sprayer near a stream. He worked alone. I knew that the stream connected to the main stream just above the place where drinking water was drawn off, but, before I asked him about it, the young man assured me that the stream connected below the tap. His clothes were wet due to spraying the parts of coffee trees which reached above his head. He protected himself with a handkerchief over his mouth. Rafael had not taken any precautions to reduce risks of endosulfan spraying. Thus what happens in the field differs from vocal accounts by Rafael.

Some employers do not intend to camouflage the health risks of biocide use and explain that investing in safety measures may lower their profits. These few employers paid up to 125% of the normal day wage in order to 'compensate' for the extra risks.

From this analysis of biocide use in El Zapote it follows that producers develop an awareness of different risks of biocide use without any environmental education programme. The idea that the causes of accidents and 'wrong use' can be explained simply by referring to 'ignorance' or a 'lack of education' should therefore be dismissed. Equally, cultural notions, for example machismo, that are part of peoples' narratives on biocide spraying cannot fully explain the continuation (or change) of specific spraying practices. Although sprayers are eager to receive more information about the consequences of biocide spraying, it does not mean that 'wrong use' can simply be corrected with education. Knowledge is not simply a product of imagination and education but relates in complex ways to the intrinsic working and effects of biocides as well as to the specific organization of labour, in which the hazards are displaced from producers to day labourers.

Beyond conventional agronomy and local discourse

This chapter has investigated the adequacy of conventional agronomy and producer perceptions for understanding environmental deterioration in Honduran agriculture through discussing four themes: the fallow crisis, burning, vegetation and climate, and biocide use. The fallow crisis lies at the heart of environmental deterioration. While most official accounts primarily focus on soil degradation as the main consequence of the fallow crisis, producers consider increasing demands on weeding and labour as crucial problems too. Official solutions aim at land use planning, capability classifications and soil conservation projects to construct physical structures in the field. In general these do not fit in with local farming systems and livelihood strategies. Many of the responses of producers to the fallow crisis fall outside the scope of conventional agronomy.

One of these responses is a change in burning practices. The anti-burning attitude of conventional agronomy appears to consist of a few simple notions as compared with the richness of conversations among producers. They use a much more sophisticated set of arguments in discussing and testing the pros and cons of burning. The official discourse contrasts modernity (nature conservation through scientific agriculture) with the traditionality and ignorance of rural people who destroy nature by burning. But, if one appraises the wide array of arguments and how they reconsider these every season, producers can hardly be called ignorant. This conclusion can be extended further: the dualism of official discourse and local knowledge is not only problematic at the level of thoughts and representations. Such a view excludes the possibility that burning can be included as a useful practice in an environmentally friendly agriculture.

Again, the issue of deforestation in official discourse brands rural people as ignorant. Villagers, however, consider deforestation a hazard to their water sources. They also link it to the rise in temperature. Equally, villagers debate the possible risks of increased biocide use. The existing knowledge of the risks of biocides is not so much a result of educational programmes undertaken by outsiders but of practical experiences gained through biocide use. The source of environmental problems is not simply ignorance, as official discourse habitually proclaims. Instead, actual spraying practices have to be explained by a more complex understanding of processes of economic and social differentiation. This includes an understanding of cultural elements such as values of machismo.

The discussion of each issue has shown that conventional agronomy cannot grasp all relevant processes and that incorporating producer perceptions on resource degradation may provide many more insights. Producers generate opinions and knowledge about environmental problems that are not any the less informative than existing documentation on environmental deterioration in Honduras. Studying these may help to overcome the shortcomings of official discourse in Honduras which mainly develops its models in the classroom - from textbooks and through educational seminars followed by technicians. Official discourse can only incorporate a few variables in its models and not the many 'social' and 'biophysical' conditions experienced by producers.

Should one therefore take producers' knowledge as the miracle solution to analyse the complexities of human-environment relations? An uncritical adoption of producer wisdom can never evaluate problematic knowledge constructs such as the *cabañuelas*. Hence, one cannot simply replace the producer's knowledge for useful concepts and methods of conventional agronomy. Hence we are stuck with the theoretical problem resulting from the separation of conventional agronomy and local knowledge, which I made at the start of this chapter following other recent critiques of conventional agronomy (e.g. Kloppenburg 1991:540 who calls them 'separate realities'). This separation is also an element of those studies that focus on the discourses of the actors involved in land use.

These studies observe that, firstly, most current scientific agronomic knowledge on land degradation supplies us with uncertainty, and, secondly, with the view that there is no one unique 'truth' about degradation and possible solutions but rather an assortment of different perspectives (e.g. Blaikie 1993, Zimmerer 1993a). Their claim that what is 'right' or what is 'wrong' is not central any longer, may incline one to an unjustified relativism. In such a relativism, perceptions and definitions exclusively emerge as a result of interests and discourses and little systematic consideration is given to the practical relations these have to biophysical processes.

Research into the perceptions of producers should not, however, necessarily lead to such relativism. In another article Zimmerer (1993b) goes beyond simply capturing perceptions and their contextualization placed within a specific social, cultural and economic history. Zimmerer leaves space for an original analysis of the causes of environmental deterioration; this encompasses an analysis of the role of nature in environmental processes. This space allows us to consider that conventional agronomy and local discourses on environmental deterioration are not separate, contingent, discourses but both emerge from an interaction with nature. From this interaction practical concepts result which can be used to refer meaningfully to environmental deterioration. The logic of local discourse on land degradation can be contemplated by using agronomic knowledge (and of course vice versa). Accordingly, agronomic knowledge can be used as a heuristic tool to understand where perceptions of producers differ from each other or differ from actual behaviour.

I have followed this method above and claim that it enlarges our understanding of environmental change. It implies that explanations and views of producers on environmental deterioration are not regarded as intrinsically better, or more informed than agronomy. One can detect some correspondence between producer perceptions and agronomy: the fallow crisis, burning, climatic change and vegetation, and biocide contamination are on the agenda of both perspectives. The fallow crisis undermines food grain production and producers can maintain yield levels only with extra inputs (labour or agro-chemicals). The conditions for burning practices have changed so that producers consider the need to alter the practice itself. Deforestation is endangering the water sources in the municipality and villagers feel a need for action, but local institutional arrangements are considered too weak to halt this process. Biocides cause health problems and water pollution, and are therefore feared by villagers. All these issues, as well as reports of the phenomena and causes, appear in both producer and agronomic accounts and may contain considerable overlap. A restriction of the value of conventional agronomy and a confined re-evaluation of local knowledge on environmental deterioration do not imply that one should plead for a farewell to reason and accept every explanation of environmental deterioration as right in its own narrative. The many arguments employed in conventional agronomy and producers' knowledge both direct agricultural practice and provide practical solutions for problems in production. Some of these practices will work better than others. This practical component of agricultural knowledge will make it possible to test knowledge and to make judgements about which knowledge is 'better', that is 'more practical'.

This does not mean that one can simply 'creolize' local knowledge with scientific investigation to obtain the most comprehensive interpretation of biophysical processes and to solve the tension. Such a blending still cannot answer two crucial questions: Whose local (and scientific) knowledge should be creolized? The descriptions on fallow crisis, burning, and biocides have shown that no single producer perception about environmental deterioration exists, only different ecological perceptions. Perception of the fallow crisis is related to control over land and specific land tenure arrangements. Perceptions and strategies are not the same for all producers but differ since the distribution of resources is unequal. A diversity in perceptions is most striking in the cases of burning and pesticide spraying. In pesticide spraying resource-rich producers try to displace risk to labourers. The following chapter will analyse in-depth such social differentiation. The second question which emerges from our discussion is: Which knowledge should be creolized? Is there really such a thing as 'local knowledge' that can be differentiated from non-local knowledge? Chapter six will address this question.

5

Social Differentiation and Labour Relations

Representations of labour relations

The foregoing chapters have discussed differential access to land, diversity in land use, and different perspectives on environmental deterioration. Chapter one defined a broad concept of social relations of production. Social relations of production refer to the mobility of land, labour, and credit, and reflect how people relate to each other in developing productive activities, such as agriculture. It should not, however, be limited to the distribution of the means of production and the associated labour relations, but also includes the role of politics, kinship, and cultural notions. This chapter will discuss how various institutions shape labour relations. In doing so it is possible to overcome the shortcomings of the functional dualism model in environmental theory (see Chapter one).

The functional dualism model has at its centre the labour relations between semi-proletarians and the modern capitalist sector. In order to classify these relations it has used groupings of farm size as they are produced in the agrarian censi of many Latin American countries (e.g. de Janvry 1981; de Janvry et al. 1989).[1] These studies classify farms below a certain size (e.g. five hectares) as semi-proletarians because such a small farm cannot sustain the reproduction of a whole family and off-farm income is a necessary condition for survival. The increase of semi-proletarians and the environmental consequences (see also Faber 1992; 1993) is explained by the specific development of the modern sector. In my view, the reduction of labour relations to farm size, and the deduction of labour relations from farm size conceals the relational character and the complexities of labour relations, and the daily struggle around labour.

This chapter therefore shows that the functional dualist model is not an adequate representation of the complexities of social differentiation in El Zapote, i.e. the complex differences in land distribution, land use, and labour exploitation as well as their dynamics and the regulation through social institutions. If it is necessary to characterize the social situation with one term, 'nickel-and-dime capitalism' would be a more appropriate one than functional dualism. It does not separate producers into two classes of semi-proletarians and the modern sector. On the other hand, it does reject the idea of a more or less homogeneous peasantry: rural people exploit each other thus generating structures of exploitation.

They do this not only through inequality in access to the means of production but also by manipulating political clientelism, kinship, gender, and friendship relations.

In order to demonstrate this, I shall compare local representations of differences in wealth, accumulation and poverty. Subsequently I explore the various ways in which control over labour is established and how control over labour is contested in the field. Thereafter it is possible to develop a typology of producers in El Zapote which highlights some of the main processes that create differences among producers in the village.

Local narratives of wealth, accumulation and poverty

The pact with the devil

Our understanding of social differentiation will improve if we investigate how people themselves experience their own situation and differences in material preconditions for rural life. I shall start with recounting the local narrative of the pact Alfredo Luna made with the devil. It is the local version of the mythology of the man who sells his soul to the devil in order to become rich and powerful. The most complete story came from Fidel (b. 1941), who lives on the outskirts of the village in a very poor house. Although he owns some land he mostly rents land or makes his milpas in the Zona. He works most of the time as a wage labourer for other producers. His story of the pact between Alfredo and the devil starts with observations of his father.[2]

> My father got to know Alfredo Luna at the time he started to buy and sell petates and other stuff in the village. Soon, Alfredo came to live in El Zapote. My father said that he travelled with mules as far as San Pedro to sell petates; eight days it took to travel from here to San Pedro. The petate was cheap but Alfredo nevertheless became richer very fast. Once when my father went with his compadre [Alfredo Luna] to his hacienda they spent the night there. On the way my father said to him that he had seen a man on a black mule counting the cattle of Alfredo. Alfredo answered: "Just leave him there, these are *sombras*, it is the friend, let him count the cattle".[3] When they went upstairs to enter the hacienda-house, Alfredo said: "Wait here for me compadre, I have to go out to do something". My father stayed in the old wooden house a while but then he left to look for his compadre. He went down and searched in a *quebradita* [a small ravine] where he saw Don Alfredo sitting at a table with a tall man. In a ravine do you understand? What tables and chairs would be there? The man had a big book on the table and a pen; well illuminated that table. The man was writing bent forward. I do not know what Don Alfredo Luna was saying because my father returned to the house. When Alfredo Luna came back my father asked him: "Compadre, where do you come from?" "I went to do something in the ravine", Alfredo answered, and he continued: "and you don't have the guts to do such a thing [*usted no tiene valor*]".
>
> Five days later one of his a farm-labourers passed away. The labourer went to bathe in the river and simply drowned, even though he was healthy. Labourers of Alfredo died from drowning, or were bitten by insects, for example by ants in the mountains, or from disease. Another died just like that. One guy went to buy eggs and when he entered the house he dropped on the floor: dead. It turned out that Alfredo handed over many people. The people worked for him because he had work to do. In this village we have poverty, we all are poor, so therefore people went to work for

the man, because he had ways to pay labourers, many ways. Also the late Santiago worked for him. The late Santiago was depulping coffee when a tall man, black and with a big sombrero, passed by on a black mule. Then one day Santiago drank milk from a black cow. I was still a boy and told him not to drink the milk. Lying on a pile of maize leaves, he was caught by cholera. There was a burial, just for drinking a glass of milk, but [I know that] the late Santiago is not there but stays in the black house.

They say it is a black house. Some say it is a white house. Only at noon and at midnight can one see the black house. People say that it is the place to enter into an agreement. I have walked a lot in San Pedro but I have never come across that house although I want to see it. [To make a contract you have to pass] seven rooms, each one with a big snake, before you meet him [the devil]. He instructs you to deal three blows to Jesus Christ, but Jesus Christ is weeping and shedding tears. Anyone who has a weak mind (*corto de espíritu*), who has no guts, will not make the pact when he sees Christ weeping because of the three blows he will receive. But he who masters his conscience will win; who indeed wants to be rich, will strike Jesus Christ three blows. The deal is for a few days only and [the devil] will come to receive.

People say Alfredo handed over his own daughter. They say that those handed over will never die. If, for example, someone is to be shot, Lucifer will make a puppet and when the shot is fired he throws it and the puppet will be hit by the bullets. The puppet will fall dead on the ground and the person will be taken alive to the black house. They say that my *madrina*, Doña Aurelia, the wife of Don Alfredo, is there too. She died during delivery along with her child.[4] Alfredo sometimes goes to San Pedro, maybe to see her. His sons also travel to San Pedro often. She has told one of her sons that they should take her out there and should construct a house outside the village. She said: "The people think that I am dead so how can they then see me alive? You have to bring me a black cat, without any white hair. If you bring it I will leave." But no one brought her the cat. All the farm-labourers who were handed over by Alfredo are there too. One of his sons told me. He knows all the labourers and had looked through a window of the house. He had seen this guy and that; he had seen about eight labourers in the black house. He had also seen my madrina with her son, already big now; also some uncles. Nobody was dead, all were alive. Who knows how he managed to bring so many people?

In this way Don Alfredo became rich. It is not nothing to make a pact. You have to love the person who is handed over very much. He had an enormous cattle herd. He had fifty pack animals, just to lug coffee. He always had ten, twenty labourers to pay.

Core elements of the belief system which recur in most stories are that Alfredo arrived rather poor and became incredibly rich very fast; that he handed over his own family and his farmworkers; that he had guts (*valor*); and that he possessed supra-human powers. That he sacrificed his own family is important because it stresses the conviction that he personally handed over his farmworkers. Someone who is capable of handing over his own family can certainly be expected to hand over his farmworkers. The fear of day labourers who do not want to work for Alfredo is therefore accepted as plausible and well-reasoned (without saying it openly, everybody knows that the pact is the motivation of such a refusal). 'Having guts' is important because it explains why only one single man made this pact and not a mass of people. At the same time it expresses a sort of esteem necessary to maintain working relationships with Alfredo. In spite of what he does to his fellow beings it is possible to deal with him. He is not totally evil, he just has the guts to connect with evil. Therefore he deserves to acquire things of value (*valor*); his richness is, in the end, a result of his own work. The stories tell two sides. Alfredo is human, but he is also supra-human as he can do things which normal people are incapable of. In one of the stories a certain Anastacio, who lived near the river, left his house on a night of torrential rainfall to check his belongings. It was midnight and he saw Don Alfredo passing on a black mule. Alfredo went to his hacienda to look for his animals. Anastacio told him not to go because he had to cross the river which was very wild and had swept away entire trees. Alfredo nevertheless crossed the river mounted on his mule and disappeared entirely under water. Anastacio thought he had died until he heard a shot on the other side of the river. Everybody still wonders how Alfredo succeeded in crossing the river. Another example of his extraordinary powers is his age, about which people say: 'eighty-nine years and he still mounts horses and keeps glaring at people with eyes full of fire. Nobody of that age is so energetic.' The pact gives him everlasting life. People take these stories as signs that Alfredo really does have a pact with the devil.

My first interpretation of this belief was that it gives people an explanation of why somebody can become rich while working under the same conditions as those who remain poor. This belief serves to relieve frustration when people lack the knowledge to understand a particular event, in this case the impossible wealth of Alfredo, who arrived poor, in trousers with patches, but obtained many properties and became rich within a few years. This interpretation, however, cannot explain why certain elements appear repeatedly in different versions of this belief and why the belief acquired its particular content and specific meanings.[5]

It is very possible that such beliefs are not so much used to explain differences in wealth, but to explain the difference in wealth and power emerging from new social conditions and changes in characteristics of the economy, as Taussig (1980) argues.[6] A central element in this story is about labour relations: Alfredo became rich because he could hand over farmworkers, i.e. exploit a stock of labour to accumulate his wealth and cause their death.[7] Alfredo was the first villager who employed a substantial amount of farmworkers throughout the year. A group of them, mostly unmarried youngsters without parents to care for them, were living in his house. Others were living in houses on his hacienda and in his finca. Until then, people regarded it as impossible for somebody to have enough money to pay or provide for so many labourers. If interpreted in this way the belief refers to a new kind of labour relation and form of accumulation (while at the same time it mystifies this relation).

Not all villagers, however, accept this belief. Let us consider the view of Excequiel:

I do not believe it: there is no such pact. That man loaned half a bag of beans to somebody who later had to return three quarters of a bag. These were loaned again and so Alfredo got more and more. Furthermore, that man sold everything in his shop. (..) Alfredo also became rich because he took animals away from the poor that were wandering free. He branded these and put them in his paddocks. In this way the rich become rich from the poor.

In this account the explanation of Alfredo's wealth shifts from production (labour relations) to accumulation through commanding exchange and credit in kind and through what has been called primitive accumulation: the violent robbery of the means of production from others. In its negation of the devil-belief this view confirms its central concern of explaining the special form of accumulation for which Alfredo stands. It only argues that one should look for other reasons why Alfredo became rich: usury, merchant profits, and dispossession.

A second rejection of this belief comes from people who follow the instructions of new evangelical religious movements to stand aloof from such 'superstition'. One villager said:

> The people say Alfredo has a pact with the devil. I do not believe this. The devil has no money to make someone rich. God has not created the rich and the poor for nothing. There have to be rich and poor. The poor can work as farmworkers for the rich and earn thus some of the wealth. The poor and the rich are there for each other.

This view of the differences recurs in the perspective of many poor people. If the rich did not exist, the poor would have no place to find work and to get paid. Although this villager rejects the mythological explanation of Alfredo's wealth he directly points to the same link between his wealth and the labourers who work for him. In his rejection of the belief he holds onto the notion that it has to do with labour relations between employers and workers. He only replaces the hand of God for the hand of the devil.

These three contrasting native representations of Alfredo's recent accumulation show it to be important to explain basic different positions in social relations of production or exchange between members of the community. Wealth is not a result of itself, that is, generated by earlier wealth or in relation to personal characteristics only, but is created in relation to others. Expanded accumulation requires reorganization of existing relations, for which the devil-belief finds an explanation which refers to asymmetry, non-reciprocity, exploitation and destructive relations between people, and not to relations as natural relations (cf. Taussig 1980).

Views on impoverishment and difference

The case of Alfredo's pact with the devil is one instance of the dualist poor-rich concept which villagers use to describe differences. *Los ricos* (the rich) are in the first place the descendants of Alfredo Luna. They live in a row of (relatively) big houses, the most expensive in the village, in the main street of El Zapote. Their land, cattle, productive large fincas, their status as traders, and cars are signs of wealth. The village poor stand in contrast to these rich. If this were, however, the only representation of the poor it would correspond well to the functional dualism model. The pact with the devil narrates how someone can become rich and develop a modern enterprise while keeping others in poverty. But there are several other representations of how one can become poor.

The poorer villagers generally view the past as a better time. One admits that there is more money now, that many houses are better, and that the children can go to school. But these people also state that they ate meat everyday in the past, while meat is not on the daily menu any more; once a month if they are lucky. There was no hunger because of the availability of enough maize and beans.[8] Villagers recall that 'permanent labourers' did not exist in the past because everybody had access to land. People only worked occasionally as farmworkers. Additionally, the treatment of labourers in the field was better. Even in the 1930s, they received three meals a day from the producer who hired them, apart from their wage, and they ate the same as the producer, meals with meat. Nowadays farmworkers only receive monetary payments. In contrast to the past the poor no longer have cattle or pigs. They have ceased to keep cattle because access to 'free land' has virtually disappeared. A prevalent explanation of villagers for their impoverishment is the loss of access to land. Many producers have less land available for cultivation than producers had in the past (see Chapter two). Moreover, the land of the village common has lost part of its production capacity.

Apart from structural and historical issues such as land shortage and market development, villagers point to personal abilities and moral virtues to explain poverty. Laziness, drunkenness, and petty-theft pop-up in most stories about poverty. Laziness in popular narratives explains both the individual poor as well as the general state of poverty in Honduras. Stories about the laziness of Hondurans appear time and again in Honduran history.[9] Many villagers in El Zapote, and in Honduras in general, have a self-image of Hondurans as 'lazybones'. It is a recurrent theme in letters to the editor of Honduran newspapers. 'We are producers of children, but things to eat, nothing. We are lazybones,' was said to me. The typical examples of such lazybones are the people who received land through the land reform. In this generally accepted view members of the cooperatives drink and sell the biocides, fertilizers, machinery and the land they obtained in the land reform process only because of their laziness and their longing for booze. They inherit this behaviour, it is said, from the earlier life in the village where they were 'accustomed to sow not more than one manzana of milpa': '*lo poquito nos encanta*' (we love the little).[10] Hondurans often compare themselves with El Salvadorean or Guatemalan people who are supposed to work much harder. The Salvadoreans who lived in Honduras (until they were repatriated in 1969) are now famous for their intensive forms of production. People argue that Honduras could export food grains in the past, when these were produced by Salvadoreans, while it has to import them nowadays. The image of rural people as lazy is sometimes complemented with a logical cause when some villagers refer to a lack of land to explain why it does not make sense to work hard.

The companion of laziness is, as in many places worldwide, alcohol. The linking of alcohol to strength, masculinity and on the other hand misery and degeneration is not typical for Honduras or this village but is nevertheless of importance here. Perceptions about drunkenness changed with the emergence of new protestant movements in the village in the 1970s.[11] Many villagers relate the protestant churches primarily to the issue of not-drinking rather than adhering to a certain religion. The new movements offer men the opportunity to remain a *macho* while, at the same time, to give up drinking. The movements control their members' drinking behaviour and sanction such behaviour by barring those who drink from privileged tasks within the church, or by expulsion. Several villagers explained how they started to accumulate money after they had stopped drinking and joined a movement. This upward mobility after 'starting to believe in the word of

God' is for some a result of investing the money which they used to consume. The cultural opportunity to give up drinking was one of the factors reinforcing the rapid spread of these movements, which in turn -through new consumption patterns without alcohol for a part of the population- increased differentiation.

The 'normal' producer is not only differentiated from the rich, the farmworker, the drunk, and the lazybones, but also from the thief. People think that far fewer crops and goods were stolen in the past. Only animal was sometimes stolen. According to villagers the increased theft of maize, fruits, and coffee, leads to changes in agricultural practices. Some see it as the main reason for the change from the storage of maize in huts in the field to storage in drums, bags and silos in the house. Some producers have cut down fruit trees in the field because thieves stole all the fruit. Producers try to snap the maize as soon as possible because the thief will be discovered much sooner in a field with snapped maize. When the maize is ripe, producers go as often as possible to the fields. Watching over the crop is a time consuming task which must be weighed against other tasks. For example, a producer chooses not to sow a postrera, even though he expected a good harvest, because he needed the time for picking coffee and not for watching the maize crop in the ripening phase. Many choose to sow particular crops in specific fields based on expectations about theft. Petty-theft happens more often in the hunger season (June-August), especially in years of drought when prospects for yields are low. It is precisely in these years that producers care more about getting in the entire harvest.

This short description of local views of impoverishment illustrates that, for villagers, poverty is more than an effect of the incomprehensible deeds of God or the devil. Both the structure of inequality in landholdings and personal agency figure in their explanations. Both generate differences in poverty.

The idiom of independence and reciprocity

The creation of difference is accompanied by the establishment of a norm about what constitutes successful farming. This norm entails an independent producer who works hard to improve the wealth of his or her family. Everyone can reach this objective provided they are not lazy or get drunk or do not work permanently for others. This norm can only obscure the tensions it generates if people continue to think that those who work for others do it on a reciprocal basis. A characteristic concept in the ideology of reciprocal relations is the concept of *ayudar* (to help), which stands in contrast to *trabajar* (to work for). Producers will say that for renting land you need the *ayuda* of other people, and to carry out work in the field people 'help' each other. It is called help, even though it is normally paid. Those sporadic cases of *mano vuelta*, i.e. non-commoditized exchange of labour for one or two days between producers, were strongly tied to the idea of helping very close friends. Quite a lot of day labourers do not like to be represented as such. If one asks for whom they *work* they are inclined not to answer such a question. In their view they help (*ayudar*) other people. They have not yet developed a proletarianized identity: they may help employers but are equal to them. They like to consider themselves still as independent producers.[12]

In order to explain poverty, villagers construct a difference between the labourer and the independent producer. Although many people in the village consider themselves poor, only a few overtly admit that they belong to the group of farmworkers. For many, poverty as such is not a source of embarrassment, while being dependent upon others is. From a position of independence one can help (*ayudar*) others. If one is dependent upon a patron, one has to work for him. Many present day labourers have been told by their parents that working for others is not a good way of living. Non-labourers look down on farmworkers; they express it in many conversations. They complain that the people they hire are lazy: 'They want to receive money only to drink.' They are people 'who love to work for others' (*trabajar en lo ajeno*). Most labourers try to deny that they are dependent on farm-labouring or oppose this attack on their dignity by reinforcing the concept of *ayudar* by stressing the mutual help between them and the producer they work for. But this form of cultural resistance towards negative representations of their way of living conceals their own exploitation.

Not all people abstain from thinking in a worker's discourse. A few farmworkers relate poverty directly to the concept of *camello* (camel) which indicates that the rich patron mounts on the back of the pobre, the camel. They do not look at poverty as a generalized state of affairs as the more wealthy villagers often do, but as a concept of class differences within the village. Less explicit but more generalized is the recognition of exploitation in quotations such as those which stress that working for others 'only provides you with money for daily expenses' and not for savings. Non-labourers and labourers agree on this point: it is better to work in your own field because 'working for others does not pay'; 'it produces nothing'; and 'sometimes you even lose more [maize from your own field] than you harvest'. Another idea which many share is that you have to work harder as a farmworker than when you work in your own field.[13] In the latter situation you can go home early, stay at home when you are ill, or hire others to do the work.

Is poverty functional?

A long stay in a Honduran village confronts one with harrowing examples of poverty which do not fall into the category of the semi-proletarian of the functional dualism model. Indeed, a group of farmworkers is indebted periodically and sell their maize after the harvest in order to pay back loans, or they borrow maize or beans during the 'hunger season' and pay back with labour later. But the poverty of a 'lumpen-peasantry' is often more grinding still. For example, the household where half the woman's earnings from petates is just enough to buy the firewood needed for cooking, because the man has no mule to bring enough firewood to the house. Or the boy of nine years who has already been cultivating a tiny plot of milpa for three consecutive years and who has to weed it during a period in which he has hardly eaten for weeks. Or the young man who is never asked by producers to work for them and who hardly harvests anything on his quarter hectare milpa, and who is so undernourished that he sometimes starts to eat earth. Or the man who is living outside the village in a cave and never shows up in the village because he is ashamed ('*le da pena*') that somebody will see his poverty. Or the woman whose partner and sons are not capable of cultivating the land around their house in the village common; this woman has no cooking utensils at all, and the family therefore never eats tortillas and beans but only uncooked roasted maize. These poor people are in no way functional to the modern sector.

The direct causes of dispossession of the means of production are generally not a function of the development of a modern sector. When people describe the loss of the means of production they refer to personal dramas and contingent processes. I shall summarize two such dramas. One villager said he expected to receive some land and cows from his father, but his father married a second wife who persuaded him to sell the land and cows, so that she could support her children financially. The children of his first marriage thus missed out on their inheritance and had to live from day-labouring and cultivating land in the Zona. The father of Mercedes Alvarez, another poor villager working in the Zona, started drinking when three of his children died in an epidemic of measles. One by one he sold his fifteen cows to buy drink until none were left for his children. The father had lived with two different women. The sons of one of them received all the land in the mountains, while the other woman received some land near the village. Mercedes said:

> My father had eight manzanas of land in the mountains. When he died the children of the other woman received that land. One day a man visited and asked me whether I would sell him my rights to that land in the mountains. I was ill and had to pay the hospital in Santa Bárbara. What do you do [in such circumstances]? I sold him my rights. But the boys of the other woman resisted and threatened to go to a lawyer. It is better to avoid lawyers getting involved in a problem. I thus went to my mother and she divided the piece of land she had received from my father. I did not like the idea of selling that land so close to the village, but after a while I told the man to whom I had sold the rights of the land in the mountains that he could take one manzana of this land down here. In the end only one manzana was left for me.

Apart from giving another lively illustration of some of the processes already analysed in Chapter two, these examples indicate the continuous struggles over the means of production. These are not just individual cases of accidental misery. Every case of decline in access to the means of production has a story of individual crisis. Drink often figures in the stories. These personal stories show that land is not a static element in 'peasant society' which is transferred through inheritance (the view of neo-liberal modernizers who like to create a land market) or by the displacement of peasants by external forces (the functionalist dualism model). Land and other means of production are sold and resold continuously among the different producers, including those who do not pertain to the 'modern sector'. If poverty and misery, which may result from and may cause loss of access to the means of production, is not a direct result of the development of a modern sector, its ascribed 'functionality' may obscure how it is created in local relations of production. The following section will further explore this issue by investigating the ordering of labour relations.

Establishing control over labour

As argued above, the supply of labour for farm work is not simply a function of capitalist development of a modern sector but an effect of daily local struggles. The prime locale for reproduction and socialization of labour is the household. After a discussion of crucial features of households in El Zapote I shall discuss relations between labour, kinship, and friendship. Subsequently the way patronage shapes labour relations and the making of the quality of labour in the field will receive attention.

The household: contradictions of labour reproduction and socialization

Labour force, basic agricultural skills and ecological knowledge in El Zapote are primarily reproduced through the household. Netting (1993) investigates this process. The strength of the household enterprise is its capacity to control consumption according to Netting. It 'can mobilize disciplined and responsible labour for intensive agriculture in a way the wage-labour farm cannot match' (p.75). It can benefit from 'specialization in various tasks, gains that exist because of age- and sex-specific differences in aptitude, strength, knowledge, and experience' (p.70). Netting's thesis brings to the fore how under constraining conditions, for example environmental stress, the smallholder-householder may adapt production systems and intensify in such a way that even higher output levels than before may be reached. This possibility of change does not appear in the functional dualism model as used by Faber.

Parents or other relatives pass on their skills to their children. Agricultural work under Honduran mountain conditions requires specific skills and a physical development of the body which can only be obtained after years of training.[14] It takes months and months before someone can properly hold the machete for cutting bushes all day long, or even just to walk in the mountains with a sharp machete. Care is taken so that boys do not work too hard when they start to do agricultural work in the fields. Educators tend to forbid them to work for other people because they are afraid that another patron will make them work too hard. Later only those patrons who do not demand too much from boys can be helped. The idea is that one should not '*quemar*' the boy, he should not cause 'burn-out', because this would make it impossible for him to work hard during the rest of his life. It takes at least three to four years for the body to develop from a school boy into a field worker.

Apart from training children for field labour they are socialized about the objectives of work. Gradually parents let boys sell some beans. First it may be a very small part of the harvest of the father. Later they may be allowed to have their own small plot beside the household plot. They believe that in this way they 'learn to work for money' and that 'working gives you something in return'. If children are not allowed to earn something 'they will steal for money'.

The household is the principal place to socialize children and this supports the creation of affection and bonds through which property is transferred. Several producers expressed how their own farm work still depends on their father or mother who owns the land or the cows they use. They face tensions with the owner and the uncertainty of never being sure

141

whether they will really receive ownership in the future. Many do not want, for example, to plant coffee because the land may be inherited later by another child or sold to somebody else by the owner before he or she dies.

The reproduction of knowledge, skills, and property, as emphasized by Netting are important features of households in El Zapote. Such a household approach, however, runs the risk of overlooking the fact that consumption, and division of tasks and property are not only strengths but may also be weaknesses of the household as they provide sources for internal conflict. Netting looks at households as corporate groups with more or less common objectives.[15]

A harmonious form of income pooling does not take place in the households in El Zapote nor does a 'rational' spending of money. Instead, conflicts in household life are discussed time and again by villagers. Issues that recur in conversations are, for example, that men spend all the money on drinking, that many women spend too much money on lottery tickets, that the youth do not want to work but instead hang around in the village, or that children go to work for an employer while the parents want to use their labour in their own fields for the benefit of the household. The severe tensions among household members constrain, what Netting calls, 'rational land use'. The case of Pedro Delgado, twenty-three years old, is, in all his innocence, illustrative.

> I am the only one who really works in this house. My youngest brother does nothing. I had to work hard directly after leaving school, but he is already sixteen years and is still sitting at home drinking coffee all day. When I come back from the milpa in the late afternoon I even have to leave again to collect firewood. My mother is ill, she has arthritis, and cannot work well. She rarely makes petates and I have to look for somebody who can wash my clothes, or I have to find time to do it myself. My youngest brother sells the maize too. He loves dancing and if he has no money he goes to harvest maize in order to sell it. In June [the season of scarcity] we then have to buy maize. I do not sow beans any more. I loved making two *tareas**. But last year my brother sold twenty pounds of the harvest, and very cheap too! Now I no longer sow beans. When I earn money I give a share to my mother and a small amount to my father. I am the only one who works here. My father, Martín Delgado, does not do much. You know how fathers are nowadays: they do not provide food for their children.

People change their behaviour to respond to the constraints posed by fellow household members. Household members may sell harvests or pieces of land while others oppose it. I was told several stories of women who sold their land against the wishes of their husbands. Constant negotiation takes place about how much different members should contribute to household expenditures and how much each can sell from the harvest for individual consumption. Some children may cultivate private plots of maize or beans and contribute to the household food stock while others may sell a part or all of the harvest, but still consume food produced by other household members. There is no single flow of product into the house which is for consumption and of which the surplus is sold. Moreover, there is no common collective process of decision-making.

Normative frameworks about which sex should do what type of work shape specific gender divisions of labour. In cases of urgency one finds a 'de facto blurring of work roles' (Netting 1993:69) but in general there are undeniable rewards for specialization, according to Netting. Household members, nevertheless, may have individual strategies which conflict with each other. One illustrative case portrays a struggle between Rosa, Excequiel, and their sons.[16] In October 1994 there was a lot of tule to be cut, but her husband, Excequiel, preferred to prepare a field for the postrera. For several days arguments about what should be done filled the house: that there was no time for cutting tule because the postrera had to be prepared (Excequiel); that making postrera is a hell of a lot of work (Excequiel); that making a postrera is little work because Rosa had bought *gramoxone** to make the work easier (Rosa); that much tule was ready to be cut and that a delay would damage the tule (Rosa); that the children should receive the tule they cut in order to sell it and buy new clothes for Christmas (Excequiel, two sons); and that without money from tule no *tamales* (a favourite dish) could be served at Christmas (Rosa). Rosa considers the tule which comes into the house as hers, and she wants to enlarge this amount of tule. She furthermore tries to establish a claim on the land by working in this field sometimes in case Excequiel should die (Roquas 1995). The result of all this friction was that the sons and a friend of Excequiel worked two days in the tular. The sons pressed continuously for a part of the harvest to sell. Excequiel gave his friend all the tule he had cut. The sons were not allowed to sell, which complied with Rosa's demand, but she was unable to negotiate over the gift to the friend. The friend would later work for Excequiel upon request; Excequiel would profit from this gift and not Rosa. Excequiel was clearly not pleased with the efforts of Rosa to control tule production. In his view Rosa could not claim all the tule, but he accepted that his sons should not receive a part of it. To give away a part of the tule to a friend was his countermove, thus showing that he was in command over the tule. Strikingly, Excequiel laughed very hard and long when somebody joked that Rosa was like a *tuleteniente*.[17] The gender division over access to the tular and the product of the labour, the tule, is continuously reproduced in struggles within the household; even in households which villagers otherwise perceive as very harmonious, such as Rosa and Excequiel's.

These cases show that the division of labour within the household is not an outcome of an optimally organized smallholder system with commonly defined objectives, but an outcome of daily struggle. Furthermore, the gender division of labour is not functionally determined as Netting argues, but has historical roots and may be changed by political struggle. Moreover, parent-child tensions, caused by the disciplining of children and the inheritance question, may change over time. The role of the child in smallholding is not functionally fixed.[18]

Kinship and friendship

The notions of kinship and friendship introduced above, may shape labour relations beyond the borders of the household and beyond pure monetary relations. But to what extent? Corporate kin groups larger than the conjugal family are of relatively no importance to most rural people in Honduras. Kendall (1983) considers family organization is fluid in rural Honduras. There is a high mobility of household personnel, fragility of connubial unions, large numbers of children without a recognized father, alternate forms of 'marriage', many couples are not officially married, and family units break up easily. Kendall disagrees with Gudeman's notion of the 'loose family structure' and provides an alternative definition which is supported by our observations. The presence of 'loose family structures' in rural Honduras does not indicate that kinship has no influence on social life. The conjugal family unit remains an important domain in which rights are vested; kinship is crucial in transferring property (see Roquas 1995) and in organizing labour among the members who live in one household. Outside this it has no dominant influence on day to day agricultural practice and kinship relations outside the household are of little normative significance for labour relations. Unlike Kendall's findings, *compadrazgo* has not been important for structuring relations in El Zapote, at least during this century. It has lost further significance since the evangelical movements began to dominate the religious sphere and the catholic church to lose strength.

Many development programmes consider the 'community' as an organized entity, much in line with the idea of the 'corporate peasant village' which Wolf (1966) observed in Middle America. In a closed corporate peasant community the central power does not or cannot intervene in direct administration, and the local village retains or builds administrative devices of its own natural and social resources. If my descriptions in earlier chapters are correct, however, villages like El Zapote are no corporate coalitions with internal solidarity and levelling of differences, but consist of very individual-centred coalitions (cf. Wolf 1966). As kinship, ritual kinship, and corporate community are relatively loose structures, room is provided for friendship to become important.

Many non-commoditized relationships pass through friendship. 'Friends' help each other, for example, in buying or renting land. The latter results in the fact that owners of neighbouring plots are often friends. This makes it easier to organize labour for clearing paths, guarding the ripe crop, or keeping an eye on assets. Many producers count on the help of friends for their day to day agricultural activities. As Wolf (1966) clarifies, there are two kinds of friendship: emotional friendship and instrumental friendship. In concrete friendship relations both aspects play a role. Instrumental friendship is important for getting access to resources but can only exist on the condition of at least a minimal element of affection. Friendships connect a person to other people. As explained above, a crucial notion within the discourse of friendship is 'to help' (*ayudar*), which expresses how an interaction is perceived as being constituted by something which lies outside a direct, non-reciprocal, market transfer, even though payments are part of the interaction. Friendship is an important notion for people in explaining why they develop activities with certain people and not with others. The role of kinship and community is therefore less important as, for example, Boyer (1982) suggests, and friendship deserves more analytical attention. Friendship, like patronage, is a bond through which labour can be contracted.

Patronage

The distinction between friendship and patronage is not very clear. Patronage in Honduras always has elements of friendship. Wolf (1966) calls patronage a lopsided friendship (citing

Pitt-Rivers). Social scientists (e.g. Pastor 1986) contend that an analysis of social relations in rural Honduras should focus on the local patron, *el caudillo*. One finds, however, few detailed descriptions of concrete patron-client relations. Crucial for patronage is the act of granting or exchanging favours between members of hierarchically arranged groups (cf. Littlewood 1980). Patrons control access to political, economic, or cultural resources that clients want or need. This, however, does not specify enough the typical Honduran 'patron', who is generally seen as somebody with much economic power. Littlewood (1980) explains that several discussions about patronage have primarily based the concept upon ownership of land instead of the reproduction of labour power through the occurrence of favouritism. This indeed occurs in Honduran discussions where a large landowner is almost by definition involved in patronage relations. In anthropology patronage often refers to social relations outside the sphere of production and in the sphere of politics and the regulation of access to resources. The patron provides protection against both the legal and illegal exactions of authority (Wolf 1966). The clients pays back the patron with his loyalty and political support which adds to the name and the fame of the patron. Patronage develops, in this view, as a result of a dysfunctional state which fails to provide access to resources.

How important are patron-client relationships in El Zapote and how should they be understood: as an extension of land-based power, as a labour relation, or as political brokerage? Does it refer to the extra favours granted by an employer to a labourer which are not directly stipulated in a labour contract (which Littlewood (1980) calls 'paternalism')? It seems that villagers use the term *patron* mainly in this latter sense. If somebody says that he is 'working for a patron' this generally means that he can expect certain favours of this patron. A patron has to care for (*cuidar*) his/her labourers. Favours may, for example, be that the patron leases or lends land to the labourer, or that a labourer may pick from the employer's fruit trees, collect fire wood on his/her land, or borrow pack animals. Most favours, however, are monetary, such as payments in advance or loans in times of crisis. The goodness of the patron will depend on the amount of money that somebody can receive and the interest which has to be paid.[19]

Villagers use overlapping concepts for different debt relations.[20] The concepts *adelantar* (pay in advance), *prestar* (to lend), and *alquilar* (lend with interest) have different meanings. Many labourers will only be willing to work if they receive an *adelantado*, a payment in advance. Producers who occasionally employ people have no long-standing relations with labourers and are particularly dependent on this form of contracting labour. They often complain that the labourers come to ask for money in advance on Saturday, become drunk, and lose their interest to work hard on the Monday because the money has been squandered already. Usually the labourer is expected to work for the received payment within a few days.[21] *Prestar* generally involves larger sums of money or maize. Poor villagers consider that a 'patron' for whom they work regularly should *prestar* money. Patrons are qualified not only by the amount of money they lend but also by their willingness to do it. Producers who employ others are constantly preoccupied by the contradiction that they may have to *prestar* or *adelantar* in order to contract labourers but that there is a risk of losing the money. Many stories circulate about people who borrowed money and left the village, labourers who borrowed and started to drink for weeks and never showed up, kin who borrowed and never showed up. 'Lending turns friends and family into enemies,' is the adage for some. Some attempt to restrict lending to *mozos de confianza* (labourers with whom you have a trust relation) but in practice this is difficult.[22] Farmworkers may change patron in times of crisis after having served a patron for many years. The relationship goes bankrupt. 'In order to *prestar*,' it is said by poor villagers, 'you have to look for coffee producers; the merchants do not *prestar* because they like to multiply their money.' *Alquilar* has the objective of making money out of money. *Prestar* is a monetary transaction, but not for making profits on moneylending capital but for getting access to labour or, as we will see below, to a marketable surplus.[23]

Gender may influence who will be approached to borrow money. Sonia is a female producer with a nine manzana, high-productive finca. In her fields one finds many female labourers picking coffee, whilst female coffee pickers are far in the minority or totally absent in fincas of male producers. When these women need money they go to Sonia to borrow (*prestar*) money with the intention of paying it back with labour in the picking season. Gender relations influence their preference for not borrowing money from males.[24]

Besides favours in the sphere of labour-relations, the term patron may also refer to political clientelism. The question is, however, whether in actuality the different aspects can be separated. I shall discuss the relationships between clients and Rafael Luna, probably the most important 'patron' in El Zapote at the time of study. The first case is Excequiel who worked as a muleteer for Rafael Luna during the first years of his marriage with Rosa.[25] During this period he never borrowed money from Don Rafael because he did not like doing so. Only later, in a period of severe crisis, did he go to Rafael to borrow money. Rafael was always asking him to come back to work for him, but Excequiel refused because he had firmly resolved to never again work as a farm labourer. Although Excequiel had problems in paying back the money he did not return to work for Rafael. He preferred instead to sell his wife's sewing machine very cheaply in order to repay the debt. Rafael did several 'favours' for Excequiel by providing him with access to land and political/juridical support. In the period 1962-1966 Excequiel borrowed land from Rafael without paying rent. Later Excequiel had problems with a sister-in-law who accused him of assault. This accusation was part of an on-going struggle between them. She intended to bring him before the court, but Excequiel asked Rafael for help. Rafael went to the local authorities and negotiated an agreement: Excequiel was fined 72 Lempira (36 US$) but would not be prosecuted further. Another typical 'favour' took place in the beginning of the 1980s when Rafael helped Excequiel to build his house: he bought him the asbestos roof covering in San Pedro and transported it to El Zapote at no extra costs.

A second case involves the brothers Paco and Saturnino Ramirez. They and several of their brothers worked for Rafael Luna for long periods. Saturnino, for example, worked for him for fourteen years. Paco started to work for Rafael at the age of seventeen. The brothers made their milpas on Rafael's land. Rafael sometimes even ordered his workers to plough the land for them using his tractor. Later, both Paco and Saturnino received a half manzana of land from Rafael, free, and with a deed of purchase. Rafael helped them in the construction of their house. He brought the zinc roofing for Paco and gave him the timber he needed, and he lent money to Saturnino to build his house. Paco and Saturnino no longer work as day labourers for Rafael but still refer to his goodness. Paco says he is much worse off with his present patron who never wants to lend him money: 'There is no better patron than Don Rafael, never'. Saturnino, at present a coffee producer, says that Rafael is now his 'father'. He sells all his coffee to Rafael: 'Sometimes buyers come with a truck and offer 500 L while the price is 400 L; in no time they have filled the truck. But I always sell to Don Rafael. Even if he has no money at that [particular] moment and will pay much later I still sell to him.' Saturnino is very disappointed that not all the people support don Rafael when there are elections. He has converted himself into a Liberal to help Don Rafael. Paco has remained Nationalist but says he now intends to vote Liberal too.

A third case is Rogelio Herrera. He regularly borrows money from Rafael to pay his day labourers. He pays it back when he sells his coffee harvest to Rafael. Rogelio does not know how much interest he would have to pay to Rafael until the cancelation of his debt. Sometimes Rafael does not charge him interest at all. In 1992 Don Rafael brought him a hand-operated drum pulper (*despulpadora*) which he needed badly although he had no money to buy one. Rafael decided that he could pay for it in two harvests with coffee, but it remained unclear for Rogelio whether he would have to pay interest or not. Nevertheless, he already considers that Rafael is doing him a favour.

Many other people tell similar stories about how Rafael 'helped' them. In emergencies Rafael offers his pick-up to take you to the hospital, Rafael may find you a cheap lawyer, or Rafael may convince authorities of your rights or innocence, and so on. Why does Don Rafael grant such favours to different people? And why do they go to Don Rafael? The gains for Rafael are often not a profit at that specific time but there may be known or unknown future benefits. These may be of a different nature: a loyal labour force, profit through trade and monopolization of a share of the market, or the creation of a political clientele which may give him more strength in the political arena (within his party at departmental level).[26] In the past both Raphael and Rafael's father could become a 'good patron' by providing land to their day labourers.[27] At present Rafael can no longer use this mechanism because he needs all his land for his own production purposes. However, the affection created by this past mechanism, for example in the case of the Ramirez brothers and to a lesser extent Excequiel, still influences people's attitude towards Rafael.

In all three cases people use notions of trust, affection, and favours to characterize the relationship. Relations of affection and trust give Rafael access to a substantial share of the marketed coffee. People sell to him because they assume that in the future they, or their family, might need to make an appeal to Rafael to borrow money. People also go to buy in his shop and not in other shops. Investing in affective relations with Rafael is a sort of 'insurance' which can be counted on in situations of severe crisis.

What may appear as favours for some can be appreciated as an important source of income by Rafael. Rafael provides a handful of pulpers to producers each year (see the case of Rogelio). They pay back later. The amount of affection which surrounds this transaction is thought to be expressed in the interest rate; the lower the interest the more the patron 'values' (*valer*) the relationship. This conceals the fact that for Rafael this pulper business is an important direct source of profit because of the interesting price difference between purchase and sale. Producers assume that Rafael brings them the pulpers to demonstrate his affection and trust, and they feel they have to respond with selling him their coffee. They assume that he is interested in the coffee and they do not see, according to him, the relatively big profits he makes on the pulpers.

People also see Rafael as a patron because they may need his help to make deals with authorities or to take part in legal procedures. As juridical defence is inaccessible to the poor they may have to resort to patronage relations in order to operate successfully in the wider state and juridical system. The cases of Excequiel and the Ramirez brothers contain examples of political clientelism. Favours in this sphere, however, are not always responded to by returning a favourite political vote (see Paco Ramirez who still does not vote for Rafael's political party despite the many favours). People may also show their affection for Rafael by working for him if he needs labourers, or by selling him their coffee.

The cases with Rafael as patron suggest that patronage is not a fixed and single relation. Political clientelism is interwoven with mechanisms of labour control and trade profits. The profits for Rafael may vary: sometimes he will never receive anything in return, sometimes he will directly receive interesting profits (e.g. in the case of the depulpers) of which the favoured will never know the value for Rafael, and sometimes the 'help' in return is clearly visible (e.g. such as why Saturnino sells his coffee to Rafael). The way patrons are able to play with such opportunities leads to their eventual success in building a clientele and making profits. Rafael has to switch between favours, affection, exploitation and use. But it is just in this way that favours are created: some people will be helped and others will not (they will pay high interest on loans, or high transport costs for an emergency drive to the hospital). The notion of favours encloses the notion of establishing differences. If the favour were to be delivered to everybody, it would cease to be a favour (and could even become a right). This may also be the case with respect to any one client: a favour will sometimes be given but not always and continuously. It is the *possibility* of favours (and not the obligation) and the *switching* from building political constituencies into profit-making through trade or labour control that characterizes Honduran patron-client relations.[28]

From this it follows that the content of the relations varies over time. Rafael's patron-type behaviour was very important in controlling a labour force in the past; nowadays it helps him to monopolize a part of the coffee trade and to reinforce his position as political leader. The current expressions of patronage are not the old *hacienda* related patronage systems which revolved around the supply of labour for the patron and access to land for the client. Nevertheless labour supply and control remain a feature of current patronage structures.

Contesting the quality of labour

The relationship between producers who employ labour and labourers is not fixed but continuously subject to negotiation and struggle. The discussion above of the negotiation to *prestar* or *adelantar* money already raised this point. Below I shall examine other arenas for negotiation and struggle such as working conditions, whether payment will be for piece-work or day work, the length of the working day, the wage level, and the length of the labour contract. These together constitute the quality of labour in El Zapote.

Working conditions are not only important for white collar employees and blue collar workers but also for poor day labourers. Day labourers are reluctant to work in fields which are far away from the house. Several coffee producers encounter difficulties in finding coffee pickers due to the distance to their fields. Excequiel, for example, always complains he cannot find people willing to pick in his finca which is a distance of two hours walking. In 1994 he tried to solve this problem by offering payment in advance. The only ones willing to accept the offer were those who drank from payments in advance. Although he therefore did not trust them so much, he had to take the risk. The result was that his labourers did not appear on the agreed date and time. For several days he had to insist that they must show up. When they finally turned up he was still not pleased: they arrived late and left early, arguing that they had to walk far. According to Excequiel they had picked too few berries compared to what should be done for a day's wage. A year later he accepted his son's proposal to bring several eight to ten year old friends who would stay overnight in the finca. In doing so Excequiel had to withdraw his earlier objection to child pickers who, according to him, only play, do not pick, and destroy the coffee trees. This example shows the complicated consequences of something as apparently simple as the distance to a field. The situation in the field may bear similar consequences. If a field is located where it is very hot and no cooling winds blow, no-one wants to go there unless the producer allows many breaks and a very early end to the working day. Producers may also find it difficult to contract labourers if the fields contain many stones. The labourer must bring his own tools for weeding (a pando and a file to sharpen the pando). One week cleaning or weeding in fields with many stones may sometimes wear out one to three files, which cost half a day's wage each. Hence, this will lower the returns on his labour. Even though the poor may urgently need to do farmwork they therefore prefer to choose certain producers to others.

A second point of struggle is whether the labourer will be paid for tasks, per piece, or per day's wage. It is a struggle over how much labour in return for a certain wage.[29] Most work is paid by day wage for which the labourer works from six a.m. to four p.m. (which generally includes the time to walk to the field; three o'clock is the usual time to stop work). Once in the field labourers often start a discussion, half in jest, about the length of the working day. They praise producers who 'set free' their labourers earlier, for example at two o'clock.

Work can also be paid per task. An example is to pay for weeding by a certain measured area, the *tarea**. A point of negotiation is who will measure the area (with outstretched arms), the day labourer or the patron. It is a favour to the day labourer when he is allowed to measure, but I know of a case of one labourer who refuses because his arms are 'much too long'. The labourer can go home when he has cleared, weeded, or sowed, the entire measured area. Larger contracts (then called a *contrato*) are made for weeding a whole finca or cleaning a paddock. A contracted labourer can subcontract other people.

Another contract form is piece-wages, a common form in coffee picking. During the picking season the wage level and the situation in the fincas are a major topic of lively conversations. In the beginning, the first picking round, the ripe beans are scattered, and labourers prefer a day wage. In the middle of the season each tree bears many ripe berries and labourers prefer to be paid per bin. Fast pickers can thus add to their income. At the end of the season, when the amount of berries per tree drops, pickers want to be paid in day wages again. Producers have different reasons. When they pay per day the pickers do not pick enough and their costs rise. This is difficult to manage. When they pay per bin the pickers want to move too fast and may destroy the trees by breaking off branches and may refuse to pick up berries that fall to the ground. The labourer tries to become informed about the fields that bear much coffee and must balance speed of picking against amount of coffee (and the relationship with the producer) to decide whether to demand a day or piece wages. The producer must weigh up a preference for fast picking against quality of work and how much he/she can trust the labourers to work according to the requested standards.

The wage level is a third point of contention between employer and labourer. Some 'patrons' (the 'misers') are notorious for their discursive efforts to lower wages, but in general the level of day wages for adult male labourers and for different type of assignments is quite uniform. Only for tasks such as spraying biocides, are a few employers willing to pay a 10-20 per cent higher wage. Young boys who have just started to work in the field receive less and women picking coffee may receive a lower day wage, but more often, they will work on piece rates (per bin of picked coffee) just like children, while adult men may work for a day wage. In general, I think, the wage level is less debated than the length of the working day or aspects of working conditions. Only at particular times do labourers talk about the need to increase remuneration. During my field work period this was twice, just before and at the beginning of the coffee picking season. It is difficult to understand the mechanisms of how wages rise. Demands for higher wages not only result from rising costs of living, but also to the levels of the employers' profits. The prospects for high coffee prices because of frost in Brazil and a lower world market supply in 1994 generated optimism. The expectations of high coffee prices were further cultivated by producer organizations and state institutions. At the village level coffee pickers started to talk about higher wages. While wages were still ten to twelve Lempiras per day (about 1.30 US$), labourers began to speculate that wages would rise to twenty or even thirty Lempira. Afraid of high wage demands coffee producers made it known in the public sphere that they were not happy with the frost in Brazil and that they needed this extraordinarily good year to compensate for the preceding bad years. The situation generated multiple instances of negotiation between labourers and coffee producers. In the end, coffee prices only doubled instead of tripling or quadrupling (as expected by producers) and the wage level stabilized at fifteen Lempira. This rise is a result of many small negotiations between individuals. The coffee pickers profited relatively much less than the coffee producers from the rise in coffee prices.

A fourth issue for struggle is the length of the labour 'contract'. Employers may contract for one or a few days or can guarantee longer periods of work. Many labourers prefer to have a 'patron' because it takes away the necessity to search for work again each day. They take the risk that they may have to work for the patron at times when they would prefer to sow or weed their own maize or beans. A bond with a patron creates dependency and obligations. Others choose to remain more independent and take the risk of not finding work at times when they need it. Producers too have a variety of strategies with regard to establishing the length of labour contracts. Some prefer to work with one or two labourers (on a temporary or permanent basis - *mozos permanentes*) and to finish the work after a longer period, since a small number are easier to control than large groups. Others prefer to work with larger groups to finish the work in short periods, for example maize weeding or harvesting in one or two days. Maize sowing in particular is better done in one day in order to have an even germination of the crop. Furthermore, with larger groups the producer will need little of his own labour to fulfil a specific task.

This point of the size of work groups relates to the more general issue of the control of labour tasks. Many producers complain that labourers were honest in the past while they cannot be trusted nowadays: 'you always have to supervise them in the field'. They argue that labourers arrive too late, that they throw too many seeds in a hole when sowing maize, that they do not care about the tule and cut the stems too low causing diseases in the plant, and that they steal biocides, fruits, and fertilizers. The stories about the mayor's problems in controlling his labourers are told with great hilarity and circulate as examples. Because of his function, the mayor cannot accompany the day labourers to his fields. Once he sent a couple of workers to fertilize his coffee. These labourers applied all the fertilizer in the first few rows and probably finished the work within an hour while receiving a day's wage. The coffee of the first rows died, burnt by the overdose of fertilizer, and the dead trees, which stood just near the path that led to all the other coffee fields, became a visible symbol to all producers. A similar story of labour defiance addresses gross misconduct in the pastures of the mayor. The labourers, paid to clear the pastures with their machete, cut the bushes far above the ground instead of just above it which is a much harder job but the way it should be done according to producers. Villagers joke that the mayor is unable to control his labourers because they are of the same political party and, if he did correct them, they (and their relations) would no longer vote for the mayor. This wisecracking replicates the main lesson that 'one should be in the field to control the labourer'. The same lesson is repeated by some women producers who complain that they, as women, cannot control labourers as they cannot or do not want to go so often to the field. They suffer for this lack of control, they say. One employee of the electricity company holds a similar view. He twice started to build up a finca but sold both times, disillusioned because the contracted and paid labourers did not apply the fertilizer or weed the finca. He has decided not to enter agricultural production while he is unable to control the labourers in the field.

Above I have outlined the many points of negotiation between producers and labourers. The day-to-day perception of inequality and relations between farmworkers and smaller and larger producers is not about differences in access to land but about the 'politics of production' (Burawoy 1985): the day-to-day organization of labour as discussed above. The daily exercise of negotiating labour conditions pushes the unequal distribution of land, which is still the decisive means of production, into the background. With the many facets of establishing labour control in mind, we can now try to model differentiation in El Zapote while going beyond a simple stratification according to farm size.

A typology of producers

The multiple and contradictory character of labour relations shows that a linear model of stratification according to farm size is not adequate to capture rural complexities. However, a notion of multiplicity of relations does not mean that any sort of modelling of social differentiation is impossible or worthless. As the idiosyncrasy of each producer is relational to other producers we need to develop a relational typology that goes beyond listing personal producer strategies (e.g. entrepreneurship) or classifying in terms of single observable morphological features (such as the size of farm, production level, composition of crops, or agro-ecological zones); a composite profile based on individual characteristics is also not adequate. Similarity in entrepreneurship, farm size or agro-ecological conditions cannot explain the quantitative and qualitative changes that have occurred and are occurring in land use. In contrast to taxonomic typologies, a relational typology attempts to comprehend why producers act differently even though their farms are of equal size, e.g. why 'producers-by-inheritance' with five hectares of land choose to cultivate very different crops on the same type of land as an 'employee-producer' with five hectares of land. Crop choice, technology choice, and other decisions may differ in spite of access to the same resource base.[30]

Table 5.1 lists the main types of producers in El Zapote. I look mainly at differences in labour relations, the origin of working capital, and the scale of the means of production. This typology situates producers within a wider network of production relations by recognizing historical causes and economic and social configurations that influence land use. This typology results from theoretical reasoning and qualitative analysis, and has been validated by confronting producers with the typology.[31] I made descriptions out of sentences gathered during interviews on labour issues. In a second stage respondents could choose among one of the described types and indicate why they differed from other types.[32]

The question served as an entry for starting a conversation about differences. Typical starting comments were: 'beautiful, so are we', 'all those people live here in the village'. Many respondents could directly make a choice among the presented types. For some it was difficult to choose between a producer type which came close to their way of life in the past or their desired situation, and another which reflected most their current situation. Such a typology always faces difficulties in dealing with historical change. 'I have passed all those stages of life', answered one producer. Others picked up elements of two or three type-descriptions. No respondent made use of the explicitly offered possibility to disagree with all the presented types. In fact, the conversations centred upon the elements which structure differences: land, labour, off-farm employment, how capital/land was accumulated and the role of inheritance, savings made elsewhere during periods of migration, and specific profits made (e.g. through coffee or pigs).

While talking over the typology it became clear that producers represent differences in a simple *pobre-rico* discourse as well as portraying a much more refined framework of differences. Villagers do not represent themselves as *campesinos* who are all alike in the village but different from the outside world, from the state or the traders.[33] The main concepts indicating opposition or difference refer to relations within the village. Below I introduce the different types and then discuss whether inequality should be theorized as an effect of structured forms of differentiation.

Types of producers in El Zapote

The **employer-producer** hires all labour and accumulates a substantial share of total capital with profits from agriculture.[34] Investments in other sectors (housing, transport, merchant activities) are quite common. The producer makes crucial decisions, such as when and what biocides to spray, even when foremen supervise the farmwork. Unlike the 'urban-based investor', the employer-producer remains a 'farmer' and develops his/her own agricultural knowledge on the farm.[35] He/she is rooted within the local cultural and social context, important for hiring and controlling labour. A producer like Rafael Luna is a typical example of this type.

The **producer-accumulator** also succeeds in accumulating capital with profits from agriculture but still uses a substantial amount of family labour. Patronage relations to bind labour are therefore less important than for the employer-producer type. This type is highly interested in commercial crop production and savings are mainly invested in coffee, land, and some animals. The producer intends to implement modern farming techniques and searches for institutional assistance in developing the farm. José (see Chapter three) represents this type of producer. He organizes production in such a way that it meets his goal of a 'profitable agriculture'. This producer type emerges when possibilities for commercial activity (coffee or cattle) grow. A starting level of the means of production (e.g. obtained through inheritance) may initially be important but is not decisive. The availability of cheap wage labour is critical for setting up profitable activities. This producer type is often active in village affairs, such as water committees, the village council, the school council, local party activities, and producer organizations.

The **saver-producer** first saved money as a wage worker outside the village or, for example, as a teacher or construction worker.[36] This money has been invested in land, farm equipment, or some animals. Cash crop production is a main objective. Most of these producers do not succeed in expanded accumulation through agriculture and production remains at a constant but substantial level. This producer type becomes more important as the number of jobs expands in Honduras. Farm labour is a combination of family labour and hired labour.

The **employee-producer** earns an income from wage labour or trade and invests part of it in lucrative crops (here coffee) and, to a lesser extent, in food grains. Employee-producers are teachers, municipality clerks, or civil servants of rural state agencies. The development of a safety net is an important stimulus for farming. Crop management may fluctuate according to expectations in future employment. Uncertainty arising from state privatization or political changes after elections may lead to increased activities in farm production. Farm work may take place during the weekends and hired and family labour are employed. Profits made through agriculture do not lead to an impressive broadening of the production base (the stock of the means of production). In response to rising or falling prices, the producer tends to shift investments to other activities.[37]

The **producer-by-inheritance** inherits a substantial part of the means of production. Producers of other types also inherit land (see Table 5.1), but for this producer type inheritance is the *only* moment in which capital (land) is obtained. The land base is sufficient to feed the family and since the stock of resources remains large enough to avoid a livelihood crisis, there is no strong pressure to change cropping systems or to work as a day labourer. Labour is only occasionally hired. Increasingly property is now subdivided under the pressure of heirs. Moreover, a rise in land prices encourages elderly owners to sell it as a commodity in order to pay the costs of living or medical treatment. The relative importance of this producer type is therefore decreasing.

The **tenant or common-land producer** cultivates land from others or cultivates his maize in the Zona. Many of these producers prefer the commons, even when yields are lower than on rented land, because it does not impose a set of (labour) obligations. They generally do not hire labour and may use herbicides to offset labour shortages. Excequiel (see Chapter two and three) is an example of this type of producer.[38] This type may continue to exist as long as a land pool is available from which land can be rented or occupied temporarily.

The **servant-producer** generally sows a small milpa which is not sufficient to guarantee family livelihood. To survive, the servant-producer works as a farmworker. Patronage relations may provide access to land for subsistence crops. Cultivation tends to be sub-optimal; labour obligations may lead to late sowing or weeding. Herbicides are not used with the objective of increasing production but to offset the labour crisis that results from the servant-producer selling his own labour power. While the tenant or common land producer intends to make his milpas as large as possible to guarantee enough food, the servant-producer counts on the availability of employment when he needs income to buy food.

154

A typology is only useful when it helps to understand important processes at work. Table 5.1 may help to discuss some of these processes. The typology is not intended to reduce structures of differences and processes of ordering to one single model of fixed positions.

Social differentiation explains how resource conservation by one producer may enhance the vulnerability to environmental deterioration of the production system of other producers. With the increasing amount of coffee revenues several producers employ strategies to become owners of more land with the intention of broadening their land base and of reintroducing or extending the fallow periods between periods of maize cultivation. From the viewpoint of natural resource conservation, such strategies can be regarded as positive. Investments in 'sustainable' subsistence production are paid for with the profits from export crops. However, this process increases pressure on land and creates land shortage for other producers. Land-poor producers find it increasingly difficult to rent land because land-rich owners cease to rent out land in order to preserve soil fertility. Once a fallow period has restored soil fertility the owner uses this fertility him/herself while in the past tenants and servant-producers often could clear such a *guamil*. From the viewpoint of servant-producers and tenant or common-land producers, such strategies threaten their livelihoods. Furthermore, individual strategies to conserve land shift the pressure on land to other areas, such as the Zona where soil degradation is taking place. The land use and conservation strategies of some producers can increase the destructive use of common land by land-poor producers.

Another aspect of social differentiation is that it shapes interventions for developing sustainable agriculture. Although development interventions often target poor producers, local contradictions and implicit assumptions about homogeneity and producers' rationality wreck the intentions of producing rural equality. The work of PRODESBA is the local example of this widespread phenomenon. This integrated rural development programme functioned in the village between 1985 and 1990 and intended to fill basic needs, to improve subsistence production and marketable output, and to conserve natural resources. To improve maize production, groups of producers received credit, improved seed, fertilizers and biocides, and courses in how to make contour ditches to slow down run-off. These maize projects encountered many technical problems and expectations were not fulfilled. Producers were therefore no longer interested in maize projects and asked for projects to improve coffee production, which PRODESBA agreed to. It increased the amount of credit while, at the same time, the number of producers in the projects decreased. The participants in the coffee groups improved their coffee production within a few years.

Despite intentions to target the poor producer the project mainly interfaced with the producer-accumulator, the saver-producer, and the employee-producer (see Table 5.2). It did not reach the servant-producer and the tenant or common land producer, nor the producer-by-inheritance. Of these latter types nobody participated in the coffee groups and only a few had joined the unsuccessful maize groups. The projects largely failed to transform these types of producers into commercial farmers and to incorporate them into

Table 5.1 Types of producers in El Zapote in the 1990s, land distribution and farm technology

producer type	N	value property	share in total land	yield milpa	harvest milpa	harvest coffee	area pastures	land in fallow	land property	external land	inherited land	fertilizer use	herbicide use %	burnt %
employer-producer	5	275.3	62.9	1475	79 (4)	126 (5)	56.00	53.1	128.2	0.0	32.6	71	20	20
producer-accumulator	9	45.4	13.4	1023	19 (9)	50 (6)	4.38	3.6	15.2	0.4	4.0	38	89	44
saver-producer	6	36.4	6.2	1358	19 (5)	29 (6)	2.81	3.2	10.6	0.7	0.4	22	67	50
employee-producer	5	44.5	4.2	1031	12 (5)	49 (5)	1.67	3.1	8.5	0.6	1.4	67	20	20
producer-by-inheritance	16	19.8	8.2	921	11 (12)	7 (14)	1.17	2.2	5.2	1.2	5.1	31	43	43
tenant or common-land producer	11	10.0	3.2	883	13 (11)	5 (7)	0.05	2.5	3.0	1.7	0.5	18	64	64
servant-producer	25	3.3	1.3	549	10 (25)	1 (6)	0.05	0.3	0.6	1.4	1.5	12	48	63
others	6	6.0	0.5	804	8 (5)	7 (2)	0.00	0.1	0.9	0.4	0.2	28	0	50

Note: N is the number of producers who belong to each category (total N = 83); 'value property' is the average value of property in 1000 L; 'share in total land' is the percentage of the total land owned by this type of producer; 'yield milpa' is the average yield of the main milpa in 1994 in kg/ha; 'harvest milpa' is the average harvest of all milpas in 1994 in qq per producer of those producers who harvested milpa (between brackets the number of producers about whom data exist); 'harvest coffee' is the average harvest in the 1993/94 season in qq of those producers who harvested coffee (N=51) (between brackets the number of producers who harvested coffee); 'area pastures', 'land in fallow', 'land property', 'external land' (is land rented, borrowed, or common land used in 1994), and 'inherited land' are averages in local manzanas; 'fertilizer use' is the average in kg/ha applied in the 1994 milpa; 'herbicide use' refers to the percentage of producers of each category who applied herbicides in maize cultivation in 1994; 'burnt' refers to the percentage of producers who burnt at least one milpa in 1994. Most differences among groups are not significant (using the conservative Scheffé test for comparing group means); only the employer-producer type differs significantly from other types for some of the variables. The small size of the sample makes it difficult to draw definite conclusions. Differences should only be interpreted as indications of hypotheses which need corroboration in further research. The category 'others' includes people who could not be grouped with one of the other types, such as two young producers who were just starting their own production.

expanding markets. When credit could be obtained, a selected group of producers preferred credit that could be invested in coffee production, while improvement of maize production and investment in soil conservation techniques did not take place. Typically, interventions for sustainable agriculture are more easily designed for the relatively resource-rich, market-oriented dynamic producers, such as the saver-producer and the producer-accumulator, and tend to subordinate ecological objectives to economic imperatives.

Table 5.2 Number of producers participating in PRODESBA groups in El Zapote

	N	Coffee	Coffee and Maize	Maize
employer-producer	5		1	
producer-accumulator	9	2	1	1
saver-producer	6	1	2	1
employee-producer	5		1	2
producer-by-inheritance	16			2
tenant or common-land producer	11			
servant-producer	25			1
others	6			

Source: survey of eighty-three producers, fifteen of them participated in a PRODESBA group; 'coffee' refers to groups in which PRODESBA supported coffee production; 'coffee and maize' refers to producers who first joined the maize groups and later the coffee groups.

Social differentiation generates inequality with regard to access to resources and use of farming techniques. Table 5.1 shows that much of the land is concentrated in the hands of the employer-producer and the producer-accumulator. The servant-producer owns a very small portion of the land. For both of them the amount of inherited land is substantial.[39] They share this feature only with the producer-by-inheritance. As with access to land, the technological performance seems to differ. The lower strata tend to have lower maize yields and they harvest much less coffee. The lower maize yields of tenants and servant-producers probably relate to a lower level of fertilizer use.[40] On the other hand they use herbicides more often than, for example, the employer-producer; this may be related to the labour crisis which these producers confront, but the available data cannot confirm this. The poorer producers produce less maize per producer than, for example, the employer-producer. This observation runs against the generalized myth that poor producers provide the countries' maize supply. Resource-poor producers in the village generally are net-consumers (see also Johnson 1997).

Inequality, differentiation, and everyday forms of small exploitation

Is this inequality of resources a result of upward social mobility due to the changing ratio of consumers to workers in the household, demographic variation, inheritance patterns, or gains from off-farm employment, as Netting (1993) argues? Or is it an outcome of social differentiation with qualitatively different positions of different types of producers, tied

157

together by polarized relations? My analysis above differs from Netting (1993) as it maintains that the contemporary smallholder is not a historically continuous category. Instead, most producer types exist as a result of contemporary and changing relations. Think, for example, about labour opportunities outside agriculture (e.g. the saver-producer), state jobs (e.g. the employee-producer), booming markets (e.g. the producer-accumulator), or increasing wage labour in agriculture (e.g. the servant producer). Netting (1993:230) suggests that mobility among ranks of smallholders is more characteristic for smallholders than polarization and the hardening of class barriers. In El Zapote mobility certainly exists as we have seen in the history of Alfredo Luna or in case of the saver-producer. The saver-producer inherits a small 0.4 mz of land while he owns on average 10.6 mz land; the inheritance is only a tiny fraction of his property. But mobility also can mean impoverishment, as discussed above. Table 5.1 shows that servant-producers on average lose most of their inheritance (they inherit 1.5 mz, while they own not more than 0.6 mz) in periods of crisis. Individual mobility, however, does not terminate the qualitative difference between types of producers. In his denial of polarization among smallholders, Netting fails to see qualitatively different characteristics that make producers act differently. For example, producers-by-inheritance or servant-producers face decisive constraints in intensifying coffee production and will not invest labour and money in a process of intensification, while, for example, employee-producers do remove constraints by buying land and employing the servant-producer.

With some caution that future developments may contradict my contention, I conclude that a process of social differentiation is taking place whereby servant-producers and tenant or common-land producers increasingly face problems in maintaining sufficient control over land. As long as the coffee industry is booming, coffee producers (the employer-producer, the producer-accumulator and the employee-producer, and to a lesser extent the saver-producer) will employ a part of their labour. The coffee boom will at the same time undermine the resource base of resource-poor producers because coffee producers continue to extend their land base with their coffee revenues. Future developments in coffee will, to a large extent, shape the profile of rural communities in mountainous Honduras. At this moment about a quarter of the producers have been able to modernize coffee during the last decade (see Table 5.1). A group of poorer producers with coffee (the producer-by-inheritance and tenant or common-land producer types) does not succeed in intensifying production and generally their meagre profits are rapidly consumed within the household. Those without coffee stay further behind and do not benefit from economic development.

Apart from inequality, which Netting considers a common characteristic of smallholders, I thus observe social differentiation and polarization. But not the differentiation Netting rightly criticizes: the idea that rural Honduras should necessarily end up in a modern sector of capitalist production and a class of proletarians. To understand rural Honduras, however, it is critical not to overlook small forms of exploitation. Relations of exploitation between the poor and the very poor in particular very often remain invisible for outsiders even though these relations structure a rural economy. To substantiate this argument I will use the case of relations in petate production described by Roquas (1994). Diverse development organizations have intended to increase the incomes of women who make petates. PRODESBA (CDI 1989, SECPLAN 1989b) developed a credit system and a cooperative commercialization programme assuming that this bypass of petate merchants would increase producer prices. The project failed because it did not understand the existing production structure and assumed that all petate makers were poor women who received the tule from their cooperating husbands. However, the man who controls the tular does not always have a cooperative relation with the woman who uses the tule. The man can choose not to pass the tule he cuts to the women in the house but to sell it. Several men sell their tule while their wives buy tule from other producers. When the tule is sold the work of the man is valued higher than the work of the woman in the end product, the petate. Women, in turn, can buy tule if they do not receive it from the men in the household.

Among women, a second set of complex relations exists. Roquas distinguishes between the possessor of tule and the petate maker. The possessor can make petates or contract other women to do so for her in different, more or less exploitative forms. In the *real por real* contract the petate maker receives tule for two petates and returns one petate. In the *hechuras* contract the possessor pays somebody else to make a petate for her with her tule. Making petates in hechuras is how the poorest women make a living. They only receive about half of what a tule possessor would earn if she were to make the petate herself. The possessor receives the other half. The real por real contract is somewhat more favourable to the petate maker, but this contract is only made in situations of personal relations and favouritism. In months when there is a scarcity of tule, the real por real contract even disappears and only hechuras contracts are made.

The result is that some women exploit the labour of other women in the labour process of petate production. Development projects have not seen such relations and as a consequence the women supported by their projects (e.g. with credit) have been able to make more hechuras contracts with poorer women. They have also been able to start to make profits in the field of commercialization. Here again small exploitation is important. For example, a petate maker may receive 7 L as a small credit on the Monday on condition that she delivers a petate, worth 7.50 L, to the buyer by the Friday. In fact the petate maker pays an interest rate of 7 per cent per week. Although the projects were intended to help empower the poorest in petate production they actually strengthened an upper layer of tule possessors.

The study of Roquas is more than a conscientious empirical description of a micro-cosmos of unequal gender relations and of the material bases of complex social differentiation. It also outlines how petate production and commercialization takes place in a social space in interaction with other forms of differential distribution of value and power within the village. The case of the petate illustrates the existence of everyday forms of small exploitation; it explains complexities in this social space and it is therefore a valuable contribution to the theoretical critique and development of what Kearney (1996) has called 'post-peasant studies'.

This latter approach recognizes the existence of a plurality of antagonisms (Laclau and Mouffe 1985). Complexities in social relations of production and multiple subject positions, however, do not lead necessarily to the abandonment of every understanding of class, as long as people occupy different positions in systems of production of value and the differential distribution and consumption of that value (Kearney 1996:153). The discussion above shows that this is the case in El Zapote. One could argue that the current absence of any signs of a shared identity of a subordinated/oppressed/dominated peasantry opposed to an external body of capitalists/traders/state/science that may be taken as a herald of future forms of organized resistance, supports the thesis of complex forms of internal differentiation. Indeed what preoccupies people is how to manage the multifarious relations with other villagers, those 'others' who are categorized as equally poor by outsiders who plan development intervention. The study of Roquas acknowledges the existence of external differentiation, petate buyers make large profits from the petates they buy cheaply from petate makers. But it also shows that we have to take into account internal differentiation (cf. Kearney 1996:136-170): smallholders are not unitary objects but complex subjects who are, for example, members of a household where a possessor of tule buys tule from a neighbour and makes her low-priced petates while she exploits other petate makers at the same time through 'hechuras' contracts. She may also share the house with a husband of the saver-producer type who sells his tule to other women, and a son who is a servant-producer and involved in patronage relations with Don Rafael. There is a complex set of structural discontinuities within the farming population based upon differences of social interest (Long 1989).

Nickel and dime capitalism

This chapter reviewed different views on inequality in smallholder agriculture. It started with local narratives, from the pact with the devil and rich-poor dualisms, to ways of talking about more intricate differences. They all point to relations of asymmetry and non-reciprocity. In their stories villagers combine both structural and actor-oriented explanations of poverty and impoverishment. They reveal that poverty as a phenomenon cannot be explained by referring to an essential functionality in the sense of a cheap labour supply for a modern sector. The typology of producers supports this conclusion as it underlines that the agrarian producers cannot be divided into two sectors. Moreover, a politics of production and reproduction present in the day to day struggles and negotiations about the quality of labour cannot be read off from the distribution of the means of production. Currently, the coffee boom plays a pivotal role in reshaping the relations between producers.

The villagers in El Zapote are related to each other through forms of small exploitation. Some producers control more means of production than others and can employ the labour of others to accumulate more wealth or at least to attain a higher level of consumption. Besides control of the means of production, the knowledge and capability to utilize (and define and redefine) rules and resources of non-commodity relations (such as patronage, kinship, gender, friendship, and household relations) is important. The notion of a nickel-and-dime capitalism is useful to capture this situation of multiple forms of small exploitation.[41] It says that the subject in El Zapote is differentiated 'internally and externally' to use Kearney's (1996) words, without denying that people merge into systems of production of value and a differential distribution and consumption of that value. The native representations of difference all stress the importance of such an understanding.

The notion also supports the argument that functional dualism cannot analyse rural society beyond a modern sector - (semi-)proletarian dualism. At the same time it intends to avoid an assessment of the diversity in producer strategies as re-introducing 'homogeneity' through the backdoor by disregarding fundamental contradictions among producers. The community is not composed of homogenous, poor, hillside producers. The typology demonstrates that those who speak of 'el campesino' or 'the farmer' and 'the community' presuppose a homogeneity of producers and disregard local contradictions in social relations or production.

The notion of nickel-and-dime capitalism may be helpful to understand why sustainable development interventions generally will tend to work against the presumed target group of poor rural people. Some types of producers in rural transformation improve their situation, accumulate capital and assure their reproduction at the cost of others who increasingly face problems in securing their livelihoods. With every re-orientation some types of producers will be privileged above others, not necessarily because only a number of them can participate in projects, but, more importantly, because of the relations between them in the competition for land and labour.

6

Knowledge: Locality, Context, and Content

Cada cabeza es un mundo. Hay muchas variedades de pensar
(Every head is a world. There are many ways of thinking)

Don Reducindo, producer from El Zapote

The Rediscovery of Local Knowledge

State officials, agronomists, and other experts characterize the burning of fields, the spraying of biocides without protective clothing, or deforestation near water sources as 'ignorant' behaviour (see Chapter four). Producers sometimes share this view attributing such practices to a lack of knowledge or to the application of wrong knowledge. On the other hand, there has recently been a growing interest in the value of local knowledge for good farming and for the development of sustainable agriculture that prevents environmental deterioration. The literature provides numerous examples (see, for example, Altieri and Hecht 1990; Brokensha et al. 1980; Chambers et al. 1989; Richards 1985; Thurston 1992; Toledo 1991; Warren et al. 1995; Wilken 1987).

This chapter examines the main claims of local knowledge approaches. Chapter four already suggested that producers' knowledge should not be seen as an intrinsically better type of knowledge for analysing farming at the local level. This chapter will push the argument further by questioning whether we really can define and describe such a thing as 'local knowledge'.

I first explore the current increasing attention for producers' knowledge in Honduras and elsewhere. The following section examines several examples of producers' agricultural knowledge in El Zapote in order to answer the question of whether or not there is a unified body of local knowledge. I then compare the nature of knowledge and of 'the local' as it emerges from the findings of my study in El Zapote. One of the conclusions is that producers' knowledge is not simply a reflection of their environment. It is constructed in a social process. To illustrate this I discuss how dominant narratives about what is good farming develop as a complex response to both exogenous ideas and local conditions. Finally, I review producers' perceptions of recent interventions which employ participatory approaches and examine whether they are able to incorporate the producers' point of view in the generation of new knowledge.

From the creation of ignorance to the rediscovery of local knowledge

The fact that rural people in non-western cultures were often labelled as ignorant by the expert-outsider was first criticized within anthropology. Anthropology argued that agricultural techniques result from centuries of active observation and testing, and that agriculture developed through the science of the concrete (Levi-Strauss 1990:11-92). This anthropological wisdom has only recently permeated official planning narratives of agricultural research and extension. Institutions which created the ignorance of the peasant in the past now accept the need for a careful understanding of local knowledge (cf. Warren 1991).[1]

To a certain extent this change has also taken place in Honduras.[2] The image of the superiority of scientific research and extension crumbles when exogenous technologies emanating from official agencies lead to disasters and tragedies. One local example concerns the work of the Honduran Coffee Institute (IHCAFE*). In the early 1980s, technicians from IHCAFE started extension services in El Zapote. They advised producers to convert existing low-input production systems into high-input coffee groves. One crucial element in their design was the removal of shade trees on coffee fields. Shade reduces photosynthesis and without shade the plant may increase photosynthesis and thus increase production. Shade, on the other hand, regulates temperature variation (it reduces maximum and raises minimum temperatures), reduces biennial bearing, overbearing and die-back, and extends the useful life of the coffee bushes (Wrigley 1988). Many of the high-input systems in Colombia and Brazil have no shade trees. These systems served as a model for the technical staff of IHCAFE. The removal of shade necessarily requires increased fertilizer application and generally demands new ways of pest management. Without heavy fertilization die-back will occur. The structure of the tree and the leaves under shade differ from plants grown without shade. A sudden removal of shade trees will expose non-adapted plants to high radiation. The technicians, however, promoted shade-less plantations and producers started to cut trees in existing groves. After a few years these groves were lost or severely damaged.[3] Some producers report a loss of 60 to 70 per cent of their fincas and most other producers who worked with IHCAFE confronted smaller disasters. A regional director of IHCAFE explained that they intended to transform traditional methods of coffee cultivation, but that the producers did not understand the recommendations.

The Institute never told them to work without shade. We recommended producers to plant *Guamo*. We wanted shade but not tall shade trees, not in the old way with heavy, unregulated, shade. The technician had criteria for shade, but the cultural level of the producer impeded the criteria being realized.

(..) We do a lot of research on shade now. (..) About *Inga* species we do not know much. The producers have always used *Inga* in their fincas, but we do not know which species they use, which species produce what type of [organic] material, how the species root, and how they are susceptible to diseases and pest, and whether diseases are transmitted to coffee.

IHCAFE officials attribute the unproductiveness of former production systems and what they call the 'little problems' associated with shade removal to the lack of knowledge of the producer, to their 'cultural' level.[4] The quotation still imputes ignorance to producers but also points at IHCAFE's new approach exploring the role of Guamo in coffee. Producers 'traditionally' select Guamo (*Inga* spp.) as their preferred shade tree in coffee. They create a Guamo dominated shade tree population through selective weeding in the finca.[5] Recently, IHCAFE has regained interest in shade trees and the way Guamo is being used, at least this is how it appears to producers. They perceive that IHCAFE now acknowledges the validity of producers' knowledge and recognizes the drawbacks of its earlier recommendations, even though the officials do not admit it overtly. The latest official thinking stresses the importance of preserving a diversity of different shade trees (and not a monoculture of one species of Guamo). The decision of which kind of shade should be developed is now left to the producer.

Local knowledge: tool-kit or a critique of modernization?

An increasing official interest in producers' knowledge raises a new set of questions. Does it reduce local knowledge to a tool-kit for context-driven technology development? Does it resemble earlier strategies of modernization by endangering the cultural integrity of rural communities? Does it really empower the poor or merely steal their good ideas? With these questions the debate on local knowledge is shifting from repeating the relevance of looking at local knowledge and discovering fascinating insights to a new debate which explores why local knowledge is being investigated and how power struggles shape linkages or gaps between local knowledge and external knowledge (e.g. Apffel-Marglin and Marglin 1996; Appadurai 1990, 1995; Banuri and Apffel-Marglin 1993; Benvenuti 1995; Fairhead and Leach 1994; Field 1991; Jansen 1995; and Thrupp 1989).

Some authors contend that much of the rediscovery of local knowledge makes use of producers' knowledge in an instrumental way (e.g. Field 1991). After the wave of romantic appraisal of the usefulness of local knowledge for agricultural research in the early 1980s, agronomic literature started to assert that many facets of farmer knowledge are not adapted to rapidly changing environments (Fresco 1986:222). Under conditions of stress or change, local knowledge does not adapt rapidly and adequately enough to new situations. It is argued that under such circumstances an optimal blend of exotic scientific knowledge and local knowledge should be made to stimulate agricultural development (see for example DeWalt 1994). This resembles traditional agronomy which used to consider local knowledge instead of simply dumping exogenous knowledge and practices, for example as Sears (1953:162) already stated for Honduras:

> What is needed is not *primarily* the introduction of labour-saving methods or the mass-production which has been so effective in other lands. Rather, (..) it is the use of science to restore and render as efficient as possible the best practices which have been indigenous in the past and which are suitable to the skills, needs and temperament of the people themselves.

This quotation illustrates that much local knowledge literature in fact has rediscovered a view which was much more common in the past (cf. Ploeg 1987).

In contrast to this utilitarian or instrumental view stands a view which develops the local knowledge concept as a critique of contemporary modernization (e.g. Banuri and Apffel-Marglin 1993). This critique includes two distinct perspectives. The first stresses that a utilitarian view will only understand what they can translate, while in fact it is impossible to disentangle the technical, social, religious, aesthetic, and other characteristics of local knowledge (Apffel-Marglin 1996:26). This approach criticizes the universal pretensions of the modern mode of thought and the delegitimization of local forms of knowledge. It does not search for an optimal blend of modern thought and local knowledge but takes local knowledge as an inspiration to overcome the separations of mind and body, subject and object, culture and nature: it does not press for reforming modern Cartesian thought but for learning from other cultures to decolonize our minds so as to abandon the Cartesian route to development.

A second type of critique of modernization pays less attention to the rationalities of forms of knowledge and gives people's control over their forms of production and reproduction a more central place. It rejects romantic or preservationist views about local knowledge (Thrupp 1989). In this approach research on local knowledge may legitimize local knowledge for the people and thus help to analyse and criticize dominant practices promoted by external agents. In contrast to utilitarian approaches, it not only investigates *what* local people do and want, but also *why* they believe particular practices work (Thrupp 1989:20). Local knowledge then becomes a source of political-economic *empowerment* of rural people. This critique of modernization embraces radical as well as more populist views. The latter in many ways resemble the utilitarian approach (but remain different to the extent that they do not proclaim technological development and economic growth as the prime objectives of development).

The political relevance of a plea for paying more attention to local knowledge is clear: 'formal' scientific research procedures on experimental stations and the transfer-of-technology paradigm do not work as expected in many situations and to improve agriculture, the skills and initiatives of producers themselves are essential (Chambers and Ghildyal 1985; Richards 1985). Another form of agricultural development prioritizes self-reliance, ecological soundness and popular empowerment (Bebbington (1996). The question, however, is whether both the empowerment and decolonization of the mind approaches need the concept of local knowledge in order to sustain their points of view. The following analysis of local knowledge in Honduras reveals that the analytical value of the concept of local knowledge is less clear than normally suggested in local knowledge literature.

Local knowledge in El Zapote

Partial, diffuse, and contradictory knowledge

During my stay in El Zapote I began to study producers' knowledge in order to document precisely their local knowledge of the biophysical environment, in the same way as anthropologists such as Levi-Strauss (1990) and Conklin (1957), and the later local knowledge scholars, had done. In conversations with producers it turned out that their knowledge was not so coherent and shared as sometimes suggested. I often was over-whelmed with the feeling so nicely expressed by Goldschmidt (1995:12) who attempted to understand the taxonomic diversity of the *Furu*, a group of fishes characterized by an incredible species diversification in the East African lakes.

> Full of expectations and very willing to become impressed by their knowledge of the cichlids, I presented the inhabitants of Nyegezi with the most wide range of Haplochromis species: big, small, elongated, stumpy, thick-lipped, thin-lipped, wine-red, bright yellow, jet black, but time and again I received the same answer: 'This fish, the name of this fish? *Furu*, the name is furu'. (my translation).

After long pondering by his respondents Goldschmidt always received the same answer: 'Westerner, you have caught a furu, really'. While there are hundreds of different species of furu with quite distinctive features, local people had only one name for them. Hence, local knowledge does not develop differentiating classifications or deep insights about every object or process in the environment, even when these objects seem relevant for the people because they live from them. I encountered producers who did not know the names of weeds or grasses in their fields. Producers who could not better distinguish trees than I did (and my tree knowledge is very limited). Producers who had never seen the leaf miner in beans (or coffee) which causes much damage and is so clearly visible, yet they showed me other insects which I never would have discovered by myself. People who do not know how long they can eat a certain stock of maize in the house; people who do not know the amount of land they possess. I once interviewed a producer about different diseases in maize and beans. He started to laugh very loudly and replied: 'These are easy to recognize for us: everything is *hielo** for us'. *Hielo* is a generic term that covers practically all diseases. In the conversation which developed he maintained his statement that people do not distinguish between diseases (in fact, several of them are not diseases but nutrient deficiencies).

Other observations made it clear to me that producers' knowledge in El Zapote cannot be described as a tool-kit with useful bits of knowledge constituting a clearly structured foundation for agricultural practice. Some examples may illustrate this.

> Producers talk a lot about when the *elotes*, the state in which maize is eaten as a fresh vegetable, are ready to eat and have their best taste. They do that every year again and again. To test the state of the *elote* they feel the tip of the cob in the field to know whether it can be harvested. Only in the house, however, after cooking and tasting, can the final judgement be given as to whether the cob had been harvested at the right time and not too early or too late. Producers

generally claim that others do not know how to harvest the cob at the right moment. In the end nobody knows exactly 'the point', the best moment of harvesting, and cobs are harvested before and after they have reached this point.

Producers tend to delay sowing in the year following drought at the start of the maize sowing season. The loss of maize seed or a bad harvest last year influences their decision to postpone the date. If rains start early (or 'normally') many complain that they were stupid to sow so late.

One of the producers came from outside the village. He settled himself in the village after he had married a woman from El Zapote. He had no farming background but started to cultivate crops. He made a *tular** where he applied the common set of local practices, including cutting tule 'with the moon'. In a short time he could harvest a lot of tule. Compared with other fields his had a much better stand. He had no problems rapidly incorporating the highly location specific knowledge of how to cultivate tule. 'I just looked at what the neighbours were doing', he said.

I investigated whether the producer in El Zapote used a complex, fine-tuned classification of soils which are locally adapted instead of using universal scientific categories. Most local concepts refer to colour, texture and structure of soils. People know black, red, and yellow soils, and gravel, sandy, clay-loam, heavy clay, and *panecito* soils.[6] *Panecito* refers to a loamy soil which can be easily worked with the *pando**. *Laja* is where soil has disappeared (erosion) and the weathered bedrock forms crumbled red particles. Most of their classifications are easy to understand with the help of universal knowledge about soils.

One late afternoon we were sitting in front of the house of Amado and talking about harvesting tule. I asked him about the present position of the moon. Amado and other friends who joined us could not answer my question but asserted that they all 'searched the moon' to cut tule. Nobody seemed to be aware that the moon was already visible in the sky at that moment. Amado went inside the house to get his almanac in order to find out the position of the moon.[7] Even though producers stress the importance of the moon they seem not to be fully cognizant of the actual positioning of the moon.

These examples inform us that local knowledge is not always complex or fine-tuned. It is not so difficult to learn how to cultivate tule successfully. The examples of the elote and the sowing date illustrate that producers' knowledge is often not clear and includes guess work and luck. Producers may have to run behind the events. Their local knowledge, which results from years of experience and learning about the probability of rainfall, does not make them stick to an optimal sowing date. Concrete forms of reasoning are much more chaotic and ad hoc. They interpret the clouds, take decisions based on known dates for the start of the rains, have doubts, awaken with a good idea, remember what happened last year, and take a decision. They themselves consider such a decision as being simply a leap in the dark. Much farming is like this: farmers do rely on their experience and a basic set of rules, but when it comes to action, it is always a 'performance' (Richards 1989), but a performance full of improvisation and failure.

In my view the uniqueness of local knowledge, in contrast to universalizing notions of science, is sometimes overstated. Local soil classification schemes may seem distinctive and attuned to local culture. When these classifications are presented in another language they tend to sound exotic and unusual. In many cases, however, they refer to no more than basic categories such as sand, loam, and clay (texture), colour, and difficulties of tilling

167

them (structure), which can be learned quite rapidly and which are not remarkably complex.

Some local knowledge concepts are attributed with explanatory meaning though primarily this may be a sort of explanation in retrospect. The cabañuelas, as discussed in Chapter four, is such a case. If it does not rain people may say that it has been caused by the cabañuelas. Likewise, producers may say that a certain tree is sown during a specific moon phase because it grows so well. But if one insists, it may turn out that they do not remember exactly with which moon a certain tree was sown or planted. Something similar can be observed for the concept of *caliente* ('warm'). Things (e.g. fertilizers, *gramoxone*[*] or manure) work in a specific way because they are *frio* (cold) or *caliente*. In conversations, however, it is clear that those producers who mention these concepts often use them to express that they do not know why certain events take place. If they do not know of another cause, they can always refer to something being *frio* or *caliente*.[8]

Divergent views on the influence of the moon

Some topics in local knowledge are hardly affected by external scientific thinking and intervention. This knowledge is often classified as superstitious beliefs (*creencias, leyendas*) and the only external shaping entailed is simply a rejection or denial. The influence of the moon on plants is such a topic. Most villagers acknowledge the influence of the moon but it was difficult to understand how they conceived this influence. It became somewhat easier to comprehend when I discovered that producers often disagreed about which moon phase generated which effects. When I abandoned the idea that they had a shared view on the moon phases I could make more sense of what they were saying. At least two views contest each other.

The first view distinguishes two lunar cycles. The first is the general cycle of new moon, waxing moon, full moon, and waning moon. The second is a cycle within the first cycle which uses the concepts of *luna tierna* and *luna sazona* (see Table 6.1). *Tierna* means fresh, young or tender, *sazona* means ripe. People can refer to one of these two cycles when indicating the effects of the moon on a practice on a specific day. The following table locates *luna tierna* and *luna sazona*, according to this view.

Luna tierna and *luna sazona* influence, for example, the ripening of fruits, the life span of (fruit) trees, the way plants will grow after planting, the moment of fruit bearing, the susceptibility for pests and diseases, and sprouting. In certain moon phases natural fibres are easier to work with. Tule is the crop that is most affected by the moon. With respect to tule people not only talk about the influence of the moon but act in crop cultivation according to the stipulated guidelines. Table 6.2 lists several activities for which producers say that one can 'search the moon' in order to obtain optimal results. Not all days in the cycle are equally important. Certain days reappear again and again in conversations, while others seem to be less important. Important moments are the new moon, day three, five and eleven after the new moon, and full moon.

The second view merges the *tierna* and *sazona* concepts with the directly visible phases of the waxing and waning moon. New moon and waxing moon is then *luna tierna* and full

168

moon and waning moon is *luna sazona*. Informants drew a certain analogy between the waxing moon and plant growth. The waning moon seems to be somewhat less decisive.

Table 6.1 Lunar cycle in El Zapote

days after new moon	phase
3	*tierna*
5	*sazona*
6-8	*tierna*
11	*sazona*
12-13	*tierna*
full moon	*sazona*
	two days *tierna?*
17	*sazona (?)*
19-22	*tierna*
23, 24 or 25 (?)	*sazona*
new moon	*tiernita*

Note: '?' refers to data which is not confirmed by other informants or which is ambiguous

Table 6.2 Influence of the moon on some agricultural activities

moon phase	action	effect
day 3 after new moon (or from day 3 until day 8)	plant tule	if planted otherwise the life span will shorten, the plant will remain short
2 days after new until 1 day before full moon (or 1 day after until 5 days after full moon)	cut tule	if cut on other days plant will rot or will remain short; shoots will be thin
full moon or *luna sazona*	snapping the maize	less pest attack and diseases
different views: day 2 or 3, or 3 days after full moon; others day 11	plant or sow fruit trees	rapidly produces first fruits (some say the tree will have a short life span)
different views: 4 days after full moon - new moon (*luna tierna*); others day 5; or day 3-5	pick fruit, especially bananas	fruit will ripen fast and good
day 3 (and subsequent 6 days)	transplant coffee	
luna sazona, full moon	cut wood	*comején* (insect) will not attack wood

The lack of a coherent view leads to a lot of discussion about the days that the moon produces certain effects. People often disagree about the influence of the moon. In general people do not conceptualize so much the influence of the moon on the plant as such but the effects on plants during a certain manipulation of the plant. In particular the first view argues that the crucial relation between the moon and the plant is the influence it has on water flows. The difference between *luna tierna* and *luna sazona* is that when you cut a young tree at *luna tierna* 'big streams of water will flow out of the plant'. At *luna sazona* the plant will remain dry. Water flows most in the first days after the new moon. Not everybody links the same days to *luna sazona* and *luna tierna* and the decisive burden of proof is whether or not such streams of water can be observed and not the number of days after the new moon. Thus, it is not the appearance of the moon you observe in the sky, as the second view assumes, but rather the streams of water in plants that are associated with *luna tierna* or *sazona*. The first view talks about 'movements' of the moon. These are the changes between *luna tierna* and *luna sazona*. According to some, these changes can take place in a few minutes. In any case these phases change from one day to another: the movements are fast and not gradual as in the moon cycle conceptualized in the second view.

People dispute each other's opinion about the way the moon acts upon plants by referring to empirical evidence, to what they have observed in the field, and to testing. With a similar procedure the view of those who deny the influence of the moon is contested. These may be other villagers as well as outsiders. Excequiel tells his story of a confrontation with an agronomist who was a friend of Neri (a higher-educated villager who irregularly practices agriculture).

A friend who visited Neri did not believe in [the influence of the moon]. He called it 'tales, legends of past people'. I told him the story of the mango that I got from Neri. Neri once came with two grafted mangos. He gave me one and went with the other to his field on the river terraces where he planted it in very good soil. When he asked me whether I would plant my mango that same day, I said no. I made a hole in the bedrock here [behind the house]. I filled it with a few bags of soil and waited until the roots of the mango came through the bag. Then I waited for the 'good moon' and planted it, with a straight root. [I added] some debris to keep it humid and a bucket of water. After a year my mango had flowers which I picked to let the plant grow. The second year was the same. The third year I left the flowers and I could already pick ten mangoes. The mango of Neri did not even flower at that time. I told this story to the agronomist but he only asked Neri what kind of man I was. 'With this man one cannot talk' he said.

This case shows how important reference to empirical evidence is for producers in order to ground views which support the influence of the moon. Producers frequently point out that they undertook specific activities with a certain moon which resulted in good outcomes. Excequiel could provide strong evidence by comparing his results with those of Neri, who had planted his mango under 'another moon'. The agronomist could not negate the evidence as Neri was there to confirm it. He therefore turned away from the subject (the influence of the moon), maybe to save face. He rejected not the evidence but the possibility of sound communication. Different from what Horton (1970) has called 'traditional thought', producers in El Zapote can imagine possible alternatives if there is new evidence. They allude to norms of reasoning and knowing but they give priority to empirical evidence and not to closed-ended predicaments. In this case it is the agronomist and not the producer who displays a protective attitude towards established theory. Discussions among producers, for example about the influence of the moon, always turn around evidence, and past and recent experiences. To ascertain that the moon is influential,

170

there must always be visible proof, such as the fruit tree that produces so well or the wood in the house that has already lasted for decades.

The discussion above reveals crucial differences of knowledge within the farming population. There is no unified knowledge even when exogenous knowledge institutions do not encroach directly upon local knowledge, such as the case of the moon. As we have seen in Chapter four, producers' knowledge about certain topics reveals a lot about why they farm in a specific way. Nevertheless, it can also be vague, incomplete, rudimentary or contradictory on other topics. The role of evidence in confronting dissimilar views suggests that local knowledge differs less from science than sometimes assumed. The next section explores this issue.

The Nature of Local Knowledge

The nature of knowledge

One implicit consequence of the concept of local knowledge is its contrast with a non-local or universal knowledge, western-scientific or 'modern' thought. From this perspective producers have other forms of reasoning than scientific: producers do not follow the nomological models used in science (if => then structure; if certain conditions are fulfilled, then a specific event will be realized) but, instead, their mode of thought is holistic (cf. Ploeg 1987). Another supposed difference is that producers do not construct hypotheses nor test them. Science is based on experimentation and local knowledge on observation (DeWalt 1994).

I think, however, that producers in El Zapote cannot be separated in these ways from science. In our conversations producers generally reacted to my questions with lists of hypotheses about what could have been the reasons for a certain outcome in their field. They followed nomological models depicting limiting conditions for certain practices. As has been illustrated in earlier chapters, they analyse differences of treatment as if they were experiments. 'I have experimented with it' is a common saying.

The denial of a break between local knowledge and science does not imply that there are no differences between them. Scientific knowledge production is much more standardized (and standardizing) and insights are systematically transferred through 'immutable mobiles' which are supposed to remain invariant through any change in spatial or social location (Latour in Kloppenburg 1991:529). Different social networks in which knowledge develops shape variations in the content and form of knowledge, as well as the language and practices in which knowledge is expressed. Scientists and producers are tied to the state and capital in different ways, and may belong to different gender and ethnic groups. These variations in the content and form of knowledge, however, do not necessarily imply that the structures of their modes of thought are essentially different (cf. Long 1992b).[9]

Local knowledge approaches often presume that producers are more capable than science in developing technology in an open, general, or holistic sense, i.e. related to field conditions and socio-economic context. What they take as the weakness of science in agricultural development, however, may also be the weakness of local knowledge. Laboratory-made artifacts or prescriptions recurrently do not work in the field. Closed systems are constructed in the laboratory to discover certain laws in nature and to generate new technologies, for example high-yielding maize with short stalks (Collier 1994). Once these technologies have to operate in an open system, many other factors interact and the high-yielding cultivar does not produce as expected because growing conditions vary and diverge much more than in the research station. The producer also 'behaves' differently than s/he 'should' according to the prescriptions that accompany a scientific innovation. Producers' expectations, forms of cultivation, and production objectives differ from the successful producer the research laboratory may have had in mind, because the producer has to respond to many more complicating factors (e.g. the needs of the household).

This problem cannot simply be solved by turning to local knowledge. It is precisely the open character of the 'system' which makes testing, experimenting and building coherent knowledge so difficult for the producer at the local level. The open character of agricultural and social systems is not a solution for successful practice but a problem which producers have to solve: how can they control the complicating factors. The system is often too open to constitute local guidelines that guarantee success.

In order to make the world comprehensible they therefore try to discover if-then relations between a few variables. Chapter four listed a series of if-then relations with regard to burning.[10] Producers display in-depth knowledge about specific relations but still are in doubt whether to burn or not. Much of the doubt stems from being unable to predict the effects of burning or not burning because of the many variables involved, because of the openness of the system.

'Experiments' are a method to construct if-then relations. The evidence which convinces producers of existing relations is constructed in situations of experimental closure. Producers who hold the opinion that burning gives better yields than not burning, state that they themselves have witnessed it. Having seen it, is their form of proof. The typical situation to which producers refer is when they have seen fields with burnt and non-burnt parts (see the case of Excequiel in Chapter three).[11]

This way of searching evidence parallels science. Just as in science closed systems are mainly abstractions. In a year after an experiment the conditions in the same field will be different; consider for example the possibility of heavy rains instead of drought, or of increased bean prices because Salvadorean traders buy all the beans on the market and push up the prices. This openness and these dynamics do not only make the results of science-based intervention so unpredictable; they are also the flaw of local knowledge.

The nature of the local

Another conceptual problem of local knowledge approaches is the status of 'local'. Producers' knowledge contains elements which seem to pertain to the field of 'the local' but which are, in fact, an outcome of pan-local processes. The belief system of the 'cabañuelas' illustrates this well. It takes the first days of January to forecast the weather of the whole year (see Chapter four). Honduran agronomists see the cabañuelas as a typical cultural product of local producers and contrast it with their own universal idea of meteorology. The system, however, is presumably a cultural heritage of the conquest as it originates from Spain (Foster 1960:50-69). In quite different climatic environments the same (thus universal) system of cabañuelas is operating. Something similar can be said for the names of many trees, agricultural practices, and so on. Hence it is difficult to link the content of knowledge to a specific locality. Producers' knowledge is in this sense not local but a hybrid of many localities.

Another problem is that contradictions and differences in local knowledge may be concealed by focusing on the problematic chasm between local knowledge and scientific/western knowledge. Local knowledge students tend to visit and interview the 'knowledgable' people, the single specialists on soils or medical properties of rainforest plants. In many cases this knowledge is extrapolated to cover the whole community or locality. I have already indicated that some Zapoteños know a lot about specific things or themes, while others are totally unaware of details. Some other observations may confirm this.

When villagers told about the grass Jaraguá (*Hyparrhenia rufa*) most people said that it had existed in the village since time immemorial. A few people however told me how a specific person introduced this grass into the village. These accounts, in turn, again differed: one villager claimed that his uncle was the first to get some seeds from Salvadorean traders and tried them. Another villager asserted that his father brought the seed returning from the North.

Information about the history of what happened with the land titles of Juniapal and Cárcamo is unequally dispersed. Alfredo Luna 'made himself owner' of sections of land within these titles (see Chapter two) and during this process titles disappeared and state officials were influenced. Few villagers, however, know details about what happened and important information has been monopolized by a close circle around Alfredo Luna. All that most people can remember is that this land once belonged to the municipality and the villagers. But few people can recall how Alfredo became the 'recognized' owner.

People who own pack animals often load up these animals, even if they hire day labourers to do the field work (e.g. the harvesting). Several day labourers who do not own nor use such animals lack the skills to carry out this task.

Several women give names to types of tule* with different qualities. The man who has tule in his field usually considers it as one and the same type of tule. The women give the names without visiting the field. Women dry the tule, split the stems and weave the petates and are concerned about whether the material is easy to work with (not too hard, not too thin, not too sharp) and whether the colour will be nice after drying.

These examples again suggest an absence of a unified body of local knowledge. There is no shared knowledge about vegetation change in the village; even about such a dominant grass as Jaraguá, which spread itself in the course of this century, contrasting histories exist. Knowledge may be highly differentiated or even monopolized, as the other examples show. Access to resources is also a struggle about access to information. This furthermore implies that distribution of skills is related to the distribution of resources. Some of the differences in knowledge arise from different relations to the object; women develop more interest in classifying different types of tule than men do. The local knowledge approach has no clear methodology to analyse and interpret these differences in local knowledge.[12]

The question becomes relevant as to how local is local. Do we investigate how producers think in Honduras or in Santa Bárbara? Do we try to discover local agricultural principles in El Zapote or in parts of El Zapote? Do we individualize knowledge and just collect knowledge of individual producers and search for new insights? Villagers regularly responded to some of my questions by saying that they could not give an answer because they never visited the relevant locality to which my questions referred.

> Many producers do not know the different areas within this small municipality. The whole day, people may see from their own field the Zona, the village common, which is lying at the other side of the river, without having any idea about soils and crop growth there. People may never have been in (parts of) the mountains and do not know whether beans grow there or which beans should be used there, and when and how these have to be sown.

This suggests that producers mainly produce meaningful knowledge about their own context of working and living. This reinforces the principle of locality: it is only in their specific fields that people can optimally manage the resources. But in a heterogenous environment and a situation of great diversity in social relations the locality is infinitely small, single and unique. The consequence is that this principle of locality undermines the idea of local knowledge. It turns knowledge to the individual experiences of people and not to the growing body of knowledge within a rural 'community'. If local knowledge is shaped by individual experience how can the assumption of smooth reproduction in the group hold?

Definitions of local knowledge define the local community as a production unit of 'learned ways of knowing' (e.g. McClure 1989:1). Local knowledge is taken as a historically determined rationality that acts in favour of group survival (Field 1991; see also Alcorn 1995). Local knowledge has, then, evolved from years of experiences and is shared and accumulated in social groups. This common view tends to assert that specific forms of knowledge are developed because of group adaptation to environmental and social context, and that inter-generational reproduction of knowledge is crucial. Local knowledge is then looked at as a system: an interconnected, multidimensional matrix of data, symbols and values rather than a miscellaneous collection of factual items (Okali et al. 1994:35).

In my view, however, knowledge cannot be seen as a system with clear boundaries, functional and hierarchical relations, and patterned input-output flows. Local knowledge is not reproduced in a smooth way. As described above, many elements of the knowledge the people of El Zapote have about their world do not have this character of group knowledge.[13] Several observations made above affirm that knowledge is non-homogeneous and not smoothly passed on to other people. Many villagers do not know at all what other producers are doing in their fields. They simply do not talk about it. In fact, much agricultural knowledge is based on learning by self-training instead of learning from previous generations. Producers learn basic skills and develop an interpretation of the environment mainly by doing agriculture. I do not deny that producers communicate and exchange information, but this is not so exhaustive and continuous as often suggested.

Furthermore, the idea that all knowledge is optimally adapted to the environment is not tenable. 'Adaptation' entails a connotation of being useful, practical, having a certain degree of completeness, or being important for survival. With these observations I do not deny existing social theories about socialization, learning, building knowledge and the development of agriculture. Rather I criticize the idea that processes of socialization, learning, and communication within the village lead to a unified knowledge system. An alternative view stresses that producers may have diverging ideas, beliefs, interests, and skills and that they often do not know what others think, experiment and discover.[14]

The differentiation of local knowledge (as well as unity with regard to some aspects) is built upon a heterogenous environment and constructed in a social world which is coherent yet chaotic, authoritative yet arguable, highly systemic yet unpredictable, consensual yet internally contradictory (Comaroff & Comaroff 1992:30). 'Local' knowledge is never local but a historical result of encounters, interfaces as well as individual experience and interpretations. Long and Villarreal (1994) call this the 'encounter of horizons' which transforms knowledge and produces discontinuity and change. This contrasts with local knowledge approaches which mainly visualize the (successful or unsuccessful) transfer of knowledge between different knowledge systems.

An alternative view of knowledge which dissolves the conceptual divide between local knowledge and exogenous knowledge has several methodological consequences. It distrusts producers' knowledge as much as scientific or policy discourse, and it studies their content and practices from a similar point of view. Producers in El Zapote tend to represent their current way of thinking and acting as a state of nature. Producers will tell you how they use fertilizers and herbicides as if they have always operated like that. Local knowledge literature often collects discursively expressed information about agriculture, but the match between narrative and practice is usually not explored. Let me take three examples of Jansen (1995) to demonstrate that narratives and burning practices are not in line with each other.

> Gollo changed his presentation of the reasons why he does not burn. In our first interview Gollo, in his theatrical style, related proudly that he was very smart because he ceased burning thirty years ago when he saw that the soil washes away after burning. A few months later, however, I visited his fields. We ate some avocados and he told me that he did not burn this field because it had two big and very productive avocado trees in the middle and care should be taken not to damage them with fire. He had changed his account of why he does not burn in this field. In the past he explained to his fellow producers that he had ceased burning because he wanted to save his avocado trees. Recently, he changed to the discourse of soil conservation in which producers who do not burn are 'good farmers'. This was the discourse he used the first time I talked with him. Only after sitting and eating together in the field, did the avocado trees regain their place in the story.

In this case the explanatory narrative changed while the practice remained the same. Both narratives matched the practice. In many cases, however, narratives dissent from actual practice.

Genaro Caballero explained to me in 1993 that he always burnt and that burning was good. In 1994, however, he told me that he had not burnt for years. Apparently he had changed his opinion and did not burn his milpa in 1994.[15] It seems that he found it important to argue that he had stopped burning many years ago. Under the dominance of the new not-burning narrative he reinterpreted his own history.

In 1993, Rosalío told me that he never burnt and that he was against burning. In 1994, when I knew him a lot better, he related with twinkling eyes and great enthusiasm that he burnt his milpa. Rosalío followed a very common custom. You say to the outsider that you do not burn, even when you do.

I suppose that Rosalío first remained within the not burning narrative because not-burning is equated with being a 'good farmer'. Genaro probably had forgotten our earlier conversation and described himself as a constant non-burning producer. Many producers want to play the 'good farmer'. This playing of the 'good farmer' means mostly conforming to a hegemonic narrative that burning is bad.

An alternative approach should also recognize that producers' knowledges tend to be forgetful about the past. For example, one can detect that Jaraguá was introduced not so long ago although it appears as a native species in the producers' speech. If only rapid rural appraisal methods are used to document local knowledge such changes remain invisible; the eternal character of local knowledge will instead be over-emphasized.

An alternative approach brings to the fore the fact that there may be less transfer of knowledge among producers than supposed. It will study how social hierarchy influences internal knowledge transfer and how people may hide insights from each other; much knowledge is not communicated. Some children will hear a lot from their parents about the environment, how to work and their social history, but many other children hardly talk with parents or other elder people about such subjects.

An alternative approach will distrust any claim of locality for knowledge. People may present information as their own invention, their own experience, which, in fact, is not more than a reproduction of a narrative which they have heard on the radio or during the latest encounter with an extensionist. Producers rapidly tend to pick up several new ideas in their discursive repertoire. People can tell exactly when, how, and how much fertilizer should be used, suggesting that they are experts on this, without ever having applied fertilizer. What is presented as locally produced/reproduced knowledge in a long term process of learning may, in effect, be the result of a complex set of encounters with many more contradictions and discontinuities than often imagined in the local knowledge literature.

Finally, the assumption must be questioned that more direct contact between producer and extensionist and a joint process of technological innovation will guarantee successful improvement of production systems. An example may illustrate this. After the debacle with the shade trees, IHCAFE extensionists became worried about the amount of shade and therefore distributed seeds of the fast-growing Cornavaca to producers they visited regularly.[16] Two IHCAFE officials gave the following comments.

(i) We do not recommend Cornavaca. Cornavaca was scattered unofficially. One technician brought seed from Guatemala. When I saw it I asked how in God's name they thought it would be good shade. (..) The roots of the Cornavaca are very bad; they develop themselves superficially and extensively and [thus] compete with coffee [for nutrients]. It is a Solanacea and therefore susceptible to diseases and pests. It's bad structure [shape] is not appropriate for shade. We now want to standardize recommendations. We hope to prevent incidents such as that which happened with Cornavaca. It was a researcher from La Fe [the research station]. Now the Cornavaca is spread by itself because producers give seeds to each other. *Madriado* has not been spread so much; that species is more for the lower elevations. Look, every extensionist makes a particular mixture of techniques.

(ii) There was no recommendation from the Institute to use Cornavaca. The plant was for research here in La Fe. That plant is not good: it causes nutrient extraction and after several years it breaks and falls on the coffee trees. (..) However, the technicians also visited La Fe and saw the shade and liked the plant, with those big leaves. They took seeds and put these in their pockets, and in the field they distributed them among the producers'.

Several producers in El Zapote have sown Cornavaca after the recommendation to do so from an IHCAFE technician. In their statements the higher IHCAFE officials evaluate the propagation of Cornavaca as a negative process and accused the technician-extensionist of ignorance. This signifies that IHCAFE as an institution cannot be held responsible for the use of Cornavaca. Through good communication between extensionist and producers, followed by a producer-to-producer transfer, the technology had been distributed rapidly and before higher levels in the institution noticed it. Extensionists informed me that they had to improvise their own technology package because they had 'to give some extension to producers' (present some new technologies) notwithstanding the constraints posed by the institution. They 'hardly received any materials to give to producers'. In fact, they expressed their problems of operating when they cannot hand out new technologies. They, and many producers, see it as the reason for their existence.

At the higher level one intends to underestimate the power of the extensionist making hybrids and mixing technologies. The management of IHCAFE wants to replace technological solutions that result from communication between extensionists and producers with standardized recommendations. A main reason for standardizing procedures is so that the organization is held responsible for the outcome of extensionist-producer interfaces. Increasing opportunities to experiment with new technologies at lower levels within the system may generate negative results which will hit back on the organization. No organization can afford to relinquish all control. Its check on technology in order to maintain control is therefore not only a question of establishing social power, but necessarily includes a test of the practical content of a technology.

As the above examples suggest, local knowledge of the environment and agricultural practices are not by definition oriented to good farming, a function of the environment, or an optimal adaptation to it. Some knowledge such as the cabañuelas have no specific value for good farming. These observations undermine the teleology in much local knowledge literature: individual or group knowledge is identified and because it exists it is concluded

177

that it is adapted to the local context. Exogenous technology which is not (yet) used is not (yet) adapted to the local context.

Dominant Narratives

Definitions of good farming do not simply result from adaptation to local environments and available technologies. They are shaped by social struggles. Can we say, then, that narratives of good farming are socially constructed? In order to answer this question I shall discuss how local perceptions of burning practices changed and how the state was involved in this change.

Chapter four showed that producers develop a whole range of different and partly contradictory arguments for or against burning. A single, non-contradictory knowledge system concerning burning practices in El Zapote does not exist. Nevertheless, a dominant narrative towards burning is in operation. A narrative is dominant when it conceals that other practices also exist and when it involves a set of rules which function as norms on how one should practice agriculture.

In the past it was unquestionable that burning was a good agricultural practice: 'it was law to burn' as people say. It was a dominant narrative because it subsumed views that argued against burning. Arguments for not burning were not overruled by counter-arguments but could be put aside simply by referring to laziness and ignorance.

This situation has been turned upside-down. At present, quite a lot of producers support the view that burning is not technological and not modern. According to this view, those who continue to burn 'do not think' and are 'stupid', 'drunkards', 'traditional', and 'unaware of the consequences'.

Outsiders have always portrayed burning producers with the mark of ignorance. The new dominant narrative coincides with the official stance towards burning, expressed in the following quotations:

It is a custom. It is difficult to control burning: they have inherited the system from the past. If one could mechanize agriculture it would be different (The director of the district office of the Ministry of Agriculture in 1992).

Burning belongs to their culture; the indians already did it before Columbus came (an official of COHDEFOR)

We advise people not to burn, but it is all tradition. (..) With the young people it may change, maybe, but first the old have to die. [The producers] think that with burning there will be *maiz muerto* and so on. They are ignorant (a technician of the Ministry of Agriculture).

These officials frame the reasons for the ignorant behaviour of burning in a modern-traditional opposition. They indicate that the traditional mode, the culture of burning, has to die, to make room for the modern mode: not burning, mechanization and technology. They attribute the role of spreading the new to the state. The state has tried to influence the practice of burning in three different ways: (i) the incorporation of fire control into

178

legislation and enforcement by central state institutions, (ii) the enforcement by local government, and (iii) the transfer of exogenous notions through more communicative approaches.

Fire control by legislation

The state tried to control fires by passing laws which forbade the burning of fields without informing the owners of adjoining fields, so that they could be present at the time of burning. They also prohibited burning on windy days in order to avoid the spread of fires to forests.[17] The legislator was not as interested in regulating burning on agricultural lands as in guarding against forest fires. Fire regulation was mainly handled by forestry laws. The Forestry Law of 1955 forbids burning without having requested permission from the local municipal authorities (Honduras 1955). These written permissions had to specify date and time of burning. The only further requirement was the trimming of a five metre wide firebreak. The Forestry Law of 1961 reinforced these regulations and decreed the total prohibition of burning in certain areas (Honduras 1961).

Some attempts were made to implement these paper laws. For example, in 1960 the district governor sent a message to the municipalities that permission for burning could only be issued after approval by the Ministry of Agriculture (RRNN):

> These permissions should be issued only in cases of absolute necessity and only when the place of burning is not a protected forest; they are meant to protect watersheds and surface water streams; exploitation is not permitted within fifty metres on both sides of streams. (..) Springs will have to be protected by forests in a circle of 150 metres, and fields with an inclination of more than 45^0 have to be protected with forests in horizontal strips of thirty metres wide, every 200 metres.[18]

In fact, this order proposed the development of a system which would be called 'agro-forestry' nowadays. In general producers ignored these laws and orders. They had few consequences for producers in El Zapote. Apart from enacting this legislation the state remained largely inactive towards burning. One exception, however, took place in 1952.

Villagers remember a governor who was called the 'enemy of burning'. He was Daniel Rápalo Bográn (b. 1881), a civil engineer who had studied in the United States (Ruiz & Triminio, 1943s. Back in Honduras he set up his own coffee plantations and a sawmill, he bred cattle, experimented with improved pastures, and cultivated rice and maize. Carlos, his son-in-law, told me that tenants, who rented land from him, were forbidden to burn. In 1952, Daniel Rápalo became district governor and issued prohibitions against tree felling and burning. His son-in-law claimed that people complied with these orders but that people regressed to 'traditional practices' after his term. However, villagers did not accept the orders of this governor. Hildebrando told me the story of his father when he was an authority who had to deal with this governor:

> There had always been a law that burning was forbidden except for *guamiles**, but none of the governors did anything about it. [Only] Daniel Rápalo Bográn prohibited burning [by sending] circulars. The order was disobeyed. The governor had his spies in the village: people whom he knew very well, or friends. He summoned a group of people including my father and gave them a

fine of ten Lempira each. My father argued that he had sent the *bando* [men who attracted attention with music instruments and promulgated orders in the village] to go round the village, and that he himself had not issued permissions to burn. He also said that people had the custom of burning and had beliefs that with burning less weeds germinate and that maize does not die. The governor replied that this was not true and he expounded the advantages of not burning. He said that burning had taken away all the *abono** which finally would end up in the sea and that the debris itself would turn into *abono*. Producers defended themselves by saying that others, because of mischief and roguery, set alight their milpa, but that was very implausible. My father had not given permission but if people came to ask for permission he told them that it was up to them if they wanted to burn; he would not do anything, and they themselves had to see what to do if they were called (..). The spies tattled to the governor. Somebody blabbed that my father had let the people burn. Therefore, he was fined.

Don Cruz was another local authority at that time:

Daniel Rápalo Bográn forbade burning; that was in the Zona, a condition for adjudication of the Zona [by the government] to the municipality. We, the municipality, gave permission to burn to the villagers. (..) That governor wanted to imprison us; he summoned us before a court. He had forbidden burning but we had issued permissions to people who had cut down thick guamiles. It was only for guamiles that we gave permission. One always had to request permission. (...) We went to a lawyer. The lawyer arranged the papers and the bail for us. He attested that the governor did not know the bush. We never heard of it again.

It seems that fire regulation through legislation in itself did not change burning practices. The efforts of Rápalo Bográn to implement legislation by imposing fines on authorities and producers neither increased the effectiveness of legislation. Producers themselves are aware of this. They say that they 'evade laws', that the 'laws are not in their interest', and that they 'are stubborn'. Despite his authority and acknowledged astuteness, Rápalo Bográn could not force people to stop burning, nor impose his view of good agriculture on the producer.

Enforcement by local government

El Zapote's history shows several attempts by local authorities to control burning and to stop deforestation but these never succeeded. The person who was mayor from 1990-1993 sketched out the dilemma for a mayor to control burning in a concise statement:

To do something about it was one of my ambitions when I started, (..) but I never could do anything: people are *compadres*, friends, sympathizers of the same party, or family.[19]

These relationships overdetermine the interest in stopping burning.

Most villagers do not consider the content of laws and regulations as problematic. Instead, the modes of enforcement are troublesome according to them. One villager, who had been an authority several times, said:

The law is good. The law does not know about relationships.[20] (..) The authorities, however, are not strict enough, because of the friendships. I have never given a fine for spreading fires. (..) Everywhere fires have spread. Even near to our water sources, some of which have been destroyed.

I asked him what he did when people came to the municipality when somebody had caused an unwanted fire. He shrugged his shoulders: 'Nothing. What can one do when the fire has already spread'. People recall many half-hearted efforts of authorities to stop burning, for example about one action of the mayor cited above:

> Two or three years ago he gave an order which prohibited burning. They fined some people who let the fire pass to another area, but the rest could go on as they liked. The authorities do not obey the law in order to avoid making the people angry (..). People keep insisting. If the law would be enforced (..) with a stiff fine, then one would refrain from burning.

Many similar stories repeat the message that there are laws to control burning but that the authorities do not apply them strictly as they do not want to incur the producer's wrath. Moreover, producers respond to any increase in control of burning by no longer applying for a permission in order to prevent a permission being denied. They believe that burning after the denial of a permission will antagonize the authorities. Burning without having applied for a permission would be less problematic.

Time and again party political strife and patronage relations shape local authority - producer interfaces. Enforcement of not burning is generally subservient to political conflicts. Esteban, for example, narrates how an *alcalde de policía* (authority who can fine people for forbidden behaviour), named Santos, wanted to fine him for having caused a fire.

> The *suplente* [another authority] from Tontolo, declared how he had seen that a spark had been blown over and had kindled the bush further up. Later the fire had come back and had burnt a part down hill. The *alcalde de policía* could not refute it because [the *suplente*] had 'seen it'. (..) Santos was from the other party. He had given the fine because of politics.

This case shows the clear subordination of such issues to party politics. Party politics influences almost every aspect of intervention by state officials. In this case, the *suplente* belonged to the same party as Esteban. Esteban had to laugh when he told this story and it was clear that the *suplente* had not seen the spreading of the fire at all. He could nevertheless make his account plausible because he lived in a hamlet near the place where the fire had spread, a place far away from the village. His argument was therefore even strong enough to explain that the unity of Esteban's own milpa fire and the fire uphill resulted from the uphill fire burning downhill and linking the two.[21] Probably everybody knew that the *suplente* was inventing this unbelievable but uncontestable story in order to defend a supporter of his own party.

Enforcement of not burning is furthermore contested by the poor by making use of patronage relations. One recent case in the Zona is widely recalled:

> Last year Juan (..) set a fire. He had only made a firebreak beneath his field and not above; precisely there you should have a firebreak. He lit the fire and went to the river to bath. The whole slope was catching fire and this threatened the coffee fields of Santos Pineda. We could make a firebreak there just in time. (..) Juan has set the Zona on fire three times already. However, he is a godchild of Don Rafael, and Don Rafael went to the municipality to speak out for him. He said that Juan was poor and so forth. He was thus saved without being fined.

Someone who is brought before the authorities because he has flagrantly broken the rules and caused a fire, will generally appeal to a patron. Up to now this has provided successful protection for the accused in most cases.

The different stories and the observations I made suggested that local government could not enforce burning prohibitions more effectively than state legislation or its implementation by Daniel Rápalo Bográn. Village authorities provide considerable room for manoeuvre to continue with burning. A difference between the central state and local government enforcement of not burning is that local authorities act in a network of local social relationships. The central state could not reinforce non-burning because the gap between its authorities, regulations, and producers' practices was too large. The local authorities could not reinforce non-burning because they were too much a part of local relationships which were given more importance than a ban on burning. This discussion also shows that party politics does not dominate local life 'from above' but is, with regard to quotidian activities, living 'from below'. It is the villagers themselves who reproduce the dominance of party politics over many aspects of daily life and relations among villagers.

The communicative shift

The efforts to control burning through legislation and coercion did not work. Extension is a third official strategy to stop burning. In 1986, the integrated rural development project PRODESBA stationed a technician in the village in order to develop soil conservation activities with peasant groups. Several producers related that PRODESBA's message not to burn was not new to them: 'before PRODESBA you could already hear on the radio that burning was bad'. At that time, the beginning of the 1980s, burning was still the normative practice and the dominant narrative. Nevertheless, several producers had already stopped burning and others were experimenting with it. Hence, it was not the information that was new, but more probably the type of interface.

Almost all informants referred to Don Modesto as the person who was influential in promoting not burning. Modesto was a technician from PRODESBA and producers showed interest in his ideas.

> Don Modesto gave talks in the communal centre. It was filled with people [who came] to listen to him. People were pleased with him; they learned a lot. (..) Don Modesto said that you should not burn anywhere, not even on slopes with stones. He said that, after burning, everything washes away with the first rains. That is true, it washes away.

Repeatedly, producers said that Modesto was not a charlatan like the other extensionists who did no more than lecture in the communal centre. Modesto, in contrast, often went with producers to their fields. Villagers pointed out that this increased his credibility considerably. People said that he did not talk like the others, who were formal engineers. Instead, Modesto was a self-trained man, without formal education.

When I talked with Modesto, however, he displayed his technical authority in the way most other technicians do. He suggested that he had more technical knowledge than producers and that the producers should be educated. He expressed himself in the same typical style of many other extensionists: 'I do not talk about 'earth' (*tierra*). You have *to knock that out* of people. Agriculture is man, capital and 'soil' (*suelo*). Not earth.' It is this style of making distinctions between technical knowledge and producer's ignorance which often obstructs communication between extensionists and producers.[22] Modesto portrayed himself as a total and consistent enemy of burning.

Modesto was nevertheless able to switch between this 'technician discourse' and one in which he left more room for interpretation and persuasion by the producer. In practice he did not rigidly abide by the not burning theorem. Producers explained that Modesto was not so strict as he had suggested to me. He informed people about negative as well as positive consequences of burning and that producers themselves had to choose. An uncompromising philosophy of not burning could not be transferred to the producers.

The arrival of Modesto can be described as a communicative shift. Producers do work with external ideas and the incorporation of those ideas into agriculture is stronger when the source is tangible or close to people. Modesto was capable of establishing a relationship of trust with the producers. People generally refer to Modesto and his field visits and not to other programmes of the Ministry of Agriculture and PRODESBA which attacked burning. Other agronomists of PRODESBA, generally higher qualified and higher in rank than Modesto, are not mentioned either. PRODESBA offered some new opportunities to work in a more communicative way with producers, but Modesto was the only one who really did it. Moreover, Modesto was only a small element of the big PRODESBA project and only lived in the village for a short period. Apart from the period of Modesto, the state was not really effective in promoting new agricultural practices without burning.

Non-burning as a new norm

Have producers gained in wisdom now they are turning towards not burning? Have they finally followed the advice of Campos (1910), Pinel (1939) and Burgos (1941) (see Chapter four) and overcome their 'ignorance'? Has local knowledge of burning retreated and given way to modern scientific insights? Have the people listened to the engineer who used to address himself to producers by saying: 'Donkeys! Don't be donkeys, don't burn the earth'? I have described how the state has tried to change producers' views through various strategies. The fact, however, that producers' views have changed recently, that non-burning is now the dominant narrative, does not imply a positive answer to these questions. That would grant too much power to exogenous notions emerging from the state and scientifically educated technicians in constructing the current dominant narrative which fosters not burning. The fact that non-burning has become the new norm does not mean that the state and science have won this battle of knowledge.

We have seen that legislation in itself has not been very forceful in changing burning habits. The failure of Rápalo Bográn to change attitudes towards burning practices marks the weakness of the executive to enforce legislation upon producers. At the local level, authorities are entangled in a myriad of social relations and the regulation of burning becomes subordinated to other fields of struggle and social cohesion.

The communicative shift was not significant enough to explain change in the dominant narrative. The arguments for and against burning (see Chapter four) are still used by producers to decide whether they will burn or not. Education by outsiders has not changed these arguments, although it may have changed the wording of some arguments. In my view, it is more changes in the local circumstances, for example the shortening of fallow periods or the reduction of organic matter, which have made possible the emergence of a new dominant narrative against burning. Only by being rooted in this changing environmental context, can legislation, enforcement, and communicative action contribute to the emergence of a non-burning narrative. This also explains why so many people still practice burning even though they support the dominant narrative: burning is still in line with how these people evaluate their particular field qualifications. They no longer contest the general idea that burning should be reduced, but add specific arguments as to why it should be done under certain circumstances.

The Transience of Intervention

This section addresses the changes in approaches of 'technology transfer' which were mentioned briefly in the previous section about the burning case. Instead of top-down regulation and distribution of technology, more participatory approaches with a focus on communication are evolving. This change parallels the increasing interest in local knowledge. I shall discuss the classical approaches to regulation and providing new technology packages, the integrated rural development approach which links new technology with social and economic projects for the rural poor, and new schemes involving a growing role for non-governmental organizations. Table 6.3 lists the main organizations which have engaged in technology and knowledge related activities in El Zapote. There is no room here to analyse in-depth all the complexities of intervention processes. I concentrate mainly on how producers interpret the different intervention efforts. Many evaluations look at what organizations have done, while a focus on producers' perceptions may also reveal what they have not done. I will explain how from this position all these activities can be called 'transient' interventions.

Classical approaches[23]

IHCAFE* started in the 1970s by concentrating on intensification of coffee fields of a few wealthy producers. In the 1980s the 'AID-IHCAFE-project' aimed to work with the 'small producer' but only some better-off producers received credit and technical assistance. Day labourers who worked for these producers had to implement the instructions of the technicians, for example how to make seedbeds. One to two decades later some of them planted their own coffee and tried to implement (and adapt) these techniques in their fields. In my view the widespread use of several of these techniques was not a result of the credit programme, which was the dominant element of the project, but of the nature of promoted techniques which fitted into existing practices and which worked, that is they were viable in this environment. During the first phase of the AID-IHCAFE project removal of shade trees was compulsory as well as the use of young coffee plants bought from fincas controlled by IHCAFE.[24] IHCAFE could impose these technologies through the credit they had extended. Producers disagreed with this project and had their own interpretations of technologies. Hence, the IHCAFE project was not an unambiguous success: producers criticized its obligatory character and few producers participated.

Table 6.3 Knowledge and technology interventions in El Zapote

organization	activities in relation to natural resource use
IHCAFE (state/USAID-project)	public extension in coffee cultivation; support to participants (credit, technical assistance)
COHDEFOR (state)	issuance of permissions to cut forest/trees; fire control
PRODESBA and SRN (state)	public extension about maize and coffee cultivation; formation of producer groups (credit, technology, extension)
Peasant unions	aborted land reform; some activities by women sections (horticulture, marketing petates, social activities)
PLAN (Foster Parents Plan)	individual clients, distribution of fertilizers and biocides; groups with coffee, cattle, horticulture
smaller NGOs	Initiatives to start nature conservation and reforestation.

Note: public extension refers to talks in the communal centre which were open to all villagers.

The state's forestry agency COHDEFOR* was an important actor in development programmes in the 1970s and 1980s. Chapter four discussed how COHDEFOR did little to protect forests in El Zapote but instead gave permission to outsiders to cut forest. Furthermore, authorities did not like COHDEFOR because they interfered in an authoritarian style in village concerns, such as the control of burning. In those cases that COHDEFOR's help was summoned it could not satisfy local demands either. In several instances villagers or representatives in the municipality tried to involve COHDEFOR in the conservation of their drinking water sources. Coffee producers, who were extending and intensifying their fields, have endangered water quantity and quality since the second half of the 1980s. They cut forest vegetation near the different springs and sprayed biocides near to streams. Inspired by the increasing shortage of water during the dry season many villagers protested and local authorities went to the fields to measure the distance (150 m) from the streams where it was forbidden to cut trees or to use biocides. COHDEFOR was invited to deal with the disobedient producers. COHDEFOR came, measured, and ordered that ten *varas* (about nine metres) on both sides of the stream had to remain free from crops. Most villagers were disappointed about COHDEFOR's support given to a handful producers. COHDEFOR's decisions were entirely at odds with the law.[25] The villagers concluded that COHDEFOR had been manipulated. They complained that on a later visit COHDEFOR officials only wanted to talk about the development of tourism and did not want to enter the issue of water resource conservation.

Regularly, it is expected that COHDEFOR should control burning by producers. A regional official from COHDEFOR said that the task of COHDEFOR has always been the exploitation of timber:

> We are not interested in *agricultural fires*, only in *forest fires*. COHDEFOR tries to regulate burning to prevent forest fires. People have to get permission from COHDEFOR in order to burn, but because it is too expensive for producers to come to the town, the municipalities can give the permission. Since 1986 we have forbidden burnings during the dry season, the critical period. The underlying idea is that people will burn only after the first rains; these start between the 10th and 15th of May. For us, however, agriculture is not a main concern. In the surroundings of Santa Bárbara we have done much regarding fires, but that is politics. Santa Bárbara is a political centre and we do not want problems. Thus we did more [control of burning] near there.

What is important to note is the disinterest of COHDEFOR in local affairs, the incapacity to transfer any idea of natural resource management, and the one-off character of most contacts. The knowledge interface was one of little communication. Villagers recall with resentment the authoritarian style in which COHDEFOR operated.

Integrated Rural Development

A major intervention in the 1980s was the integrated rural development project PRODES-BA, coordinated by the Ministry of Agriculture (SRN) and linked to ten other state agencies. It undertook activities in very different fields (agricultural credit, adaptive agricultural research, extension and social organization, commercialization, food security, health, infrastructure, technical assistance).[26] PRODESBA's main agricultural activities in El Zapote were improvement of maize and coffee production with groups of producers. In 1985 and 1986 two groups (one of sixteen and one of seventeen male members) started to sow maize under guidance of SRN-personnel. Credit was provided to buy rucksack sprayers, seed of a high-yielding variety, and to apply fertilizers and manure, herbicides and pesticides. During field visits producers were taught not to burn, to prepare the soil (in-row tillage) and to sow along contour lines, and to build physical soil structures against erosion. The group was collectively responsible for reimbursement of the debt. The producers had to sow maize at narrower spacing, which was possible because of fertilizer application and short stalk cultivars.

In 1986 the maize of most participating producers grow too tall and did not yield very well. PRODESBA had supplied bad maize seed to the producers; it was a mixture of short stalk cultivars and long stalk cultivars instead of pure *Planta Baja*. The fertilizer and narrow spacing caused the long stalk cultivars to shoot up and yield very little. The producers nevertheless had to repay the debt and it was never explained to them what went wrong. Some wanted to withdraw but were not allowed to; they had to accept the fertilizer for the following postrera because the bank concluded that the money had already been spent on them.[27]

After the maize disaster PRODESBA offered the opportunity to participate in coffee groups. Two groups were started (twelve and seven members respectively). The nurseries were made with their own investment, while PRODESBA provided credit for the

186

preparation of the field, fertilizers, and biocides. Technically, most of these fincas became a success. With the formation of coffee groups the poorer producers of the maize groups dropped out (see Chapter five). Other resource-poor producers who showed interest in participating were also excluded. PRODESBA only accepted producers with land, 'moral capacity' to pay back the loans, and those who found somebody who was willing to act as guarantor for them. Accepted group members tended to exclude resource-poor applicants because everybody was held responsible for the debt of the group and more poor producers would increase the risk. Many others who initially had an interest in participating said they feared the bank. It was for the first time that larger groups of people took bank credit.[28] A third group was initiated two years later. However, at the time when their plantations were sown but not yet in production, the government changed in party affiliation after national elections (December 1989). The agronomist who covered El Zapote was fired and PRODESBA was terminated. Technical assistance and credit stopped and producers had to improvise solutions in order to remain in coffee production and to avoid the loss of their investments.

All groups, including those of the maize disaster, showed a good record in debt repayment during the first years. Several years later, however, public discussion started at the national level about writing off debts in agriculture. Technicians and producers alike took the view that one could not require the poor producer to pay back when large debts of hundred of thousands of Lempiras of wealthy producers (among them important congress members) were written off. Producers started to negotiate at the office of SRN, arguing that they could not pay back their loans. The technicians told how they stopped putting pressure on the producers to repay. One technician said: 'the producers reasoned with me why they should not pinch 2000 L of the money from the gringos when those others put millions into their pockets'. Later, many of the debts were officially written off.[29]

PRODESBA completed few activities as projected. This becomes especially transparent in the case of a women's group that was formed to foster horticultural skills. The group first borrowed land from a wealthy producer, but after one season he ordered them to leave because he was afraid that the group would invade his land and take it. Next year, the group received land from Carlitos Salgado who said:

> I lent three *tareas** of the land behind my house to PRODESBA; they wanted to make a vegetable garden for women's groups. The soil, however, is not appropriate for vegetables. The women received seeds and had to sow chilli, but they did not do anything. The women participated in the groups because they received food for working in the garden, such as oil and tins of sardines.[30] They did not sow anything but PRODESBA visited us proudly to show the group and to take photographs while the women were 'working'. A lot of people came to look. At the very height of it, about fifteen cars stood before my house. Very beautiful, fifteen cars (laughing loudly), one [person] in every car!

Officials told me similar stories. Once they even went to a successful commercial vegetable grower nearby. They 'took' a women's group and put the women in his field to take photographs in order to show these to their foreign visitors.

Without analysing in detail the causes of the failures of PRODESBA it is clear that producers, technicians and officials feel that such a large development project cannot be executed satisfactorily, in spite of the good elements of the proposed methodology of the project, due to organizational and technical incapacities and the politicized institutional context. Nevertheless, despite the failures of the project, people still felt they were abandoned when PRODESBA left the village. The fifteen cars which came to see the fabricated image of the successful women's project constitute the main local metaphor for the whole project: a waste of money, technically inadequate, too many personnel who mainly came for their own pleasure or when foreign visitors needed to experience a donor-sensitive image (women working in the field), but nevertheless leaving some useful things (silos, rucksack sprayers, tins of sardines and several new insights in coffee cultivation and biocide use). The fifteen cars left as soon as the show was over, and PRODESBA left with the next political change.

The different moments of failure are of course specific incidents, each with its own particular dynamics. Together, however, they make up the way PRODESBA functioned in daily practice. Viewed from the perspective of villagers, PRODESBA was not much more than these 'incidents': instances of a fleeting interface. The whole idea of an integrated rural development project is transient almost by definition. It defines holistically all the needs the programme must address. Within a short period the project has to demonstrate results; this leads to the formulation of measurable but unrealistic targets and excludes the building of in-depth knowledge of specific problems by the executing agencies. Moreover it promotes easy shifts to new fields of work when the old are exhausted. On a large scale, the latest evaluation of PRODESBA confirms this (SECPLAN 1989b): it recommends new activities relating to the environment, housing, literacy, and community development, while also illustrating the failures in earlier fields of activity. On a small scale, this is illustrated by the easy shift from failing maize groups to coffee groups in El Zapote.

The communicative shift, discussed before in relation to the building of a dominant narrative against burning, can now be contextualized. Modesto was a lower ranked technician and subordinate to an agronomist ('engineer'). The personal capacities of such technicians to communicate are individual, that is, they are not built into a long term working programme of SRN. Even the local success of PRODESBA was significantly linked to the personal abilities of the communicative Modesto who only lived for a short time in the village. In his words: 'we just started the things we could not continue. If PRODESBA had worked longer the results would have been much better. It takes time to work with the people.'

Knowledge generation and non-governmental organizations

The view that state initiatives have failed to bring about knowledge and technology development often suggests that successful knowledge exchange and knowledge progression is better reached through the privatization of the state and an increased role for new NGOs (non-governmental organizations). But recent literature casts some doubts on the role of NGOs and subdues an ideologically fuelled optimism (e.g. Benvenuti 1995; Jansen 1992;

188

Kaimowitz 1993). This section discusses NGO activities in El Zapote in order to explore whether they have the potential to overcome crucial constraints of state-driven and controlled intervention.

Before the wave of new NGOs in the 1990s, non-governmental development activities in El Zapote were undertaken by peasant unions and PLAN (Plan International or Foster Parents Plan). Peasant organizations have largely been transient. One peasant group linked to the peasant union UNC* occupied the land of Alfredo Luna but this land reform initiative failed (see Chapter two). Another group obtained land in one of the hamlets but is no longer connected to the UNC and has since transformed itself into a PLAN-group. INA documents registered, until the late 1980s, that the UNC supported four peasant groups in El Zapote, but in fact the UNC displayed no activity at all. Peasant unions keep registering such groups in order to sustain the number of member groups as high as possible. Locally there is no feeling of a link to peasant unions.

PLAN had a difficult start in El Zapote since it could not get sufficient foster children listed because of a rumour circulating that the foster parents would later come to take away the children. With regard to agricultural development, PLAN was more or less copying what was in vogue in other agencies. Since 1981, PLAN mainly distributed fertilizers to its clients and started to rent or buy some land for groups to plant tule, to keep cattle, or (with women) to start a vegetable garden.[31] The most successful PLAN group established a joint coffee field. Two groups with cattle still manage to carry on. These producers did what all the people around them were doing and no new knowledge was introduced. Most other groups failed: one group with tule lost the land to two members; another group sold the land they had received for maize cultivation; all the chickens of a chicken farm died; and so on. People who left the groups said that they did not like working in groups: 'the group ruins, it decomposes the good'. They believe that only some people work for the group while the others profit. PLAN started a process of withdrawal from the region in 1994. Instead of working with individuals and client groups, PLAN erected local committees to include authorities. The committees were required to write applications for new projects and address these directly to the headquarters in the capital. People view PLAN as getting worse; 'it does not give any longer'. The change from a donating and imposing organization to a more participatory one is not particularly welcomed by villagers. They criticize the growing influence of local politicians in distributing donations from PLAN.

A new shift took place in the 1990s. The efforts of peasant unions to obtain land for the landless had failed, and the PLAN strategy to donate goods to some of the poor had alleviated their life somewhat but did not change their relative poverty. New NGOs emerged whose focus of attention became the environment and sustainable agriculture. Two experiences in El Zapote identify some of the problems of this shift.

In September 1994 an NGO, which promotes the conservation of the National Park of Santa Bárbara, visited El Zapote. In a lecture in the communal centre an agronomist of this environmental NGO explained the utility of trees. He attempted to capture the attention of the audience by asking questions such as: 'What are the functions of trees?' However, dialogue was minimal. In the style of a teacher he summed up the many functions: from providing fruits and firewood to solving the national energy crisis. He argued that deforestation and agriculture on slopes leads to erosion and causes inundations in the north of Honduras. He finished with an incomprehensible exposition on CO_2 and the global climate. During his whole lecture the villagers remained silent and many of them were sleeping. Nobody answered the questions the lecturer posed to stimulate participation of the audience. The agronomist had plans to collaborate with the village. He announced that there was 'money because people in the rich countries do not know what to do with their money' and that they would like to give it to save the Honduran forest. He proposed to set up local committees for conservation and environmental education.

The audience showed no interest and remained silence. Many left the centre before the talk was over. Afterwards, however, many people gave their comments. They said that they did not know who had lectured and from which organization he was. They could only remember that the visitor talked about trees. Resentfully they said that they always worked with trees and knew well how useful trees were: 'How can that man say that we do not know what trees are for?' The NGO worker had not shown any interest in the agricultural production systems of producers. Consequently the producers reacted with silent defiance.

Another NGO had talked about agro-forestry on the 19 July 1994. A producer narrated:

> We were summoned to go to a meeting at the municipality with people from outside. Eighteen villagers appeared. The institution said that it was prohibited to burn. They wanted to reafforest the Zona with pine. People said that they would not accept that their land be taken. They [the outsiders] replied that in that case they would only reafforest the river sides; [they reafforest] for [their own] profits. They made a list of the people who work in the Zona, about sixty. They would come again on the 4th of August, but they never returned.

The villagers directly viewed this NGO as their opponent and a new threat to their livelihoods. The mayor had summoned people to come to the meeting, otherwise nobody would have appeared to listen to the visitors.

These two examples of short-lived interfaces, and of the absence of long-term communication, exemplify much of the current NGO practice in Honduras. I believe they are not just accidental anomalies. NGOs vary, of course, in the quality of their programmes but there is no conceptual framework to characterize adequately the different NGOs.[32] For the moment NGOs are defined not by what they are, but by what they are not: *non-governmental*. The underlying connotation is that they are better than the bureaucratic state in providing services. There is no reason, however, to assume a priori that NGOs are any better than the state. In many aspects they may reflect the shortcomings of the state.

In both examples the NGOs had little knowledge of the local ways of utilizing nature. Notwithstanding the interest in participation expressed by many NGOs, they do not have the technical capability to initiate processes of knowledge innovation together with producers (see also Kaimowitz 1993). Most NGOs limit themselves to working with existing technologies. They tend to approach technologies as artifacts (at the present, green manure, living barriers, and agro-forestry are the most popular, fertilizer and improved cultivars are outdated) and not as processes (what does phosphorus do in the ground and to the plant?). Hence, just as the state did in the past, they believe they have things to 'transfer' to rural people.

NGOs have no qualifications which guarantee that they will be less transient than former state-led interventions. Many NGOs are populated by individuals formerly working in the state system. As the examples above illustrate, similar forms of awkward communication, reflecting different perspectives, interests, and discourses of NGOs and producers, characterize the new interfaces. When I asked villagers afterwards about visits by outsiders, they generally could not recall the name of the organization to which the person belonged nor the objectives of his or her visit. The NGO worker of the first example tried to convince villagers of the need to enter environmental activities by saying: 'The environment is the latest fashion, we have to exploit it, there is much help'. Current practices of many NGOs in Honduras reflect what happened previously with the state. There are few coherent policies and most programmes mimic international development themes and float on foreign interests.[33] Personnel employment is often subordinated to party politics in a way that is not much different from the state.[34] The local politicians who become involved in distributing PLAN donations are an example of shifts in rent-seeking behaviour. Rent-seeking behaviour within the state shifts to the funds circulating in NGOs.

Many activities of NGOs are transient in character. The two NGOs did not return to El Zapote after their first presentation. NGOs may be more efficient than the state in shifting to new fields of activities when earlier fields are not of interest any more. But this is not always a gain, for example, when the problems in these earlier fields have not yet been solved. NGOs focus on ('poor' but) successful producers or villages, leaving aside those people with whom organization and extension does not work. They do this perhaps even more than the state since the government still has to please wider groups in society: the party in government needs the political vote.

Apart from organizational differences NGO work was not very distinct from former state intervention. All these activities appeared as transient to villagers for several reasons. The amount of producers participating was in general small, the largest with PRODESBA. The time that an activity endured was generally short, often less than one year. Many producers did not show much interest in the different extension activities because of the low quality of the information offered. Quite a lot of the technological interventions were not very successful or non-recurring events (e.g. the soil conservation promoted by PRODESBA). Furthermore, the intervening organizations learnt little from the past.[35] PRODESBA is now described as paternalistic; people seem to be unaware that it intended initially to employ a participatory approach which nowadays is said to be a specific characteristic of NGOs.[36] The transience of intervention is reproduced by single unrelated visits by outsiders, technologies which are in many ways useless, programmes which stop as soon as they start, unreliable and unstable organizations, and organizations which are floating on every new development fad.

Locality, Context, and Content

Critiques of current forms of modernization analyse how official agencies and experts label rural people as ignorant. They propose a re-evaluation of local knowledge. Local knowledge approaches call for a rehabilitation of hitherto disregarded producers' knowledge by incorporating it into technology generation and rural development. The concept of local knowledge, however, seems to be more a normative expression than a useful analytical concept.

Several arguments substantiate this claim. The concept cannot provide procedures for evaluating differences in producers' knowledge (other than drawing upon science). How can it evaluate which of the two views on the moon better explains the moon's influence on plant growth? Should a local knowledge study build upon the producer who can name hundreds of trees and plants or the one who uses no names at all for the plants he is weeding? The concept of local knowledge is unable to answer such questions. This chapter has shown that local knowledge is often differentiated and partial. The concept in itself pays little attention to the differential character of knowledge, for example, the uneven way in which villagers understand the effects of pesticides, burning, or the history of land distribution in the village. Finally, local knowledge formulations are unclear about the nature of knowledge and the nature of the local. Knowledge is not a thing that can be incorporated, utilized, or empowered. Science and rural development organizations cannot simply 'go out there' and incorporate (or 'empower') what they find. Evaluations of knowledge on the basis of the locality of its origin (local, farmer, scientific, western) tend to fragment knowledge into separated bodies of knowledge. The review of agricultural knowledge in El Zapote, in contrast, found little evidence that essential differences between scientific and non-scientific thought exist. Both operate in open systems while at the same time needing some form of temporal closures in order to test hypotheses and to experiment (which both do). Both can design and perform, and both can be partial as well as general or holistic. This is not to say that they are the same: there may be different degrees of dealing with these variables, different prospects for systematization and testing complexities, different interests in certain topics, and so on. Withdrawing from a dichotomized view on knowledge that ties knowledge to its origin, we see multi-layered forms of knowledge which interweave, hybridize, and creolize continuously (cf. Long and Villarreal 1994). And we no longer assume a fixed boundary between locality and context.

There is also a practical problem of applying the local knowledge approach in Honduras. The proposition that we need participatory approaches which take local knowledge seriously does not yet clarify what kind of actor can implement successfully such an approach. Current appeals to participatory approaches point to NGOs as the most qualified actors but tend to overlook the political and economic constraints that brought about similar previous attempts. Although I have not analysed in-depth these constraints, there is some evidence that recent participatory approaches as propagated by young NGOs remain as transient as earlier interventions. Despite their critique of earlier intervention rationalities they fail to establish the much-wanted communicative shift.

My argument that there is no such thing as local knowledge parallels a central argument of the social constructionist perspective that there are differentiated (but not fragmented) and diverse bodies of knowledge and that power differential and struggles over social meaning are central to an understanding of knowledge processes (cf. Long and Villarreal 1994:50). Two clarifications have to be added to this argument.

Firstly, although knowledge is an element in power relations (a resource as well as an outcome) it cannot be fully equated with power. The struggle over the dominant narrative around burning was power-laden, but not power-determined. Producers' knowledge does not only have social meaning but it also has a practical and instrumental content. Knowledge is only partly socially constructed, not totally.

Secondly, the normative drive to work with producers' knowledge (to contest/undermine power relations in the process of modernization) and the instrumental utility of much of producers' knowledge has not been discarded with the dissolution of local knowledge as a concept. An instrumental or tool-kit approach *does* collect important information. Although the producers in El Zapote provide no recipes for curbing soil erosion nor generate very successful techniques to improve soil fertility or halt deforestation, they do impart a lot of wisdom about issues such as crop-soil interaction or reasons to burn. The instrumental approach has shown that the successful development and use of sustainable technologies may require such situation-specific information and local participation (Warren 1991). In fact, science and policy would be bad science and (generally) ineffective policy if it did not explore all existing information or fail to communicate with rural people to learn jointly about constraints for developing a sustainable agriculture. If such science and policy drops its populist negation of difference at the local level and its romantic interpretation of locality versus western/scientific context, it can still retain its normative objective of eliminating inequality and poverty.

7

Explaining the Social Origins of Environmental Deterioration: Relativist 'Post'-theories or 'Realist' Political Ecology?

The foregoing chapters have discussed how social relations, historical and environmental conditions, and external factors are shaping environmental deterioration in mountain agriculture in Honduras. Attention has been paid to land distribution, technological change, perceptions of land use and degradation, social relations of production, and knowledge struggles. This concluding chapter brings together the different lines of argument. The first section compares the explanations that are used in the Honduran debate on the social origins of environmental deterioration. Most of these explanations fail to specify structuring principles although each of them refers to existing phenomena. Those explanations that refer to structural causes generally tend to point to one structural root cause. The second section sorts out the different explanations and aims to understand the multiple factors that shape environmental deterioration instead of representing it as a linear outcome of one root structure. The argument that causation of environmental deterioration is plural rather than singular does not mean that there are no structures which shape the occurrence of events, but only that there is no single or central structure. The last section argues that this approach to political ecology is an alternative to recent influences from post-modernism which tend to reduce the study of the social origins of environmental deterioration to a relativist interpretation of knowledge struggles.

Emerging Environmentalism in the Honduran Agricultural Sector

The formation of a host of environmental NGOs, federations of NGOs and professional groups (such as the environmental journalists), as well as the publication of the second Environmental Profile (SECPLAN 1989a) and the first Environmental Law in 1993 (Honduras 1995) are signs that environmental deterioration has become a dominant development issue in Honduras during the past decade. Nevertheless, a coherent intellectual debate about environment, poverty and agricultural development has yet to be developed.

The most elaborated and explicit views have been developed with regard to the expansion of cattle and its effects on deforestation (e.g. Howard 1995, Kaimowitz 1996b, Stonich & DeWalt 1989). Other views or interpretations of the relations between environment, poverty and agricultural development have to be identified by more careful reading and interpretation of texts, newspaper clippings, or through interviews. Explanations of environmental deterioration are mostly built upon earlier analyses of agrarian change and poverty. The following series of key words together cover most of the existing explanations:

· ignorance and ecological unawareness (the 'ignorant peasant', the 'lazy Honduran'),
· overpopulation,
· lack of economic growth,
· crisis-generating forms of capital accumulation: (i) the 'colonial legacy', and (ii) the 'hamburger thesis' or 'displacement thesis',
· failing authority,
· insecure property relations (title insecurity),
· lack of adapted scientific methods.
· undiscovered or hindered peasant rationality

The explanations do not strictly belong to specific authors or social groups. In many cases different arguments are mixed and they do not necessarily exclude each other. At this point it is most fruitful to discuss the arguments separately from the authors. The few references given are only for clarification and there is no intention to argue that these authors stick to one specific argument.

Ignorance

The poor are often blamed for causing environmental destruction by reference to their 'ignorance'. According to this argument Honduran peasants clear forests and burn their fields due to a lack of education. The burning of fields is seen as a continuation of traditional Indian culture.[1] Other examples of supposed ignorance are the careless use of pesticides and the deforestation of water sources. The ignorant producer is sometimes made the scapegoat for destructive activities which were initially induced by governmental organizations, for example the removal of shade in coffee plantations (see Chapter six). A further extension of this argument is present in the supposed 'laziness' of the Honduran in general and the poor peasant in particular. The refusal of producers to make efforts to practice soil conservation has been attributed to their laziness. Chapter five discussed how images such as the 'pig-peasant' in a hammock or the rural drunkard are created to support this argument.

Supporters of this view can be found in many arenas: NGOs (see note ten in Chapter five), the media, state organizations, and so on. The virulence of the argument is astonishing: villagers habitually explain their own behaviour by pointing to ignorance. This reflects a deep rooted feeling of inferiority, or at least the cultural expression of such a feeling.

195

The proposed solution that accompanies this explanation is education. The producer must be made aware of his or her responsibility to protect natural resources and to invest in soil conservation. The content of environmental education programmes usually presumes the villager to be an unknowledgeable individual who does not understand environmental processes. To what extent, however, can one speak of ignorance?

It is difficult to sustain this argument when producers know that their practices are harmful but see no opportunities to act otherwise.[2] The material in this book shows that villagers have always been aware of some of the important environmental consequences of land use. Local awareness of resource deterioration has existed at least from the beginning of this century when villagers were debating the deforestation and drying up of water sources (Chapter four). I have also outlined how producers use a sophisticated set of arguments about the reasons and effects of burning. Producers are the first to acknowledge the need for soil conservation but may see it as impracticable in their situation. It does not fit with their current organization of production. The argument of ignorance presupposes that ideas determine actions. However, a producer may well perceive the environmental consequences of his actions but still refrain from changing his actions due to the conditions he faces. Agro-ecological intensification may require an increase in labour-input or monetary investment without direct returns. Labour (costs) and the low short-term return on 'investments' seems a crucial factor as to why soil conservation is not practised. Chapter three shows that many producers do not have slack periods or labour time available to practise soil conservation or restoration.[3] Insufficient access to resources may also limit soil conservation. The poorest sector of the villagers have no land to improve (Chapter two) or have to work as day labourers (Chapter seven). In general terms the problem with this explanation is that environmental deterioration is seen as a result of the individual mind-set and not of social relations.

Overpopulation

A second explanation refers to increasing pressure on land through population growth. It is argued that population growth leads to subdivision of landholding, to land deterioration and impoverishment, and, subsequently, migration to the city or agricultural frontier areas.

This view is disseminated by several means. The fear of rural poor invading the city is regularly expressed in letters to the editor in Honduran newspapers. It also appears as introductory statements in professional publications which highlight the importance of soil conservation projects (e.g. Thompson 1992). Villagers also remark that the problem of land will further increase because they have too many children.

Solutions that follow from this explanation are family planning and modernization of agriculture. Family planning is silently promoted as a solution, widely practised by the women of El Zapote, but does not figure very prominently in the Honduran debate as a remedy for growing population pressure.[4] A more frequently proposed solution is the modernization of agriculture. It is believed that the application of new technologies can improve soil conservation and feed the increasing population.

196

It is possible to criticize this naturalist perspective on the population problem. Population growth appears as a natural fact in order to legitimize technological intervention to intensify agriculture. The proposed solution to modernize agriculture does not generally specify its relation to population pressure although, paradoxically, overpopulation is considered a hindrance to sustainable land use. These proposals to modernize fail to offer concrete propositions of how to upgrade smallholder agriculture of resource-poor producers without pushing out large numbers of them and thus increasing the pressure on other land. Durham (1979) provides a detailed case study in southern Honduras in which land scarcity for poor producers cannot be interpreted as a result of population growth, but as a result of commercialization and new forms of land use. Chapter two showed the increasing commercialization in El Zapote raised land pressure in specific areas of the municipality while other areas were used in a more extensive way. The naturalist perspective overlooks distributional dynamics. A second critique has been formulated by Boserup (1965), Fairhead and Leach (1995), Netting (1993), and Tiffen et al. (1994), who set the naturalist perspective on population growth on its head. Population growth and land pressure do not necessarily lead to land deterioration, but instead are the driving forces of land intensification. Technology generation and use of labour change in a dynamic interaction with demographic growth. The emergence of intensive coffee cultivation in El Zapote is an example. One of the conditions of its recent expansion was the increasing availability of labour. To conclude: land pressure as a result of demographic growth is not a natural, unmediated process but a result of complex combinations of social practices, their contextual conditions, and cultural perspectives.

Lack of economic growth

A third explanation of the causes of environmental deterioration refers to the lack of economic growth or the incapacity to make profit which can be invested in environmental management and sustainable use of resources. The explanation varies somewhat according to the type of economic actor. For the individual poor producers it is the social conditions of consumption, the need to support a family, that limit prospects for capital accumulation and investment in a sustainable reproduction of agricultural resources. The Honduran hillside producer is too poor, and the income which food grain cultivation on slopes can generate too low to meet the costs of soil conservation and sustainable agricultural practices. For the enterprise, a lack of resources signifies a lack of economic efficiency, that is, low administrative and organizational capacity, low education levels, and a lack of technological knowledge. This makes such an enterprise an irresponsible user of the environment. By plundering the environment it is still possible to make a profit even with inefficient production systems.

This thinking particularly predominates in official policy documents of different kinds: those focusing on state intervention and project planning (Brzovic 1990, SECPLAN 1989a) or those which advocate liberalization and neo-liberal policies after the LMDSA had been launched (Honduras 1992, for an application in environmental issues see SRN n.d.:31-2; CODA 1995). The structural adjustment programme is supposed to set real prices instead of artificially low agricultural prices. Real prices would open possibilities for both type of economic actors to invest in the environment (for example see Walker et al. 1993).

Solutions are formulated at two levels. At the atomized level of individual producers and enterprises, an improvement of conditions through development intervention is proposed. Poor producers should be supported to meet the basic needs of their families and to get access to technology and inputs to modernize their production system in a sustainable way. Enterprises should receive managerial training, access to capital and access to knowledge. At a second level the solutions are formulated in macro-economic terms. At present these are generally interpreted as follows: producers cannot participate efficiently and competitively in markets because of imperfections in markets and lack of infrastructure, both an effect of improper functioning of the state and bad macro-economic policies. This squeezes their profits and, hence, their capacity to invest in the environment.

A weakness of this explanation is that the problem of a lack of resources is reduced to the economic efficiency of individual producers and enterprises. Little attention is paid to how resource distribution is produced and reproduced through social structures. The proposed solutions may therefore constitute a danger of creating new poverty and environmental deterioration. Those producers who have been ousted may still need to survive; they remain poor or become even poorer. Furthermore, this explanation assumes that the replacement of inefficient producers by efficient producers leads to a rational use of resources without spoiling inputs (Strasma and Celis 1992). However, rationality in economic terms does not necessarily mean a rational use of resources in ecological terms. The environmental problems in, for example, Dutch or North-American agriculture, are illustrative. Poverty limits investment in the environment, but this truism does not make the opposite true that more profit and affluence necessarily lead to agricultural systems which are environmentally friendly.

Crisis-generating forms of capital accumulation

This explanation of environmental deterioration starts from the issue of a lack of resources and poverty too, but, in contrast to the former argument, it poses the question of how poverty is reproduced in structures of relations of production. Poverty -or marginality- is a result of the skewed distribution of land and of the economic dominance of an export sector. The latter is reinforced by preferential state policies. This explanation links the poverty of many to the affluence of some. Two interpretations have gained influence in Honduras (see Chapter two). The first model views the unequal distribution of land as a 'colonial legacy'. In this model, an agrarian bourgeoisie monopolizes the land and constitutes an archaic class not willing to modernize unless forced by state intervention and social struggle. A second model is represented by the 'displacement' thesis or 'hamburger' thesis. In this model the export sector appropriates the land and state support, and accumulates to the detriment of the poor. Poor producers are displaced to hillsides or frontier zones, where they can do nothing other than practice unsustainable forms of agriculture and contribute to land degradation. Expansion of the export sector is dependent on foreign investments in commercialization structures and on external demand. The direct

198

environmental consequence is contamination with biocides. Critical export categories in Honduras have been banana, cotton, cattle and, recently, shrimp and various tropical fruits. The hamburger, as a symbol for what happens, refers to the US-demand for beef. This demand spurred the building of commercialization structures and generated high beef prices in Honduras after World War II. Large landowners responded by enlarging their herds and converting crop land and forests into pastures; tenants were evicted and national and ejidal land was appropriated by powerful people. Their cattle were 'eating the forest' (see Chapter three). The state supported this process by favourable credit arrangements.

The colonial legacy view is primarily reproduced in studies of Honduran intellectuals (e.g. Benavides 1984; CONSUPLANE n.d.) while critical North-American scholars are the main carriers of the displacement or hamburger thesis (e.g. Brockett 1988; DeWalt 1983; Howard 1987; Stonich 1993; Williams 1985).

These explanations of environmental deterioration have various shortcomings. Despite its historical thrust, the colonial legacy argument is a very static explanation. Chapter two emphasizes the many differences in local histories of land distribution. At the beginning of this century land was available to poor producers at low costs in El Zapote. The current skewed land distribution and problems of access to land for the poor has been mainly created recently and not in the colonial period (see Chapter two). Furthermore, I have argued that census data should be interpreted differently by paying more attention to the position of the middle categories of producers. The dynamics of this group hardly receive attention in the colonial legacy model, though it has excited interest in the question of power and control over land.

A problem with the displacement thesis is that it cannot explain land use changes in El Zapote. The area in pasture increased and land was appropriated by a powerful cattle owner. Chapter three indicated how an increase in pasture area cannot be interpreted only in terms of the expansion of cattle. It is also a result of how land use appears in census data (much land used by cattle in the past was not registered as such) and of a rise in the number of pack animals. Furthermore, expansion of cattle has arisen not only from large landowners but also from middle size producers. In fact, the hamburger thesis over-emphasizes the role of the large landowner and cattle holder, and disregards important diversity in land use and the types of producers involved.

Another problematic issue is the portrayal of export production as the main cause of environmental deterioration. This may lead to an export determinism: each export activity is automatically related to environmental deterioration and unequal distribution of resources. The importance of coffee in fragile mountain areas, as discussed in this book, defies such a determinism. Coffee, to a large extent, is cultivated by middle size producers and some poor producers. This export crop is, in the context of El Zapote's agriculture, less deteriorating for the land than food grain production (see also Jansen 1996).

Failing authority

This view considers failing authority as a main social cause of environmental deterioration. It attributes the function of defending and regulating the common good to local and national authorities. Environmental deterioration will take place when the authority is incapable of performing this function. An example is the deforestation of water sources in El Zapote by coffee producers who plant coffee near the springs. Many villagers perceive it as natural that people strive for their own profit and thereby damage the environment. It is up to the authorities to intervene: they should regulate or stop this deforestation. When the issue of water is raised villagers do not criticize the coffee producers but the local authorities who 'don't do anything'. For villagers failing authority is a result of the dominance of political clientelism in the implementation of state policies, the travesty of the juridical system, the social networks which regulate the decisions of authorities, and the lack of technical ability of state functionaries (see Chapter five and six).

This explanation, which blames authorities for encouraging environmental deterioration, is produced in everyday conversations and public discussions. One can hear it in conversations with producers, in taxis, in interviews on the radio, or in articles in the newspapers. In official documents or written studies, however, the precise role of authorities and political clientelism is less analysed, though some reference may be made to it in a more neutral formulation, for example in terms of the inefficiency of the state bureaucracy (e.g. Wachter 1992).

In these discussions various solutions are proposed. The first entails tackling the existing authorities and candidates for political posts about their moral standards, their honesty and their patriotism.[5] It is suggested that a moral clean up could improve state institutions at all levels. The second solution does not interpret the failure of authority vis-à-vis environmental conservation in personal or party-political terms. Instead, it presumes that a lack of legal instruments and sound organization leads to the failure of authority. As a solution, it proposes the improvement of the repressive and controlling function of the state. This, for instance, is attempted by formulating a new Environmental Law and introducing environmental delicti into the penal code in 1997, together with the call for the formation of new institutions and coordinating organizations.[6] Furthermore, the military is assigned a role in the control of deforestation and natural reserves, thus promoting their green image with 'green battalions'.[7] In general, better state planning is called for (e.g. SRN n.d.).

Each of these solutions has its limitations. The first faces the problem that a simple replacement of individuals occupying positions within the state apparatus does not alter the political structures and the role of political clientelism in Honduran society. Moreover, even if individuals who operate without political clientelism and rent-seeking behaviour were appointed one would still need to define the desired form of environmental conservation. The second solution does not solve the problem either, since it merely restates what the state should do (and what many citizens think the state is not doing). This also counts for the proposal to include the military in the control of environmentally-destructive behaviour. In fact the military receive little credibility from the population because of their recent involvement in illegal deforestation and their linkages with COHDEFOR, which, according to villagers, actually made deforestation possible and prohibited local use of the forest.[8] The proposal for an improved state planning can also be questioned. Why would the Honduran state succeed in implementing demanding ('rational') planning schemes for environmental management (demanding in terms of funds, political impartiality, and technical and organizational capacity) where it failed to do so in the recent past? An answer to this question entails identifying the new conditions that make successful planning likely where it has failed in the past, which to my knowledge is usually not attempted. In general, proposals to improve state functioning do not confront the central issues of how the structure of power within the Honduran state and the networks of dominant economic groups, party-politics and the military intervene and mediate in any project to restructure the state (cf. Brzovic 1990; SRN n.d.; CODA 1995).[9]

Insecure property relations

In this explanation not merely the lack of resources but the lack of control through insecure property relations, and the related absence of long-term interests, on the side of the farmer limit rational use of resources and investment, for example, in soil conservation.

This explanation is mainly found in literature that deals with land titling in Honduras (e.g. Strasma and Celis 1992; Wachter 1992, 1994, 1995) and land reform cooperatives (Ruben 1997). Short references to this explanation are sometimes made in NGO-related documents, since their practioners observe this problem in the field (e.g. Bunch and López 1995; Mejía 1993).

The land titling literature proposes a solution that requires altering institutions in such a way that individual producers obtain stable and legally-guaranteed private property rights.

A critique of this explanation concurs with the observation that poor producers often face the problems of a lack of control and insecure property rights. It will differ, however, with how insecurity is analysed and the type of solution proposed. The case of El Zapote shows how property relations shape agricultural practices. For example, whether burning or not is practised by tenants may depend on the landowner's perception and burning and fertilizing practises. People also use fire differently in their private plots and in the village common. Hence, property rights influence environmental behaviour. Can the proposed solution of private titling of land, then, contribute to environmental conservation by providing certain guarantees to the producers? This book has provided arguments to the effect that the titling process cannot provide such guarantees. Chapter two reveals that it is not so much the absence of a legal registration of private ownership that act as a constraint on producer strategies. In fact, the titling project increased insecurity about rights and it has not led to a reduction in conflict, a better availability of credit, changes in agronomic practices, or investment in soil conservation.

Lack of advanced scientific investigation

It is often argued that Honduras lacks advanced scientific investigation for protecting the environment. This implies that a lack of information about the environment promotes its 'wrong' use. Information is absent because relevant scientific knowledge and instruments are missing. Indeed, this study shows how little is known about environmental change in

Honduras, thus any pronouncement on the sort and magnitude of environmental deterioration is necessarily filled with uncertainty.

Generally, however, this explanation does not stand alone but must be added to other related arguments. The view that the environment has to be better mapped is present in several recent official documents (e.g. Honduras 1995; SECPLAN 1989a; SRN n.d.). Currently, the use of new satellite imaginary interpretation and geographical information systems (GIS) are seen as crucial new technologies for helping to solve environmental problems. In this way it is assumed that optimal monitoring and control of land use is possible.

One problem with this argument is that too much is expected from new GIS technologies. The training of Honduran GIS scientists creates a few experts whose studies tend to become disarticulated from lower-level data on agricultural practices. Socio-economic data collection is currently very limited and existing official data collection in rural areas is deficient. GIS techniques in Honduras tend to make use of a few selected technical data (those which result from satellite imaginary interpretation). Qualitative social analysis as to why some processes take place is not yet incorporated into these studies. This problem is not totally restrictive but there is a danger that the half-hearted introduction of costly new scientific techniques results more from fashionable thinking and prestige seeking than being a basic necessity. Indicative of this is the fact that the rich series of aerial photographs of Honduras lie idle in the archives.

A more serious problem is that this technological fix distracts attention away from political and socio-economic constraints of land use. It reinforces the expectations of an external -not yet known- technological input to solve problems. In this way, it clings to a kind of religious hope and belief in a better future without scrutinizing existing social structures.

Undiscovered or hindered peasant rationality

The view which resolves environmental deterioration by reference to a hindered peasant rationality was introduced in Chapter six. This view maintains that modern, western forms of agriculture based on the exploitation of soil and people are the principal cause of present land deterioration. This argument is a response to the negative appreciations of culture which emphasize 'ignorance', the lack of knowledge of producers, and the 'traditional' character of Honduran mountain agriculture. It aims, that is, to offer an antidote to classical modernization thinking in agricultural development. It takes a positive view of local culture and reappraises peasant rationality.[10] The harmonic relationship with nature ascribed to ethnic groups is a specific form of this argument (for example in the Regulations of the Environmental Law (Honduras 1995:art.65).[11]

It seeks solutions to environmental deterioration in local culture which can provide the knowledge and practice on which to base sustainable forms of agriculture. Proposals for change focus on removing the constraints which inhibit the inventiveness of small producers to develop sustainable land use. NGOs and a limited number of academics are the main carriers of this view (see Chapter six).

The problem with this argument is the same as that with the concept of local knowledge discussed in Chapter six. There is, in fact, no homogeneous peasant knowledge or agriculture. Knowledge and practices are partial and diverse, and shaped by social differentiation, local forms of small-scale exploitation, unequal access to resources, and differential incorporation into more or less powerful networks of political parties, kinship and friendship ties. Furthermore, peasant inventiveness may well opt for new non-sustainable forms of land use, entailing for example deforestation near water sources by coffee producers or the spraying of paraquat by very poor producers. Another problem is that the proposed solutions may remain constrained by the local character of bottom-up development. Also many programmes based on this analysis of the causes of environmental deterioration do not develop views on macro-economic policies and the modernization of the state.

Contrasting or overlapping explanations?

A broad set of explanations of the causes of environmental deterioration circulate in Honduras. In El Zapote, people use most of them (according to their own formulations). Chapter four mentions that, unlike producers in the studies of Blaikie (1993) and Zimmerer (1993b), the producers of El Zapote do not have a shared explanation which differs markedly from the views adhered by people within the state or other social groups. To some extent there are clear local differences in views: people without land may interpret soil degradation as resulting from the shortening of fallow periods, and increased land pressure more readily in terms of unequal access to land, expansion of cattle and land appropriation, while some larger landowners promptly point to the ignorance of the peasants who burn. These divides are almost never sharp and people mix up some of these explanations. The blurring of explanations is also clear in government documents (e.g. Honduras 1995; SECPLAN 1989a; SRN n.d.) and in interviews with state officials and extensionists. On these grounds it does not seem productive to associate a specific explanation with a specific text. Furthermore, perceptions are not direct reflections of actors' positions as they are in the cases of Blaikie (1993), Biot et al. (1995:2), and Zimmerer (1993b).

The blurring of explanations is in part a result of the fact that they overlap. Nevertheless, many of them also have strongly contrasting elements. The next section outlines the useful elements of different explanations. It starts with the type of explanation that refers to crisis-generating forms of capital accumulation. More than other ones, it analyses the practices of producers in terms of broader socio-economic processes. These other explanations, however, contain insights that are overlooked by the focus on capital accumulation. These will be discussed later.

Environmental deterioration and its multiple relations with society

Linearity, chaos, or stratified relations between society and environment?

This section argues that from an understanding of the socio-economic relations in which a producer is embedded one cannot straightforwardly draw conclusions about the producer's use of the environment. The view that not only individuals cause land deterioration but that structures also underpin causation of environmental deterioration does not, of course, imply a linear relationship between social structure and environmental deterioration. I will develop my argument through a critique of one of the variants of the functional dualism model applied in the environmental debate in Central America.

The model of functional dualism was introduced in Chapter one. It basically argues that capitalist forms of land use produce pollution and deforestation through the exploitation of semi-proletarian labour which is left with marginal, overexploited lands, subject to soil erosion. The work of Faber (1992, 1993) is exemplary. His analysis is useful in documenting that the continuing deterioration of natural resources is not only a product of misuse, mismanagement or overpopulation, but is intrinsic to the model of accumulation and the domestic power constellation associated with it. Faber's model recognizes a linear relationship between the type of command over the means of production and the pattern of environmental deterioration: semi-proletarians = hillside erosion, and capitalists = pollution.

The application of this model for explaining environmental deterioration in Honduras faces two problems: (i) the patterns of social relations which Faber observes cannot be traced in such a dichotomized way since the situation is much more diverse, and (ii) we cannot observe the suggested linear relation between command over the means of production and environmental deterioration.

(i) Chapter two furnishes evidence that unequal land distribution, the basis of this model, should not be conceptualized in terms of two categories. Spatial distribution is not bi-modal, and the concept of space is highly confusing because the constructed farm size classes do not capture the dynamics of production. Likewise, the division of rural people into capitalist landowners and land-poor semi-proletarians in Faber's model is not in line with the diversity of land-value distribution, as perceived by rural people. Furthermore, mediating institutions, such as personal relations, markets, and the state, shape land value and do not do this necessarily along farm size classes. Chapter three shows that trajectories of technological change do not follow the division into two classes either, i.e. a capitalist sector, characterized by the use of industrial inputs in cash crops, and a subsistence sector using traditional technologies. The discussion of the more complex configuration of various types of producers presented in Chapter five further invalidates the dichotomized model. Not only is the history of the division of land too dynamic to be captured in functionalist terms; the same counts for labour relations and multiple forms of household reproduction. The local power constellation cannot be depicted as a simple semi-proletarian - capitalist farmer dichotomy.

(ii) A second argument is that erosion patterns are not identical to power relations: one side of a power relation is not necessarily associated with specific types of erosion

204

problems. Small and large producers, capitalists and semi-proletarians, provoke soil degradation, deforestation, and pollution with pesticides. There are no grounds to suppose a simple linearity between types of social structure and environmental deterioration. This critique is also valid if we replace the dichotomized model with a more differentiated view on producer-types. Of course, it would have been convenient if every type of producer discussed in Chapter five was linked to a special type of resource use, and hence to a specific form of ecological degradation.[12] This, however, turned out to be impossible.[13] While the typology suggested in Chapter five does not define categories of resource degradation, it is, nevertheless, helpful in discussing how economic and social conditions constrain or enable resource use and conservation for different types of producers. I will turn to this issue below.

If agrarian relations are characterized by diversity instead of linearity, how then do we account for this diversity? One way would be to see it as some kind of 'chaos'. That means that there exists no central social structure which can explain environmental deterioration: producers respond as it were individually as knowledgeable and capable actors to a heterogeneous environment. The outcomes of these responses do not follow any consistent and replicated pattern and the multiple factors that influence producers' behaviour cannot be seen as conditions because they are not stable and bounded factors but fluid and permeable. Another way to perceive diversity is to see it as the result of the working of many different structures, forces, and producer's agency at the same time. If one observes diversity instead of generalized patterns of events which challenge structuralist theories of environmental deterioration (e.g. poor-producers with sustainable systems in fertile river terraces, large estates on eroding slopes, subsistence maize treated with the newest herbicides, or export crops cultivated without biocides), this does not mean that structures (e.g. relations of production) do not cause certain things to happen. It merely suggest that other mechanisms may be at work which produce other, unexpected effects. Social structures condition agricultural practices but do not pre-determine the events.

This latter perspective makes it possible to reintroduce into our analysis a critique of capital and reinterpret models of functional dualism. There is no one root cause for environmental deterioration but multiple causes. These multiple causes will partly be located within the working of enduring structures: that is, they are rooted in different interacting physical, cultural, social and economic structures, and in continuous interaction with more contingent, exogenous, triggering actions by humans and nature.

Reinterpreting existing explanations

At this point it is time to return to the different explanations discussed in the previous section. Even though these explanations contain incompatibilities one may reinterpret them in order to develop an account of the social causes of environmental deterioration in mountain agriculture in Honduras.[14] None of these explanations is capable of grasping the complexity of the relations between society, resource use and environmental deterioration, but linking them provides a broader perspective, so long as we can circumvent the pitfalls of an eclectic mix. In many aspects the explanations are contradictory. For example, the 'lack of economic growth' and 'crisis-generating forms of capital accumulation' arguments dispute each other's assumptions; the arguments about 'ignorance' and 'hindered peasant rationality' project opposing views about the nature and value of local culture.

From the former, we learn that 'ignorance' and 'laziness' are explanations used by people to make moral judgements. Calling some behaviour ignorant because it generates environmental deterioration is a labelling mechanism to define what is good and what is bad agriculture. Looking at what people call ignorant therefore reveals their view of agriculture. The argument about 'ignorance' can in our case be reinterpreted as an expression of the cultural distance between the TATE and most of the producers. What remains invisible in this explanation is that the imputation of ignorance to people is a form of disempowering people.

The 'overpopulation' argument recalls that population pressure may lead to problems in sustainable land use. In such general terms it may be true for El Zapote. Functionalist-marxist approaches contest a naturalist perspective on overpopulation by arguing that population pressure should be conceptualized as an effect of capitalism in creating a reserve army of labour (Faber 1993:75-6). In Faber's view, the economic conditions in Central America have spawned rapid population growth as a survival strategy of smallholders in order to maintain a constant stock of working children. Economic strategies, though, may shape demographic behaviour but they do not directly determine the number of children. There is more complexity about child making and nurturing in El Zapote than the 'bearing of children as production agents to increase the few productive sources of poor peasant families' (Faber 1993:74). A functionalist view of population pressure cannot explain, for example, why birth control has expanded enormously in El Zapote. Population pressure therefore cannot simply be seen as a consequence of capitalist accumulation and the creation of a reserve army of labour. Indeed one can dismiss the notion that population growth is a natural process without viewing population pressure as functional to capitalism. On the other hand one can accept the possibility that under certain conditions population growth does not cause land degradation and may even encourage land conservation, without making technology development and land conservation functional to demographic patterns. Instead I view demographic development as a structure independent of the social relations of production and with its own dynamics. Such structures are contingently related. Durham's (1979) study is an illustration of how these structures may co-determine the occurrence of events, in this case the struggles around land and the conflicts between El Salvador and Honduras.

The 'lack of economic growth' argument points to several phenomena I observed in El Zapote. Many producers are poor in resources. Production of food grains only is no sound economic basis in situations of actual land pressure to guarantee sustainable reproduction of resources, especially if the producers are supposed to market a surplus (and thus to compete indirectly in a world market) in order to invest in soil conservation or restoration. Sufficient investment capacity and economic efficiency (in the sense of return to labour) seems to be a condition for soil conservation. However, improvement in economic conditions does not necessarily lead to an ecological rationality.

206

Furthermore, the explanation of 'crisis generating forms of capital accumulation' highlights the fact that a lack of resources should not be seen as accidental individualized poverty but as a result of power differences, e.g. in control of land, and the specific processes of capital accumulation. One can agree with this argument and still reject that the colonial legacy, the displacement thesis, or the reference to export agriculture can explain current patterns of environmental deterioration.

Explanations which point to 'failing authority' may bring to our attention the need to consider the specific dynamics of the state apparatus even though this is generally not analysed in any depth or studied in terms of power. An important point, according to me, is that the state (the organization of authority and laws) continues to be an important structure in shaping environmental deterioration and conservation, even when state authority fails to set the necessary conditions for the development of sustainable agriculture. One cannot develop an alternative, for example, bottom-up NGO type of sustainable agriculture, without rethinking the organization of the state apparatus.

The explanation of 'insecure property rights', again, tends to exclude issues of political and economic power in institutions. This explanation nevertheless points to the importance of understanding and changing institutional arrangements concerning access, control and use rights of existing resources.

Explanations that refer to the 'lack of advanced scientific investigation' and 'hindered peasant rationality' can both be interpreted as explanations which bring to the fore issues of rationality, knowledge, and technology. Thus implicitly they bring technology development into the field of politics, even when the former tries to express its view in neutral and supposedly objective language. There may be a lack of knowledge about current processes of environmental deterioration, but this observation can be made without the common technological fix which makes it difficult to analyse how knowledge and power struggles shape technology development and use of the environment. The latter explanation is important as it recognizes the possibility of different paths of technology development and the need for political organization and practical work to redirect existing paths. Its explanation, however, may be improved by incorporating an analysis of the crisis generating forms of capital accumulation and the state, doing away with any notion of a homogeneous peasant culture which generates intrinsically better technologies.

Causes of environmental deterioration

This book opened with a series of producers' quotations about the origins of environmental deterioration. Their explanations were followed in the subsequent chapters by an historical analysis of socio-economic change in the village of El Zapote. To a large extent, environmental deterioration in El Zapote is typical for many mountainous areas of Central America. Shortened fallow periods, overgrazing, and burning may contribute to soil erosion and soil degradation. Deforestation induces micro-climatic alterations and changes in hydrology. Biocide use may pollute the environment and cause health problems. This section summarizes the main mechanisms, discussed throughout the book, that shape these particular forms of environmental deterioration:

· unequal distribution of land and type of exploitative relations,
· a sustained demand for cattle and coffee
· population pressure,
· authority structures which fail in regulating common property,
· technology and knowledge configurations which are partial and differential,
· natural mechanisms.

An **unequal distribution of land** and the existence of exploitative relations may provide a better explanation of the continuation of environmental deterioration than simple poverty. Poverty leads to low investments in soil conservation and a deplorable use of resources which is inconsistent with the long-term need to reproduce these resources. For poverty to exist, it needs relations that make possible an unequal distribution of resources and produced value. During this century a few large estates emerged which controlled a substantial area of the land in El Zapote. Chapter two argued that these estates, or latifundios, did not totally dominate the local agrarian structure. The few large estates co-existed with farms of many different compositions in terms of farm size, land value, property relations, and forms of land use. The *ejido** system guaranteed for a long time at least some land to all those who wanted to till their own parcel. Unrestricted land accumulation to form large estates by a small group of people is now history in the sense that it no longer takes place (although it does take place in other areas of Honduras). At the time that this land accumulation took place other producers could always find access to land to cultivate their food grains. It is only recently that land-poor producers face increasing problems of getting access to good soils which have been sufficiently regenerated by long fallow-periods. Increasing land pressure leads to impoverished soils and land degradation, but on the other hand it leads to people experimenting with changed production methods, for example, not burning, *postrera de agosto**, and the reintroduction of fallow periods. Due to unequal land distribution and a raising awareness that land degradation may take place, landowners are less willing to rent out land and the pressure on the village commons is increasing. Unequal land distribution concentrates the negative effects of land pressure in specific areas.

Chapter five introduced the concept of 'nickel and dime capitalism' in order to argue that class relations cannot be reduced to a struggle between capitalist landowners and land-poor semi-proletarians. Exploitative relations are omnipresent but small in monetary terms in El Zapote. The wealth some villagers acquired originated, until recently, from small-scale trade, sometimes reinvested in land. During the last decades intensive coffee cultivation is increasing and is generating wealth for a part of the population. Increased capitalization of these competing petty commodity producers will push out resource-poor producers. These coffee producers may invest some of their profits in soil conservation, but the somewhat poorer people, who work for the coffee producers, will not earn enough to pay for soil conservation in their own fields.

The most characteristic land use changes in El Zapote have been the expansion of permanent pasture for livestock after World War II and the expansion and intensification of coffee production during the last three decades. These expansions were a response to a *sustained demand for coffee and cattle* (see Chapter three). The expansion of cattle in El Zapote followed national patterns and was conditioned by a combination of high beef prices (US demand), dynamic market structures, the availability of cheap credit, a low land value and relatively easy ways to obtain large tracts of land. Land formerly used in a forest-maize-pasture system was converted into permanent pastures. Maize, cultivated by practically all producers, became increasingly sown in rotations with a short or no fallow period at all. Many resource-poor producers saw their access to fertile land constrained by the expansion of pasture. After the decline of beef exports to the US in the 1980s, the national market generated sufficient demand to sustain El Zapote's cattle. Cattle expansion however, was not the only source of conversion of crop land and forests into pastures. A significant increase in pack animals, mainly related to coffee expansion, contributed to this conversion as well.

The expansion of coffee should not be understood as a result of producers simply responding to market opportunities and high coffee prices. Such a vision cannot explain why coffee expansion took place only recently and not in the former century such as it did in neighbouring countries. Although infrastructure was less developed in Honduras it is not the single explaining factor.[15] Lack of a dispossessed poor-peasantry which could supply cheap labour was probably a more important factor.[16] Recently, such cheap labour (demographic growth and impoverishment) has become available locally (cf. de Janvry et al. 1989). Moreover, the market structures to commercialize coffee developed slowly but gradually. In itself the expansion of coffee was not a major force of deforestation in El Zapote. The area is relatively small, and the replacement of forest vegetation by a permanent crop such as coffee with many shade trees is not so harmful to soil degradation as, for example, maize cultivation or (generally overexploited) pastures. In the second instance, however, clearing of forest vegetation took place after the Coffee Leaf Rust disease arrived, which compelled producers to move coffee from lower to higher altitudes. One of the consequences was deforestation around water sources and changes in micro-climate. I presume that expansion and intensification of coffee will continue. Even years with low prices does not stop smallholders in El Zapote from investing labour and capital in coffee.

The occurrence of *population pressure* in El Zapote was mentioned in Chapter one. Demographic growth and increasing land pressure gave rise to a reduction in farm size and fallow periods, with negative consequences for soil degradation. Although I did not analyse the population dynamics in detail I would like to repeat that population growth is not an autonomous natural process. Patterns of demographic growth may well be shaped by, for example, gender notions in society, social valuations of birth control methods, loose family structures, and the role of child labour in the rural economy. As indicated above, the relationship of other social structures and population dynamics can be seen as contingent. After all the ejido land had been divided into concessions to villagers, population growth contributed to more and, on average, smaller farms. Only very recently, a process of out-migration has started. It cannot be predicted whether population growth in the near future will increase the number of producers further or whether people will move out of agriculture. It cannot be assumed that a further reduction of farm size will continue. It is, for example, possible that the growing strength of small size coffee producers may enable them to control the land and restrict access to less fortunate people.

Environmental deterioration in El Zapote is partly a result of *authority structures* which failed in regulating common property. The state's most influential role in structuring agriculture was the definition of property relations in land (Chapter two). With the ejido adjudications the state displayed a certain capacity to pass land to resource-poor producers. The case of the aborted land reform in El Zapote, however, exemplifies the Janus-faced character of the state: neither smallholder farming, nor entrepreneurial, large scale, intensive farming, nor large estate extensive farming were selected as a single option to be promoted. During this century land became increasingly commoditized (see Chapter two). The state incorporated commodity values into its interventions. Ejido land was distributed because it was thought that villagers had the right to grow their own food. The land reform to some extent repeated this idea, but was mainly carried out with the idea of modernizing agriculture and production for the market. With the land titling programme the right of smallholders to land became finally defined as the right to private property. The ejidos were abolished and there was even less thinking and intervention concerning how common properties could be regulated. It is exemplary that the producers who deforest near the village's water sources argue that they have received a private title over this land. The municipal authorities complain that it is difficult for them to forbid clearing now it is no longer ejidal land.

Within the state apparatus, apart from the law, other normative frameworks operate. A system of political clientelism shaped much of the behaviour of individual authorities as well as the functioning of state bodies. Above I described how this led to a failure to protect the drinking water sources of the village. Chapter six I analysed how it constrained the control of burning practices. In fact, the Honduran state has contradictory relations with its citizens. State authority in itself, as a regulating power, has been weak. I gave examples of how the state was not able to regulate land use (including burning), control defor-estation, guarantee property rights, or treat its citizens equally in state interventions. On the other hand, the state system tightly constrains human behaviour: independent organizations soon become dependent on the state for their functioning and thus become integrated into the *system of political clientelism* and party politics. In El Zapote actions in the public sphere, such as accusing somebody of causing forest fires or deforestation, are directly interpreted in terms of power distribution between the Nationalist and Liberal party.

There are no other structures of local relationships which may serve as an entrance to organizing alternatives for behaviour which endangers resources of common interest. The role of two political parties (with little or no difference in political programme at the village level) in Honduran society is relatively dominant compared to other types of group formation. Other types of social relationships within the village are characterized by a low degree of social cohesiveness. Group formation is low, class-based organizations are absent, and even kinship structures can be characterized as loose (see Chapter five). Recently (during the last two decades) the emergence of various protestant denominations

210

has led to new, and relatively strong social groupings. However, the denominations do not yet impinge in issues of livelihood and environment. Producer groups that are formed through the various development interventions are as transient as the interventions themselves (Chapter six). The relatively individualized character of social relationships, combined with the authority structures described, hinders organized protest against land usurpation, deforestation, contamination of water sources, and uncontrolled burning in the commons.

Technology and knowledge configurations have specific dynamics which shape environmental deterioration. Knowledge has been discussed in two ways as a central problem for environmental deterioration. One argument stresses that the ignorance, traditionality, and lack of awareness of peasants is the core of the problem of environmental deterioration in the mountains of Honduras. The introduction of modern views on agriculture and education would provide a solution. An opposite argument emphasizes that it the penetration of scientific rationality into farmers' styles which cause a disharmonious interaction with the environment. A reappraisal of local knowledge would be a solution.

Chapter six proposes that both these arguments overlook the differential character of knowledge. Some of the recently introduced 'modern' technologies, such as new maize varieties, spraying with biocides, the building of soil conservation structures, and new production systems for coffee seem to be not very 'sustainable'. On the other hand, contour cropping and fertilizer use seems to contribute to better plant growth and ground cover and, possibly, a reduction of soil erosion and an improvement in the percentage of organic matter in the soil. Local knowledge similarly developed 'good' and 'bad' technologies. It has not yet developed effective answers to soil erosion, it has not provided successful modes to manage common property, and the so-called 'farmer-to-farmer transfer' of knowledge probably diffused more effectively the knowledge of how to use biocides than how to use biological pest control. On the other hand, local knowledge has led to the selection of important shade trees in coffee and very sustainable systems of tule production.

Chapter Four argued that villagers have always perceived certain practices to be harmful to their environment. The forest vegetation around their water sources was highly valued and people knew that the deforestation in the first decades of this century threatened these water sources. This awareness, however, did not generate effective action to change environmental management. People also perceive that the problem is becoming much more critical. Villagers claim that for a long time land was abundant. Trees too were abundant. The environment was resilient in the sense that with a fallow period the natural fertility would be restored. In recent decades, however, producers have seen that soil fertility can degrade to the point of fields becoming useless: 'we will get a desert here'. Lowering of fertility is no longer a cyclical event as in a fallow-based cropping system, but is perceived in a linear time perspective: soils can keep losing fertility. People relate current events to what may happen in the future. Most of the recent educational efforts limited to stressing the need for conservation seem to spread a message which is not new.

There seems to be no clear body of local knowledge in El Zapote which can provide guidelines for environmental conservation; exogenous knowledge is not very successful either. Chapter six took this argument one step further by questioning the fragmentation of knowledge into separate entities of local knowledge and scientific or modern knowledge. Although one can discern interesting bits of knowledge, this does not mean that there is a unified body of local knowledge. Producers' knowledge is differentiated, partial and is an historical result of a continuous process of hybridization of transferred and transformed information coming from many sources. I have only looked at processes in this century. Traders have always been important sources for new knowledge. Travelling became easier and temporary migration more frequent. The space for learning was no longer limited to the village or the region but encompassed a much larger area. This brought new production ideas to the village, while social networks extended over larger areas, cross-cutting rural-urban frontiers. New cultivars, production methods, and equipment, were brought to the village and tested. Vegetation changed through the introduction of new grasses. It is impossible to define what is local and what is non-local.

A central problem is to find how local knowledge can inform environmental restoration if there is no clear unified body of local knowledge. Whose knowledge and which knowledge? Among villagers struggles about information take place; the political economy of expertise causes an uneven distribution of knowledge. Furthermore, villagers may display very different knowledge about vegetation, weeds, insects, climate, and so on. The concept of local knowledge cannot offer us a definitive clue for confronting environmental crises. The problem of the local knowledge approach seems to be located in the adjective local. In fact, the place of origin of ideas or technologies does not necessarily delimit their practical usefulness. The effects that views and technologies generate cannot be deduced from their place of origin. The recent efforts to construct an absolute difference between scientific reasoning and local knowledge tend to develop an over-culturalization of knowledge which denies the overlapping practical aspects of local and scientific knowledge and the overlapping parts of the outer world to which these knowledge configurations refer.

One can conclude that a reduction of the causes and solutions of environmental deterioration to a question of knowledge is unjustified. I have tried to show that knowledge is indeed a part of the environmental problem and thus may be part of the solution, but knowledge cannot be seen as the root problem of environmental deterioration. We have to look for ways to avoid the reductionism of those who construct a producer's ignorance, a religious belief in scientific resource management, or a romantic view of local knowledge.

A last problem, but not the least one, is how environmental deterioration is structured by **characteristics of nature** (non-human causality). My explanation of human activity has not abstracted from these natural properties. Human behaviour in El Zapote has been shaped by the heterogeneity of the environment. Slope, rainfall patterns, soils, the arrival of the fungal Coffee Leaf Rust disease, effects of fallow periods, characteristics of crops and cattle, vegetation changes, stones and thorny weeds, or qualities of biocides all work upon agricultural practice. Their properties are not socially constructed but naturally defined (although they may be socially redefined; see Chapter three and four).

This summary of the central processes discussed in earlier chapters brings me to the conclusion that any explanation of environmental deterioration in Honduras should focus

212

on how structures that underlie property relations, market, state, political clientelism, knowledge, demography, non-commoditized relations, and the elements of nature generate various mechanisms that influence the actual state of the environment. Properties of these structures encompass power relations. Environmental deterioration in Honduras cannot be reduced to one root cause (Faber 1993) but instead should be conceptualized in terms of multiple causes. This makes intervention in this area so difficult. One-factor solutions, in themselves not unimportant, cannot solve problems which are configured as a result of the working of various structures.

Political Ecology in Reconstruction

In the foregoing section I developed an account of the social origins of environmental deterioration in El Zapote which defies approaches that explain such environmental deterioration with the functional dualism model. I rejected the idea of one essential root cause, and analysed structures which interact in complex ways with producers' strategies. In this section I shall discuss how this approach of political ecology may be an alternative to the relativism that originates in post-structuralist approaches. The relativist argument implies that social structures do not exist as real entities. The social origins of environmental deterioration can only be located in discourse.

Political Ecology

Anthropological approaches to human ecology study the relations between social organization, culture and the environment. In Chapter one, it was argued that these older approaches could be revitalized by dispelling their a-historical framework and preoccupation with adaptation, and, instead, integrating the politics of production into the object of study. This approach is commonly referred to as 'political ecology'. Wolf (1972) used the term in a loose way to indicate that the dynamics of ownership are not merely an outcome of local or regional ecological processes, but that it is connected to changes in jural rules of ownership induced by the progress of capitalism. A greater knowledge of specific social and political histories and the study of inter-group relations in wider structural fields, should be combined with our inquiries into multiple ecological contexts. The term 'political ecology' gained the status of a theoretical approach in the 1980s. In the field of development studies the term is generally associated with the work of Blaikie and Brookfield (1987) and denotes an approach that combines the concerns of ecology and political economy.

The political ecology of Blaikie and Brookfield asserts that environmental deterioration can be both a cause and a consequence of social marginalization. To understand the processes at stake one has to locate the decisions of the 'land manager' within a chain of relations: land manager - other groups in society - state - world economy. Blaikie and Brookfield focus on the intersections of strategies and context. In their view, any assessment of sustainable production should include issues of access to land, capital, extension, and state assistance. The state is an important arena of struggle with regard to land use decisions (see also Blaikie 1985). The work of Blaikie and Brookfield has given rise to debate about the link between agrarian change and land degradation. Political ecology does *not* claim that patterns of state policy, multinational investments or market conditions inherently produce inevitable deterioration of the environment (Grossman 1993). But any analysis of the impact of modernization requires an inquiry into both the political economic and environmental contexts, historically as well as in the present. Blaikie and Brookfield further defend a 'plurality of purpose and flexibility in explanation'. They notice that there will always be multiple perceptions of the phenomena, causes and solutions to land degradation (see Chapter four).

Recently, revisions have been proposed to the political ecology of Blaikie and Brookfield. Stonich (1993:26) argues that in their framework political economy is 'exogenous' to land-use decision-making. She proposes that the ways in which local actors mediate the impact of external forces should be integrated into the analysis, that is, how 'human agency and local level initiatives influence the broader political economy'. Peet and Watts (1996:7-8), on the other hand, conclude that despite the theoretical claims of Blaikie and Brookfield to identify complexity and social structural antecedents, they present an ad hoc view of degradation and a theory which is 'an extremely diluted, diffuse, and on occasion voluntarist series of explanations' which lack sensitivity to social struggle and politics inscribed in various social arenas. Peet and Watts propose, furthermore, that Blaikie and Brookfield's point about the plurality of perceptions and definitions of environmental and resource problems should be elaborated by engaging with discursive approaches emerging from post-structuralism.

This book has taken up several of the issues proposed by a refined political ecology. It has collected producer perspectives on environmental degradation to examine how local struggles over natural resources and land use take place. It has located these perspectives in an historical exploration of social institutions, and changes in technology and nature, thereby giving full attention to strategies of producers and workers. In trying to make rigorous and explicit the causal connections between the logic and dynamics of capitalist growth and specific environmental outcomes (Peet and Watts 1996:9) it has used a broad interpretation of social relations of production by including the role of institutions, non-commodity relations and knowledge struggles, expressed in discursive practices.

The conclusions presented in the foregoing section may be helpful for commenting on the central idea in political ecology of a 'chain of explanation' (see Chapter one). The metaphor of the chain suggests a sequence in time, a logical succession and a causation in one direction whereby the different links move in the same way in a coordinated fashion. One broken link would stop the chain moving. This metaphor of causation and its application to the methodology of political ecology, contrasts with the idea of multiple causes and stratified structures that has come out of my analysis.

The idea of multiple structures is not the same as the plurality of perceptions which both Blaikie and Brookfield, and Peet and Watts consider an important area of study. Throughout this book I have recorded how the perception, diagnosis and explanation of

214

environmental deterioration in Honduras is subject to pluralistic interpretations, which may differ as much between different resource users as between those based in 'local' and scientific knowledge (cf. Biot et al. 1995:68). In their description of this pluralism of perceptions, however, Biot et al. explicitly refrain from exploring whether the different propositions are 'true or false' (p.67). It is unclear whether this reflects a relativism which states that truth is only convention and has nothing to do with correspondence between what a proposition says about the social origins of environmental deterioration and a real socio-natural world. Or whether it is only a reflection of the fact that no theory can claim privileged access to reality because theories are always fallible as the world often does not conform to the theories' construction of it (cf. Sayer 1993:322-324). The latter differs from the former as it presupposes that it is possible to test theories as there are practical references in theory (or language, or discourse). Empirical evaluation of this reference is possible. In our daily life our language continuously refers to a material world which makes it possible for us to live in it. As language refers meaningfully to the material world we use it, for example, to produce, to distribute, and to consume food. Peet and Watts (1993), who suggest combining post-structuralism and political ecology, do recognize that post-structural theory is often missing a sense of concrete reality. However, in my view it does not make sense to support post-structural theory while dismissing an important consequence of the central crux of this theory. Below I will argue that discursive analysis and evaluation of different perceptions of the environment are possible and desirable without flirtations with 'post'-theories.

The 'post'-turn

This study has tried to contribute to an environmental social theory which takes seriously analytical problems regarding issues such as diversity, difference, conflicting perceptions, the social construction of nature, and plurality of causation and explanation. In my view the study of these issues is not the exclusive terrain of post-theories. In order to evaluate the contributions of recent environmental theories which call themselves post-theories (post-structuralism, post-modernism, post-marxism; e.g. Blühdorn 1996, Escobar 1996) I pose the question: what is the new element of these theories?[17] This question assumes that the prefix 'post' stands for a decisive rupture in theory (in contrast to, for example, the prefix 'neo'). I think three possible answers can be traced in this literature.

The first meaning of 'post' refers to 'new' events or phenomena in current capitalism, the second to discursive analysis, and the third to the idea that progressive politics can be based on the fully relativist pair epistemology-ontology. In my view, the last one is the only candidate to receive the label 'post'. At the same time, this view is not an acceptable theoretical option for critical social analysis of environmental problems. In order to demonstrate this I shall discuss how these three meanings appear in an article of Escobar which proposes a post-structural political ecology. The work of Escobar is influential among Latin American intellectuals (an Honduran example is Mendoza 1994) and is interesting because it deals not only with environment but also with development issues.[18]

Escobar's use of the 'post' prefix partly refers to the first meaning of 'post' as new phenomena. Escobar discusses the example of rainforest diversity. The modern form of capital is the appropriation of 'traditional' or pre-modern cultural contents by scientific knowledge and the regulation of vast areas of life by expert discourses. Recently a post-modern form of 'ecological' capital, a conservationist one, is emerging in contrast to the modern exploitative form. Through new processes of capitalization, previously uncapitalized aspects of nature and society become internal to capital. This second, 'post' form of capital requires 'the semiotic conquest of local knowledges'.[19] Nature and local people are valued not so much as 'resources' but as reservoirs of value (p.57). In its post-modern form ethnic and peasant communities in the tropical rainforests are 'recognized as owners of their territories (..) to the extent that they accept seeing and treating territory and themselves as reservoirs of capital'. Other post-modern entities are cyborgs (hybrid creatures, composed of organism and machine, which can be assembled with current techniques and biotechnology), the language of biodiversity and sustainable development, and phenomena as post-Fordism.

It can be questioned whether it makes sense to label such changes in the world as post-modern phenomena. Clearly, the observation is important that the 'protection' of rainforest people is crucial for certain new forms of capital and that it depends on guaranteeing the reproduction of their culture. But does this observation mean that the rainforest people are in a post-modern situation while, for example, the people of El Zapote still live in a modern world because capital in El Zapote is merely exploitative towards nature? I think it is ludicrous to think that the rainforest people are more post-modern than, for example, the producers of El Zapote or the high-tech farmers in Holland.[20] Escobar does not really provide arguments to sustain the distinction. The only argument is that the 'post' form of capital relies on the 'the pre-eminence of the sign' and the 'semiotic conquest of nature and life'. It begs the question, however, whether these concepts are more characteristic for post-modernity than for modernity, or whether they have *always* been important. It might be argued that signs and language have always been important to deal socially with nature, and thus are as post-modern as they are modern or even pre-modern. Likewise, recent forms of technological change cannot be viewed as post-modern. Escobar's examples of new technologies - including cyborgs, biodiversity, and biotechnology - are rooted in historical processes of capitalist development and a progress of technoscience. In my view there is no decisive rupture with former forms of technological change. This, of course is not meant to deny change, nor even the possibility of drastic change and discontinuities. Imagining a new (post) world, however, with clearly different social rules and sign systems as an outcome of a new technology or ecological insight would be a rather technologically deterministic view of social evolution. It is possible that 'post' refers not so much to new social relations, discourses, or technologies, but to new avenues to analyse all such processes. This leads us to the second and third meaning of 'post'.

A second possibility is that 'post'-theories stand for discursive analysis - it is in this sense that Watts and Peet (1996) intend to link political ecology to post-structuralism. For Escobar discursive analysis is not only linguistic theory but a social theory 'which includes the analysis of representations as social facts *inseparable* from what is commonly thought of as "material reality" '(p.46, my emphasis). According to Escobar language is not simply a reflection of 'reality' but constitutive of it. Furthermore, he draws attention to a discursive materialism, a fruitful trend that political ecologists are beginning to use (citing Yapa), 'where ideas, matter, discourse, and power are intertwined in ways that virtually defy dissection'.

In my view, however, dissection is possible and a characteristic of critical theory. Social analysis entails the unravelling of elements and crucial relations instead of considering social reality and material reality as one heap of discourse. Social reality is something different from material reality, and both are different from the way reality is represented. Representations may be considered as reality too, in the sense that they exist and can be attributed certain powers. Chapter six described how the continuous labelling of people who burn as 'ignorant' producers helped to establish a dominant narrative which equates burning with bad behaviour. The state promoted this anti-burning view. However, this representation does not make the whole social world dependent on it (cf. Sayer 1993:331). In fact, non-burning behaviour increased as a result of changing social reality (for example coffee became higher valued and protection against fire more required) and changing material reality (in many fields there is simply not enough vegetation to burn). Such an analysis requires dissection and cannot be made with discursive analysis only.

The use of 'post' for discursive analysis suggests that discursive analysis is a totally new approach. However, granting an important power to discourse is not exclusively an activity of post-structural perspectives. For example, Marxist debates have been as much about production and the dynamics of capitalism as about its linkages with ideology and representations (Laclau & Mouffe 1985, Marx & Engels 1972, McLennan 1996). Knowledge construction and discursive practices have been issues dealt with long before post-theories by many other schools of thought, among them the Frankfurt School (see Billig & Simons 1994:4-5; Reijen 1981) and the sociology of knowledge of Berger and Luckmann (1967). Critical studies of images created in environmental discourses can draw upon these approaches without a total immersion in the esoterics of post-theory (see for example Hecht 1995, Jansen 1992).[21] Modern discourse analysis and a critique of scientific rationality is possible and can build on older (modernist) intellectual modes of critical analysis.

A third way of understanding 'post'-approaches in environmental studies is that no shared universal claim about the *true* nature and causes of environmental problems can be made. 'Post' then implies a particular *type* of discursive analysis which analyses different claims, different voices in an exercise of power. Oppression begins with epistemological certitude (Billig & Simons 1994:7) whereby one claim is privileged above another. This meaning of 'post' has two problematic implications. Firstly, it may suggest that claims about environmental change cannot be tested as they do not refer to a real world but exist only within discourse. Such a suggestion can be found in Escobar (1996) where he discusses the reinvention of nature in the sustainable development discourse which declares nature's symbolic death: nature is transformed into the 'environment' and this entity should be managed. The point here is that together with a critique of this discourse, Escobar tends to accept this death of nature, as if the discourse has mediated in a real *total* transformation of materiality: 'Nature as such (unconstructed) has ceased to exist, if indeed it ever existed' (p.60). This contrasts with my approach in this book which views nature as something that has powers which are independent of human society and discourse, but which, when known by producers or scientists (although this knowledge is partial and fallible) may be triggered or curbed in order to carry out agriculture.

A second implication of this third meaning of 'post' is the impossibility to ground policies which privilege, for example, distributional politics. In the post-view the mere existence of multiple perceptions have 'radically democratized' social life and our interpretation of nature. I think that Blühdorn (1996), who proposes post-ecologist politics is consistent in elaborating the implications of this third meaning of 'post'. According to him there is no single nature which was given to humanity and which provides the framework for human life and for moral principles and ethical ideals (see Blühdorn 1996, see for an opposite position McLennan 1996). '(..) there are neither rules for the social distribution of opportunities of life, nor are there criteria by which to criticise a distributive practice (..)' (Blühdorn 1996:6). 'Post-ecologist politics radicalise rational self-determination and self-control at the level of the individual, but consider the development of societal structures as largely evolutionary and beyond rational control' (Blühdorn 1996:6). In this way democratization in the post-project, which entails a rejection of the existence of universal claims, involves a theoretical acceptance of exploitation and oppressive differences by granting different voices equal 'rights'.

Although Escobar pleads similarly for a plural political ecology of knowledge his whole analysis tends to privilege one political view, namely those of social movements in opposition to capital and local culture/community, and not the view of sustainable development propagandists. In doing so he seems to reject the idea that both types of claims are equally true. In fact, he wants to generate a new productive rationality which entails the definition of an ecological utopia (what he calls a 'new narrative of life and culture') based on the work of Leff: production, away from the cultural constructions and pure market mechanisms; rationality, away from the dominant reductionistic and utilitarian views; and management, away from bureaucratized practice and towards a participatory approach. He adds that such a strategy implies 'political organizing to ensure a minimum of *local* control over the entire process' (p.62 my emphasis). I would say that this is indeed a critical but still modernist project that rests on human associations. When it comes to politics the third meaning of 'post' is no longer sustained.

Post-theories are caught in the paradox that discourse analysis, not least the post-modern narrative, destroys certitudes about environmental deterioration, poverty, social differentiation, development and knowledge, yet relies on claims of truth in order to be taken seriously as social theory. At least it has to argue that its theory is superior to rivalling paradigms. In my view this paradox may be solved by recognizing the existence of a link between a real ontology and a relativist epistemology (cf. Bhaskar 1989, Collier 1994). Discourse is not more than a part of reality instead of reality being a part of (or the same as) discourse. The different voices, perceptions, narratives about environmental deterioration and development can never claim to be the absolute true ones, they are essentially fallible. However, this fallibility is not a result of the possibility that just another arbitrary narrative or perception can be constructed, but of the existence of a real ontology which makes it possible that (scientific and common-sense) knowledge claims can be tested, compared in communicative processes, and judged as the best existing practical theory. Hence, knowledge claims are not only an element of power-games - which privilege certain claims over others - but also of continuous experiments and practical tests as to whether they are 'true' or not. The claim that environmental deterioration or sustainable agricultural practices take place is not only a result of processes of social construction, of strong claim-making and culture, but also of experiments and good reason which are related to a (social and material) reality, even though our knowledge of it will always be power-laden and discursively mediated.

Social constructionism in environmental sociology

The recent social constructionism perspectives on the environment (Hannigan 1995, Yearly 1996) is another approach of discursive analysis. Social constructionism has mainly taken an interest in how the rise of environmental consciousness and movements should be comprehended.

> Social constructionism does not uncritically accept the existence of an environmental crisis (..). Instead, it focuses on the social, political and cultural processes by which environmental conditions are defined as being unacceptably risky and therefore actionable (Hannigan 1995:30). (..) what a constructionist analysis has in common is a concern with how people assign meaning to their world (p.33).

One possible criticism is that social constructionism does not take seriously the problem of how socially constructed representations of environmental crisis relate to environmental crisis. Its main focus is on the struggles and negotiations between the different representations. Do biophysical conditions and processes dissolve then entirely in social definitions?

In many social constructionist approaches this does not seem to be the intention of the authors. Short statements can often be found which say that there is real nature outside discourse: 'that environmental risks and problems are socially constructed entities need not undercut legitimate claims about the condition of the environment, thereby denying them an objective reality'. Social constructionism 'does not deny the independent causal powers of nature' (Hannigan 1995:30). Berger and Luckmann, who are among the founding fathers of the social constructionism approach wrote: 'This does not mean, of course, that there are no biologically determined limitations to man's relations with his environment' (1967:47).

Another form of response to this type of criticism is to distinguish between strict and contextual constructionism (recognized as strong and weak constructionism by Watts and Peet 1996, and extreme and moderate by Milton 1996). Strict social constructionism refers to the view that no assertion at all can be made about conditions outside social constructions. Any common reality is denied. It resembles various 'post' arguments. Contextual constructionism, in contrast, argues that claims can be evaluated on the basis of, for example, statistics, polls, or sociological surveys and tests, even if these are in themselves social constructions (Hannigan 1995:34). It considers possible diverse representations of environmental crisis as different interpretations of a common reality. However, this correction of strict constructionism seems not to result in another definition of the research subject.

Hannigan, for example, investigates the process of claim making (divided into three elements: the claims themselves, the claim-makers, and the claim-making process) towards acid rain, biodiversity loss, and biotechnology as environmental problems. The analysis of claims includes the rhetoric of the problem, what involved actors say about the problem, and how it is typified, and no explicit consideration of the 'truth' of the claim itself. Outside this process of claim-making there seems to be no object for environmental sociology. Another example is Yearly (1996) who analyses scientification in the (international) process of defining and formulating problems of global warming, the ozone layer, and the loss of biodiversity. He argues convincingly that values and value-laden assumptions enter into the formulation of environmental problems even before the 'facts' are established. Scientific depictions of environmental problems and political assessment are not completely separable. Yearly describes the universalizing tendencies of the sustainable development discourse which formulates a goal that can hardly be contested, but which at the same time excludes Third World interests and ways of approaching environmental problems. He also deconstructs effectively how the development of environmental economics further colonizes political discourse by suggesting that economics is the crucial vehicle to rationalize optimum choice about the use of the environment. As long as social constructionism focuses on the intricacies of human knowledge about environmental problems it can contribute to social theory. Hannigan and Yearly provide interesting examples.

It becomes a problem when the intention is to fully grasp the causes of environmental deterioration. Hannigan is rather ambivalent about this issue. At the beginning of his book he describes the causes of environmental destruction as one of the two main subjects of environmental sociology, but typically, his book deals almost entirely with the second subject: the emergence of environmental consciousness and movements. He is supportive of the view that 'pollution did not become a social problem until environmental activists were able to convince others to show concern about conditions that had actually existed for some time' (Hannigan 1995:39). In an ensuing comment Hannigan suggests that existing perceptions of environmental problems are the only issue that matters and not processes that people are unaware of. Typically, Hannigan (p.31) considers it an advantage of social constructionism that it is a distinctly sociological paradigm in contrast to 'extra-disciplinary' discourses which have been labelled as 'environmental sociology'. He proposes an agnostic stance towards different views on the environment in order to optimally assess how environmental problems are '*socially* assembled' (p.31). In the concluding chapter this point is taken one step further to argue that it is doubtful whether environmental sociologists are qualified to evaluate the veracity of environmental claims. The role of the environmental sociologist:

should lie not in a quest for some elusive new model which causally links ecosystem breakdown with social variables (..) but in a return to classical sociological questions of perception and power. In this context, biophysical changes in the environment are meaningful only insofar as cultural groups affected by these changes come to acknowledge them through self-redefinition (p.189).

Instead of pushing forward the frontiers of the discipline, which he sees as a goal for environmental sociology (p.31), social analysis is reduced to questions of perception. The problem of how perceptions refer, or do not refer, to causal links between social processes and environmental deterioration is not a central object of study.

This discussion of Hannigan's work supports the view of Milton (1996:51) that the difference between strict and contextual constructionism is rather illusory. In the strict form reality is unknowable, since even its truths are constructed. In the contextual form, reality without cultural interpretation is empty of significance (see also Ingold 1992:39). In both forms of constructionism culture is determining the environment by defining it, by imbuing it with truths or meaning which become indistinguishable. 'Descriptions of culture based on the constructivist model make no reference to anything outside themselves and their process of construction' (Milton 1996:52).

Challenges for a realist political ecology

From my discussion of the contextual social constructionism of Hannigan and the post-structural political ecology of Escobar there follows a different approach as to how to sharpen the conceptual framework of political ecology. This approach intends to go beyond reducing the man-nature relationship to a narrow concept of relations of production such as the functional dualism model. It incorporates the issues of knowledge struggles, but it does not grant them a central position either. This realist perspective on political ecology faces four main challenges. Firstly, how materiality should enter social analysis. Secondly, how the pluralist perceptions of environmental crisis should be approached. Thirdly, how political ecology deals with the gap between social and natural sciences, and fourthly, how, despite plural and conflicting views on the use of nature, progressive politics can be made possible.

A first challenge to a political ecology of agriculture is how materiality (e.g. soils, slopes, plants, water) should be theorized as part of the labour-process.[22] Two main theoretical views of the limits to increase possible production with the given materiality (limits to growth) are essentially social or, on the other hand, natural. A first position is to view environmental deterioration mainly as a societal problem; that is, that environmental deterioration is not an absolute constraint for agricultural production but just a frontier which has not been pushed back sufficiently by technological progress, which is a function of the social organization of production. This position is implicit in, for example, explanations of environmental deterioration which consider producers' ignorance or unequal access to resources as inhibiting the required technological progress. In an opposite position, it is nature which poses absolute limits to successful agriculture and the only thing one can do is adapt to it. To a certain extent this view is implied in, for example, land use capability classifications (see Chapter four) but also in agro-ecology approaches.

Political ecology is about developing a perspective which combines both the natural and the social limits. Therefore, limits are not fixed but produced when human social activity encounters and deploys nature. Natural limits cannot be adequately conceptualized independently of the social processes through which they are approached (Benton 1992). One of the examples of this approach in this book is how I analysed the possibilities of soil conservation in El Zapote. The need to practice soil conservation has increased due to social processes which distribute the land unequally and keep many people dependent on land for subsistence production. Due to socio-economic processes people have low incomes and no resources to invest in soil conservation. In this sense the fallow crisis is a crisis because of the social organization of production. At the same time, however, it is important to note that the fallow crisis hits so hard because of the low production quality of hillsides. Within the current socio-economic situation this is a natural limit. On some soils and slopes soil conservation will probably never be practised since they will never produce enough to pay for the investments because of their soil quality and slope. Although this example may sound obvious and common-sense, I think that the theoretical implications are not commonly accepted. Each concrete situation is an outcome of a specific form of natural/social articulation for which a double set of social/natural constraints for human activity in agriculture can be analysed.

Although the existence of sets of social and natural constraints on farming has been a common assumption of positivist farming systems research (see Chapter three) it has been neglected by more sophisticated social theories. The point here is that these 'constraints' are not just factors which can be observed directly, read off from the observable world, - as in farming systems research - but have their origin in stratified and differentiated social and natural structures. The argument that in order to explain our use of nature we have to analyse specific forms of social/natural articulations and that this is more than listing them as observable events consequently means that more theory is required about different types of articulation. I believe that this is an important area for future research.

An initial step could be to make a distinction between different types or 'intentional structures' of concrete labour-processes (Benton 1989, 1992). Benton distinguishes the eco-regulatory process from transformative processes. In agriculture, nature does not enter the labour process simply as a subject of labour or instruments of labour to be transformed by human activity. The agricultural producer differs from the tailor who uses cloth and transforms it into clothes. In practising agriculture, however, parts of nature can be regarded as the relatively or absolutely non-manipulable *contextual conditions*. For example, the producer in El Zapote does not *transform* nature but only *sustains or regulates* the environmental conditions under which seed or animals grow and produce. Fallow vegetation is removed, maize seeds are soaked, coffee seeds are planted in a prepared seedbed, coffee plants are transplanted into prepared holes, weeds are removed, fallow vegetation is given a chance to grow in order to restore soil fertility and suppress weeds, and so on. One can see these activities as being regulatory instead of

222

transformative. The transformative moments are brought about by naturally-given organic mechanisms, not by the application of human labour.[23] In the process of capitalist accumulation, agriculture is one of the pressure points towards which the ever-growing material requirements of many other social practices are conducted and through which they must flow (Benton 1992).[24] This may entail the use of more technical innovations in agriculture to adapt to ecological constraints, but not the transformation of ecological constraints. Soil conservation, such as the construction of terraces, may counter the erosive powers of gravity and rainfall, but have to be maintained annually in order to reproduce the conditions of agriculture. If not, the same gravity and rainfall will destroy these terraces in the end.

This account of different types of labour process is only acceptable if nature is not taken as something out there, 'given' to the labour process as some unified non-human world. Nature, instead, consists of many different things and elements, biophysical processes, energy, and so on. Some elements are easier to manipulate than others and for some elements the range of choices to be manipulated is much larger. Examples of the latter are for example the possibility of choice among a large gene stock to sow an adapted cultivar; weeds can be reduced through fallow vegetation, burning, hand weeding or herbicide spraying; producers can select from different crops and activities to develop their own type of land use. Other elements are more difficult to manipulate, for example soil erosion or the spreading of some diseases. Nevertheless, to a certain extent some manipulation is still possible. Producers can make terraces or take agronomic measures to reduce disease infestation. Finally, there are elements that can be seen as almost non-manipulable, for example the rainfall pattern, the physiological cycles in plants, or the forces of gravity which cause water to run downhill which may lead to soil erosion. The point of non-manipulability can even be taken one step further. Although new maize or coffee varieties can be created, terraces can be constructed, vegetation patterns can be changed completely, diseases can be manipulated, crop growth can be made dependent on biocides and fertilizers, or new crops can be created by biotechnological manipulation of gene composition, these transformations (this making of new kind of substances and ways of being which go beyond eco-regulation) 'both *presuppose* constancy of structure and causal powers at a *deeper* structural level, and are *limited* by the nature of that deeper-level structure' (Benton 1992:66), for example genes, plant physiological processes and photosynthesis, or gravity.[25]

One important outcome of this way of theorizing nature is that it emphasizes that not only is society differentiated but also nature. This is, in my view, a strong critique of social theories which tend to view nature as a homogeneous category, whose internal elements and structures are not of interest to social analysis. Escobar (1996) can be read as a text which perceives nature as a homogeneous category. It puts emphasis on the socially constructed character of nature. Where Escobar refers to human alteration of nature, e.g. in the creation of cyborgs, he refers primarily to what we might think of as the 'empirical surface' of the world (cf. Benton 1992:66): the body parts that are replaced by machine equivalents, the elements that are remade through technology and which will finally become artificial.[26] However, such alterations do not mean entire social control of all the different layers of nature. These may continue to exist outside history, cyberculture and social construction. Sociologically it will become interesting to study which parts of nature are more socializable and which escape any form of artificializing, and why. The development of such research will only be possible if a totalizing concept of nature is rejected.[27]

A second challenge to a political ecology of agriculture is to develop a clear theoretical position towards environmental knowledge and contrasting perspectives on environmental crises. One can use post-theories positively by keeping in mind that there is an epistemological choice: contrasting perceptions exist on the environmental crisis. For example, burning, pesticide use, and the fallow crisis are evaluated differently within the village. The diverse broader explanations of environmental crisis in Honduras discussed above are other examples of contrasting perspectives. The analysis of burning (Chapter four and six) has shown that these perspectives are rooted in a social and natural context. Different views on burning do not just contest each other or serve the interests of specific social forms of power. They are in a more complex way a reflection of the heterogeneity and differentiations in the natural and the social. This makes it difficult and complex to understand the variety of discourses. The domain of social understanding is quite pluralistic (McLennan 1996:74), but it is not impossible to evaluate the plausibility of specific discourses. In contrast to post-theories I think that it is possible to test explanations and to advance our knowledge, at least in a practical sense, of concrete problems and underlying structures of environmental deterioration and livelihood. Although philosophically there might be no argument to sustain a belief in truth, in daily life (and thus social and natural science) there will be arguments and tests for worse and *better* explanations.[28] This makes human activity possible.

The acknowledgement of the practical truths of knowledge opens possibilities for transcending the opposition of scientific knowledge and local knowledge. Transcending the opposition does not imply a return to a utilitarian use of local knowledge by science nor a denial of problems of power and oppression through (the use of) science. Instead, the possibilities depend on the restoration of the importance of critical argument and good reason. It is our only instrument for judging whether a specific scientific or local/indigenous explanation makes sense, and our only instrument for understanding how a certain explanation may be related to a specific exercise of power.

This view also holds for the knowledge encapsulated in the text of this book. I intended to provide a *best possible* description and theory of why producers in fragile mountain areas of Honduras farm as they do, based upon the 'imaginative and hard work of learning about other's lives' (Gudeman & Rivera 1990:4) and not just on rhetorical text production. My theory will be rejected, converted, contested, but, contrary to a relativist point of view, it continues to have some roots in a world which exists outside my theory, outside this text.

A third challenge is whether political ecology can bridge the gap between social and natural science. It has been argued above that social constructionism and discourse analysis

224

tend to over-socialize environmental problems and to retreat to the classical boundaries of sociology. An agnostic stance or relativist approach of the problems and the causes form no part of political ecology. In contrast to social constructivism, political ecology should be based on a methodology which helps to explain the object of analysis: our relation to nature and the causes of environmental deterioration. This necessarily includes a position on the biophysical processes that are bound up with environmental deterioration. Existing explanations of biophysical processes should not only be located in power games but also tested to see whether they provide insights into (deeper) social or natural structures.[29] This also makes social science less arrogant and more open to the specificities of the work of natural/technological science. Not only do the power games and the cultural categories of natural scientists matter but also the content and methods of their work since these are shaped by the deeper structures of nature.[30] With regard to this aspect, the political ecology of Blaikie and Brookfield is more imaginative than the recent post-structuralist political ecology of Escobar and the Liberation Ecology of Peet and Watts (1996). We need a more open debate with, and critique of, positivist-managerial approaches in agriculture and rural development which, likewise, try to bridge the social-natural science gap, such as systems modelling, linear programming and farming systems research.

A fourth challenge concerns the politics of political ecology. Branches of post-structuralism develop important critiques of dominant development discourse and ecological ideologies of current mainstream environmental managerialism (cf. Escobar 1996, Nederveen Pieterse 1991). Above, it has been indicated that post-structuralism as an attempt to relativize notions of truth, is rather contradictory or ambivalent in sustaining a political project that focuses on equal distribution. Blühdorn (1996:6) sees the post-ecologist politics of nature as strongly individualized and without further attempts to construct all-inclusive ecological utopias or to devise strategies and incentives for social change towards ecological sustainability. The contradiction is that he takes the post-modern condition as a given state (almost natural), and not as a specific outcome of political struggles and negotiations in which intellectual positions themselves may be influenced by capital, science (reason), and hegemonic power (or power, knowledge and institutions if you wish). Escobar (1996), instead, is ambivalent. His post-structuralism at some points seems to reject development planning in environmental and social issues altogether thus supporting the view of Blühdorn that ecological sustainability cannot be devised. However, in other parts of his article he clearly develops a utopia with 'new productive rationalities'. His strategy to reach this utopia is via *local* knowledge and local cultures. Local cultures are able to struggle for a redefinition of the boundaries between nature and culture which will have an effect on the discourses and practices of nature, capital, and modernity.

The granting of a centre place to local knowledge (see also Chapter six) runs parallel to a tendency in progressive intellectual discourse to shift attention away from the idea of a socialist movement that controls state power to a stress on everyday forms of resistance and local knowledge/culture. For the moment I will call this 'the subaltern/civil society shift' (see Brass 1991, Hecht 1995, Peet and Watts 1993, Scott 1985).

The undeniable contribution of the subaltern shift is an increase in our awareness of how ideology (power/knowledge) and the 'dull compulsion of economic relations' (Scott 1985) function in everyday peasant life. It helps us to understand why people in El Zapote do not defy in organized form the persistent everyday forms of exploitation and blatant appropriation of resources. The subaltern/civil society shift, however, has pushed the central question of state power to the back stage. This is, for example, exemplified in the proposal for a 'liberation ecology' by Watts and Peet (1996) in which the question of the state is only marginally dealt with. The arenas for struggle are much more located in discourse, civil society, development NGOs and new social movements; if the state appears then it is to oppose it, not to struggle within and over the state. Likewise, the 'left' in Honduras is less than ever endowed with a coherent project towards the state and progressive opposition (critical to essential features of the existing social system) remains confined to some NGOs and new social movements (human rights, feminist/women's movement, ecological movements). Most of them develop few ideas of how the state should be rebuilt.[31]

A reshaped political ecology confronts the challenge to separate theoretically and politically the subaltern/civil society shift from the neo-liberal project of decentralizing the state and making it more efficient, that is reorienting the state along the requirements of international finance capital and corporate interests. This implies that the apparent paradox that the state may form part of an oppressive hegemonic project, but that control over or substantial influence in legislative, juridical, and executive power seems to be a requisite for any society-wide project which responds to social differentiation and exploitation, appalling life conditions, poverty, ecological crisis, and ethnic and gender conflicts, has to be solved. It is what the villagers of El Zapote express: the negotiations between the interests of coffee producers, who cut the trees and endanger the drinking water sources, and the other villagers, has to go through a certain kind of authority, even though the current authorities are deficient for several reasons. Local control and the state are not necessarily opposed to each other. The state is to a certain extent inseparable from local culture, since it defines laws influencing access and control of resources, gender relations, producer-market relations, and development activities and the concomitant redistribution of resources. The view of the state as external leads to an anti-state tendency in much local knowledge/local culture literature. The state is not replaced with another entity which could negotiate and settle conflicting interest and contradictory perceptions on how to use the environment. Political ecology will have to contribute to solving this problem in order to counteract environmental destruction resulting from individual profit seeking under current political-economic conditions.

Notes

Chapter 1 Environment and Agriculture in Honduras: the Study of Producer Strategies

1 *: The words marked with an * are explained in the Glossary.

2 Gender differences in agricultural work will be discussed shortly.

3 For example Stonich (1993:4) uses data of the World Resources Institute and concludes that by 1992, 24 per cent of the land in Central America exhibited moderate to extreme soil degradation (77 per cent is due to water and wind erosion and 11 per cent is the effect of chemical deterioration). But these global estimates taken from WRI 1992 cite a global GLASOD study as the original source. In this study data were gathered by asking soil scientists to estimate land degradation in the region where they work. But it is totally unclear how these scientists derive their data. Few studies on measuring land degradation and soil erosion have been done in Honduras. What are no more than rough estimates, not based on research, become 'facts' in studies similar to that of Stonich. Stonich also cites USAID data saying that soils are being lost at the rate of 10,000 hectares per year (Stonich 1993:3 citing USAID 1990:3), but the sources of this estimation are rather unclear (see USAID 1990). One can only assume that USAID has taken this data from some other source. A similar practice of uncritical use of rough and disputable estimates is Faber (1993:29). Biot et al. (1995) recognize such practices as a more generalized problem.

4 This formulation is influenced by reading Thompson and Warburton (1985, 1988).

5 These views can be read in the Honduran newspapers and heard on the radio very frequently.

6 Giddens (1996:375) puts this in fashionable sociological terms: '(..) poorer people, by the very nature of their circumstances, are often forced to adopt life-style practices which are ecologically damaging'.

7 El Zapote and names of people are fictitious in order to protect informants.

8 Source: SRN (1996:113-115): I use here the data given for 1992. A recent report of the Central Bank of Honduras suggests that the importance of agriculture for employment is declining (the percentage of labour force dropped from 48 per cent to 37 percent between 1988 and 1995), although it is still twice as high as the employment in the industrial sector (see *Tiempo* 11 March 1997).

9 Source: SRN (1996:104). In 1991-1992 coffee prices were very low and in periods with higher prices the share of coffee is much higher. For example, coffee was the most important export product in 1995 (its export value was 236 per cent higher than in 1992) and it made up 32 per cent of the total export value.

10 Paine and Freter (1996), in fact, see environmental degradation as a single factor explaining the collapse. Other research has argued that the collapse of Maya civilizations in places like Copán cannot be attributed solely to environmental deterioration. An understanding of the collapse needs to include political and economic factors at that time as well (Culbert 1974; Freter 1989). Furthermore, Mayan production systems were not simple slash-and-burn systems of maize cultivation whose continuous application led to soil degradation. The Mayas applied intensive (short fallow) forms of cultivation using a wide variety of intensifying techniques to exploit diverse micro-environments, including multi-cropping and a vast amount of cultivated plant species (Drucker & Fox 1982; Turner & Miksicek 1984; cf. Bennet 1967). This, however, does not invalidate the broader conclusion that the collapse of Maya civilizations prefaced a period of reafforestation in this particular area.

11 The North-East part of Honduras and several islands were never really controlled by the Spanish (Newson 1992).

12 For the district of Gracias a Dios, now a frontier region, the archaeologist George Haselmann (personal communication) confirmed to me the presence of many such relicti of earlier extensive occupations.

13 It was then called Cálcamo; which may have its Nahuatl origin in 'Cacamotic', a Nahuatl word for a plant species with tubers, used for diseases of the bladder (Membreño 1994). The Spaniards often adapted names to existing Spanish words: Cárcamo is a Spanish family name. In later colonial documents the word Cárcamo is used instead of Cálcamo (e.g. Cadiñanos 1893).

14 The original document was a letter from Adelantado don Francisco de Montejo to the king of Spain, written in 1539.

15 Some remnants of Indian buildings of stone can still be observed. George Haselmann (personal communication, Instituto Hondureño de Antropología e Historia, Tegucigalpa) has undertaken excavations and assumes

that the local culture was influenced by the Maya from Copán during the Late Classic period (A.D. 650-950). It is not clear whether these excavations were the buildings which made up the village as mentioned in historical documents.

16 The name continued to exist in land titles however, see Chapter two.

17 Many intellectuals in Honduras dislike the pine felling and burning by peasants and sawmills. The pine tree is the 'national tree', the symbol of Honduran pristine nature and thus of the naturalness of the Honduran nation-state. Johannessen (1959) shows that these pine forests are, to a large extent, man-made environments, an outcome of recurrent burning by pre-colombian people. They used fire to establish grasslands and open forests to create optimal habitats for game (see also Stewart 1956). The Honduran symbol of pristine nature is itself a product of man's use of fire.

18 Important family names stem from ancestors who had migrated to El Zapote from Erandique (Lempira), Cucuyagua (Copan), El Salvador (several names), Guatemala, Corquín (Copan), or Mapulaca (Lempira).

19 Several oral histories refer to the demise of one or two hamlets because of infectious diseases. These were not uncommon in the nineteenth century, e.g. the Gobernación Política of Santa Bárbara warns in a circular of 7 February 1887 that an epidemic of cholera is spreading.

20 In the past people used to live much more dispersed. The better availability of drinking water, and consequently less diseases, is often mentioned as reason why people have moved to the main centres.

21 Honduras incurred an enormous debt in the 1867 and 1869 to construct a pan-oceanic rail road, a project which dramatically failed. Due to the failures and incapacity to pay off the loans it was almost impossible for Honduras to attract money from the international capital market (Molina 1976).

22 The state was not capable of, or willing to implement a policy to develop smallholder agriculture. The elite expected more from an agro-export economy based on foreign investment and immigration ('*gobernar es poblar*').

23 Some evidence shows that coffee may have been more important in the nineteenth century than generally recognized. Guevara-Escudero (1983) describes how the local economy in the municipality of Trinidad, Santa Bárbara was already completely transformed through the emergence of coffee production between 1838 and 1866. Trinidad is at present still an important centre of coffee production. In Colinas, Santa Bárbara it was reported that coffee plantings were spreading in the 1870s and that the number of coffee trees had grown to 303,600 (Source: newspaper *El Progreso*, 15 March 1879). In the *Padrones* (censuses preserved in the Archivo Nacional; see also Rosa 1929) of villages in the districts of Gracias and Santa Bárbara which were drawn up in 1860, coffee is mentioned as an important product. The village of Ocotepeque, for example, was exporting coffee to El Salvador and Guatemala and the *padron* mentions that coffee had been propagated for twelve years. Lemus and Bourgeois (1897) report that 50,000 qq of the 1895-1896 harvest were exported with a total value of $ 750,000. The total exports valued $ 3,125,000 and coffee occupied the second place after gold and silver. Cattle and banana export each valued $ 400,000. This is the only source that mentions such high values for coffee. Export values, however, were mainly measured at the sea ports and coffee may have passed over the borders to Guatemala and El Salvador without being recorded as of Honduran origin.

24 The value of banana export was still ten times higher than that of coffee (respectively about 71 million and 7 million Lempira). During the 1950s exports of coffee and timber competed for this second position.

25 Meza Cálix (1916) mentions that Santa Bárbara cattle were exported to El Salvador and Guatemala at the beginning of this century; *pimienta* (probably all spice pepper) was exported to Nicaragua, and coffee, zarzaparilla, hides and panama hats to Europe and the United States.

26 Ponce (1986) shows how formal credit mainly went to the cattle sector during the 1970s.

27 Many villagers of El Zapote recall very concrete stories which prove that they used to eat a lot more meat (including beef) in the past.

28 1922 is an approximation. The famine in 1954 is still a point of reference for many people. There was little trade of food grains (partly because of limited purchasing capacity) and one survived on bananas and roots from undomesticated species.

29 See *Actas Municipales*', several volumes.

30 For descriptions of the developmentalist state and its involvement in agriculture see: Arriaga (1986), Posas (1979), Posas & Del-Cid (1981), Villanueva (1986), White (1978), and World Bank (1983).

31 It was foreseen that COHDEFOR would generate revenues and contribute to the state budget, but instead its projects depended on international funding. At the end of the 1980s it had lost most of its credibility, but the appointment of a former INA director, Rigoberto Sandoval Corea, by the Reina administration (1994-1997),

228

has again made it attractive for international funding, whereby forest conservation is given more priority. Efforts, however, to really control illegal exploitation and deforestation have lead to several killings of COHDEFOR officials (source: diverse Honduran newspapers 1992-1997).

32 See Posas (1979), Ruben (1989), Thorpe (1995b), and World Bank (1983); see also Posas (1996), Ruben and Fúnez (1993), Richards (1988), and Salgado (1991) on INA and cooperativism; Brockett (1987, 1988), Del-Cid (1977), IHDER (1980), Peek (1984), Ruhl (1984, 1985), Sieder (1995) and Stringer (1989) on land reform; Hernández (1991) and Walker et al. (1993) on COHDEFOR; SECPLAN (1989b) on PRODESBA.

33 The LMDSA itself does not provide any substantial contribution with regard to the management of natural resources. The Environmental Law passed in 1993 (Honduras 1995) is fragmentary and does not provide guidance for developing a sustainable agriculture.

34 For example see: Brockett (1988), Kay (1995), Llambí (1991), Long and Roberts (1994), and Redclift (1989).

35 Ecological modernization theory is one approach of environmental sociology which places the industrial character of Western society at the core of its explanation (cf. Mol 1995, Spaargaren and Mol 1992). It takes up the issue of globalization but does this from a core perspective: globalization spreads from the modern institutions of the industrialized societies. The theory of ecological modernization tends to deny the interwovenness of the emergence of industrialism and the historical plundering of resources in frontier areas and the former colonies in the process of capitalist development (see e.g. Sauer 1956, Wolf 1982).

36 The concept of culture has very different interpretations in anthropology (see Milton 1996). Milton observes a shift from a broad definition of culture, encompassing actions, ideas, and material objects of specific peoples, to a small definition. The latter refers to what people know, think and feel. Agri-culture as a term seems to be part of the broader definition. The smaller definition makes it possible to investigate people's actions in doing agriculture as a different object to how people think about agriculture and environment.

37 See Goldblatt (1996:16-17) for this description of capitalism.

38 Important texts are: Bernstein (1979, 1988), Chayanov (1987), de Janvry (1981), Friedmann (1980), Gibbon & Neocosmos (1985), Kearny (1996), Long et al. (1986), Mann & Dickinson (1978), Netting (1993), and, for Honduras, Torres (1985).

39 Redclift (1987) shows that this is also the case for social theory in general.

40 The fear for non-human causality and thus for environmental or biological determinism is continuously fuelled by ill-considered statements from natural scientists. For example, Weischet and Caviedes (1993) argued recently that the North-South socio-economic disparity could be better explained by the ecological disadvantage of many tropical regions than by any socio-economic theory about colonialism and history of societies. Their conclusion, however, was based on a limited research focus: they only investigated the environmental conditions in different parts of the world without undertaking any serious study of socio-economic issues.

41 In this context, the statement of Ellen (1996:18) is interesting: 'Every social anthropologist who asserts that there is no need to take heed of biological explanation is re-asserting the nature-culture opposition, even if the terms are not used'.

42 Critiques of the fourth view, in general, fail to distinguish it from one of the other three views.

43 For this summary, I rely on reviews of ecological anthropology by Barlett (1980), Bennett (1976), Ellen (1982), Milton (1996), Orlove (1980), and Smith & Reeves (1989).

44 Boserup (1965) provides a similar view from development economics.

45 This concept turns out to be very broad. Giddens (1984:233-5) argues that, in its expanded interpretation, adaptation is so wide and vague that it is useless as a means of explaining anything at all. It becomes a diffuse notion which includes all possible sources of influence upon social organization and transformation. Giddens seems to be right in his observation that an expanded concept of adaptation cannot be considered as a general mechanism of social change. However, Giddens' idea of 'reflexive monitoring of action' by knowledgeable and capable actors is similar to, or comes very close to what Bennett calls 'anticipation' (see also Giddens 1996). Both relate change to purposive or intentional human action in cognitive forms of learning.

46 See the review of farming system research literature by Brouwer and Jansen (1989, 1990); see also Chapter three.

47 Structures can be seen as emergent structures, as the multiple ways in which things are tied together, depending on specific locations, or as interlocking projects and practices (cf. Long 1992). This concept seems to refer mainly to structures as empirical outcomes of actions —as patterns of events— in contrast to structures

as underlying relations as in critical realism. I have no space here to elaborate on the foundations of this latter view (see Bhaskar 1989, Collier 1994, Sayer 1992).

48 Long and van der Ploeg (1994), for example, substantiate their critique of structuralism on the grounds that different farm styles develop under *similar* structural conditions, e.g. factor compositions and market opportunities (see also Bolhuis & van der Ploeg 1985). Although the point that diversity exists within one political-economic context underlines their general argument it limits, in my view, a good actor-oriented understanding of structures. It shows that a room for manoeuvre of individuals exists, but it does not explain how structures result from reproduced social practices. This book presents cases of differences between producers, which transcend a longer period, and which have been analysed by structuralist approaches (for example, in terms of differential access to land and quality of land). These structuralist approaches have focused on simple characterizations of phenomena, such as farm size, and have often neglected strategies, negotiations, and struggles, which reproduce structural contradictions in social relations. It would be a challenge to explain such structures in actor-oriented terms, instead of ignoring such unequal positions by simply referring to diversity under similar structural conditions.

49 Operating in structures, especially in social structures, means (in general) reproducing and transforming them. Social structures are by any means fixed entities (see Bhaskar 1979).

50 'Political Ecology' is becoming an important branch of environmental social science, see also: Amanor (1994), Buttel and Sunderlin (1988), Durham (1995), Escobar (1996), Greenberg & Park (1994), Grossman (1993), Harvey (1993), Hayward (1994), Hecht (1985, 1995), Martinez-Alier (1995b), Munshi (1990), Peet and Watts (1996), and Wolf (1972). In Chapter seven I will indicate how several conclusions of this study may contribute to a further development of political ecology.

51 The national censuses are based on producer information. The *manzanas* they report are transformed into hectares through multiplying by a factor of 0.7. The data in the censuses which refer to area are therefore systematically too low by a factor of 1.1944 (almost 20 per cent). Immigrants from other parts of Honduras affirmed that 'the *vara* is thirty-six *pulgadas* by law' and that in their district of origin the *manzana* has the same area. It is thus possible that the 20 per cent difference displayed in the census not only matters for El Zapote, but also for other parts of Honduras.

52 Many of these issues could not have been discussed in the same way in their homes. Even with my best friends I spoke differently in the field than the house. Apparently there are two domains. The domain of the house and the village is more of a place where they rest, joke, or argue with their neighbours or authorities. The domain of the field is where they talk more about plants, soils, weeding, sowing, and so on, and where these elements are related to the particular field and its environmental characteristics, as well as to its social history. The progression in conversations was different in both locales.

53 In my view, every formulation is context-laden; a neutral formulation is a fiction. Questionnaires should preferably be completed by the person who develops the survey and does the analysis.

54 More information about gender relations in El Zapote can be found in Roquas (1994 and 1995).

55 An exception is picking coffee. But also here women's participation is very low. The season of 1996/97 was an exception due to high wages for coffee picking (producer prices for coffee were extremely high) and extraordinarily low petate prices. In other years women prefer to do household work or to make petates instead of coffee picking.

56 My main interest is in agricultural activities that define how the land is used and less in processing and storage at home, in which women take a larger share of the work. Recent efforts to make women's work visible and to emphasize their contribution to agriculture (e.g. SECPLAN 1994) do not distinguish between different labour activities and, in my view, tend to distort our view of gender differences in Honduran agriculture instead of clarifying them.

Chapter 2 Fencing in Value: Land and Social Institutions

1 The Land Law of 1835, the decrees of 17-2-1846 and 15-5-1888, and the Agrarian Law of 1898 (art. 3-11) contained regulations for ejidos (Vallejo 1911). The nature of the Honduran ejido should not be confused with the much better documented Mexican ejido, which principal characteristics are a product of a revolutionary process in the beginning of this century (see for example Nugent 1993). Municipalities lost control over their ejidos with the Land Reform Law of 1974 which returned control over this land to the state (Honduras 1975).

2 The H and I titles (see Figure 2.1) have initially been obtained by non-villagers. These titles crossed municipality borders and caused conflicts with neighbouring municipalities which had to be solved by higher

level authorities. The actas municipales mention conflicts in 1921, 1925, 1940, 1947, 1950, 1952, and 1953. A recurring argument in such conflicts is that the original measurements (sometimes from decades earlier) were not carried out according to the law. Title J is in the hands of a single person who had offered it for sale to the municipality a few years ago, but without result. The title G (121 ha 34 a) was bought for 270 pesos in 1918 by a rich inhabitant of El Zapote, when heirs of the original applicants (first application in 1899) could not pay for it. The land of titles H, I, and G are used by people from the hamlets and title G by a inhabitant of a neighbouring village. As I mainly studied the inhabitants of the main village of El Zapote I do not include the histories of these titles in my descriptions.

3   After protests INA argued that the title had never been paid and that it was thus national land falling under the land titling regime. A small note of 12 October 1865, indicates that 4.40 pesos had yet to be paid. This note was probably a proof that this sum had been paid (as 31 lbs. in tobacco and 2.30 pesos cash). The fact that the title was signed and registered (again registered in 1903) indicates that the state saw it as a legal title (which had been paid). Paying the state in goods, such as tobacco, was not uncommon in the nineteenth century.

4   In the course of the 1970s the main title of the Yoreños had been wheedled out of a villager who saved it by the owners of a sawmill. This opened up the way for this sawmill to cut many pine trees in this area. They had permission of COHDEFOR and the people from the hamlet Yoro were not successful in protesting because they could not show their legal ownership of the land. After the sawmill had left they regained the document.

5   Some documents mention two hamlets, Cablotal and El Ladino. Presumably, the applicants came from both hamlets which lied near each other. Hamlets acted with a certain autonomy and had a local level authority (*Alcalde auxiliar*) who was also a member of the municipality council.

6   Source: the data in this section is taken from the *actas municipales*.

7   During subsequent disputes he promised to other villagers that his lease would be temporary.

8   The regulations were enacted on 22 December 1950. In 1951 villagers contributed 1115 Lempira to pay the legal representative in Tegucigalpa, the work of the land surveyor and further bureaucratic costs. The ejido title was never issued, however. It was not uncommon that activities stopped or changed orientation after a replacement of authorities (which happened every year before 1954). After the division the threat, that the village could not use Juniapal at all, disappeared.

9   Several people confirm that a title of Juniapal existed in the municipality in the past, and they can remember in detail when and where they had seen the original title. Eduardo Ramírez confirmed to me this story in general terms, not mentioning his own involvement. Some informants say that a secretary of the municipality burnt the title somewhere in the 1950s. Others confirm to have been present when money was transferred for the title. Several informants said that Eduardo burnt the title by order of Alfredo Luna in exchange for money. The Archivo Nacional de Honduras preserves the original measurement and title.

10   In 1955 it was decided to divide a part of Cárcamo-Juniapal between the inhabitants of El Zapote. Money was first borrowed from Agapito Delgado, a well-to-do villager who disputed regulations with respect to cattle grazing made by the municipality about the use of El Salto. When not enough money could be collected thirty-three manzanas of Cárcamo land were sold to Alfredo Luna (this sale was cancelled afterwards by higher authorities who ordered that the money should be collected by contributions from villagers). This took place in the same year that the municipality disputed claims of land by Alfredo.

11   'Alfredo was *vivo*' and '*el pueblo dormido*' (the villagers were sleeping). *Vivo* and *avivar* have important meanings in El Zapote: clever use of violence, being active, knowing how to develop and manipulate connections, having ambitions, not being timid, and having 'balls' (*huevos*). It could be considered as a cultural expression of material power. Only the combination, land/capital **and** being *vivo*, is effective.

12   Economic dependency and related patronage ties explain the absence of massive opposition. 'You could waken him in the middle of the night to receive some medicines. (..) He was a man of prosperity; we saw him as our father, all we asked he gave us, he did not refuse'. Other people stress the 'visionary' performance of Alfredo. 'After the mayor had divided the land in the 1950s many people sold their parcels to Alfredo, and he bought everything, but cheaply. I remember that my family sold eight *manzanas* for 100 L, which they spent on drinking. For booze they sold the land; they went to drink, together with Alfredo in his shop'. This view includes a appreciation for the crafty Alfredo who managed to take over recognized ownership of land from other people.

13   Elections of the municipality council took place yearly. Not all changes were democratic: central state rulers sometimes appointed the municipality. A further restriction was the prerequisite that the candidates could read and write. Nevertheless, this did not lead to a specific separate class of village rulers. Many families provided municipality authorities and no social distance between authorities and villagers existed.

231

14 See Spalding (1980) for a similar argument made for Southern Peru.

15 This conclusion does not exclude the possibility that the large estate in many cases took control over land of better quality. However, the peasant cash crop *par excellence* in Honduras is coffee and, until recently, land was no decisive constraint for its expansion.

16 The idea of 'Family Plots' was already propagated by earlier administrations and, according to Argueta (1975), was derived from the idea of the family farm or homestead prevalent in the United States.

17 El Zapote had 1228 inhabitants in 1926; in the population census of 1988 (DGECH 1990) one of each five inhabitants was economically active in agriculture (from both sexes, older than ten years). If we assume that this was not substantially different in 1926 one could estimate that about 245 people were active in agriculture. A part of these were dependent workers (children). The percentage of producers can be estimated at 15 per cent. The number of producers can thus be estimated to be 184. In the 1920s and 1930s at least 290 concessions were issued. It may be concluded that most producers have probably received at least one concession.

18 The proportion of concessions of transferred land rose from 12 per cent in the period 1931-1940 to 39 per cent in 1941-1950. The real percentages may be higher because the information is presumably not always presented in the actas.

19 Nevertheless, in a few cases, conflicts surfaced between concession holders and the municipality which claimed its right to take back parts of this ejidal land to construct roads or to extract construction wood for its public works. Such cases of falling back on legal interpretations of concessions were incidental, however.

20 For 918 of the 983 parcels which were measured in the 1980s data are available about the type of documents with which producers supported their claim to the land. Thirty-five per cent of the plots were occupied without any document. Most of this land has probably never been part of a concession because earlier concession holders would have transferred it with a deed of purchase (*documento privado*).

21 Together with three producers I made a map of the Zona with producer estimations of the different plot sizes in 1993. Sixty-eight producers (from sixty-one households; about 15 per cent of the households active in agriculture) use the Zona. Of these only 23.5 per cent cultivate coffee, and mostly they only have small coffee plots; of all producers in the village 46 per cent cultivates coffee. This indicates a tendency that mainly resource-poor producers use the Zona for maize cultivation.

22 The mean age of Zone users is 40.8.

23 Rent in the 1990s is about four times a day-wage of a day-labourer, that is about 7-8 US$ per manzana for one maize season. Sharecropping does not exist, apart from an occasional exception.

24 Many people were asked whether this was the case, but almost all denied it, irrespective of their party affiliation. Only one person, a well-known political activist, blamed party-politics for unequal land distribution in the past.

25 Stokes' interpretation is only based on official documents and laws and not on collected data in field work. His view is part of a liberal political project of modernization (see Stokes 1947 and 1966).

26 This section and the section on land titling are based on research with Esther Roquas, published in Jansen & Roquas (1998).

27 Coles (1988) defines customary rights in Honduras as nearly unchanging rules which are transmitted from generation to generation, and which are socially recognized by local people. Wachter (1992) considers informal rights to be existing norms and rules in society which can boast about a clear social recognition. Both Coles (1988) and Wachter (1992) think that the system of customary rights over land worked out well; people respected each other's property and hardly any conflicts emerged. Their conclusion is that customary rights provide security for property holders, and that the system is effective, cheap and socially accepted (e.g. Melmed-Sanjak, 1993). Jansen and Roquas (1998) discuss these views and argue that they draw a strict opposition between 'customary' and 'formal' rights. These studies do not succeed in specifying the exact nature of different types of regulation and they do not result in a profound understanding of the characteristics of these so-called 'customary' rights, for example their origins and working, the way they change, and the concrete problems or sense of security they create for property holders. The 'informal' in Honduras has elements of rules that are unaltered former state laws, local adaptations and transformations of former laws mingled with local norms. A dichotomy between state law and 'customary' or 'informal' law cannot be maintained for Honduras. This also questions the applicability of the concept of 'legal pluralism' for Central America as most local norms have their foundations in laws (cf. Benda-Beckmann 1995).

232

28 Roquas (1995) describes in greater detail how gender notions are used as a resource in struggles for land between men and women within families and among heirs. For example, the idea that a married daughter has no need to receive land through inheritance because to work the land is not a woman's task.

29 The role of municipality officials has diminished lately. Data from the municipal archives show that in the past conflicts concerning land concessions, boundaries, right of way, fences, or access to water sources, were mediated by the council, who listened to the parties and possibly some witnesses before presenting a solution. Nowadays, the council no longer concerns itself with such conflicts because these have to be solved officially by the 'peace judge' (*juez de paz*) or, in the case of a more violent crime, by the court in the district capital. The institution of the 'peace judge' is heavily politicized according to villagers. The peace judge is a local person whose appointment is controlled by the political party in power and thus has to leave when another party wins the elections. The job does not require any professional skills except some level of literacy.

30 For instance, the *Ley de Policía* of 1906 (art.361, see Honduras 1961) stipulated that one should build a fence of at least seven *cuartas* (a spread hand) height. Only with such a fence could one demand an indemnification if cattle had entered a field and damaged a crop.

31 The Gini-coefficient for land distribution in El Zapote is 0.67 for 1952 (calculated from DGECH 1954). Land distribution in El Zapote is a little bit less unequal than in the Santa Bárbara district as a whole. The pattern of distribution for Santa Bárbara has not changed very much between 1974 and 1993 (DGECH 1978 and SECPLAN 1994). Regrettably, the census of 1993 has not published the land distribution at municipal level, but I assume that the similarity of Santa Bárbara's distributions of 1974 and 1993 may well be the same in El Zapote.

32 The children are from two official spouses and several *pegados* ('sticked on' other women). He is not the only merchant and *terrateniente* in the region with such a large amount of children.

33 Between 1952 and 1963 at least 906 people received credit from Alfredo (source: accounting books of Alfredo Luna). A part of these 906 have been counted a couple of times, when earlier loans had been repaid and a new account was made.

34 Alfredo says: 'I gave it to him cheaply, for 36.000 L (18.000 US$), everything, more than 400 hectares land, thirty-three milk cows and all fenced, but he did not know how to use it. Now Rafael has a part of it. And he has a good *hacienda*'.

35 The land was measured before the land reform law was decreed (794 hectares) and with copies of the measurement Alfredo Luna wanted to obtain a official title in 1961 (source: copy of a notarial act).

36 Most people use the term 'invade' for this practice, the counter-term used by peasant organizations is 'to recuperate' land; however, participants in El Zapote use the term '*invasión*', and only one person, who was trained by a peasant organization, was aware that '*recuperación*' 'should' instead be used. With this in mind the term 'to occupy' acknowledges both the political character of the terms used as well as the fact that the use of the political correct term is not common in El Zapote.

37 The group consisted of people from the village of El Zapote and of people from one hamlet. The latter formed the core group and the initiators of the plan. Juan Martínez was from the hamlet.

38 Villagers generally consider that he sold the land because of his lifestyle, including spending a lot of money on women.

39 Several resource-poor people argued that many of the occupants already had enough land: 'it were not the landless who invaded the land. All people with large amounts of land. That Hugo Portillo has deprived his own family of land'.

40 The national electricity company took a part of this land for the construction of an electric power station in the beginning of the 1980s. It was considered to be national land because nobody could show an official title. If Rafael obtains the legal title he is entitled to compensation for the land taken by the company. Rafael Luna commissioned to remeasure the land at the end of the 1980s. His title also includes land possessed by smallholders. Part of the hamlet Robledal protested and Rafael assured them in a meeting he would not expel the people from their land and houses, although the land was his property. However, he could not take responsibility for what his heirs would do in the future with the property. During the meeting the point was raised that Rafael might have a title but that 'maybe he could end up somewhere else' (threat of murder).

41 A central idea of USAID was that PTT could lead to a system of land taxes; later the idea of land taxes was raised again with the formulation of structural adjustment policies, but the Honduran government gave way to pressure from large landowners and peasant organizations and disregarded recommendations of foreign

consultants to develop a land tax system (source: interviews with two former directors of PTT, one former staff member of USAID, and staff of SRN).

42 This conclusion is valid for El Zapote too: few producers receive credit, and titles are not an important collateral for formal credits. Most titled land has a low value, for example, hill side land for maize values about 60-90 US$ per hectare in 1992. In an interview the regional director of BANADESA (rural development bank) underlined the importance of the value of the improvements (which do not appear on the original title). Furthermore, properties like houses are far more important as a collateral than land. The few coffee producers with loans at the bank have mortgaged their house (many coffee producers tend to invest profits first in their house) or their coffee production.

43 Coles (1988) investigates the effects of titling on land transactions. Coles is probably the best informed researcher about producer perspectives, and, although his approach starts like the other impact studies, he comes closer to our approach by reflecting on the rejection of PTT by landholders. He concludes that producers do not have information about laws, that the costs for procedures are too high, and that INA often does not approve sales of titled land, which drives titles holders to despair. Prices which sellers can ask for parcels with a PTT title are lower than for un-titled land, due to the obstacles posed by INA.

44 The concept of the agricultural family unit already appeared in earlier agrarian laws (e.g. 1924 and 1934, see Honduras 1943). The Land Reform law (Honduras 1975) establishes a minimum farm size. It was thought that this would eliminate minifundios and subsequently eradicate poverty.

45 A high INA official denied to us that the brigade did this, saying that ten parcels within the title had been the maximum and that one person could receive more than one title. INA personnel involved in implementing the project, however, confirmed the practice experienced by the landholders. One reason could have been that INA personnel had to process a targeted amount of titles within a specified period. In the 1990s implementation altered and more parcels could be put into one title, in order to reach the minimum limit of titling. The minimum of five hectares was also lowered to one with the enactment of the LMDSA.

46 A contrasting development was that some men with too many parcels were forced to title land in the name of their wife. Several women considered these parcels as theirs afterwards and took control decisions (e.g. renting, (not) selling, transfer to children) which were discordant with the view of the original holder.

47 Equal to 19.5 per cent of the total original amount to be paid; calculated from INA, 'PTT: Listado de Saldos Por Municipio (1994)'. People considered the payment as unreasonable because the land was already their property. This view was in fact backed up by the Callejas government of the Nationalist Party (1990-1993); Callejas, being a candidate for president criticized the unwarranted and illegal payments imposed by the Liberal government on the poor during his electoral visit to El Zapote.

Notwithstanding the low appreciation of PTT, the rate of debt payment may rise in the future, because the real value is 80 per cent lower due to inflation (a decline from 30 US$ per hectare to 6 US$ between 1984 and 1995). This will make it easier for villagers to accept payment. Since 1994, real land prices also tend to rise in El Zapote.

48 INA distributed a document which stated that all producers with a debt regarding their land title had to visit the nearest INA office within fifteen days and to pay the title, otherwise INA would proceed legally to valorize the improvements and to recover the land. The document was stamped and signed by the director of INA. The director of PTT in 1997 told us that land had never been confiscated.

49 Coffee producers received this subsidy for each bag of coffee. In 1994 however, this system was already replaced by other intervention systems in coffee. Without knowing what was precisely going on in coffee, INA personnel used the subsidy issue to convince the producer to pay.

50 From the viewpoint of popular ideology, PTT is somewhat similar to some cases of state action which triggered peasant resistance to the ejido in Mexico as analysed by Nugent (1993:114): that it 'signifies and materializes an illegitimate intervention of state power into the community'. How could the state give property titles to land which the producers already had? Villagers' conduct of not paying is not only a rejection of the particular policy but may also be understood as a repudiation of the state's attempt to circumscribe the political terrain organizing and invading a material terrain, namely their land and the way it is worked (Nugent 1993:135, cf. Brouwer 1995).

51 It might even be questioned whether such a complexity has ever existed in Honduras on such a scale that it really defined crucial relations.

52 This also becomes clear when considering contestation of inequality. Each plot has a different social history. The history of Juniapal and the aborted land reform explains why the land occupation took place on land of Alfredo Luna while land of other large estates remained undisputed.

53 The category of medium-size producers is not a result of a recent process of re-peasantization which Llambí (1991) observes in Latin America, but instead emerged in a context of population growth and social differentiation of a peasantry.

54 Kay (1995:20) suggests that this observation may be valid for many other regions in Latin America.

55 How one interprets the Gini-coefficient is important here. This indicator of the inequality of distribution of land hardly changed between 1952 and 1974 (respectively 0.67 and 0.70; the difference can be ignored in the context of possible census errors). In the same period the mean farm size in El Zapote declined from 13.6 ha to 8.2 ha (sources DGECH (1954 & 1978); mean farm size in 1993 was 4.0 ha (SECPLAN 1994). The expansion of the latifundio and the multiplication of the minifundio (at cost of middle-size farms) cannot explain the constant Gini-coefficient which points to the fact that farms in all farm size classes have been split up. Del-Cid (1977:80-1) tries to explain this reduction in farm size in terms of the economic rationality of the latifundio (with the intention to perpetuate the latifundio-minifundio model) arguing that, for example, the large banana companies have rationalized their production in the 1950s and concentrated their production on the most productive land while marginal lands were passed on to the peasantry. This explanation of rationalization and selective shrinkage does not hold for large estates in El Zapote. The Luna brothers have divided the property of their father Alfredo among themselves. All type of farms were under the influence of the increasing land pressure.

56 See Del-Cid (1977) for a profound analysis of details in the law which provided opportunities for large landowners to manoeuvre and to contest the land reform process.

57 Many villagers do not talk about having little land but express the problem mostly in terms of *'ya no hay guamiles'* (there is no forest fallow any more). Richer peasants and large estate holders are not criticized for their appropriation of the land but for the fact that they have sown the land with pastures (*enzacataron todo*). The concept of land scarcity is in this representation not a spatial concept but an ecological concept that questions the types of vegetation on the land and forms of land use.

58 An example is the land in the mountains of El Zapote which had a much lower value than land near the village up until seventeen years ago. A disease (coffee rust) devastated coffee at lower altitude. New groves were started in the mountains. Those who had land there had it acquired at low or no monetary costs in times when the land was valued to be of low importance. Land prices at lower altitudes used to be much higher. These relative prices were put upside down after coffee was replaced from lower to higher latitudes.

Chapter 3 Land Use Dynamics: Heterogeneity and Diversity

1 Several sections of this chapter use material published earlier in Jansen (1996) and Jansen (1997).

2 Brass' (1995) critique of research on diversity tends to conflate a research interest in diversity with post-modernism. For Brass such research contains a hidden conservatism because it celebrates traditional culture by emphasizing it as a room-for-manoeuvre of the oppressed. By conflating research on diversity with post-modernism Brass accepts the unjustified annexation of this terrain by post-modernists. An interest in the origins or diversity is, however, not necessarily connected with post-modernism. From a neo-marxist perspective, for example, Byres (1986) acknowledges the existence of many different paths of agrarian transition. His work could be taken as an illustration of research that 'enhanced enormously our sensitivity to historically grounded variations in national political economies' (Booth 1994:8). More important than denouncing any research interest in diversity is the question as to what extent one should describe empirical diversity and how these descriptions could be used for developing theories of structural diversity and causing mechanisms. In fact, Brass may have this in mind when he accuses his 'post-modern' opponents (such as Booth 1994) of retaining a basic state-peasant dichotomy and the concept of a pan-historical, stereotypical peasant proprietor.

3 Although these authors share this particular view, they do not develop the same critique of capitalism and modernization. This is not the place, however, to analyse how these views are quite different with respect to other aspects.

4 Data on soils in El Zapote appear in unpublished research by Zamora (1994); other relevant sources are Almendarez (1986), Castellanos and Simmons (1984), Chávez et al. (1986), FHIA (1989), Kozuch et al. (1990), and Plath (1967).

5 Geographical and temporal distribution of crops is not only a response to environmental heterogeneity but also relevant to spread labour input. However, to refer solely to the labour issue would be reductionist, as it is

concomitantly an adaptation to biophysical factors. The type of soil and its water–holding capacity determine the optimal period for sowing, not the labour availability.

6 The data in Stonich's own work do not support her conclusion. The change mentioned does not take place in the village where she carried out research (Stonich 1993); Stonich reports that it was in the highlands where area in pasture rose and food-crop production fell, which challenges the earlier depiction of expanding cattle in the valleys and displaced peasants on the hillsides.

7 Stonich uses census data in a similar way to identify changes in land use patterns. Prudence is called for, however. The smaller differences shown in this figure are not independent from variation caused by errors in the censuses. Stonich and Howard use census data rather uncritically to compare areas in production. The total area in production in El Zapote is supposed to be less in 1992 than in foregoing years. In the context of environmental debates it is tempting to conclude that a part of the land is no longer suitable for production due to environmental degradation. In this case, however, errors and uncertainties of the censuses themselves may have produced the decline. I estimated the number of not-interviewed producers by calculating the population in El Zapote from data of population censuses between 1940 and 1988. Subsequently, the percentage of producers was estimated at 15 per cent on the basis of the author's survey data and the produced list with households in the village. This allowed for an estimation of the percentage of not-interviewed producers: 29 per cent in 1952, 20 per cent in 1965, 35 per cent in 1974 (the largest share) and 13 per cent in 1992. Although the 1992 census scored better in the number of producers interviewed it has the largest amount of under-enumerated area. For example, the census reports 375 hectares with coffee in El Zapote in 1992, while the National Coffee Census of 1979 already reported 392 hectares in 1979 and 575 hectares with coffee (of which 116 hectares young, not yet producing, plantings) in 1992 (IHCAFE 1993). The land titling programme which included only a part of the village area already covered 4113 hectares of measured agricultural plots. As only a part of the village was ejidal or national land and thus measured the total agricultural land in the village must be much higher. Flaws in the census are thus not the same in the different years. It is possible that in one census some large areas with a few producers are left out, while in another census many small producers with little land. This severely constrains the interpretation of census data. Only very large shifts may indicate tendencies.

8 In 1952, 31 per cent of the producers had cattle, but by 1992 this had fallen to 11 per cent (the absolute number of producers with cattle remained constant). This is only the last phase of a longer period of concentration of cattle in the hands of fewer people. Of the sixty-one households in 1890 thirty-four people had legalized branding irons (of which seven were women). Hence, about half of the households had a branding iron (data about branding irons in Honduras (n.d.); according to Vallejo (1888) 430 people lived in El Zapote in 61 houses). Probably more producers had livestock because many people kept livestock without having their own branding iron. Today only 40 per cent of the producers has livestock (calculated from SECPLAN (1994); in 1974 this was 45 per cent; calculated from DGECH 1978).

The concentration of cattle ownership probably received a push during the second half of the 1940s, when the so-called 'free lands' came under control of individual people.

9 Kaimowitz (1996b) refutes the Cattle Republic thesis, but does not analyse the precise role of pack animals.

10 Factors that have contributed to this change are the feeling that theft of maize in the field has increased and the new storage techniques in silos and drums in the house.

11 Cross tabulation of the survey data clearly shows the association between pack animals and coffee production.

| | | Producers with producing coffee fields | | |
		no	yes	totals
Producers with pack animals	no	26	10	36 (43.9%)
	yes	9	37	46 (56.1%)
		35 (42.7%)	47 (57.3%)	82 (100%)

Source: producer survey. The association is statistically significant.

12 The counter-tendencies did not halt the general rise in demand. Before 1965, local traders used pack animals to carry local products to the city and to return with merchandise for their shops in the village. Vehicles replaced these animals after the road construction to El Zapote.

Indicative is that transactions in pack animals increased from 164 in 1974 to 228 in 1978 (source: Municipality El Zapote, 'Libro para Vistas Buenas'). Trade in livestock in general had increased; while 170 animals (all cattle) were sold to outsiders in 1950 (see Table 3.2) this rose to 330 in 1978, the peak year of livestock transactions (imports increased too: forty animals were purchased from outside El Zapote; respondents suggest that these were mainly pack animals although the data is not clear about this).

13 Probably the percentage of producers with pack animals remains under-reported: the producer survey reveals that 56 per cent of the producers have one or more pack animals (mean of animals in this group of producers is 2.0; range 1-7).

14 The total number of livestock increased by 71 per cent (cattle increased by 56 per cent, horses by 125 per cent, and mules by 134 per cent) while pasture area only increased with 40 per cent between 1952 and 1992, resulting in a growth of 25 per cent of livestock per hectare pasture.

15 Between 1930 and 1950, the introduction of the grasses Jaraguá (*Hyparrhenia rufa*) and Calinguero (*Melinis minutiflora*) to this system changed the vegetation in a short period. Both grasses are very competitive with other species in a slash–and–burn culture. Producers started to weed woody vegetation (by using fire) to transform the system into permanent pasture.

16 The practice of 'free grazing' animals has been forbidden and regularly leads to a tug-of-war between local authorities, the electricity company, and producers. In 1994 the guards of the power plant drove a dozen of free grazing packing animals into a paddock; according to the electricity company, they grazed on their belongings (the company constructed several of the roads). Once enclosed the animals remained without drinking water until a young boy could convince the soldier on duty that his horse needed water urgently. The thirsty animals had gathered at the gate and when the boy opened the gate all the animals got away in search for water. In front of the authorities, the boy stuck to his point that he had not been capable to prevent the escape and that he only wanted to give his horse some water so that it would not die. The way he had 'saved the poor', as villagers detailed, may be hailed as a weapon of the weak. It is, however, not only the poor who use such a type of 'illegal' action. For maintenance the electricity company has sometimes to open the closing doors of the dam of the reservoir. Behind these doors, in the dry old river bed, many animals used to graze freely. By opening the doors without notice these animals drown in the powerful flow of water. Furthermore, producers suspect that the soldiers drive animals into the river to drown them. Thus, both parties develop small, not organized, action: the 'strong' state and the 'weak' poor. For this state institution it seems the most effective strategy to counter free grazing.

17 The share of pasture was 47 per cent in 1965, 51 per cent in 1974 and 46 per cent in 1992 (DGECH 1968, 1978; SECPLAN 1994). The growth of the national cattle herd between 1974 and 1992 is based on growth in the districts with frontier expansion, and in Choluteca, a traditional cattle area. In all other districts, including Santa Bárbara, the number of cattle declined between 1974 and 1992 (cf. Kaimowitz 1996b:173). Growth of other forms of land use has thus not been constrained by cattle expansion in the absolute way suggested by the students of the cattle sector in the 1980s.

18 The contribution of the cattle sector to the gross value added in agriculture was in 1994 practically the same as in 1978, after having somewhat recuperated from a dip at the end of the 1980s (26 per cent and 22 per cent respectively, calculated from SRN, 1996:90). Its share in the export value is much lower. The value of export beef in 1994 was thirty-nine million US dollars, while for example, coffee generated 200 million, banana 155 million (with depressed prices) and shrimp 134 million dollar (SRN 1996:104).

19 Howar's emphasis (1987) on the extensive character of cattle ranching needs rethinking too: the amount of milk and beef production more than doubled between 1974 and 1993 (cf. SRN 1996:31) while the increase in pasture was less than 14 per cent. This indicates a process of intensification.

20 It is possible that the current expansion of roads into coffee producing areas, financed by funds filled by export revenues, may suppress a further expansion of pack animals.

21 In contrast to his earlier article, Baumeister (1996) conceptualizes a more diversified spectrum of coffee producers. Ruben (1997), however, repeats the Baumeister (1990) view and contends that coffee has been adopted as a 'last resort by peasants expelled to hillside areas'.

22 Remarkably, the percentage of coffee producers has declined from 57 per cent of all producers in 1952 to 46 per cent in 1992/3. With growth of coffee production, relatively fewer producers seem to be able to cultivate coffee. This conclusion, however, is not confirmed at district level. In the whole of Santa Bárbara the participation of producers with coffee increased from 37 per cent to 45 per cent between 1952 and 1992.

23 The smaller area under coffee reported in 1992 is probably due to census errors (see above). Despite these errors, however, the trend in the table is clear: initially expansion of the area was important; more recently an intensification of production has become more important.

24 It cannot be assumed, however, that this relation is linear.

25 Local brand names of this insecticide are Thiodan and Thionex. Endosulfan is a non-selective organochlorine pesticide and is moderately toxic to humans, but nevertheless causes many health problems. While spraying tall coffee trees the worker walks in a mist of insecticide, and the product also drips from the bushes on his clothes and body.

26 Roquas (1994) provides a detailed description of petate making.

27 In 1859 the state issued a regulation to support handicraft production such as the making of panama hats. Every workshop that educated at least four young people every six months received exemption from public duties (source: document of the 1859 pile in the Archivo Nacional).

28 Source: Actas Municipales of 1 October 1918. On one occasion women from El Zapote travelled to Tegucigalpa to teach others how to make petates.

29 No institution has anything to recommend about tule, because its cultivation is localized into very few villages in different parts of the country. Nevertheless, several producers have experimented with fertilizers and biocides to control disease problems.

30 A male producer can either sell tule to women in the village or pass it to female household members; in the latter case it is less likely that eventual saved profits will be invested in larger purchases, e.g. land.

31 Yield variation appear to be high at this level of aggregation but seem to diminish at a higher level of aggregation, such as the national agricultural census reports (cf. Steenhuijsen Piters 1995).

32 This data are for the *milpa* and calculated from DGECH (1954, 1978) and SECPLAN 1994; the harvested area is used for calculation and not the sown area; thus, actual yields are lower.

33 The respective yields were 0.83, 1.11 and 0.89 metric tons per hectare. The difference in yields (at least in 1952 and 1974) is probably due to climatic differences in different years.

34 Difference of means of sown area (milpa 1994 and postrera 1993) is significant: t-value = 6.59. In 1994 96.4 per cent (80 of N=83) of the producers sowed milpa, while in the 1993 postrera 79.6 per cent (66 of N=83) sowed maize (source: own survey). The rest of the area remains in fallow.

35 54.4 per cent of the producers applied fertilizer in the milpa of 1994 (N=79); in the postrera of 1993 only 27.7 per cent (N=65). However, those who fertilize the postrera as well as the milpa do not apply different quantities of fertilizer (t-value for difference of means is 0.05 for those sixteen producers who have fertilized their maize in the postrera 1993 as well as the milpa 1994).

36 To obtain a uniform field with few losses because of seeds being eaten by birds and small animals, and to have the work done rapidly, sowing is preferably done with larger working groups (if producers have the resources to hire labourers).

37 They sow tall cultivars in a lower density (otherwise the plant would even grow higher and become more susceptible to winds). To give an indication of possible differences: a 'normal' spacing for the cultivar Planta Baja is 30-35 cm x 103 cm with two seeds per hole; leading to a density of about fifty-five to sixty-five thousand plants per hectare, while a tall Maizón sown *en cuadro* (121 cm x 121 cm) may reach a density of about twenty (three seeds per hole) to thirty-four (five seeds per hole) thousand plants per hectare.

38 Notwithstanding this intercropping the yields of maize are for producers the main point of reference whether a certain field yielded well. Therefore it remains useful to compare yields per unit area. It is impossible to investigate the influence of intercropped climbing beans on maize, although it is quite probable that there may be some influence. As only some producers sow frijol de milpa (see below) this is a further source of variation.

39 Almost all fertilizers are urea or compounds (with nitrogen, phosphorus and potassium percentages of 15-15-15 or 12-24-12). Producers consider a fertilization with one bag (100 pounds) of urea and one bag of 12-14-12 or 15-15-15 per manzana, in two applications, as good. In the future, acidification might become a problem due to the continued fertilizing without liming and the reduction of burning (after burning pH rises). Several producers experiment with mixing urea and wood ash from the kitchen. Adding ash could help to counter this tendency, but quantities may, in the long run, be too low to halt acidification.

40 The most important disease is 'Maíz Muerto' ('dead maize'), caused by a complex of *Diplodia*, *Fusarium* and *Gibberella* spp.

41 The most critical pests are 'Gallina Ciega' (*Phyllophaga* spp.), 'Gusano Cogollero' (*Spodoptera frugiperda*) and the 'Gusano Elotero'. In storage the 'Gorgojo' (*Sithophilus zeamais*) is important. Furthermore, birds (e.g. 'Piana' and 'Zanate', *Piaya* sp.) and wild animals (e.g. Mapache, Pizote) can cause severe damage. During the first decades of this century many plagues of locusts were reported.

42 Producers estimate that on average weeding takes sixteen days per hectare, but it varies of course with the amount of weeds.

43 One load is about 480 cobs.

44 Producers state that they have always cultivated beans. It is remarkable that in the national agricultural census bean production is reduced to something insignificant in El Zapote. According to the latest census (SECPLAN 1994), only 165 of the 787 interviewed producers had sown beans (in June or in September). This is 21 per cent which is much lower than the 67 per cent in the producer survey of 1994. The census techniques and criteria lead to an underestimation of this important survival activity; small plots are not enumerated.

45 *Frijol de milpa* yields generally about one qq/mz (54 kg/ha) but once sown in a higher density than normal one can harvest up to three qq/mz. Each hole with maize plants needs then at least one bean plant.

46 Some producers report that they have doubled their seed use: from seven lbs/tarea (61 kg/ha) to fourteen lbs/tarea. If one assumes that yields have remained the same the harvest index (the amount of kg harvested beans divided by the kg of seed) has diminished by 50 per cent for these producers. Producers say that yields have not changed. It is likely that the producers' strategy was to keep yields constant per sown area. Environmental deterioration is thus not expressed in lower yields per area but in a lower harvest index.

47 The producer survey provided the data to establish this wealth ranking in which the ownership of the means of production (land, cattle, mules, and so on) constitute the predominant part. Production levels of cash crops, forms of land use and non-agricultural property (house) add up to a measurement of relative wealth.

48 He does not sow frijol de milpa because he sometimes does not weed with labourers but with *gramoxone* which kills the frijol de milpa. He hardly uses the remainders of maize to feed his animals, and his animals do not graze on the stubble. Thus the maize harvest is a good measure for what he gets from the field.

49 Of course, this abstract exercise only provides a relative indication: maize prices rise during the year and may double in 'the months of scarcity' (June-August). Furthermore, maize prices and yields fluctuate over the years.

50 Up to now his brother is the legal owner of the land.

51 They received with seven group members a loan of 18.000 L (about 9000 US$), to be redeemed in seven years of which in the first three years only payment of the 11 per cent interest was obligatory. The only work they carried out together was a collective nursery.

52 The underlying gender identities will be further analysed in the forthcoming work of Roquas.

53 Remarkably, his social networks related to party-politics and religion do not seem to influence the relations with his day labourers. The same can be observed for many other labour employers.

54 Although he was thrown out because he had danced and taken some beer on a celebration of the election results of his political party.

55 Chapter two describes the land history of Excequiel.

56 See Roquas 1994 about the different contractual arrangements.

57 Data about the composition of labour and input use by Excequiel and his family cannot be collected as in the case of José because Excequiel does not use any form of book keeping. Unlike José, Excequiel had only some vague idea about how much labour they use for different activities. I therefore studied them with different methods. The family of Excequiel filled in a form each week about their daily main activities in the field. These forms were discussed with them afterwards and used as a database to construct the presented figures.

58 Total work hours on the farm was 7933 hour, of this 1153 hour was non-family labour (14.5 per cent) which was mainly used for coffee (957 hours; 624 hours coffee picking).

59 His yields were respectively 463 kg/ha and 217 kg/ha; the milpa of 1994 was a bad harvest; in the better year 1993 his milpa yielded 788 kg/ha.

60 Yield of first main bean harvest was 521 kg/ha and of the second harvest 372 kg/ha. Field sizes were different as well as the amount of seed per area. The harvest index (amount of harvest per unit of seed) of the first harvest was 4.6 and of the second 2.3.

61 Only in sowing maize he follows the same strategy as José by doing it preferably with day labourers in one day. He may use hired labour for weeding maize when he calculates that he will not finish in time with family labour only.

62 As we will see in the following chapters, however, it is José, the one with the highest sales of the export crop coffee, who can invest in making his maize cropping system more sustainable through buying more land to reintroduce a fallow.

63 Other limitations of the concept of cultural repertoires are that firstly, the producers' cognitive maps are not necessarily identical to the concrete forms of the agricultural labour process. Secondly, a danger of tautological explanation is present when folk taxonomies of differences (as with scientific taxonomies) which themselves emerge from the dynamic structures and processes under investigation, serve to explain the causes of these differences.

64 A methodological consequence of this observation is that one cannot criticize structuralist approaches by pointing at local diversity (defying thus the determining effect by macro-structures) without exploring whether there are local sets of structures or not. However, this step often remains absent.

Chapter 4 Spotting environmental change: beyond conventional agronomy and local discourse

1 SECPLAN (1989a) encompasses not only this conventional view but shifts at times to other views. Jansen and Lara (1996) analyse some of these other perspectives on environmental issues in Honduras.

2 Biot et al. 1995 provide a good and concise review of the literature which substantiates this argument.

3 Ruthenberg (1980) summarizes the general agronomic view on this kind of fallow system. Critical elements in fallow systems are soil-fertility maintenance (declining yields) and labour shortages (increased labour demands for weeding). He states that any lasting improvement would require an intensive fertilizer economy and thus a change in the system.

4 Campanella et al. (1982:66) write: 'Migrant agriculture, the traditional cropping practice in Honduras, is realized in piedmont and mountainous areas (..). With little or no appropriate sowing practices the soils generally lose their nutrients or erode in two to five years, and afterwards they are left in fallow, abandoned or sown with grasses and sold to cattle breeders'. Also Fúnez (1989:3): 'Subsistence agriculture, especially that of maize and beans, continues to follow the same pattern in the whole country: felling, burning, cultivating about three years, *abandoning the area and searching again*, resulting in a remarkable deterioration' (my translations and emphasis).

5 The contrasting term to *tierra trabajada* is *tierra descansada*. *Tierra descansada* is not the same as *tierra fertil*. *Tierra fertil* mostly does not refer to soil fertility -the nutrient availability for the crop- (as the author for a long time presumed), but to the water holding capacity of the soil, the extent to which crops could grow successfully notwithstanding periods of drought. Some producers mentioned that the soil is more *fertil* after a fallow than after cultivating it for a long time without fallow.

6 This perceived change coincides with other data. The land pressure that resulted from demographic growth and the withdrawal of the fallow period in cattle areas led to a general reduction of land under fallow and the length of fallow periods. Statistical data confirm a reduction of land under fallow with 23 per cent of total agricultural land in El Zapote between 1952 and 1992 (see Table 4.1). The mean farm size dropped in that period from 13.6 to 4.0 hectare. At this moment producers consider three manzanas (two and a half hectare) of land an acceptable area for sustained household production of maize; one manzana is then cultivated and two are lying fallow.

Table 4.1 Percentage of the land that lies fallow in El Zapote (1952-1992)

	% of total enumerated land		
	1952	1974	1992
Fallow & Guamil	46	20	23
Forest	7	4	4

Source: calculated by the author from DGECH (1954, 1978) and SECPLAN (1994).

7 Documents in the municipal archive sometimes refer to yields. In February 1953 participants in a municipal meeting estimated that the mean yield for postrera in the Zona, a piece of land which just had become available to villagers, was six *fanegas* per manzana (about 652 kg/ha). There is no reason to assume an interest in under-estimating the yields. At present unfertilized fields yield about 600-700 kg/ha.

8 This same view is regularly filtering through in soil conservation literature (e.g. Tracy & Pérez 1987), especially now the attention is no longer geared exclusively towards terraces but also towards 'what happens between the terraces' (see Mejía 1993 for this shift in Honduras). Physical conservation structures, consisting of terraces and diversion channels, were promoted in the 1980s. More recently it has been noticed that labour demands to construct and maintain such structures are too high if compared with the value of short term gains. In the 1990s the emphasis of most development efforts has shifted to 'living barriers' which are rows of

perennial grasses or other suited species along the contour to reduce erosion (compare Tracy & Pérez 1987 with Mejía 1993). The construction of stonewalls, for example, may take 238 days of work per manzana of land while making living barriers can be done within sixteen days (Mejía 1993:41). Blaikie (1985:21) argues that although *total* benefits from soil conservation may be more than the total costs, individual farmers usually lose income from these practices. In general, however, a definitive judgment cannot be formed. Cárcamo et al. (1994) calculate that under actual conditions the more costly erosion control structures (such as those promoted by PRODESBA) lead to lower incomes and higher risks. In developing their model Cárcamo et al. make some problematic assumptions. They exclude erosion control on steeply-sloped land from their model. Their conclusions are therefore not strong enough to refute certain successes in soil conservation recorded by, for example, Bunch and López (1995). On the other hand some studies formulate strong conclusions that current practices of soil conservation have positive effects on farmers' incomes, but again the data seem, in my view, much too weak to support such strong conclusions (for example, see Mausolff & Farber 1995; Valdés 1994). What can be concluded is that labour *can be* a mayor constraint, which in some contexts can be released by intervention, but which in most cases will lead to abandonment of conservation structure maintenance after project funding ceases.

Another problem of many commentaries is that they do not consider the nature of fallow systems. Most proposed forms of soil conservation cannot go together with fallow periods and the presence of animals which have to live from grazing the stubble because both will have a damaging effect on conservation structures (cf. Boserup 1965). Most maize rotations contain a fallow period (see Table 4.2) and conservation structures thus mean not just adding a supporting technique but changing the whole cropping system.

9   Other producers claim that the *postrera de agosto* germinates and grows very irregular and that yields are uncertain.

10 Producers have opinions about the causal relations involved. They remark that plants do not grow as vigourously as in the past and that one needs to sow closer because otherwise the plants will not cover the ground and they will not 'save humidity'. One producer said: 'Now there are more people, the soil is more worked [exhausted], there is more *laja* and the earth is dryer, therefore one has to sow closer, in this way it produces more'.

11 According to informants total maize seed per hectare seems not to have changed, whereas the total seed needed for bean cultivation has increased by 50-100 per cent because of closer spacing (the past quantity was about 60 kg/ha). Not all informants, however, support this observation, but the differences in answers might well relate to individual variation in spacing. When it is true that yields of beans have not changed very much, as producers state, the harvest index must have been declined considerably.

12 The ratio land in fallow to maize area is significantly correlated with farm size: $r=0.57$, $p<0.001$; available fallow ($r=0.73$, $p<0.001$), and area with *milpa* in 1994 ($r=0.59$, $p<0.001$) are also significantly correlated with farm size (N=82).

13 The percentages for the farm size classes in Figure 4.1 are respectively: 2.4, 13.8, 20.7, 34.0, 30.2, 36.7, and 39.3.

14 A significant correlation exists between farm size and area with maize ($r=0.58$, $p<0.001$) and between farm size and yield ($r=0.49$, $p<0.001$).

15 The correlation between farm size and years of fallow of the last felled guamil was not significant ($r=0.12$).

16 Land in fallow which producers do not expect to use for food grain production has been excluded. It was not possible to distinguish between good quality river terraces and hillsides. One can expect that on river terraces producers use less fallow years and longer periods of cultivation (cf. Loker 1986).

17 Well known is dry Calinguero grass (*Melinus minutiflora*), also named as Calindero or Jediondo.

18 Note the difference between the Honduran urban view and that of Goudsblom (1992). Goudsblom considers the control over fire essential for what makes humans distinguishable from animals, the start of civilization.

19 In modern organic agriculture, sophisticated equipment uses fire to replace agro-chemicals for weeding (CRABE 1984; Hoksbergen and Jager 1985). Open Field Burning has been in use in Oregon (USA) for the production of grass seeds since the late 1940's when a fungus endangered grass seed production. Interrelated benefits of burning were the stimulation of plant growth, increased fertilizer efficiency, increased effectiveness of herbicides, reduced pesticide needs and extended productive life of stands. Prescribed burning has been investigated to understand the improving effects on forage production (e.g. Mutz et al. 1985), to reduce risk of hazards by large forest fires, and its use to prevent forest encroachment into wildlife habitat (Donoghue & Johnson 1975). And even for safeguarding endangered plant species fire may be useful in some cases (Worster 1993:150).

20 Twenty-four out of forty-six producers who burnt before the 1994 milpa (N=83) mentioned evading maíz muerto as the first reason to burn.

21 Producer Flavio explained that one day he was very angry because many birds attacked his milpa. He burnt the maize, so the birds lost their meal. Afterwards he realized that he had also lost his maize. But he was fortunate, because the maize sprouted for a second time and yielded reasonably. Relating this activity to some sort of 'rationality' would abstract from the fact that he did it in an act of outrage and not as part of a well thought out plan.

22 One producer remarked that in red coloured clay only after burning maize will develop deeper roots because of the produced warmth. He linked the need to burn to a certain soil type.

23 Of the forty-six producers (N=81) who acknowledged they had burnt for their 1994 milpa, seven (15 per cent) mentioned that burning induces 'washing'. Of the not burning producers fourteen (40 per cent) out of thirty-five mentioned 'washing' as a problem.

24 About twenty years ago slash used to be burnt but now producers prefer not to burn, in order to leave 'the organic' [matter] in coffee fields.

25 The data of the producer survey do not show a significant association between burning and yield. Any improvement from not burning will not be easy to observe.

26 *Pica pica* (or *rabia rabia*) is *Mucuna pruriens*: non-irritating cultivars of *Mucuna* are promoted as green manure (velvet bean) (CIDICCO 1991). Pica pica has probably been introduced as green manure by foreign banana companies during the first decades of this century (cf. Post n.d.).

27 Many producers remark that burning in the mountains is more difficult because rains fall earlier and the debris does not dry very well and is difficult to burn after rain.

28 From the forty-five producers (N=83) who rented or borrowed land for maize in 1994, thirteen were not allowed to burn on one of the fields they rented. This might be an underestimation because some of those who burn will not be willing to say that it was forbidden by the owner. Some told me they did burn although it had not been permitted.

29 Paraquat causes the weeds to dry out and to get a yellow appearance, as if a nearby fire has burnt them.

30 Some producers start now to discuss whether prolonged use of *gramoxone* does not lead to more grasses; this mirrors the agronomic understanding that continuous use of one type of herbicide can cause a dominance of certain weed species. Paraquat seems to be not very good with stoloniferous grass weeds and sedges (David Gibbon, personal communication).

31 Source: *Libro Público de Actas Municipales*, Volumes I and II.

32 It was still allowed to extract trees for house construction with a permit.

33 Nowadays sources which provide water the whole year round do not exist in this area.

34 Illustrative is likewise that many producers try to protect water sources in their own fields by keeping small lots of wood around sources. However, many of these protection lots have also disappeared because of the pressure of expanding agricultural activity.

35 See art. 5 of the law on COHDEFOR (Honduras 1974).

36 Corruption is considered to be widespread in COHDEFOR. In 1994 a former director and several other officials were charged with corruption. In daily conversation it is common sense to believe that all COHDEFOR officials are involved in bribing and many Hondurans can give illustrative examples. No systematic analysis of the role and functioning of COHDEFOR in Honduran society has been undertaken yet. Existing reports limit themselves to conclusions about organizational flaws. Some short remarks about concrete functioning of COHDEFOR can be found in Jones (1990) and Richards (1997).

37 One leaflet started with a 'Creed of Protection': 'I give my promise as Honduran, to conserve, not to destruct, and to defend faithfully the natural resources of my country, its soils and minerals, its forests, waters and fauna' (Departamento de Información Agrícola (1970), *Instructivo para los comites locales de los recursos naturales*. Tegucigalpa). This merging of forest conservation and nation-building is not unique to Honduras; see Brouwer (1995) about a similar organic link between state formation, military repression, development of a patriotic hegemonic ideology and forest management in Portugal.

38 This beautiful image is extremely local: petates (from which *petateado* stems) are a typical product of El Zapote, and the cloud structure indeed is a picture of the interweaving tule in petates.

39 The *cabañuelas* system is known in other countries in Central America and Mexico, and probably originates from Spain (Foster 1960).

40 Paraphrasing Staal (1989:298) one could say that it is central to this ritual that you say something, not what you do, believe or think. Considering these type of talks as rituals reinforces the view of Staal that rituals have no objective, meaning or sense. Considering the talks about techniques as rituals does not mean that I consider these techniques as 'erroneous beliefs'. Part of the ritual are those people who contest the beliefs in *cabañuelas*: 'Si Dios no quiere no hay *cabañuelas*'. During the fieldwork the researcher seems to have contributed to the continuation of this ritual as several informants talked more and more about the *cabañuelas* without any consequences for their practices.

41 In 1994, for example, practically all people burnt in May (seventy-nine permits issued), while only four people burnt during the last week of April (source: municipal archive of permits).

42 FHIA detected a Chlordane concentration of 0.015 ppm while it considers 0.0003 as the highest acceptable level of contamination. Most contaminations of water sources in Santa Bárbara district were with Chlordane and Dieldrin (FHIA 1989).

43 Of the producers who have used herbicides 16 per cent started before 1979. But half of all producers who have used *gramoxone* (at least one time) did their first spraying after 1988. Initially, its use was limited to maize cultivation.

44 There are several indications that the use of *gramoxone* and other herbicides has put pressure on intercropping of maize with squash and beans (always climbing cultivars), but in El Zapote most producers circumvent in the field squash and bean plants while spraying, if they apply intercropping.

45 PRODESBA's role as instigator of fertilizer use was much more prominent than with herbicides. Of the actual users of fertilizers (N=53) only 7.5 per cent was user before 1986, and 15.1 per cent started in 1986; for herbicides (N=50) these percentages are 32 per cent and 10 per cent.

46 Fungicides such as Benlate -with benomyl as active component- and those from the Dithane-group, based on dithiocarbamates such as mancozeb or nabam.

47 PCNB (brand Terrachlor) is most widely used against fungi in nurseries and soil insects are combatted with carbofuran (brand Furadan). Nematodes have not yet been reported as a problem in coffee in Honduras.

48 PH_3 in the form of a pill. The gases kill the *gorgojos* (*Sithophilus zeamais*) during a short period.

49 The sellers of the main pesticide sale outlets in Santa Bárbara could not display much knowledge about the risks of the products they retail. Some of them told me they got their information about the products from the buyers, the producers.

50 Endosulfan (brand names: Thiodan and Thionex) is used against the Coffee Berry Borer.

51 Cynically, many pesticides are more detrimental when alcohol is consumed.

Chapter 5 Social Differentiation and Labour Relations

1 Various texts on environmental deterioration in Honduras, e.g. Campanella (1982), SECPLAN (1989), and Stonich (1989, 1992) present typologies based on farm size.

2 This story of Fidel has been taped and is reproduced here in summarized and arranged form.

3 Local concepts for referring to different non-human souls are: *sombras, el malo, mala espíritu, sueño, duende, el susto, la sucia*, and *el gritón*.

4 In the stories of others about the pact of Alfredo, she died because a pig that was hanging from the ceiling fell off and dropped into a bin with water just beside her. She died of fright.

5 In building an alternative interpretation I am influenced by Taussig (1980) who opposes interpretations that refer to emotions. The psychological features of my first interpretation, which reduces beliefs to an emotion of anxiety, may, however, still hold some relevance for explaining why some specific people like very much to reproduce this belief system. The proof for this goes beyond the borders of this research project (see also Meyer 1994 for devil contracts in Ghana). Other references in literature on Honduras to contacts or contracts with the devil to increase wealth are Chapman (1985:168) and Aguilar (1989:150-151).

6 Other Honduran cases of the devil contract also involve this aspect of a new element of the outside world which is entering 'peasant' life. In one story -which took place at the turn of this century- a poor man from a neighbouring village wanted to send a son to study in Mexico or in the USA to become an engineer. He signed a pact with the devil to obtain money for the expenditures. Other stories refer to the banana companies who have a contract with the devil. The sugar plantation firms also have pacts. In another story a white foreign mine-engineer settled in a village and married a Honduran woman. She died young as well as some of her children because of the devil contract of this man. In El Zapote the engineering company that constructed the

power plant is thought to have made a pact. The souls of the men who died during the work still wander around as *malas espíritus* on the land near the power plant.

7   Edelman (1994) summarizes the critiques on Taussig's work. Edelman rightly points out that Taussig contains the devil contract into one single perspective of peasant reaction to a wage-labour-based agrarian capitalism. However, I think that in *this* situation the people of El Zapote use the belief system to deal with labour relations.

8   The famine years were an exception. When case harvests failed due to drought or locust plagues, the whole village had problems with food supply. Nowadays the development of a transport system and the money economy prevents the occurrence of village-wide famines. Nevertheless, some social groups face severe hunger periods every year because they lack entitlements to food, not because of the absence of food.

9   The Spanish colonial regime used similar classifications: In 1804 the *intendente* Anguiano informed that the indians lived 'in the bush left to indolence, to which they are naturally inclined' (cited in Barahona 1991:207).

10 This representation of the lazy Honduran who needs a mental transformation appears in the *finca humana* solution for sustainable agriculture propagated by Elías Sánchez. In this view development is 'located in the head' of the poor *campesino*. A poster is pinned down on the wall in the class room of the Loma Linda extension centre which shows a sleeping pig lying in a hammock: a depiction of the Honduran *campesino* according to Sánchez. The work of Elías Sánchez serves as model for most other NGOs and government interventions in sustainable agriculture in Honduras (e.g. see Smith 1994; SRN n.d.).

11 The following religions, apart from the Catholics, held gatherings in El Zapote: the *Centroamericana* (two churches), *la Philadelphia*, the *Pentecostés (Asamblea de Dios)* , the *Adventistas del Séptimo Día*, and the *Testigos de Jehová*.

12 Here we see the manifestation of front-stage and back-stage discursive fields. In public, a day labourer may use the term *ayudar* while in private conversation he will easily say that he is 'working for'. An employer may ask somebody if he is willing to *help* him tomorrow, while to other employers or to this interviewer he/she may say that he/she is *hiring* farm-labourers. He will then reserve the term *ayudar* for the help of other producers, not of labourers.

13 This is the view of acknowledged labourers as well as of producers who themselves never work for others. Quite as few smallholders in El Zapote work less hard than people who work a lot as a farmworker. This observation weakens theories which build the explanation of the existence of smallholders on the drudgery of family labour, that is that family labour exploits itself by working harder than hired labour.

14 Development interventions which intend to convert '*amas de casa*' (housewives) into agricultural labourers (based on the idea that being a producer means working yourself in the field) often fail to notice the importance of these requirements. When women work in the field they limit themselves to tasks for which less skills are required, such as picking coffee or harvesting beans. If they control agricultural production they will hire male labour to do the manual work.

15 Netting is aware of the critique, especially from feminist studies, that households are not harmonious (p.80-82), but this does not return in his household model; the household remains a coherent unit throughout the book.

16 Roquas (1995) analyses this case more extensively.

17 A *terra-teniente* is a large landowner.

18 It is a widely shared feeling in El Zapote that relations between parents and children have changed over time. Many detailed accounts are given of how parents treated their children in the past and that children have much more freedom today. It seems that educator-child relations were much more hierarchical and authoritarian than nowadays. This change cannot be related to any function it could have in the agricultural holding. Another point is that many children become much later (or never) a worker on the farm of their parents, as they go longer to school compared to the past.

19 In general the lender will determine the interest rate although sometimes the borrower can determine the rate. There is no fixed interest and the rate may vary between 0 and 20 per cent per month. Very often, those who have borrowed do not know how much the interest will be until the moment of reimbursement.

20 I use here the term 'overlapping' because the meaning of each concept is not exclusive and in some cases one of the other concepts may be used.

21 From people who are indebted (*adelantado, prestado*) it is expected that they keep their promise and appear on the agreed day. It is accepted that people who have not received any money do not appear, even if they have promised to do so.

22 Some elder people suggest that in the past it was much less risky to give *adelantados*. This may indicate a shift in relationships.

23 My impression is that *prestar* forms a much larger share of the outstanding debts within the village. There are many methodological difficulties in quantifying the amount of *prestar*, *adelantar*, and *alquilar*. Therefore I have no aggregated quantitative data about these actions.

24 Another reason why women prefer to work for Sonia is the preference of picking coffee where other women are picking. The action that women go to pick coffee is perceived in the sexual sphere. A single woman (who mostly will be accompanied by her brother, father, or husband) picking coffee is a subject for sexual joking. This disappears when a large part of the labour force consists of women.

25 Chapter two and three describe other aspects of Excequiel's life.

26 This may give Rafael access to higher level resources. Recently, for example, he received an exclusive licence for a certain public transport route; to get such a licence often requires political influence.

27 Lending land free to labourers gave Rafael also direct profits in the period that he changed from a system with forest fallow to permanent pasture: these labourers-tenant were helpful in clearing the forest.

28 Breman (1993:18) considers rights and obligations as characteristic of patronage. The patrons in El Zapote, however, have few obligations. What patrons do is mostly seen as 'favours', and, more importantly, a patron can abandon a favour without many consequences.

29 Labourers are usually paid on Saturday afternoon. A patron who cannot pay on Saturday is ridiculed. He/she should have borrowed money from others to avert this. Saturday is also a favourite day to look for payments in advance.

30 Whatmore et al. (1987a&b), Allen (1983), and Whatmore (1994) provide the theoretical justification of this relational typology. I agree with Lockie (1996) that Whatmore et al. perceive an external determination of the farm business. However, I think that their undue preoccupation with a subsumption process does not undermine the theoretical value of their model.

31 This typology was first presented in Jansen (1996) and is here refined after discussions with villagers. Within one household more than one type of producer was sometimes identified.

32 One example of these descriptions of producer types is as follows: Mr./Mrs. Posas says: 'I survive because I have inherited enough land from my parents. Therefore I am lucky, for the help of my parents. I work on my land, but I do not have money to make a good finca or to cultivate technified (*tecnificado*).'

The idea of choosing was strange to several respondents who did not understand the question, that is, that they had to *select* among those types. Nevertheless, they all started to tell that they *recognized* those producers.

After each interview I related the respondent to a specific producer type, whereby I based myself on their answer and the subsequent conversation in combination with other data they had provided. Hence, in last instance the types are not folk-categories but analytical types, corroborated through a hermeneutical approach to connect theory with 'views from the field'.

33 One single exception was a person who had been following different workshops organized by a political party and producer organizations.

34 Women producers generally employ wage workers. Many of them are of the employer-producer type, but in some cases they resemble more the employee-producer type or the producer-by-inheritance type, taking the modification into account that they themselves do not work in the fields.

35 Urban-based investors (often military or white-collar power) invest capital in lucrative agricultural activities although he/she remains city-based. This type has often been associated with a rapid plundering of natural resources (Williams, 1986, Stanley 1990 a&b, Stonich 1991b). I have excluded this type, as well as land reform cooperatives and large plantations, from the typology because they are unimportant in the research area. I only use the urban-based investor as a point of reference.

36 As long as agricultural wages in El Zapote remain at the current low level day labourers in agriculture will never save enough money to follow this path.

37 A related type is the small merchant-producer. This producer juggles profits from small-scale commerce to small-scale production (cattle and coffee) and back again while searching for the most lucrative activity at any given moment. The small-merchant producer can be considered as an employee-producer because calculations and strategies towards agriculture are similar.

38 Recently, Excequiel had some success with coffee and could expand his land base. He is relatively better-off than all the other producers in the sample that resemble this producer type. He increasingly uses hired labour.

39 This contradicts Netting's thesis who sees so much mobility between ranks of smallholders that relative wealth and poverty is not preordained at all by former generations.

40 This relation between maize yields and fertilizer applied is not linear however: the saver-producer seems to obtain high maize yields with low fertilizer level.

41 I do not use the concept of 'petty capitalism' coined by Tax (1953) although it similarly refers to a society which is 'capitalist' on a microscopic scale. Penny capitalism refers to 'undeveloped communities' which will (and must be) changed, according to Tax. The difference between poor and rich is for Tax a difference in modern economy and primitive underdeveloped societies. In contrast to penny capitalism 'nickel-and-dime' capitalism refers not to poverty and the fact that every person works in his own firm, but to labour relations between people in one society which are exploitative but which seem of an insignificant nature for outsider observers who only perceive large processes of capital accumulation and labour exploitation, and clear forms of opposition and polarization.

Chapter 6 Knowledge: Locality, Context, and Content

1 The term 'indigenous' knowledge is criticized because it refers to the concept of 'native' (DeWalt 1994). A shared element in different studies on this topic is the *locality* of such knowledge production (Kloppenburg 1991). How much locality is different from context, independent from context, determined by context, or shaping context part, is a point of discussion (see, for example, Appadurai 1995).

2 For more conventional studies of local knowledge on classification and plant taxonomy in Honduras see Ardón (1993), Bentley (1989b), Lentz (1986, 1989), and Williams (1981); for more novel studies which intend to incorporate producers' knowledge into technology development see: Bentley (1994), Bentley and Andrews (1991), and Goodell et al. (1990); or into health care programmes see Milla et al. (1994).

3 Higher officials at IHCAFE deny that technicians advised to remove shade in existing groves, whereas producers maintain that this happened. Both are contemporary 'texts' about the past but it seems that the producers' text explains more, as it makes clear why clever producers, who in fact had an aversion towards the idea of removing shade, felled the trees. Producers do not always criticize the extentionists but say that they had to follow the orders to give certain advice to participants in the AID-IHCAFE project. Producers explained that they only could get credit after they had removed all shade trees.

4 I do not argue here that all internal IHCAFE explanations of the 'shade'-problem refer to ignorance of producers. Other explanations of why some extensionists advised shade removal, point to the domination of credit supply over technical support and control in the project, or to the political conjuncture which means that sometimes personnel is employed which 'enjoys the confidence of the government but is less professional'.

5 Local names for different *Inga* species or cultivars are 'Guajiniquil hoja ancha', 'Guajiniquil hoja fina' (or 'Guajiniquil de río'), 'Guajiniquil velludo', 'Guachipilín', 'Guamo negro', 'Guamo blanco', 'Guamo paterno', and 'Paterno'. Other shade trees which producers prefer are 'Guanacaste' (*Entorolobium cyclocarpum*) and 'Madriado' or 'Cacahuanance' (*Gliricidia sepium*; recently promoted by IHCAFE). All are Leguminosae. Producers consider, for example, 'Lesquín' or 'Liquidámbar' (*Liquidambar styraciflua*) harmful to coffee and classify it as 'caliente'.

6 *Negra, roja, amarilla; piedra o playa, granzosa (instead of granosa), arenosa, arcillosa, lodo y barrial, vega, panecita or panecito.*

7 *Almanaque Pintoresco de Bristol* has been published every year by Lanman & Kemp-Barclay & Co. (USA) since the 1830s. Many producers use this almanac which announces the phases of the moon and weather forecasts.

8 I do not suggest here that this means that *frío* and *caliente* never guide peoples actions.

9 Appadurai (1990), Horton (1970), Knorr-Cetina (1997), and Marglin (1990) describe, each in their own specific way, shifts in the way of knowing. They describe important ongoing processes and emphasize the role of modern science. However, there is a danger of a dichotomized view which conceptualizes an absolute rupture between 'traditional' thought and western science. Knorr-Cetina conceives the locality of modern science, the laboratory, as a model for our modern society: it is the metaphor for a shift to object-centred sociality, compared to the actor-networks of Law (1992) and Latour (1994). For Latour, however, actor-networks have always existed, and are not a specific characteristic of modern society.

10 Here follow two quotations which may illustrate how producers reason in if-then relations:
(i) When it rains and one does not burn, much *maíz muerto*˙ results, [but] if one burns very little will rot. If it does not rain, yields will be as good as the earth is [then it does not matter if you have burnt or not]. Without

246

burning and fertilizers maize turns out discoloured. When you burn there is a difference, the maize germinates beautifully, and one evades the damage by animals because there is no debris.

(ii) With burning you have less weeds, sometimes, that depends. In a *guamil** you have less weeds, but when the earth is worked you have maybe more weeds. People go on burning, the difficulty is the immense debris. But weeds are more weak when one does not burn. If you burn then weeds are hard.

11 This is a type of proof analogous to conventional agronomy: the two treatments (burning and not burning) have to be situated in the same field and have to grow in the same year under equal conditions. The only difference with the scientific experiment is that replication is (usually) missing. Richards (1993) found interesting parallels between Mende people in Sierra Leone and research of primatologists with regard to observing chimpanzees, experimentation with crops and building a natural history.

12 Soulé (1995:151-3) argues that intracultural differences in the intricacy and accuracy of classifications of the biophysical environment are likely to be much greater than intercultural differences. For intercultural differences see Apffel-Marglin & Marglin (1996).

13 This critique of views which situate the reproduction of crucial agricultural knowledge in the community also counts for authors who situate this reproduction primarily in the household (e.g. Netting 1993).

14 This differentiation, of course, will not be the same for all cultures; the intensity of knowledge exchange may differ from place to place.

15 Through other informants I checked that he did burn until 1993, but did not burn in 1994.

16 This is the way it is more or less pronounced in the village and by some extensionists. Other people use the name Cuernavaca.

17 *Ley de Policía* 1906; art.365.

18 Circular nr.11, 9-2-1960, *Archivo Gobernación Política Santa Bárbara* (my translation).

19 Although he said he was a fervent adversary of burning this may be not more than official front stage talk. This mayor ordered his day labourers to clear one of his fields, a former coffee grove, and to burn it one day after he had received an USAID-sponsored course about environmental management (in part dealing with the need to put an end to burning).

20 The word used is *parentesco*, which, in El Zapote, can mean kinship as well as relationship. One regularly uses it in the broader sense.

21 COHDEFOR officials assert that the producer who burns a field is responsible for a sparkle that blows over and causes a fire. In local rules, however, these sparks can not be ascribed to the person who makes a milpa fire. Only fires that spread over the borders, passing the firebreak to a nearby field are the responsibility of a producer. The situation is more vague when a producer has not asked permission to burn. According to some, this is of no influence, but others argue that in such case he is also responsible for sparks that cause fires.

22 In this context it is interesting to recall the concept of *conservación de suelos* (soil conservation). A question in the agrarian census of 1993 asked the producers on how much land they had applied *conservación de suelos*. At that time, however, nobody understood what this meant. Hence, the answers to this question are useless. Later I visited a talk of an extensionist of IHCAFE. He kept going on talking about *conservación de suelos* while most people were falling asleep or were leaving the centre. Afterwards, the man was described as an old blockhead who does not understand anything about agriculture. Even relatively high-educated producers (one is a certificated bookkeeper) did not know the meaning of the word. People I talked with afterwards thought *conservación de suelos* had something to do with the floor in their house. For them the soil in their fields is *tierra*.

23 The first extension activities took place in the 1950s by STICA (*Servicio Técnico Interamericano Cooperativo Agrícola*) with an approach that imitated US extension systems. The extensionists of STICA worked mainly with the rural elite (see Apodaca 1954; White 1978:242). In El Zapote only Alfredo Luna visited a few meetings.

24 This is the producers' interpretation: officials denied the obligation to remove shade trees and brought forward that it was only during the first phase that young plants had to be bought. The underlying idea was that control by IHCAFE would guarantee quality (which would lead to better production and thus repayment of loans). Plant quality, nevertheless, was low, because the producers who were contracted to supply the project with young plants had a guaranteed sale and profit, and did not pay sufficient attention to quality. Later, participants of the project could make their own nursery.

25 The municipality council decided not to accept any further order of COHDEFOR because the municipality felt they had 'the obligation to assert the rights of the villagers' (i.e. to provide drinking water).

26 PRODESBA started in 1985 with a budget of more than 62 million L (31 million dollars of which 78 per cent came from international funding agencies). It was targeted on smallholders (with less than ten hectares of land) and mainly focused on agriculture. SECPLAN (1989b) presents a moderate critical inventory of the failures and problems of PRODESBA. The project as such was closed down in 1989/1990, but several of the activities (mainly credit recuperation from groups, but also technical assistance) were continued by SRN.

27 Most producers did not use this fertilizer for the postrera because they viewed that fertilizing the postrera was not worthwhile. Instead they sold the fertilizer, applied it in coffee or saved it for the next year.

28 The credit system for coffee was a term of seven years, instalments had to be paid after three years, and the interest was 11 per cent (later 17 per cent). This interest rate was below the commercial interest rate.

29 The corresponding law (*Ley para el saneamiento de la cartera en mora de BANADESA e INA*) was approved in March 1992. It applied to all agrarian debts in default at/before 30 April 1991.

30 All vegetable gardens of women's groups in El Zapote failed in a technical sense: the products did not value economically against the labour input. Many women, however, expressed that they were pleased to participate although they would have earned much more money while staying at home and making petates. They viewed the activities mainly as a social gathering, to meet other women and to relieve their dull daily labour tasks with some new experiences.

31 PLAN works primarily outside agriculture: house improvement (zinc roofing, cement floors), scholarships, cooperative shops, construction of schools, wood-burning stoves, latrines, and drinking water systems.

32 Evaluations of NGO-activities may point to successful activities; see Kaimowitz et al. (1992).

33 The future of NGOs may be endangered now international funding agencies seem to have lost interest in Central America since the signing of peace agreements in various countries (Kaimowitz 1993).

34 Kaimowitz (1993:182) indicates splits in the NGO movement because of political polarization.

35 Particularly state agencies fail in learning. A lot of documentation is thrown away with every extensionist or official who leaves. A new employee normally starts from scratch again. It was hard to find any documentation in the regional SRN office about PRODESBA in 1993. Few people knew what had been done, what had been the results and what went wrong, except for in very general terms (bureaucratization, dissipation of funds, and politicization). The directorate of PRODESBA changed much faster than the political cycle. According to one former official it had seven or eight different directors between 1982 and 1990, each with his (her?) own staff. Most agencies do not build their own history. NGOs which are managed by the same directors for a long time may know more of their own past.

36 In a similar fashion COHDEFOR aimed to develop social forestry programmes (Honduras 1974).

Chapter 7 *Social Origins of Environmental Deterioration*

1 '[E]stos incendios (..) son deliberados, (..) para continuar con la ancestral milpa maya' (Editorial of 7 April 1997, newspaper *Tiempo*.

2 Stonich (1993) has used this problem to open her book with. A poor producers says 'I am degrading the land', but that he has no means to stop this.

3 The success of green manuring with velvet beans depends to a large extent on the little extra labour required or even the reduction of labour input due to weed suppression (cf. Bunch 1990).

4 The Honduran Catholic Church continuously argues against artificial contraceptives and still dominates much of the official political discourse on this topic. The leftist critique of family planning of the 1980s (when it was considered an imperialist project) appears to have faded away in the 1990s.

5 Appeals to patriotism, for example, were typically made in February and March 1997, when trees were felled and transported to El Salvador by inhabitants of land which until recently had been disputed between El Salvador and Honduras. The problem of supposed illegal deforestation was entirely recalled in the language of patriotism (see, for example, newspaper *Tiempo* 28/02/97).

6 See newspaper *Tiempo* 10/03/97.

7 The so-called 'green battalions' were, for example, involved in environmental education. In March 1996 seventy trained officials gave classes to a total of 35,000 school children about environmental issues, deforestation, and reafforestation. See *Tiempo* 23 March 1996.

8 Another critique is the military support for the Nicaraguan *contras* in the 1980s, who, apart from social disruption, engendered deforestation of large parts of Honduras (see Almendares 1989, Faber 1993). Furthermore, the military forces are distrusted due to violation of human rights (CNPDH 1994)

248

9 These issues have not been a subject of my study and thus do not receive full attention here. Although many Hondurans have far reaching opinions about how these networks function, they have received hardly any scholarly attention, apart from Euraque (1996).

10 It could be argued that the 'ignorance' explanation represents the modernist urbancentric view that emphasizes the backwardness of rural life, whereas the hindered peasant rationality argument is a romantic view that depicts a moral economy (cf. Kearney 1996:75).

11 See Milton (1996:109-114 and 199-204) for a summary of the anthropological critique on this myth of primitive ecological wisdom.

12 Nevertheless, in specific cases such a methodology *may* show coincidence, see for example Ashby (1985).

13 In fact, comparative methods of anthropology, as proposed by Milton (1996), maintain a similar assumption since they suppose that cultures may differ in environmental perspectives and practices, thus assuming that each culture develops as an entity its specific use of the environment.

14 I thus object to taking these explanations as incommensurable local knowledges, narratives, or discourse, as well as considering them as ideological notions which deviate from one true narrative of history (cf. Sayer 1993). Each explanation may refer to causalities which we wish to understand and in some sense we have to engage with such analysis, even if the explanations seem incommensurable at first sight.

15 The improvement of infrastructure and accessability to coffee fields in neighbouring countries in the nineteenth century is mainly an *effect* of successful coffee production (e.g. Cardoso 1977).

16 A labour pool was created with force in El Salvador and Guatemala (see Browning 1971; Williams 1994).

17 I do not pretend to analyse post-modernist thought here, but only how some arguments, which are said to be taken from post-theories, emerge in environmental theory.

18 After completion of this chapter I read Lehmann (1997): a commentary on another book of Escobar. Lehmann makes several observations which coincide with my reading of Escobar.

19 Escobar reproduces here the fragmentation of knowledge into local knowledge and expert discourses. Chapter six argued that knowledge is not fragmented in this way.

20 It must be emphasized again that it is not the other way around either: that the high-tech farmers in Holland are more modern than the rainforest people.

21 Escobar's explicitly negative assessment of 'sustainable development' discourse, in fact, poses rather classical questions. Instead of the Foucaultian analysis of discourse he claims to make, he does not view discourse unconnected from representations, thus as a more or less independent system unconnected to the carriers of representations. Escobar does not focus so much on the 'how' of power in discourse (what Foucault would do), but more on the 'why' (p.51) and the 'who' (p.50) (cf. McLennan 1996:65). He claims to have some reason to be sure that in this discourse a global environmental problem was invented by a white male Western scientist-turned-manager (p.49-50). I think his methodology is interesting although the argument seems incorrect to me. He has to counter a possible refutation of his assertion which could put forward that the World-Commission for Environment and Development was headed by a woman (Mrs. Brundtland) and that it had Third Worlders as members, which may prove his assertion to be incorrect. He maintains his rather simplistic view of a hegemonic sustainable development project by arguing that the first one was a 'matriarch-scientist' and the latter were 'cosmopolitans', thus enforcing his picture of a patriarchal, western project which simply oppresses the other: the woman, the non-western, and the non-scientist. The analysis is interesting, however, as it tries to explore the reasons *why* a certain discourse emerges. According to Escobar, there was a need for a discourse that could justify further economic growth despite poverty and environmental deterioration. The sustainable development discourse fulfilled this role as it rationalizes both the need for economic growth to alleviate poverty and the need to halt environmental deterioration in economic terms. Without further discussing the rights or the wrongs of this analysis it can be argued that the methodology does not seem to be very different from past approaches.

22 The following argument is based on Benton (1989, 1992). For comments on Benton see Bellamy Foster (1995), Grundmann (1991), and Hayward (1994). Foster argues that Benton incorrectly attributes a productivist position to Marx. Grundmann, on the other hand extends and defends Marx's perspective on production, and characterizes Benton's position as romanticist. I think both emphasize only one part of the argument by Benton who recognizes different contrasting perspectives in Marx's work. Hayward comments on the focus of Benton on the 'conditions of *production*' while a reconstructed political ecology should go beyond the paradigm of production and reconceptualize the role of reproduction. Benton has already pointed to this need by elaborating on the 'domestic labour-debate'.

23 Drawing a distinction between transformative and eco-regulatory processes is a theoretical exercise. By giving examples (agriculture) we turn to the empirical level whereby differences seem to be more gradual and can be seen as degrees.

24 The distinction between transformative and eco-regulatory processes, in fact, underlies the argument of Mann and Dickinson (1978) which states that the difference in penetration of capitalist relations in agriculture and manufacturing industry can be traced back to a non-identity of production time and labour time. Cultivation of crops faces seasonal constraints and the periods of long biological processes during growth cannot easily be socially modified or manipulated as in industrial processes. The tailor in our example works in relatively unspecific spatial and temporal conditions.

25 Benton discusses gene technology which in the end depends on natural mechanisms of molecules. Scientists use the term recombination of DNA, which interestingly does not transform the basis structure of DNA but recombines the different elements.

26 'Empirical surfaces' are the shapes, sizes and mixtures of things, their spatial distributions, concentrations and relation to one another. 'Factories, railways, telegraphic cables, hedgerows, fields and so on all bear the imprint of this restless human activity of moulding, shaping, rearranging things to suit our purposes' (Benton 1992:66).

27 My analysis is limited to the sphere of production but I suppose that it could be extended to theorize also in the sphere of consumption a similar combination of natural limits and social/ culturally defined characteristics. An illustration is Eder (1996), although in this work the naturalist element of consumption is subsumed to a cultural determination of consumption.

28 However, I think that philosophically the argument also cannot be sustained. If it were true that every theory or discourse is right in its own perspective, then the view that theories making such claims are nonsensical, would also have to be taken as correct.

29 It may be true that people trained in social sciences are generally unqualified to evaluate the veracity of environmental claims (Hannigan 1995:188), but this is no theoretical argument as to why political ecology should refrain from transgressing a confined social science perspective. Doing so would imply a surrender to the current disciplinary ordering of science (in fact negating the social construction of science but taking it as a direct and true reflection of the world), instead of theorizing which type of knowledge expansion is wanted.

30 I think that the actor-network theory of Latour (1987) and Law (1992), despite the deep insights they provide about science, tend to dismiss the acting of nature upon the experiments and theories of scientists and influencing the outcomes. A discussion goes beyond the theme of this book.

31 On the one hand, this is partly a result of the unsuccessful earlier efforts to establish socialist oriented parties and political movements with mass support, the increasing awareness of the failure of the bureaucratic developmental state, the corruption within and cooptation of labour and peasant unions, and, on the other hand, the crucial donor-push which stimulated the formation of a wide array of NGOs operating as dependent entities in all the fashionable fields of development. I am well aware of the provisional character of these statements.

Glossary

This glossary explains local Spanish terms, acronyms and abbreviations, and a few agronomic and sociological concepts.

Abono	*Abono* encompasses many substances such as ash, manure, fertilizers, debris, and so on.
Actas Municipales	Records of the minutes of meetings of the municipality council, including official agreements and measurements of concessions carried out by the *síndico*. These records have been well preserved in numbered volumes.
AHPROCAFE	*Asociación Hondureña de Productores de Café*: Honduran Association of Coffee Producers
BANADESA	*Banco Nacional de Desarrollo Agrícola*; the National Agricultural Development Bank, formerly BANAFOM
Caballería	One *caballería* is equivalent to 45.03 hectares or 64.6 *manzanas*.
Clordano	Chlordane is an insecticide of the organochlorine type. Other organochlorines such as dieldrin, DDT, lindane, and aldrin were sold under the local name *Clordano* in the past. Therefore, I will use this local Spanish term to refer to this group of biocides. The persistency of organochlorines has received widespread research attention.
COHDEFOR	*Corporación Hondureña de Desarrollo Forestal*: the Honduran Corporation for Forestry Development. With the LMDSA its name has changed in AFE-COHDEFOR; AFE means *Administración Forestal del Estado*.
Concession	Usufruct rights given by the municipality to producers, mostly considered as property by producers. In official terms this is *dominio útil*.
Commoditization	The process whereby goods (use values) become commodities (with exchange value) and where the production, distribution, and consumption of these goods is increasingly incorporated into global capitalist economies and shaped by commodity values and relations. This process may entail that producers increasingly produce for exchange instead of for their own use, and come to depend more upon purchases for at least some of the things they require.
Cultivar	In botany the term cultivar is applied to a recognizable variant that originates under cultivation and can be distinguished from other plant groups of the same species.
Ejido	The *ejido* or *ejidal* land is national land designated to the municipality. The municipality could grant usufructuary rights to *ejidal* land to its inhabitants on an individual basis.
Escritura pública	A deed, provided by a lawyer, that a plot holder has legal property rights to a plot (or other items, e.g. a house). In many cases it is inscribed in the official property register and used as collateral for loans. In official terms land with an *escritura pública* is in *dominio pleno*.

Finca	Locally used for coffee plantation. As many readers associate the word plantation with large-scale enterprises this would provide a wrong representation. *Finca* is also used for 'farm' in Honduras, but in El Zapote this is not the case. It might be used too for a small banana plantation, but these hardly exist in the village. Therefore, in the text *finca* refers to a plot with coffee, often with a small house to store tools and processing installations, and to sleep during the harvest.
Gramoxone	Gramoxone is the brand name of a non-selective herbicide produced by ICI with paraquat as an active ingredient. Producers also call other brands (e.g. Exprone) with paraquat '*gramoxone*'. When italicized in the text *gramoxone* refers to a product having paraquat-similar effects and not to the brand. Other non-selective herbicides may be indicated by producers with this name.
Guamil and *Guatal*	Sometimes written as Huamil/Huatal). A *guamil* is a secondary growth of bush or forest, considered by producers to be substantial enough to give good yields when burned and sowed. A *guatal* is composed of small herbs, crop residues and grasses. *Guamil grueso* is a guamil with thick trees, for which the axe might be necessary for clearing.
	According to Membreño fallow systems must have existed before the arrival of the Spaniards because the word *guamil* has Nahuatl roots: it may stem from *guammilli* which refers to 'bastón, palo delgado' (Membreño 1908) or from *ouatl*, espiga tierna de maíz, y *milli*, campo: tierra preparada para sembrarla de maíz (Membreño 1982). Chapman (1985 citing F. Santamaría (1959), *Diccionario de Mejicanismos*) thinks it stems from *huac-milli*; of *huacqui* 'dry', and *milli* 'field': field where one has harvested and where only the dried stems remain.
IHCAFE	*Instituto Hondureño del Café*, Honduran Coffee Institute
INA	*Instituto Nacional Agraria*, the National Agrarian Institute; its main task is to implement the land reform.
L or Lempira	Honduran currency: fixed exchange rate until 1990 was 2 L = 1 US$; during the field work period the exchange rate was 1 US$ = 5.40 in June 1992 and 5.53 L in August 1993 (use 5.50 for 1993), 6.20 L in June 1993 and 7.05 L in December 1993 (use 6.50 in 1993), and 1 US$ = 8.84 L in August 1994 and 9.2 in December (use 8.80 in 1994) 1994.
lbs or libra	A pound, 0.454 kg
LMDSA	*Ley para la Modernización y el Desarrollo del Sector Agrícola*; Agricultural Modernization Law enacted in 1992; generally viewed as the legislation of structural adjustment policies in agriculture.
Machete vuelta	see *pando*
Materiality	Materiality refers to the non-social world: this includes, for example, material things such as raw materials, the natural environment, human made artifacts, and forces such as gravity and magnetism.
Maíz muerto	*Maíz muerto* literal means 'dead maize'. It is caused by a complex of fungi (*Fusarium* sp. and *Giberella* sp., and probably also *Diplodia* sp. (cf. CATIE 1990).
Manzana or mz	An area measure: officially 0.697 hectare; the manzana in El Zapote measures 0.8361 hectare (see Chapter one).

Milpa	The first maize crop in the season, sown in June (sometimes May); elsewhere *milpa* may be used to indicate every maize crop, but in El Zapote and in this book, *milpa* has a more restricted signification and is distinguished from *postrera*.
Pando	Tool for weeding. The *machete vuelta* and the *pando* have both a curved blade which is sharpened at the inside and which can also be sharpened at the outside. The *machete vuelta* is for the rest flat and does not enter the soil, while the *pando* is concave and can therefore be used to uproot weeds.
Petate	Sleeping mat made from tule; word originates from the Nahuatl word 'petlatl' (Siméon 1977).
Planta Baja	High-yielding maize cultivar with short stalks.
Postrera	Second maize crop, sown in October-November; see *milpa*. *Postrera de agosto* is a maize crop sown in August.
PRODESBA	*Proyecto de Desarrollo Rural Integrado del Departamento de Santa Bárbara*: the integrated rural development project of Santa Bárbara.
PTT	*Proyecto de Titulación de Tierra para los Pequeños Productores*; Honduran Land Titling Project for Smallholders
Quintal or qq	Quintal, weight unit, 1 bag of 45.4 kg or 46 kg; one quintal is 100 lbs (the Spanish lbs is 0.46 kg, the English lbs is 0.454 kg); most texts use 46 kg, but I have used 45.4 kg for calculations as this is consistent with the balances people use.
Silo	A *silo* is a bin of aluminium to store maize; most silos in El Zapote can store eighteen quintals.
Síndico	Authority who is responsible for land measurements, settling border lines and solving border conflicts. In some periods it has been the person who safeguards the land titles of the municipality (e.g. the *ejidos*).
SRN	Secretaría de Recursos Naturales, the Ministry of Natural Resources; in 1997 its name has changed to SAG (Secretaría de Agricultura y Ganadería)
Tarea	1/16 of a *manzana*; measured as 12 x 12 *brasadas*, one *brasada* is the wide of two outstretched arms or two *varas* of 36 inches. Some producers comment that a tarea should be 12.5 x 12.5 *brasadas*.
TATE	TATE or Technical-and-administrative-task-environment (Benvenuti 1982), refers to the institutions to which agricultural producers are tied (agro-industry, banks, extension services, cooperatives, and so on). Benvenuti uses the concept to explain that these ties not only include economic relations, but also technical and organizational prescriptions and standardization.
Tule and *Tular*	Tule is *Cyperus canus* (fam. Cyperaceae), a perennial crop of which the stems are used for weaving *petates*. A *tular* is a field with tule.
UNC	*Unión Nacional de Campesinos*, National Union of Peasants
USAID	United States Agency for International Development (USAID)

Bibliography

Agudelo C., Nelson, (1988), *Ecosistemas terrestres de Honduras*. Asociación Hondureña de Ecología, Tegucigalpa.

Aguilar Paz, Jesús, (1989 [1930]), *Tradiciones y Leyendas de Honduras*. Museo del Hombre Hondureño, Tegucigalpa.

Alcorn, Janis B., (1995), Ethnobotanical Knowledge Systems - a Resource for Meeting Rural Development Goals. In: D.M. Warren, L.J. Slikkerveer & D. Brokensha (eds), *The Cultural Dimension of Development: Indigenous Knowledge Systems*. Intermediate Technology Publications, London, p.1-12.

Allen, J., (1983), Property Relations and Landlordism- a Realist Approach. *Environment and Planning D: Society and Space* 1:191-203.

Almendares, Juan, (1989), Efectos ambientales de la ocupación militar norteamericana. In: I. Hedström (ed.), *La situación ambiental en Centroamérica y el Caribe*. DEI, San José, Costa Rica, p.61-101.

Almendarez, Hugo E., (1986), *Zonificación Agroclimática de Honduras*. Tomo III Region Nor-Occidental, Santa Bárbara. Secretaria de Recursos Naturales, Tegucigalpa.

Altieri, Miguel A., (1987), *Agroecology: The Scientific Base of Alternative Agriculture*. IT Publications, London.

Altieri, M. & S. Hecht (eds), (1990), *Agroecology and Small Farm Development*. CRC Press. Florida.

Alvarado, Pedro de, (1908 [1536]), Repartimiento de la Ciudad de Gracias á Dios y su fundación por Pedro de Alvarado (año de 1536) *Revista del Archivo y de la Biblioteca Nacional de Honduras* 4(5-6):132-142.

Amanor, Kojo Sebastian, (1994), *The New Frontier. Farmers' Response to Land Degradation: A West African Study*. Zed, London.

Apffel-Marglin, Frédérique, (1996), Introduction: Rationality and the World. In: F. Apffel-Marglin & S.A. Marglin (eds), *Decolonizing Knowledge: From Development to Dialogue*. Clarendon Press, Oxford, p.1-39.

Apffel-Marglin, F. & S. A. Marglin (eds), (1996), *Decolonizing Knowledge: From Development to Dialogue*. Clarendon Press, Oxford.

Apodaca, Anacleto G., (1954), *Enseñando al Agricultor. Enseñanza Agrícola en un Pais Latinoamericano*. American Embassy, Tegucigalpa, Honduras.

Appadurai, Arjun, (1990), Technology and the Reproduction of Values in Rural Western India. In: F. Apffel-Marglin & S. Marglin (eds), *Dominating Knowledge: Development, Culture, and Resistance*. Clarendon Press, Oxford, p.185-216.

Appadurai, Arjun, (1995), The Production of Locality. In: R. Fardon (ed.), *Counterworks: Managing the Diversity of Knowledge*. Routledge, London, p.204-225.

Ardón Mejía, Mario, (1992), Inventario de técnicas de conservación de suelos utilizadas en zonas de laderas en la República de Honduras. Informe de estudio. Tegucigalpa, Honduras.

Ardón Mejía, Mario, (1993), Aproximaciones al Manejo de Cultivos en Mesoamérica durante el Siglo XVI. In: M. Ardón Mejía (ed.), *Agricultura Prehispánica y Colonial*. Guaymuras, Tegucigalpa, p.83-136.

Argueta, Mario, (1975), Política Agraria de la Administración Soto. Aspectos Agrícolas y Ganaderos. *Revista de la Universidad* 9:16-23.

Argueta, Mario R., (1992), *Historia de los sin historia*. Editorial Guaymuras, Tegucigalpa.

Arriaga, Ubodoro, (1986), Recent Evolution of Honduran Agrarian Policy. In: M.B. Rosenberg & P.L. Shepherd (eds), *Honduras confronts its future. Contending Perspectives on Critical Issues*. Lynne Rienner, Boulder, Colorado, p.153-159.

Ashby, Jacqueline A., (1985), The Social Ecology of Soil Erosion in a Colombian Farming System. *Rural Sociology* 50(3):377-396.

Atwood, David A., (1990), Land Registration in Africa: The Impact on Agricultural Production. *World Development* 18(5):659-671.

Bandy, D.E., D.P. Garrity & P.A. Sanchez, (1993), The Worldwide Problem of Slash-and-Burn Agriculture. *Agroforestry Today* 5(3):2-6.

Banuri, Tariq & Frédérique Apffel Marglin, (1993), A Systems-of-knowledge Analysis of Deforestation. In: T. Banuri & F. Apffel Marglin (eds), *Who Will Save the Forests? Knowledge, Power and Environmental Destruction*. Zed, London.

Barahona, Marvin, (1991), *Evolución Histórica de la Identidad Nacional*. Guaymuras, Tegucigalpa.

Barahona, Marvin, (1994), *El silencio quedó atrás. Testimonios de la huelga bananera de 1954*. Guaymuras, Tegucigalpa.

Barlett, Peggy F., (1980), Adaptive Strategies in Peasant Agricultural Production. *Annual Review of Anthropology* 9:545-573.

Barraclough, Solon, (1973), *Agrarian Structure in Latin America*. Lexington Books, Lexington, Massachusetts.

Barrett, Michèle, (1984), *Links en de vrouwenbeweging. Het wankele verbond*. Het Wereldvenster, Weesp. (translation of: Women's Oppression Today: Problems in Marxist Feminist Analysis. New Left Books, London, 1980).

Bartlett, Harley H., (1957), *Fire in Relation to Primitive Agriculture and Grazing in the Tropics*. Annotated Bibliography, Vol II. Ann Arbor, University of Michigan.

Baumeister, Eduardo, (1990), El Café en Honduras. *Revista Centroamericana de Economía* 11(33):33-78.

Baumeister, Eduardo, (1996), Rasgos básicos y tendencias estructurales de la actividad cafetalera en Honduras. In: E. Baumeister (ed.), *El agro hondureño y su futuro*. Guaymuras, Tegucigalpa, p.267-325.

Bebbington, Anthony, (1996), Movements, Modernizations and Markets: Indigenous Organizations and Agrarian Strategies in Ecuador. In: R. Peet & M. Watts (eds), *Liberation Ecologies: Environment, Development, Social Movements*. Routledge, London, p.86-109.

Bellamy Foster, John, (1995), Marx and the Environment. *Monthly Review* 47(3):108-123.

Benavides, Jorge A., (1984), La Reforma Agraria en Honduras. *Economía Política* 23:5-29.

Benda-Beckmann, F. von, (1995), Anthropological Approaches to Property Law and Economics. *European Journal of Law and Economics* 2:309-336.

Bennett, Charles F., (1967), A Review of Ecological Research in Middle America. *Latin American Research Review* 2(3):3-27.

Bennett, John William, (1976), *The Ecological Transition. Cultural Anthropology and Human Adaptation*. Permagon, New York.

Bennett, John W., (1993), *Human Ecology as Human Behavior*. Transaction Publishers, New Brunswick, USA.

Bennholdt-Thomsen, V., (1980), Toward a Class Analysis of Agrarian Sectors: Mexico. *Latin American Perspectives* 7(4):100-114.

Bentley, Jeffery W., (1989a), What Farmers Don't Know Can't Help Them: The Strenghts and Weaknesses of Indigenous Technical Knowledge in Honduras. *Agriculture and Human Values* 6(3):25-31.

Bentley, Jeffery W., (1989b), El Lexico Agroecológico de Honduras. Departamento de Protección Vegetal, Escuela Agrícola Panamericana, Tegucigalpa, Honduras, (unpublished draft).

Bentley, Jeffery W., (1994), Science and People: Honduran Campesinos and Natural Pest Control Inventions. *Agriculture and Human Values* 11(2/3):178-182.

Bentley, Jeffery W. & Keith L. Andrews, (1991), Pests, Peasants, and Publications: Anthropological and Entomological Views of an Integrated Pest Management Program for Small-Scale Honduran Farmers. *Human Organization* 50(2):113-124.

Benton, Ted, (1989), Marxism and Natural Limits: An Ecological Critique and Reconstruction. *New Left Review* 178:51-86.

Benton, Ted, (1992), Ecology, Socialism and the Mastery of Nature: A Reply to Reiner Grundmann. *New Left Review* 194:55-74.

Benton, Ted, (1994), Biology and Social Theory in the Environmental Debate. In: M. Redclift & T. Benton (eds), *Social Theory and the Global Environment*. Routledge, London, p.28-50.

Benton, Ted & Michael Redclift, (1994), Introduction. In: M. Redclift & T. Benton (eds), *Social Theory and the Global Environment*. Routledge, London, p.1-27.

Benvenuti, Bruno, (1982), De technologisch-administratieve taakomgeving (TATE) van landbouwbedrijven. *Marquetalia* 5:111-136 (the Netherlands).

Benvenuti, Bruno, (1995), How to Utilize 'Local Knowledge': A Likely Case of Scientifically Created New Ignorance? *Tijdschrift voor Sociaal-wetenschappelijk Onderzoek in de Landbouw* 19(1):5-20.

Berger, Peter L. & Thomas Luckmann, (1967 [1966]), *The Social Construction of Reality: a Treatise in the Sociology of Knowledge*. Anchor Books.

Bernstein, Henry, (1979), African Peasantries: a Theoretical Framework. *The Journal of Peasant Studies* 6(4):421-443.

Bernstein, Henry, (1988), Capitalism and Petty-Bourgeois Production: Class Relations and Divisions of Labour. *The Journal of Peasant Studies* 15(2):258-271.

Bernstein, Henry, (1990), Agricultural 'Modernisation' and the Era of Structural Adjustment: Observations on Sub-Saharan Africa. *The Journal of Peasant Studies* 18(1):3-35.

Bhaskar, Roy, (1979), On the Possibility of Social Scientific Knowledge and the Limits of Naturalism. In: J. Mepham & D.H. Ruben (eds), *Issues in Marxist Philosophy Vol. III. Epistemology, Science, Ideology*. Harvester Press, Brighton, p.107-139.

Bhaskar, Roy, (1989), *Reclaiming Reality. A Critical Introduction to Contemporary Philosophy*. Verso, London.

Billig, Michael & Herbert W. Simons, (1994), Introduction. In: M. Billig & H.W. Simons (eds), *After Postmodernism: Reconstructing Ideology Critique*. Sage, London, p.1-11.

Biot, Y., P.M. Blaikie, C. Jackson & R. Palmer-Jones, (1995), *Rethinking Research on Land Degradation in Developing Countries*. World Bank Discussion Papers no. 289, The World Bank, Washington.

Black, Nancy Johnson, (1989), *Transformation of a Frontier Mission Province; The Order of Our Lady of Mercy in Western Honduras, 1525-1773*. PhD dissertation, State University of New York at Albany.

Blaikie, Piers, (1985), *The Political Economy of Soil Erosion in Developing Countries*. Longman, Harlow, Essex.

Blaikie, Piers, (1988), The Explanation of Land Degradation in Nepal. In: J. Ives & D.C. Pitt (eds), *Deforestation: Social Dynamics in Watersheds and Mountain Ecosystems*. Routledge, London, p.132-158.

Blaikie, Piers, (1993), What Glasses Are We Wearing? Different Views of Environmental Management. In: C. Cristiansson, A. Dahlberg, V.M. Loiske & W. Ostberg (eds), *Environment, Users, Scholars. Exploring Interfaces*. ESDU Stockholm University, Stockholm.

Blaikie, Piers M. & Harold Brookfield, (1987), *Land Degradation and Society*. Methuen, London.

Blühdorn, Ingolfur, (1996), A Theory of Post-Ecologist Politics. Paper given at the Euroconference on Environment and Innovation, October 23-26, 1996.

Bolhuis, E.E. & Ploeg, J.D. van der, (1985), *Boerenarbeid en stijlen van landbouwbeoefening*. Leiden Development Studies 8, Leiden.

Booth, David, (1994), Rethinking Social Development: an overview. In: Booth, D. (ed.), *Rethinking Social Development. Theory, Research and Practice*. Longman, Harlow Essex, England, p.3-34.

Boserup, Esther, (1965), *The Conditions of Agricultural Growth. The Economics of Agrarian Change under Population Pressure*. George Allen & Unwin, London.

Boyer, Jefferson C., (1982), *Agrarian Capitalism and Peasant Praxis in Southern Honduras*. PhD dissertation, University of North Carolina. University Microfilms International, Ann Arbor, Michigan.

Brand, Charles Abbey, (1972), *The Background of Capitalistic Underdevelopment: Honduras to 1913*. PhD dissertation, University of Pittsburgh.

Brass, Tom, (1991), Moral Economists, Subalterns, New Social Movements, and the (Re-) Emergence of a (Post-) Modernised (Middle) Peasant. *The Journal of Peasant Studies* 18(2):173-205.

Brass, Tom, (1995), Old Conservatism in 'New' Clothes. *The Journal of Peasant Studies* 22(3):516-540.

Bravo H., (1989), Konkurrenzbeziehungen zwischen pflanzlicher und tierischer Produktion. *Agrarwirtschaft und Agrarsoziologie* 1/89:22-38.

Breman, Jan, (1993), *Beyond Patronage and Exploitation: Changing Agrarian Relations in South Gujarat*. Oxford U.P., Delhi.

Brockett, Charles D., (1987), Public Policy, Peasants, and Rural Development in Honduras. *Journal of Latin American Studies* 19:69-86.

Brockett, Charles D., (1988), *Land, Power and Poverty. Agrarian Transformation and Political Conflict in Central America*. Unwin Hyman, Boston.

Brokensha, D., D.M. Warren & O. Werner (eds), (1980), *Indigenous Knowledge Systems and Development*. Univeristy Press of America, Lanham.

Brouwer, Roland, (1995), *Planting Power. The Afforestation of the Commons and State Formation in Portugal*. PhD dissertation, Wageningen Agricultural University, Wageningen.

Brouwer, Roland & Kees Jansen, (1989), Critical Introductory Notes on Farming Systems Research in Developing Third World Agriculture. *Systems Practice* 2(4):379-395.

Brouwer, R. & K. Jansen, (1990), FSR: Model en Werkelijkheid. In: R. Brouwer & K. Jansen (eds), *Het systeem, de som en de delen: 5 opstellen over FSR*. SG-paper 115, Studium Generale LU, Wageningen, p.5-53.

256

Browning, David, (1971), *El Salvador: Landscape and Society*. Oxford U.P., London.

Brundtland G.H. et al., (1987), *Our Common Future*. World Commision on Environment and Development. Oxford U.P., Oxford.

Brush, Stephen B. & B.L. Turner II, (1987), The Nature of Farming Systems and Views of Their Change. In: B.L. Turner II & S.B. Brush (eds), *Comparative Farming Systems*. The Guilford Press, New York, p.11-48.

Brzovic Parilo, Francisco J., (1990), Crisis Económica y Medio Ambiente en Honduras. Mimeo, CEPAL.

Bulmer-Thomas, V., (1987), *The Political Economy of Central America since 1920*. Cambridge University Press, Cambridge.

Bunch, Rolando, (1982), *Dos mazorcas de maíz*. World Neighbors, Oklahoma City.

Bunch, Rolando & Gabino López, (1995), La recuperación de suelos de Centroamérica: midiendo el impacto de 4 a 40 años después de la intervención. Mimeo, COSECHA, Tegucigalpa, Honduras.

Burawoy, Michael, (1985), *The Politics of Production. Factory Regimes under Capitalism and Socialism*. Verso, London.

Burawoy, Michael, (1991), The Extended Case Method. In: M. Burawoy (ed.), *Ethnography Unbound. Power and Resistance in the Modern Metropolis*. University of California Press, Los Angeles, p.271-287.

Burgos, Jorquin, (1941), *Economía Rural. Exposición de aspectos agrícolas y económicos de la vida rural hondureña, con motivo de experiencias de trabajo práctico durante veinte años*. Tegucigalpa.

Buttel, Frederick H. & William Sunderlin, (1988), Integrating Political Economy and Political Ecology: An Assessment of Theories of Agricultural and Extractive Industry Development in Latin America. Paper presented at the 46th International Conference of Americanists, Amsterdam, 4-8 July 1988.

Byres, T.J., (1986), The Agrarian Question, Forms of Capitalist Agrarian Transition and the State: An Essay With Reference to Asia. *Social Scientist* 1986:3-67.

Cadiñanos, F. de, (1893), Censo levantado por fray Fernando de Cadiñanos, obispo de esta diócesis, en 1791. In: A.R. Vallejo (ed.), *Primer Anuario Estadístico Correspondiente al Año de 1889, República de Honduras*. Tipografía Nacional, Tegucigalpa, p.101-118.

Campanella, P. et al., (1982), *Honduras. Perfil ambiental del país. Un estudio de campo*. JRB Associates, McLean, Virginia.

Campos, Guillermo, (1910), La supresión de la quema en la práctica agrícola. *Revista Económica* 2(11):602-4 (Boletin mensual, Tegucigalpa).

Cárcamo, Julio A., Jeffrey Alwang & George W. Norton, (1994), On-site economic evaluation of soil conservation practices in Honduras. *Agricultural Economics* 11:257-269.

Cardoso, Ciro F.S., (1977), The formation of the coffee estate in nineteenth-century Costa Rica. In: K. Duncan, I. Rutledge & C. Harding (eds), *Land and Labour in Latin America. Essays on the Development of Agrarian Capitalism in the Nineteenth and Twentieth Centuries*. Cambridge, U.P., Cambridge, p.165-202.

Carrière, Jean, (1991), The Political Economy of Environmental Degradation in Costa Rica. In: Reclift, M. & D. Goodman (eds), *Environment and Development in Latin America. The Politics of Sustainability*. Manchester U.P., UK, p.1-23.

Castellanos, V. & C.S. Simmons, revisado por C.V. Plath, (1984 [1967]), *Uso Potencial de la Tierra (Republica de Honduras)*. Mapa, Dirección Ejecutiva del Catastro. SRN, Tegucigalpa.

Castillo, L., C. Wesseling, H. Aguilar, C. Castillo & P. de Vos, (1989), Uso e Impacto de los Plaguicidas en Tres Paises Centroamericanos. *Estudios Sociales Centroamericanos* 49:119-139.

CATIE (Centro Agronómico Tropical de Investigación y Enseñanza), (1984), *Alternativa de manejo para el sistema maíz-frijol (El Rosario, Honduras)*. Serie Técnica, Informe técnico No 48, Turrialba, Costa Rica.

CATIE (Centro Agronómico Tropical de Investigación y Enseñanza), (1986), *Alternativa de manejo para el sistema maíz-maicillo (Comayagua, Honduras)*. Serie Técnica, Informe técnico No 83, Turrialba, Costa Rica.

CDI (Centro de Desarrollo Industrial) - RRNN, (1988), *PRODESBA: Componente de crédito artesanal*. CDI-RRNN, Tegucigalpa, Honduras.

Chambers, Robert & B.P. Ghildyal, (1985), Agricultural Research for Resource-Poor Farmers: The Farmer-First-and-Last Model. *Agricultural Administration* 20:1-30.

Chambers, R., A. Pacey & L.A. Thrupp (eds), (1989), *Farmer First. Farmer Innovation and Agricultural Research*. Intermediate Technology Publications, London.

Chapman, Anne, (1985), *Los Hijos del Copal y la Candela. Ritos Agrarios y Tradición Oral de los Lencas de Honduras (tomo I)*. UNAM, México.

257

Chávez M., Sergio, Guadalupe Cruz & Jose Ricardo Pérez, (1987), *Estudio del caso de la cuenca del rio Palaja.* ENEE/CATIE, Tegucigalpa.

Chayanov, A.V., (1987), The Family Farm as a Component of the National Economy and Its Possible Forms of Development. In: A.V. Chayanov, *The Theory of Peasant Economy.* Oxford U.P., Delhi.

CIDICCO, (1991-), *Noticias sobre Cultivos de Cobertura.* Tegucigalpa.

CNPDH (Comisionado Nacional de Protección de los Derechos Humanos), (1994), *Los hechas hablan por sí mismo. Informe preliminar sobre los desaparecidos en Honduras 1980-1993.* Guaymuras, Tegucigalpa.

Cochet, Hubert, (1993), Agriculture sur brulis, élevage extensif et dégradation de l'environnement en Amérique Latine (Un exemple en Sierra Madre del Sur, au Mexique). *Revue Tiers Monde* 34(134):281-303.

CODA (Conesjo de Desarrollo Agrícola), (1995), *Plan Agrícola para el Desarrollo del Campo 1995-1998: PROAGRO.* SRN, Tegucigalpa.

Coles, Alexander, (1988), Transacciones de parcelas y el proyecto de titulación de tierras en Honduras. Mimeo, Land Tenure Center, University of Wisconsin, Madison.

Collier, Andrew, (1994), *Critical Realism. An Introduction to Roy Bhaskar's Philosophy.* Verso, London.

Comaroff, John & Jean Comaroff, (1992), *Ethnography and the Historical Imagination.* Westview Press, Boulder.

Conklin, Harold C., (1957), *Hanunóo Agriculture. A Report on an Integral System of Shifting Cultivation in the Philippines.* FAO, Rome.

CONSUPLANE, (n.d.), Reforma agraria, desarrollo y empleo rural. Unidad de recursos humanos, CONSUPLANE, Tegucigalpa (unpublished draft).

Contreras, Alonso de, (1991 [1582]), Relación hecha a su Majestad por el gobernador de Honduras, de todos los pueblos de dicha gobernación. In: H.M. Leyva (ed.), *Documentos Coloniales de Honduras.* Centro de Publicaciones Obispado de Cholutca/CEHDES, Tegucigalpa, Honduras, p.58-74.

Conway, Gordon R., (1985), Agroecosystem Analysis. *Agricultural Administration* 20:31-55.

Cook, O.F., (1909), *Vegetation affected by agriculture in Central America.* U.S. Department of Agriculture, Bureau of Plant Industry, bulletin no.145, Washington.

Cook, O.F., (1921), Milpa Agriculture: a Primitive Tropical System. *Annual Report Smithsonian Institution 1919,* Government Printing Office, Washington, p.307-326.

CRABE, (1984), *Flame Cultivation for Weed Control.* Proceedings of the International Meeting 20-22 November 1984, Namur, Belgium.

Croll, Elisabeth & David Parkin, (1992), Cultural understandings of the environment. In: E. Croll & D. Parkin (eds), *Bush Base: Forest Farm. Culture, Environment and Development.* Routledge, London, p.11-36.

Culbert, Patrick, (1974), *The Lost Civilization: the Story of the Classic Maya.* Harper and Row, New York.

de Janvry, Alain, (1981), *The Agrarian Question and Reformism in Latin America.* Johns Hopkins U.P., Baltimore.

de Janvry, A., E. Sadoulet & L. Wilcox Young, (1989), Land and Labour in Latin American Agriculture from the 1950s to the 1980s. *The Journal of Peasant Studies* 16(3):396-424.

Deere, Carmen Diana & de Janvry, Alain, (1979), A Conceptual Framework for the Empirical Analysis of Peasants. *American Journal of Agricultural Economics* 61:601-611.

Del-Cid, J. Rafael, (1977), *Reforma Agraria y Capitalismo Dependiente.* Editorial Universitaria, Tegucigalpa.

DeWalt, Billie R., (1983), The cattle are eating the forest. *The Bulletin of the Atomic Scientists* 39(1):18-23.

DeWalt, Billie R., (1985a), Microcosmic and Macrocosmic Processes of Agrarian Change in Southern Honduras: The Cattle Are Eating the Forest. In: B.R. DeWalt & P.J. Pelto (eds), *Micro and Macro Levels of Analysis in Anthropology.* Issues in Theory and Research. Westview Press, Boulder, Colorado, p.165-186.

DeWalt, Billie R., (1985b), The Agrarian Bases of Conflict in Central America. In: K. H. Coleman & G.C. Herring (eds), *The Central American Crisis.* Welmington, Deleware, SRInc, p.43-54.

DeWalt, Billie R., (1994), Using Indigenous Knowledge to Improve Agriculture and Natural Resource Management. *Human Organization* 53(2):123-131.

DeWalt, Billie R & Kathleen M. DeWalt, (1984), *Sistemas de cultivo en Pespire, Sur de Honduras: un enfoque de agroecosistemas.* Report no.1 del proyecto entre la Universidad de Kentucky y el Instituto Hondureño de Antropología e História.

DGECH (Dirección General de Estadísticas y Censos de Honduras), (1954), *Censo Agropecuario 1952.* San Salvador.

DGECH (Dirección General de Estadísticas y Censos de Honduras), (1968), *Segundo Censo Agropecuario Nacional, 1965-1966.* Tegucigalpa.

DGECH (Dirección General de Estadísticas y Censos de Honduras), (1978), *Tercer Censo Nacional Agropecuario 1974.* Tegucigalpa.

DGECH (Dirección General de Estadísticas y Censos de Honduras), (1990), *Censo Nacional de Población y Vivienda 1988.* Tegucigalpa.

Donoghue, L.R. & V.J. Johnson, (1975), *Prescribed Burning in the North Central States.* North Cent. For. Exp. Stn., St. Paul, Minnesota.

Drucker, P. & J.W. Fox, (1982), Swidden Didn' Make All That Midden: The Search for Ancient Mayan Agronomies. *Journal of Anthropological Research* 38(2):179-193.

Durham, William H., (1979), *Scarcity and Survival in Central America. Ecological Origins of the Soccer War.* Stanford U.P., Stanford California.

Durham, William H., (1995), Political Ecology and Environmental Destruction in Latin America. In: M. Painter & W.H. Durham (eds), *The Social Causes of Environmental Destruction in Latin America.* The University of Michigan Press, Ann Arbor, p.249-264.

Edelman, Marc, (1994), Landlords and the Devil: Class, Ethnic, and Gender Dimensions of Central American Peasant Narratives. *Cultural Anthropology* 9(1):58-93.

Edelman, Marc, (1995), Rethinking the Hamburger Thesis: Deforestation and the Crisis of Central America's Beef Exports. In: M. Painter & W.H. Durham (eds), *The Social Causes of Environmental Destruction in Latin America.* The University of Michigan Press, Ann Arbor, p.25-62.

Eder, Klaus, (1996), *The Social Construction of Nature.* Sage, London.

Ellen, Roy, (1982), *Environment, Subsistence and System. The Ecology of Small-Scale Social Formations.* Cambridge University Press, Cambridge.

Ellen, Roy, (1996), Introduction. In: R. Ellen & K. Fukui (eds), *Redefining Nature: Ecology, Culture and Domestication.* Berg, Oxford, p.1-36.

Ellis, Frank, (1993), *Peasant Economics. Farm Households and Agrarian Development.* Cambridge U.P., Cambridge.

Escobar, Arturo, (1996), Constructing Nature: Elements for a Poststructural Political Ecology. In: R. Peet & M. Watts (eds), *Liberation Ecologies: Environment, Development, Social Movements.* Routledge, London, p.46-68.

Euraque, Darío, (1992), Zonas regionales en la formación del Estado Hondureño 1830-1930: el caso de la Costa Norte. *Revista Centroamericana de Economía* 13(39):65-102.

Euraque, Darío, (1996), *El Capitalismo de San Pedro Sula y la Historia Política Hondureña (1870-1972).* Guaymuras, Tegucigalpa.

Euroconsult, (1989), *Agricultural Compendium for Rural Development in the Tropics and Subtropics.* Elsevier, Amsterdam.

Faber, Daniel, (1992), Imperialism, Revolution, and the Ecological Crisis of Central America. *Latin American Perspectives* 19(1):17-44 (Issue 72, Winter 1992).

Faber, Daniel, (1993), *Environment under Fire. Imperialism and the Ecological Crisis in Central America.* Monthly Review Press, New York.

Fairhead, James & Melissa Leach, (1994), Declarations of Difference. In: I. Scoones & J. Thompson (eds), *Beyond Farmer First: Rural People's Knowledge, Agricultural Research and Extension Practice.* Intermediate Technology Publications, p.75-79.

Fairhead, James & Melissa Leach, (1995), False Forest History, Complicit Social Analysis: Rethinking Some West African Environmental Narratives. *World Development* 23(6):1023-1035.

Fandino, Mario, (1993), Land Titling and Peasant Differentiation in Honduras. *Latin American Perspectives* 20(2):45-53.

FAO & Conservation Foundation, (1954), *Soil Erosion Survey of Latin America.* Reprint from Journal of Soil and Water Conservation.

Farah, Jumanah, (1994), *Pesticide Policies in Developing Countries: do they encourage excessive use?* World Bank discussion papers 238, Washington.

FHIA, (1989), *Caracterización Físico-ambiental de la Región Cafetalera de Santa Bárbara, Honduras.* Informe Final. Fundación Hondureña de Investigación Agrícola, La Lima, Honduras.

Field, Les, (1991), Tools for Indigenous Agricultural Development in Latin America: An Anthropologist's Perspective. *Agriculture and Human Values* 8(1/2):85-92.

Foster, George M., (1960), *Culture and Conquest: America's Spanish Heritage*. Wenner-Gren Foundation for Anthropological Research, New York.

Fresco, L.O., (1986), *Cassava in Shifting Cultivation: a Systems Approach to Agricultural Technology Development in Africa*. Royal Tropical Institute, Amsterdam.

Fresco, L.O. & E. Westphal, (1988), A Hierarchical Classification of Farm Systems. *Experimental Agriculture* 24:399-419.

Freter, AnnCorinne, (1989), *The Classic Maya Collapse at Copan, Honduras: a regional settlement perspective*. PhD dissertation, The Pennsylvania State University, UMI, Ann Arbor, Michigan.

Friedmann, Harriet, (1980), Household Production and the National Economy: Concepts for the Analysis of Agrarian Formations. *The Journal of Peasant Studies* 7(2):158-184.

Fúnez Martínez, M.L., (1989), *Problemática Ambiental en Honduras*. Asociación Hondureña de Ecología & FOPRIDEH, Tegucigalpa.

Gibbon, P. & M. Neocosmos, (1985), Some Problems in the Political Economy of 'African Socialism'. In: H. Bernstein & B.K. Campbell (eds), *Contradictions of Accumulation in Africa. Studies in Economic and State*. Sage, Beverly Hills, p.153-206.

Giddens, Anthony, (1984), *The Constitution of Society*. Polity Press, Cambridge.

Giddens, Anthony, (1996), Affluence, Poverty and the Idea of a Post-Scarcity Society. *Development and Change* 27:365-377.

Goldblatt, David, (1996), *Social Theory and the Environment*. Polity Press, Cambridge.

Goldschmidt, Tijs, (1995), *Darwins hofvijver. Een drama in het Victoriameer*. Prometheus, Amsterdam (3rd edition).

Goodell, Grace, Keith L. Andrews & Julio I. López, (1990), The Contributions of Agronomo-Anthropologists to On-farm Research and Extension in Integrated Pest Managment. *Agricultural Systems* 32:321-340.

Goud, Benoit, (1986), *Empresas campesinas en Honduras: el modelo y la realidad*. Proyecto Forge, IICA, Tegucigalpa.

Goudsblom, J., (1992), *Vuur en beschaving*. Meulenhoff, Amsterdam.

Greenberg, James B. & Thomas K. Park, (1994), Political Ecology. *Journal of Political Ecology* 1(1):1-12 (http://www.library.arizon.edu/ej/jpe/jpeweb.html).

Grossman, Lawrence S., (1993), The Political Ecology of Banana Exports and Local Food Production in St. Vincent, Eastern Caribbean. *Annals of the Association of American Geographers* 83(2):347-367.

Grundmann, R., (1991), The Ecological Challenge to Marxism. *New Left Review* 187:103-120.

Gudeman, Stephen, (1978), *The Demise of a Rural Economy. From Subsistence to Capitalism in a Latin American Village*. Routledge & Kegan Paul, London.

Gudeman, Stephen & Alberto Rivera, (1990), *Conversations in Colombia. The Domestic Economy in Life and Text*. Cambridge U.P. Cambridge.

Guevara-Escudero, José, (1983), *Nineteenth-Century Honduras: A Regional Approach to the Economic History of Central America, 1839-1914*. PhD-thesis, Department of History, New York University.

Guivant, Julia, (n.d.), The Social Construction of Risks: Pesticides from the Farmers' Point of View. (forthcoming).

Hannigan, John A., (1995), *Environmental Sociology: a Social Constructionist Perspective*. Routledge, London.

Hart, Robert D., (1982a), An Ecological Systems Conceptual Framework for Agricultural Research and Development. In: W. Shaner, P. Philipp & W. Schmehl (eds), *Readings in Farming Systems Research and Development*. Westview, Boulder, p.44-58.

Hart, Robert D., (1982b), One Farm System in Honduras: A Case Study in Farm Systems Research. In: W. Shaner, P. Philipp & W. Schmehl (eds), *Readings in Farming Systems Research and Development*. Westview, Boulder, p.59-73.

Harvey, David, (1993), The Nature of Environment: the Dialectics of Social and Environmental Change. *The Socialist Register 1993*. Merlin, London, p.1-51.

Hayward, Tim, (1994), The Meaning of Political Ecology. *Radical Philosophy* 66:11-23.

Hecht, Susanna B., (1985), Environment, Development and Politics: Capital Accumulation and the Livestock Sector in Eastern Amazonia. *World Development* 13(6):663-684.

Hecht, Susanna B., (1995), Nature, Myths, Epistemes, and Policy in Tropical Politics of Biotechnology. In: Agrarian Questions Organising Committee (ed.), *Agrarian Questions: the Politics of Farming anno 1995: proceedings*. Wageningen Agricultural University, Wageningen, p.588-606.

260

Hengel, Eduard van, (1987), Waarom technologie zich leent voor kritiek. *Spil* (61/62):9-18.

Hernández, Alcídez, (1991), *La política económica y la situación del sector forestal*. Boletin Especial No. 57, Diciembre 1991, CEDOH. Tegucigalpa.

Hesse-Rodríguez, Monika, (1994), *Sembradores de esperanza. Conservar para cultivar y vivir*. Guaymuras-COMUNICA, Tegucigalpa.

Hoksberger, F. & K. Jager, (1985), *Mogelijkheden en beperkingen van onkruidbestrijding met stootbranders*. Rapport nr. 404, De Dorschkamp, Wageningen.

Honduras, República de, (n.d.), *Matrícula de fierros y marcas de los dueños de ganado vacuno y caballar*. Tegucigalpa. (printed before 1893, Cortés is not yet named as a seperated district; according to historian Mario Argueta it was published during the presidency of Luis Bográn (1883-1891).

Honduras, (1914), *Memoria del Secretario del Estado en el Despacho de Fomento, Obras Públicas, y Agricultura presentada al Congreso Nacional, 1913-1914*. Tegucigalpa.

Honduras, República de, (1924), *Ley agraria, Decreto No. 34, 20 de noviembre de 1924*. Tipografía Nacional, Tegucigalpa.

Honduras, Secretaría de Estado en los Despachos de Fomento, Agricultura y Trabajo., (1943), *Lotes de familia. Su creación, legislación y designación*. Tip. La Democracia, Tegucigalpa.

Honduras, (1955), *Ley Forestal. Decreto-Ley No. 184, 1955*. Secretaría de Recursos Naturales, Tegucigalpa.

Honduras, Congreso Nacional, (1961), *Ley Forestal. Decreto No. 117, 27 de Mayo de 1961*. Talleres Tipolitográficos, Tegucigalpa.

Honduras, (1961), *Ley de Policía (de 22 de Enero de 1906) y sus reformas*. AMHON (Asociación de Municipios de Honduras). Tegucigalpa.

Honduras, (1974), *Decreto-Ley No. 103 (Ley de COHDEFOR), de 15 de Enero de 1974*. Tegucigalpa.

Honduras, República de, (1975), Ley de reforma agraria, Decreto-Ley No. 170, 1974. *La Gaceta* nr.21482, 08-01-1975, Tegucigalpa.

Honduras, República de, (1992), Ley para la modernización y el desarrollo del sector agrícola. *La Gaceta* 6-4-92; Decreto 31-92.

Honduras, República de, (1995), *Ley General del Ambiente (1993, decreto número 104-93) y su Reglamento General (1993, acuerdo número 109-93)*. Secretaría del Ambiente (SEDA) and Guaymuras, Tegucigalpa, Honduras.

Horton, Robin, (1970), African Traditional Thought and Western Science. In: B.R. Wilson (ed.), *Rationality*. Basil Blackwell, Oxford, p.131-171.

Howard, Patricia Ballard, (1987), *From Banana Republic to Cattle Republic: Agrarian Roots of the Crisis in Honduras*. PhD dissertation, Ann Arbor, Michigan University Microfilms.

Howard-Borjas, Patricia, (1989), Implicaciones de la expansión ganadera en la población, el empleo y la alimentación. Alternativas de política a la actual crisis. Resumen ejecutivo. Documento de trabajo, Proyectos SECPLAN/OIT/FNUAP, Tegucigalpa.

Howard-Borjas, Patricia, (1995), Cattle and Crisis: the Genesis of Unsustainable Development in Central America. In: Agrarian Questions Organising Committee (ed.), *Agrarian Questions: the Politics of Farming anno 1995: proceedings*. Wageningen Agricultural University, Wageningen, p.617-646.

Hudson, N.W., (1988), Conservation Parctices and Runoff Water Disposal on Steep Lands. In: W.C. Moldenhauer & N.W. Hudson (eds), *Conservation Farming on Steep Lands. Soil and Water Conservation Society*. Ankeny, Iowa, p.117-128.

IHCAFE (Instituto Hondureño del Café), (1993), Censo cafetalero 1992-1993. Unpublished data. IHCAFE, Tegucigalpa.

IHDER, (1980), *84 meses de reforma agraria del gobierno de las Fuerzas Armadas de Honduras*. IHDER, Tegucigalpa.

IHDER, (1981), *La Tenencia de la Tierra en Honduras*. Tegucigalpa, Honduras.

INA (Instituto Nacional Agrario), (1990), Proyecto Titulación de Tierras. Informe final 1982-1990. Mimeo, Tegucigalpa, Honduras.

Ingold, Tim, (1986), *The Appropriation of Nature. Essays on Human Ecology and Social Relations*. Manchester University Press, Manchester.

Ingold, Tim, (1992), Culture and the Perception of the Environment In: E. Croll & D. Parkin (eds), *Bush Base: Forest Farm. Culture, Environment and Development*. Routledge, London, p.39-56.

261

Jansen, Kees, (1992), Agrarische ontwikkeling en het ecologisch denken: de vergankelijkheid van duurzaamheid. *Derde Wereld* 92(3):39-58.

Jansen, Kees, (1993), Café y Formas de Producción en Honduras. *Revista Centroamericana de Economía* 14(41):58-96.

Jansen, Kees, (1995), The Art of Burning and the Politics of Indigenous Agricultural Knowledge. In: Agrarian Questions Organising Committee (ed.), *Agrarian Questions: the Politics of Farming anno 1995: proceedings.* Wageningen Agricultural University, Wageningen, p.676-708.

Jansen, Kees, (1996), Ecological Dilemmas of Coffee Exports and Local Food Production in North-West Honduras. *European Review of Latin American and Caribbean Studies* 60:7-30.

Jansen, Kees, (1997), Diversity and the Nature of Technological Change in Hillside Farming in Honduras. In: J. de Groot & R. Ruben (eds), *Sustainable Agriculture in Central America.* MacMillan, Basingstoke, p.108-126.

Jansen, Kees & Tatiana Lara, (1996), Producción Agrícola y Cuestión Ecológica: Desenmarañar el Nudo Gordiano. In: A.A. Khan (ed.), *Economía Agrícola: Recorrido Teórico y Debates de Interés Actual.* Prografic, Tegucigalpa, p.103-130.

Jansen, Kees & Esther Roquas, (1998), Modernizing Insecurity: the Land Titling Project in Honduras. *Development and Change* 29:81-106.

Johannessen, Carl L., (1959), *The Geography of the Savannas of Interior Honduras.* Department of Geography, University of California, Berkeley.

Johnson, Hazel, (1997), Food Insecurity as a Sustainability Issue: Lessons from Honduran Maize Farming. In: J. de Groot & R. Ruben (eds), *Sustainable Agriculture in Central America.* MacMillan, Basingstoke, p.89-107.

Jones, Jeffrey R., (1990), *Colonization and Environment. Land Settlement Projects in Central America.* United Nations University Press, Tokyo.

Kaimowitz, David, (1993), NGOs, the State and Agriculture in Central America. In: A. Bebbington & G. Thiele (eds), *Non-Governmental Organizations and the State in Latin America.* Routledge, London, p.178-198.

Kaimowitz, David, (1996a), The Political Economy of Environmental Policy Reform in Latin America. *Development and Change* 27:433-452.

Kaimowitz, David, (1996b), La ganadería hondureña: entre la esperanza de un crecimineto incluyente y sostenible y las amenazas del latifundio y la deforestación. In: E. Baumeister (ed.), *El agro hondureño y su futuro.* Guaymuras, Tegucigalpa, p.167-208.

Kaimowitz, D., D. Erazo, M. Mejía & A. Navarro., (1992), Las organizaciones privadas de desarrollo y la transferencia de tecnología en el agro hondureño. *Revista Centroamericana de Economía* 12(37):46-88.

Kay, Cristóbal, (1991), Reflections on the Latin American Contribution to Development Theory. *Development and Change* 22:31-68.

Kay, Cristóbal, (1995), Rural Development and Agrarian Issues in Contemporary Latin America. In: J. Weeks (ed.), *Structural Adjustement and the Agricultural Sector in Latin America and the Caribbean.* MacMillan, London, p.9-44.

Kearney, Michael, (1996), *Reconceptualizing the Peasantry: Anthropology in Global Perspective.* Westview Press, Boulder.

Kendall, Carl, (1983), Loose Structure of Family in Honduras. *Journal of Comparative Family Studies* 14(2):257-272.

Kincaid, Douglas, (1985), "We Are the Agrarian Reform": Rural Politics and Agrarian Reform. In: N. Peckenham & A. Street (eds), *Honduras: Portrait of a Captive Nation.* Preager, New York, p.135-147.

Kloppenburg, Jack, (1988), *First the Seed. The Political Economy of Plant Biotechnology, 1492-2000.* Cambridge University Press, Cambridge.

Kloppenburg, Jack, (1991), Social Theory and the De/Reconstruction of Agricultural Science: Local Knowledge for an Alternative Agriculture. *Rural Sociology* 56(4):519-548.

Knorr-Cetina, Karin, (1997), De epistemische samenleving. Hoe kennisstructuren zich nestelen in social structuren. *Kennis en Methode* 21(1):5-28. (translation of: Epistemics in Society: On the nesting of knowledge structures into social structures).

Kozuch, M.J., J.W. Carter, R.C. Finch & F. Ramirez, (1990), *Geología del cuandrangulo de La Unión, Lempira.* Mapa Geológico de Honduras, Instituto Geográfico Nacional, Tegucigalpa (scale 1:50,000).

Kramer, Frank, (1986), *Market Incorporation and Out-migration of the Peasants of Western Honduras*. PhD dissertation, University of California, University Microfilms International, Ann Arbor, Michigan.

Laclau, Ernesto & Chantal Mouffe, (1985), *Hegemony and Socialist Strategy. Towards a Radical Democratic Politics*. Verso, London.

Lacroix, A., (1981), *Transformations du procès de travail agricole, incidenced de l'industrialisation sur les conditions de travail paysannes*. Grenoble.

Lapper, Richard, & James Painter, (1985), *Honduras: State for Sale*. Latin America Bureau, London.

Latour, Bruno, (1987), *Wetenschap in actie. Wetenschappers en technici in de maatschappij*. Bert Bakker, Amsterdam, (translation of: Science in Action, 1987).

Latour, Bruno, (1994), *Wij zijn nooit modern geweest: pleidooi voor een symmetrische antropologie*. Van Gennep, Amsterdam, (translation of: Nous n'avons jamais été modernes. La Découverte, Paris, 1991).

Law, John, (1992), Notes on the Theory of the Actor-Network: Ordering, Strategy, and Heterogeneity. *Systems Practice* 5(4):379-393.

Lehmann, David, (1997), An Opportunity Lost: Escobar's Deconstruction of Development. *The Journal of Development Studies* 33(4):568-578.

Lemus, M. & H.G. Bourgeois, (1897), *Breve notícia sobre Honduras. Datos geográficos, estadísticos e informaciones prácticas*. Tipografía Nacional, Tegucigalpa.

Lentz, David L., (1986), Ethnobotany of the Jicaque of Honduras. *Economic Botany* 40(2):210-219.

Lentz, David, (1989), Contemporary Plant Communities in the El Cajon Region. In: K. Hirth, G. Lara Pinto & G. Hasemann (eds), *Investigaciones Arqueológicas en la Región de El Cajon, Tomo I*. University of Pittsburgh, Latin American Archaeology Publications, Pittsburgh, p.59-94.

Leonard, H.J., (1987), *Natural Resources and Economic Development in Central America*. Transaction Books, Oxford.

Lévi-Strauss, Claude, (1990), *Het wilde denken*. Meulenhoff, Amsterdam. (translation of: La Pensée Sauvage. Librarie Plon, Paris, 1962).

Littlewood, Paul, (1980), Patronage, Ideology and Reproduction. *Critique of Anthropology* 15(4):29-45.

Llambí, Luis, (1991), Latin American Peasantries and Regimes of Accumulation. *European Review of Latin American and Caribbean Studies* 51:27-50.

Lockie, Stewart David, (1996), *Sociocultural Dynamics and the Development of the Landcare Movement in Australia*. PhD dissertation, Charles Sturt University.

Loker, William, (1986), *Agricultural Ecology and Prehistoric Settlement in the El Cajon Region of Honduras*. PhD dissertation, University of Colorado. Ann Arbor, Michigan.

Long, Norman, (1986), Commoditization: Thesis and Antithesis. In: N. Long et al., *The Commoditization Debate: Labour Process, Strategy and Social Network*. Papers of the Department of Sociology 17, Agricultural University Wageningen, p.8-23.

Long, Norman, (1989), Conclusion: Theoretical Reflections on Actor, Structure and Interface. Norman Long (ed.), *Encounters at the Interface. A Perspective on Social Discontinuities in Rural Development*. Wageningen Sociologische Studies 27. Landbouwuniversiteit Wageningen. p.221-243.

Long, Norman, (1992a), Introduction. In: N. Long & A. Long (eds), *Battlefields of Knowledge. The Interlocking of Theory and Practice in Social Research and Development*. Routledge, London, p.3-15.

Long, Norman, (1992b), Conclusion. In: N. Long & A. Long (eds), *Battlefields of Knowledge. The Interlocking of Theory and Practice in Social Research and Development*. Routledge, London, p.268-277.

Long, Norman & Jan Douwe van der Ploeg, (1994), Heterogeneity, Actor and Structure: Towards a Reconstitution of the Concept of Structure. In: Booth, D. (ed.), *Rethinking Social Development. Theory, Research and Practice*. Longman, Harlow Essex, England, p.62-89.

Long, Norman & Bryan Roberts, (1994), The Agrarian Structures of Latin America, 1930-1990. In: L. Bethell (ed.), *The Cambridge History of Latin America Vol. VI. Latin America since 1930: Economy, Society and Politics*. Cambridge U.P., Cambridge, p.325-390.

Long, Norman & Magdalena Villarreal, (1994), The Interweaving of Knowledge and Power in Development Interfaces. In: I. Scoones & J. Thompson (eds), *Beyond Farmer First: Rural People's Knowledge, Agricultural Research and Extension Practice*. Intermediate Technology Publications, p.41-52.

Mann, Susan A. & James M. Dickinson, (1978), Obstacles to the Development of a Capitalist Agriculture. *The Journal of Peasant Studies* 5(4):466-481.

263

Marglin, Stephen A., (1990), Towards the Decolonization of the Mind. In: F. Apffel-Marglin & S. Marglin (eds), *Dominating Knowledge: Development, Culture, and Resistance*. Clarendon Press, Oxford, p.1-28.

Martínez Alier, Juan, (1993), El ecologismo de los pobres. In: J. Barba (ed.), *Nuestro futuro: desafíos ambientales*. Istmo editores, El Salvador, p. 31-49.

Martinez-Alier, J., (1995a), In Praise of Smallholders. In: Agrarian Questions Organising Committee (ed.), *Agrarian Questions: the Politics of Farming anno 1995: proceedings*. Wageningen Agricultural University, Wageningen, p.935-942.

Martinez-Alier, J., (1995b), Political Ecology, Distributional Conflicts, and Economic Incommensurability. *New Left Review* 211:70-88.

Marx, Karl & Friedrich Engels, (1972), *De duitse ideologie; deel 1, Feuerbach*. SUN, Nijmegen.

Mausolff, Cristopher & Stephen Farber, (1995), An economic analysis of ecological agricultural technologies among peasant farmers in Honduras. *Ecological Economics* 12:237-248.

McClure, Gail, (1989), Introduction. In: D.M. Warren, L.J. Slikkerveer & S.O. Titilola (eds), *Indigenous Knowledge Systems: Implications for Agriculture and International Development*. Studies in Technology and Social Change no. 11, Iowa State University, Ames, p.1-2.

McLennan, Gregor, (1996), Post-Marxism and the 'Four Sins' of Modernist Theorizing. *New Left Review* 218:53-74.

Mejía, Francisco S., (1993), *Las actividades de conservación de suelos en las organizaciones privadas de desarrollo de Honduras*. FOPRIDEH/COSUDE-p/ONG, Tegucigalpa, Honduras.

Melmed-Sanjak, Yoline, (1993), The Proyecto de Titulación de Tierras. Paper presented at the seminar on the land titling research project, POSCAE, Tegucigalpa.

Membreño, Alberto, (1982), *Hondureñismos*. Guaymuras, Tegucigalpa, (reprint of second edition of 1897, Tegucigalpa).

Membreño, Alberto, (1994), *Toponimias Indígenas de Centroamérica*. Guaymuras, Tegucigalpa, (reprint of Nombres Geográficos Indígenas de la República de Honduras, 1901, Tegucigalpa).

Mendoza, Breny, (1996), *Sintiéndose Mujer, Pensándose Feminista. La Construcción del Movimiento Feminista en Honduras*. Guaymuras, Tegucigalpa.

Meyer, Birgit, (1994), Satan, slangen en geld. Betekenissen over duivelse rijkdom in christelijk Ghana. In: H. Driessen & H. de Jonge (eds), *In de ban van betekenis. Proeven van symbolische antropologie*. SUN, Nijmegen.

Meza Cálix, (1916), *Geografía de Honduras*. Tipografía Nacional, Tegucigalpa.

Milla, F., J. Almendares, L. Sarvide & M. Smith, (1994), *Tierra, Vida, Amor y Esperanza*. Litografía López, Tegucigalpa.

Milton, Kay, (1993), *Environmentalism. The View from Anthropology*. Routledge, London.

Milton, Kay, (1996), *Environmentalism and Cultural Theory. Exploring the Role of Anthropology in Environmental Discourse*. Routledge, London.

Mitchell, William P., (1991), *Peasants on the Edge: Crop, Cult, and Crisis in the Andes*. University of Texas Press, Austin.

Mol, Arthur P.J., (1995), *The Refinement of Production. Ecological Modernization Theory and the Chemical Industry*. Van Arkel, Utrecht.

Molina Chocano, Guillermo, (1975), Población, estructura productiva y migraciones internas en Honduras (1950-1960). *Estudios Sociales Centroamericanos* 12:9-39.

Molina Chocano, Guillermo, (1976), *Estado liberal y desarrollo capitalista en Honduras*. Editorial Universitaria UNAH, Tegucigalpa.

Montaner Larson, Janell B., (1995), *An Economic Analysis of Land Titling in Honduras*. PhD dissertation, University of Oxford.

Montes Maldonado, Carlos, (1928), *Cultivo racional del café*. Tipografía Nacional, Tegucigalpa.

Moore, Briscoe, (1969), *From Forest to Farm*. Pelham Books, London.

Morris, James A., (1984), *Honduras: Caudillo Politics and Military Rulers*. Westview Press, Boulder, Colorado.

Munshi Saldanha, Indra, (1990), The Political Ecology of Traditional Farming Practices in Thana District, Maharashtra (India). *The Journal of Peasant Studies* 17(3):433-443.

Murga Frassinetti, Antonio, (1977), Estructura agraria y latifundio: el caso de Honduras. In: *Lecturas sobre la realidad nacional*. Departamento de Ciencias Sociales, Editorial Universitaria, Colección Realidad Nacional No. 9, Tegucigalpa, p.43-74.

Murga Frassinetti, Antonio, (1978), *Enclave y sociedad en Honduras*. Editorial Universitaria, Tegucigalpa.

Murray, Douglas L., (1991), Export Agriculture, Ecological Disruption, and Social Inequity: Some Effect of Pesticides in Southern Honduras. *Agriculture and Human Values* 8(4):19-29.

Murray, Douglas L., (1994), *Cultivating Crisis. The Human Cost of Pesticides in Latin America*. University of Texas Press, Austin.

Murray, Douglas L. & Polly Hoppin, (1992), Recurring Contradictions in Agrarian Development: Pesticide Problems in Caribbean Basin Nontraditional Agriculture. *World Development* 20(4):597-608.

Mutz, J.L., T.G. Greene, C.J. Scifres & B.H. Koerth, (1985), *Response of Pan American Balsamscale, Soil, and Livestock to Prescribed Burning*. The Texas Agricultural Experiment Station, Texas.

Nations, James D. & Daniel I. Komer, (1987), Rainforests and the Hamburger Society. *The Ecologist* 17(4/5):161-167.

Nederveen Pieterse, Jan, (1991), Dilemmas of Development Discourse: The Crisis of Developmentalism and the Comparative Method. *Development and Change* 22:5-29.

Nesman, Edgar G. & Mitchel A. Seligson, (1987), *Baseline Survey of the Honduran Small Farmer Titling Proyect: Descriptive Analysis of the 1985 Sample*. LTC-Wisconsin Madison, USAID-Honduras.

Nesman, E.G., M.A. Seligson & A. Coles, (1989), El impacto de la titulación de tierras en Santa Bárbara, Honduras. Paper presented at the Seminar 'Políticas de tierra en Honduras', Wisconsin (7-11 August 1989).

Netting, Robert McC., (1993), *Smallholders, Householders. Farm Families and the Ecology of Intensive, Sustainable Agriculture*. Stanford U.P., Stanford, California.

Newson, Linda, (1992), *El costo de la conquista*. Editorial Guaymuras, Tegucigalpa, (translation of: The Cost of Conquest: Indian Decline in Honduras under Spanish Rule. Dellplain Latin American Studies no.20, Westview Press, Boulder Colorado, 1986).

Noé Pino, Hugo & A. Thorpe (eds), (1992), *Honduras: el ajuste estructural y la reforma agraria*. CEDOH-POSCAE, Tegucigalpa.

Noé Pino, Hugo, A. Thorpe & R. Sandoval Corea, (1992), *El Sector Agrícola y la Modernización en Honduras*. CEDOH/POSCAE, Tegucigalpa.

Nugent, Daniel, (1993), *Spent Cartridges of Revolution: an Anthropological History of Namiquipa, Chihuahua*. The University of Chicago Press, Chicago.

O'Connor, James, (1989), Uneven and Combined Development and Ecological Crisis: a Theoretical Introduction. *Race and Class* 30(3):1-11.

OEA (Organización de los Estados Americanos), (1962), *Informe Oficial de la misión 105 de asistencia técnica directa a Honduras sobre reforma agraria y desarrollo agrícola*. Union Panamericana, OEA, Washington D.C.

Okali, C., J. Sumberg & J. Farrington, (1994), *Farmer Participatory Research. Rhetoric and Reality*. Intermediate Technology Publications, London.

O'Neill, John, (1995), *The Poverty of Postmodernism*. Routledge, London.

Ooyens, J., (1988), Boerenbeweging en landhervorming in Honduras. In: J. Weerdenburg (ed.), *De Verenigde Staten van Amerika*, Studium Generale, Utrecht, p.83-97.

Orlove, Benjamin S., (1980), Ecological Anthropology. *Annual Review of Anthropology*. 9:235-273.

Ortega, Pompilio, (1951), *El cultivo del cafeto en Honduras*. Talleres Tipográficos Nacionales, Tegucigalpa.

Paine, Richard R. & AnnCorinne Freter, (1996), Environmental Degradation and the Classic Maya Collapse at Copan, Honduras (A.D. 600-1250). *Ancient Mesoamerica* 7:37-47.

Painter, Michael, (1995), Introduction: Anthropological Perspectives on Environmental Destruction. In: M. Painter & W.H. Durham (eds), p.1-21.

Painter, M. & W.H. Durham (eds), *The Social Causes of Environmental Destruction in Latin America*. The University of Michigan Press, Ann Arbor.

Pastor, Rodolfo, (1986), *El ocaso de los cacicazgos: historia de la crisis del sistema político hondureño*. CEDOH Especial 21. Tegucigalpa, Honduras.

Peek, Peter, (1984), *Agrarian Structure and rural poverty: the case of Honduras*. World Employment Programme research, ILO working paper WEP10-6/WP68.

Peet, Richard & Michael Watts, (1993), Introduction: Development Theory and Environment in an Age of Market Triumphalism. *Economic Geography* 69(3):227-253.

265

Peet, Richard & Michael Watts, (1996), Liberation Ecology: Development, Sustainability, and Environment in an Age of Market Triumphalism. In: R. Peet & M. Watts (eds), *Liberation Ecologies: Environment, Development, Social Movements*. Routledge, London, p.1-45.

Peters, William J. & Leon F. Neuenschwander, (1988), *Slash and Burn. Farming in the Third World Forest*. University of Idaho Press, Moscow, Idaho.

Pinel, Emilio, (1939), *Elementos de agricultura indispensables para todo buen agricultor*. Tegucigalpa.

Plath, C.V., (1967), *Uso potencial de la tierra. Parte V de un estudio Centroamericano, Honduras*. FAO, Roma.

Ploeg, Jan Douwe van der, (1987), *De verwetenschappelijking van de landbouwbeoefening*. Wageningen Studies in Sociology, Wageningen.

Ploeg, Jan Douwe van der, (1990), *Labor, Markets, and Agricultural Production*. Westview, Boulder.

Ploeg, Jan Douwe van der, (1991), *Landbouw als Mensenwerk. Arbeid en Technologie in de Agrarische Ontwikkeling*. Coutinho, Muidenberg.

Ploeg, Jan Douwe van der, (1994), Styles of Farming: an Introductory Note on Concepts and Methodology. In: J.D. Ploeg & A. Long (eds), *Born From Within. Practice and Perspectives of Endogenous Rural Development*. Van Gorcum, Assen, p.7-30.

Ponce, Mario, (1986), Honduras: Agricultural Policy and Perspectives. In: M.B. Rosenberg & P.L. Shepherd (eds), *Honduras confronts its future. Contending Perspectives on Critical Issues*. Lynne Rienner, Boulder, Colorado, p.129-152.

Posas, Mario, (1979), Politica Estatal y Estructura Agraria en Honduras (1950-1978). *Estudios Sociales Centroamericanos* 24:37-116.

Posas, Mario, (1981), *El Movimiento Campesino Hondureño*. Guaymuras, Tegucigalpa.

Posas, Mario, (1992), *La Autogestión en el Agro Hondureño. El caso de la Empresa Asociativa Campesina "Isletas" (EACI)*. Editorial Universitaria, Tegucigalpa.

Posas, Mario, (1996), El Sector Reformado y la Política Agrario del Estado. In: E. Baumeister (ed.), *El agro hondureño y su futuro*. Guaymuras, Tegucigalpa, p.131-166.

Posas, Mario & Rafael Del-Cid, (1983 [1981]), *La construcción del sector público y del estado nacional en Honduras (1876-1979)*. EDUCA, San José.

Post, T., (n.d.), A Literature Review on Topics Related to the Use of Leguminous Cover Crops, Particularly Velvet Bean, Mucuna pruriens, by Resource-Poor Farmers in Southern Mexico and Belize, Central America. Mimeo.

Puerta, Ricardo A., (1990), *El pequeño agricultor en Honduras: situación y perspectivas de desarrollo*. Instituto de Investigación y Formación Cooperativista & Fundación Friedrich Naumann, Tegucigalpa.

Redclift, Michael, (1987), *Sustainable Development: exploring the contradictions*. Methuen, London.

Redclift, Michael, (1988), Sustainable Development and the Market. A framework for analysis. *Futures* (dec. 1988):635-650.

Redclift, Michael, (1989), The Environmental Consequences of Latin America's Agricultural Development: Some Thoughts on the Brundtland Commission Report. *World Development* 17(3):365-377.

Redclift, Michael & David Goodman, (1991), Introduction. In: M. Redclift & D. Goodman (eds), *Environment and Development in Latin America. The Politics of Sustainability*. Manchester U.P., UK, p.1-23.

Redclift, Nanneke & Sarah Whatmore, (1990), Household, Consumption and Livelihood: Ideologies and Issues in Rural Research. In: Marsden, T., P. Lowe & S. Whatmore (eds), *Rural Restructuring. Global Processes and their Responses*. David Fulton Publ., London, p.182-196.

Reijen, Willem van, (1981), *Filosofie als kritiek. Inleiding in de kritische theorie*. Samsom, Alphen aan den Rijn.

Repetto, Robert, (1989), Economic Incentives for Sustainable Production. In: G. Schramm & J.J. Warford (eds), *Environmental Management and Economic Development*. Johns Hopkins U.P., Baltimore, p.69-86.

Reyes, Felipe, (1927), *Anotaciones sobre el cultivo de café*. Tipografia Nacional, Tegucigalpa.

Richards, Michael, (1988), Final Progress Report: Michael Richards, INA, Honduras 1986-1988. Mimeo, Tegucigalpa.

Richards, Michael, (1997), Alternative Approaches and Problems in Protected Area Management and Forest Conservation in Honduras. In: J. de Groot & R. Ruben (eds), *Sustainable Agriculture in Central America*. MacMillan, Basingstoke, p.142-156.

Richards, Paul, (1985), *Indigenous Agricultural Revolution*. Unwin Hyman, London.

Richards, Paul, (1989), Agriculture as a Performance. In: R. Chambers, A. Pacey & L.A. Thrupp (eds), *Farmer First. Farmer Innovation and Agricultural Research*. Intermediate Technology Publications, London, p.39-43.

Richards, Paul, (1993), Natural Symbols and Natural History. Chimpanzees, Elephants and Experiments in Mende Thought. In: Milton, Kay (ed.), *Environmentalism. The View from Anthropology*. Routledge, London, p.144-159.

Robleda, Roberto, (1982), Latifundio, Reforma Agraria y Modernización. *Economía Política* 21:5-34.

Roquas, Esther, (1994), *Las petateras producen más que artesanía. La economía del tule y del petate*. Documentos de Trabajo No. 8, POSCAE-UNAH, Tegucigalpa.

Roquas, Esther, (1995), Gender, Agrarian Property and the Politics of Inheritance in Honduras. In: Agrarian Questions Organising Committee (ed.), *Agrarian Questions: the Politics of Farming anno 1995: proceedings*. Wageningen Agricultural University, Wageningen, p.1383-1406.

Rosa, J.M. Tobías, (1929), Datos geográficos e históricos del departamento de Santa Bárbara (publicado el año de 1902 y hoy corregidos y aumentados por su autor). *Revista del Archivo y Biblioteca Nacionales* 8(4):228-238.

Ruben, Raúl, (1989), Notas sobre la cuestión agraria en Honduras. Mimeo, Consultorías para el Desarrollo Rural en Centroamérica y el Caribe - VU Amsterdam, San José, Costa Rica, 57p.

Ruben, Ruerd, (1997), *Making Cooperatives Work. Contract Choice and Resource Management within Land Reform Cooperatives in Honduras*. PhD dissertation, Free University Amsterdam.

Ruben, Raúl & Francisco Fúnez, (1993), *La compra-venta de tierras de la Reforma Agraria*. Guaymuras, Tegucigalpa.

Ruhl, J. Mark, (1984), Agrarian Structure and Political Stability in Honduras. *Journal of Interamerican Studies and World Affairs* 26(1):33-68.

Ruhl, J. Mark, (1985), The Honduran Agrarian Reform under Suazo Córdova, 1982-85; An Assessment. *Inter-American Economic Affairs* 39(2):63-80.

Ruiz, J.T & R. Triminio, (1943), Daniel Rápalo Bográn. In: *Apuntes biográficos hondureños e informaciones para el turista*. Imp. Hernández, Tegucigalpa, p.110-111.

Ruthenberg, Hans, (1980), *Farming Systems in the Tropics*. Clarendon Press, Oxford, (3th ed.).

Salgado, Ramón, (1987), El Proyecto de Titulación de Tierras en Honduras. *Cuadernos de Realidad Nacional* 1:36-41 (Tegucigalpa, Dept. de Ciencias Sociales, UNAH).

Salgado, Ramón, (1991), Observaciones sobre la situación actual del sector agrícola de Honduras. *Puntos de Vista* 4:45-55 (Revista de análisis político-social, CEUG-UNAH/CEDOH, Tegucigalpa).

Salgado, R., P. Jiménez, H. Chávez, H. Noé Pino, J. Melmed-Sanjak, A.L. Restrepo, & A. Thorpe, (1994), *El Mercado de Tierras en Honduras*. CEDOH, Tegucigalpa, Honduras

Santos de Morais, Clodomir, (n.d.), *El Modelo Hondureño de Desarrollo Agrario*. PROCARRA, Tegucigalpa.

Sauer, Carl O., (1956), The Agency of Man on the Earth. In: W.L. Thomas (ed.), *Man's Role in Changing the Face of the Earth*. The University of Chicago Press, Chicago, p.49-69.

Sayer, Andrew, (1992), *Method in Social Science: a Realist Approach*. Routledge, London (2nd ed.).

Sayer, Andrew, (1993), Postmodernist Thought in Geography: a Realist View. *Antipode* 25(4):320-344.

Schrader, Ted, (1990), *Milieukunde en ontwikkeling. Milieuproblemen in de derde wereld en de samenwerking tussen vakgebieden*. Leiden Development Studies No.10, Leiden.

Schuurman, Frans, (1996), Post-impasse ontwikkelingstheorieën: Deel II. *Derde Wereld* 14(4):370-395.

Scott, James C., (1985), *Weapons of the Weak. Everyday Forms of Peasant Resistance*. Yale University Press, New Haven.

Sears, Paul B., (1953), An Ecological View of Land-Use in Middle America. *Ceiba* 3(3):157-165.

SECPLAN/DESFIL/USAID, (1989a), *Perfil Ambiental de Honduras 1989*. Tegucigalpa.

SECPLAN, (1989b), *Evaluación pre-terminal del Proyecto de Desarrollo Integrado de Santa Bárbara (1984-1988)*. SECPLAN, Unidad de Planificación Departamental de Santa Bárbara, Honduras.

SECPLAN (Honduras, Secretaría de Planificación, Coordinación y Presupuesto), (1994), *IV Censo Nacional Agropecuario 1993*. Graficentro Editores, Tegucigalpa, Honduras.

Semple, Arthur T., (1963), Soil Conservation: Who is Responsible? In: *Central America and Mexico. Soil Conservation in the Pacific*. Tenth Pacific Science Congress Series. University of Hawaii Press.

Shaner, W.W., P.F. Philipp & W.R. Schmehl, (1982), *Farming Systems Research and Development: Guidelines for Developing Countries*. Westview Press, Boulder.

Shiva, Vandana, (1988), *Staying Alive: Women, Ecology and Development*. Zed, London.

Sieder, Rachel, (1995), Honduras: The Politics of Exception and Military Reformism (1972-1978). *Journal of Latin American Studies* 27(1):99-127.

Siméon, Rémi, (1977 [1885]), *Diccionario de la lengua Nahuatl o Mexicana*. Siglo XXI, México.

267

Slutzky, Daniel & Esther Alonso, (1980), *Empresas transnacionales y agricultura: el caso del enclave bananero en Honduras*. Editorial Universitaria, Tegucigalpa.

Smith, K., (1994), *The Human Farm. A Tale of Changing Lives and Changing Lands*. Kumarian Press, West Hartford, Connecticut.

Smith, Sheldon & Ed Reeves, (1989), Introduction. In: S. Smith and E. Reeves (eds), *Human Systems Ecology: Studies in the Integration of Political Economy, Adaptation, and Socionatural Regions*. Westview, Boulder, p.1-18.

Soulé, Michael E., (1995), The Social Siege of Nature. In: M.E. Soulé & G. Lease (eds), *Reinventing Nature?: Responses to Postmodern Deconstruction*. Island Press, Washington, p.137-170.

Spaargaren, Gert, (1997), *The Ecological Modernization of Production and Consumption: essays in environmental sociology*. PhD dissertation, Wageningen Agricultural University.

Spaargaren, Gert & Arthur Mol, (1992), Sociology, Environment, and Modernity: Ecological Modernization as a Theory of Social Change. *Society and Natural Resources* 3:323-344.

Spalding, Karen, (1980), Class Structures in the Southern Peruvian Highlands, 1750-1920. In: B.S. Orlove & G. Custred (eds), *Land and Power in Latin America: Agrarian Economies and Social Processes in the Andes*. Holmes and Meier Publishers, New York, p.79-97.

Squier, E.G., (1856), *Apuntamientos sobre Centro-América, particularmente sobre los estados de Honduras y San Salvador: su jeografía, topografía, clima, población, riqueza, producciones tec. y el propuesto camino de hierro*. Paris, (translation of: Notes on Central America. Harper and Bros, New York, 1855).

SRN (Secretaría de Recursos Naturales), (n.d.), Agenda Ambiental de Honduras. Documento Preliminar. Internal preparatory document for the UNCED conference in Rio de Janeiro, Brazil, 1992. SRN, Tegucigalpa.

SRN, (1996), *Compendio Estadístico Agropecuario*. Secretaría de Recursos Naturales, Unidad de Planeamiento y Evaluación de Gestión, Tegucigalpa.

Staal, Frits, (1989), *De zinloosheid van het ritueel. Zin en onzin in filosofie, religie en wetenschap*. Meulenhoff, Amsterdam, p.295-321 (2nd ed.).

Stanfield, David, (1989), La tierra vista como un recurso económico: el mercado de tierra y las fincas familiares. Paper para un seminario sobre Políticas Agrarias, Tegucigalpa.

Stanfield, David, (1992), Titulación de Tierra: Alternativa a la Reforma Agraria en un Contexto de Ajuste Estructural. In: Noé Pino H. & A. Thorpe (eds), *Honduras: el ajuste estructural y la reforma agraria*. CEDOH-POSCAE, Tegucigalpa, p.181-206.

Stanfield, D., E. Nesman, M. Seligson & A. Coles, (1990), *The Honduras Land Titling and Registration Experience*. The Land Tenure Center, University of Wisconsin, Madison.

Stanfield, D., R. Zeledón, S. Moquete, A. Coles, M. Fandiño, L, Caballero & R. Stringer, (1986), *Land Titling in Honduras: a Midpoint Evaluation of the Small Farmer Titling Project in Honduras*. The Land Tenure Center, University of Wisconsin, Madison.

Stanley, Denise, (1990a), Capitalist agriculture and differentiation in Southern Honduras. Unpublished paper Rural Sociology 619, Department of Agricultural Economics, University of Wisconsin, Madison.

Stanley, Denise, (1990b), Development Processes and Deforestation in Southern Honduras: Reflections on the Shrimp Farming Debate. Unpublished paper CALS Interdisciplinary Seminar 375, Land Tenure Center, University of Wisconsin, Madison.

Steenhuijsen Piters, Bart de, (1995), *Diversity of Fields and Farmers. Explaining Yield Variations in Northern Cameroon*. PhD dissertation, Wageningen Agricultural University.

Steensberg, Axel, (1993), *Fire-Clearance Husbandry*. Poul Kristensen, Herning, Denmark.

Stewart, Omer C., (1956), Fire as the First Great Force Employed by Man. In: W.L. Thomas (ed.), *Man's Role in Changing the Face of the Earth*. The University of Chicago Press, Chicago, p.115-133.

Stokes, William S., (1947), The Land Laws of Honduras. *Agricultural History* 21:148-154.

Stokes, William S., (1966), Honduras: Problems and Prospects. *Current History* 21:22-26 and 51-52.

Stone, Lucy, (1990), The Peasant Movement in Honduras (1960-1990): Division and Fragmentation. Thesis, Institute of Latin American Studies, La Trobe University.

Stonich, Susan C., (1989), The Dynamics of Social Processes and Environmental Destruction: A Central American Case Study. *Population and Development Review* 15(2):269-296.

Stonich, Susan C., (1991a), The Political Economy of Environmental Destruction: Food Security in Southern Honduras. In: S. Whiteford & A.E. Ferguson (eds), *Harvest of Want. Hunger and Food Security in Central America and Mexico*. Westview Press, Boulder, p.45-74.

Stonich, Susan C., (1991b), The Promotion of Non-Traditional Agricultural Exports in Honduras: Issues of Equity, Environment and Natural Resource Management. *Development and Change* 22(4):725-755.

Stonich, Susan C., (1992), Struggling with Honduran Poverty: The Environmental Consequences of Natural Resource-Based Development and Rural Transformations. *World Development* 20(3):385-399.

Stonich, Susan C., (1993), *"I Am Destroying the Land!" The Political Ecology of Poverty and Environmental Degradation in Honduras*. Westview Press, Boulder.

Stonich, S.C. & DeWalt, B.R., (1989), The Political Economy of Agricultural Growth and Rural Transformation in Honduras and Mexico. In: S. Smith and E. Reeves (eds), *Human Systems Ecology: Studies in the Integration of Political Economy, Adaptation, and Socionatural Regions*. Westview, Boulder, p.202-230.

Strasma, John D. & Rafael Celis, (1992), Land Taxation, the Poor, and Sustainable Development. In: S. Annis (ed.), *Poverty, Natural Resources and Public Policy in Central America*. Transactions Publishers, New Brunswick and Oxford, p.143-169.

Stringer, Randy, (1989), Honduras: Toward Conflict and Agrarian Reform. In: W.C. Thiesenhusen (ed.), *Searching for Agrarian Reform in Latin America*. Boston, Unwin Hyman, p.358-383.

Stürzinger, Ueli & Benjamín Bustamante, (1997), *La Distribución de Tareas entre Hombres y Mujeres en el Area Rural*. Intercooperation/PROASEL, Tegucigalpa.

Taussig, Michael T., (1980), *The Devil and Commodity Fetishism in South America*. The University of North Carolina Press, Chapel Hill.

Tax, Sol, (1953), *Penny Capitalism. A Guatemalan Indian Economy*. Smithsonian Institution, Institute of Social Anthropology Publication, no.16, Washington.

Thompson, Paul, (1989), *The Nature of Work. An Introduction to Debates on the Labour Process*. MacMillan, London.

Thompson, Marc, (1992), The effect of stone retention walls on soil productivity and crop performance on selected hillside farms in Southern Honduras. Mimeo, Tropsoils, Texas A&M University.

Thompson, Michael & Michael Warburton, (1985), Decision making under contradictory certainties: how to save the Himalayas when you can't find out what's wrong with them. *Journal of Applied Systems Analysis* 12:3-34.

Thompson, M. & M. Warburton, (1988), Uncertainty on a Himalayan Scale. In: J. Ives & D.C. Pitt (eds), *Deforestation: Social Dynamics in Watersheds and Mountain Ecosystems*. Routledge, London, p.1-53.

Thorpe, Andy, (1991), *"America Central no pude tener democracia con hambre": Las politicas de la reforma agraria en Honduras antes de 1982*. Documento de trabajo No.3, POSCAE-UNAH, Tegucigalpa.

Thorpe, Andy, (1995a), Agricultural Modernisation and its Consequences for Land Markets in Honduras. In: Agrarian Questions Organising Committee (ed.), *Agrarian Questions: the Politics of Farming anno 1995: proceedings*. Wageningen Agricultural University, Wageningen, p.1673-1696.

Thorpe, Andy, (1995b), Adjusting to Reality: The Impact of Structural Adjustment on Honduran Agriculture. In: J. Weeks (ed.), *Structural Adjustement and the Agricultural Sector in Latin America and the Caribbean*. MacMillan, London, p.205-228.

Thrupp, Lori Ann, (1989), Legitimizing Local Knowledge: From Displacement To Empowerment For Third World People. *Agriculture and Human Values* 6(3):13-24.

Thurston, David, (1992), *Sustainable Practices of Plant Disease Management in Traditional Farming Systems*. Westview, Boulder.

Tiffen, Mary, Michael Mortimore, & Francis Gichuki, (1994), *Population Growth and Environmental Recovery: Policy Lessons from Kenya*. Gatekeeper Series No.45, IIED, London.

Toledo, Victor M., (1991), Pátzcuaro's Lesson: Nature, Production, and Culture in an Indigenous Region of México. In: M.L. Oldfield & J.B. Alcorn (eds), *Biodiversity: Culture, Conservation, and Ecodevelopment*. Westview Press, Boulder, p.147-171.

Torres Adrián, Mario J., (1985), *Familia, trabajo y reproducción social. Campesinos en Honduras*. PISPAL/El Colegio de México.

Tracy, Frederick C. & J. Ricardo Pérez Munguía, (1987), *Manual práctico de conservación de suelos*. Proyecto Manejo de Recursos Naturales. Tegucigalpa.

Turner II, B.L & W.B. Meyer, (1993), Environmental Change: The Human Factor. In: G. Likens & W. Cronon (eds), *Humans as Components of Ecosystems*. Springer-Verlag, New York-Berlin, p.40-50.

Turner II, B.L. & Charles H. Miksicek, (1984), Economic Plant Species Associated with Prehistoric Agriculture in the Maya Lowlands. *Economic Botany* 38(2):179-193.

USAID-Honduras, (1990), *Agricultural Sector Strategy Paper*. USAID, Office of Agriculture and Rural Development, Tegucigalpa, Honduras.

Valdés P., Antonio, (1994), Economic Analysis of Soil Conservation in Honduras. In: E. Lutz, S. Pagiola & C. Reiche (eds), *Economic and Institutional Analysis of Soil Conservation Projects in Central America and the Caribbean*. World Bank environment paper no.8, Washington, p.63-73.

Vallejo, Antonio R., (1888), *Censo general de la República de Honduras, 1887*. Tegucigalpa.

Vallejo, Antonio R., (1911), *Guía de agrimensores o sea recopilación de leyes agrarias*. Tegucigalpa.

Vargas, Gilbert, (1992), Estudio del uso actual y capacidad de uso de la tierra en América Central. *Anuario de Estudios Centroamericanos*, Universidad de Costa Rica, 18(2):7-23.

Velasquez Lambur, Rosa Melida, (1990), *AHPROCAFE, su historia*. Asociación Hondureña de Productores de Café, Tegucigalpa, Honduras.

Velsen, J. van, (1967), The Extended-Case Method and Situational Analysis. In: A.L. Epstein (ed.), *The Craft of Anthropology*. Tavistock, London, p.129-149.

Villanueva, Benjamin, (1968), *The Role of Institutional Innovations in Economic Development of Honduras*. PhD dissertation, University of Wisconsin.

Vinelli, Paul, (1986), General Characteristics of the Honduran Economy. In: M.B. Rosenberg & P.L. Shepherd (eds), *Honduras confronts its future. Contending Perspectives on Critical Issues*. Lynne Rienner, Boulder, Colorado, p.97-110.

Wachter, Daniel, (1992), Die Bedeutung des Landtitelbesitzes für eine nachhaltige landwirtschaftliche Bodennutzung. Eine empirische Fallstudie in Honduras. *Geografische Zeitschrift* 80(3):174-183.

Wachter, Daniel, (1994), Land Titling: Possible Contributions to Farmland Conservation in Central America. In: E. Lutz, S. Pagiola & C Reiche (eds), *Economic and Institutional Analysis of Soil Conservation Projects in Central America and the Caribbean*. World Bank environment paper no.8, Washington, p.150-156.

Wachter, Daniel, (1995), Landbesitzunsicherheit - Bedeutung für die Bodendegradation in Entwicklungsländern. *Geografica Helvetica* 50(1):29-34.

Walker, Ian, Jenny Suazo, Alison Thomas & Herold Jean-Pois, (1993), El impacto de las políticas de ajuste estructural sobre el medio ambiente en Honduras. Mimeo, Postgrado Centroamericano en Economía y Plancificación del Desarrollo, UNAH, Tegucigalpa.

Warren, D. Michael, (1991), *Using Indigenous Knowledge in Agricultural Development*. World Bank Discussion Papers no.126, The World Bank, Washington.

Warren, D.M, L.J. Slikkerveer & D. Brokensha (eds), (1995), *The Cultural Dimension of Development: Indigenous Knowledge Systems*. Intermediate Technology Publications, London.

Watters, R.F., (1971), *Shifting Cultivation in Latin America*. FAO, Rome.

Watts, Michael, (1983), *Silent Violence. Food, Famine and Peasantry in Northern Nigeria*. University of California Press, Berkeley.

Watts, Michael & Richard Peet, (1996), Conclusion: Towards a Theory of Liberation Ecology. In: R. Peet & M. Watts (eds), *Liberation Ecologies: Environment, Development, Social Movements*. Routledge, London, p.260-269.

Webster, C.C. & P.N. Wilson, (1980), *Agriculture in the Tropics*. Longman, London (2nd ed.).

Weeks, John M. & Nancy J. Black, (1991), Mercedarian Missionaries and the Transformation of Lenca Indian Society in Western Honduras, 1550-1700. In: D. Hurst Thomas (ed), *Columbian Consequences: vol. 3, The Spanish Borderlands in Pan-American Perspective*. Smithsonian Institution Press, Washington, D.C., p.245-261.

Weeks, J.M., Black, N. & J.S. Speaker, (1987), From Prehistory to History in Western Honduras: The Care Lenca in the Colonial Province of Tencoa. In: E.J. Robinson (ed.), *Interaction on the Southeast Mesoamerican Frontier: Prehistoric and Historic Honduras and El Salvador*. BAR International Series 327 (i), BAR, Oxford, p.65-94.

Weinberg, Bill, (1991), *War on the Land. Ecology and Politics in Central America*. Zed, London.

Weischet, Wolfgang & Cesar N. Caviedes, (1993), *The Persisting Ecological Constraints of Tropical Agriculture*. Longman, Harlow.

Wells, William V., (1982 [1857]), *Exploraciones y Aventuras en Honduras*. Educa, San José, Costa Rica.

Whatmore, Sarah, (1994), Farm Household Strategies and Styles of Farming: Assessing the Utility of Farm Typologies. In: J.D. Ploeg & A. Long (eds), *Born From Within. Practice and Perspectives of Endogenous Rural Development*. Van Gorcum, Assen, p.31-37.

Whatmore, Sarah, Richard Munton, Jo Little & Terry Marsden, (1987a), Towards a Typology of Farm Business in Contemporary British Agriculture. *Sociologia Ruralis* 27(1):21-37.

Whatmore, Sarah, Richard Munton, Terry Marsden & Jo Little, (1987b), Interpreting a Relational Typology of Farm Business in Southern England. *Sociologia Ruralis* 27(2/3):103-122.

Whitaker, M.J., (1989), Normas de Manipulación y Uso de Paraquat por los Pequeños Productores de Maíz en Centroamérica. *Turrialba* 39(2):260-274.

White, Robert A., (1978), Prestación de Servicios Públicos en el Sector Agropecuario. Reprinted in: Ministerio de RRNN, CONSUPLANE, AID (eds), *Compilación de los estudios básicos del diagnóstico del sector agricola, Tomo II.* Tegucigalpa. p.175-363.

Wilken, Gene C., (1987), *Good Farmers. Traditional Agricultural Resource Management in Mexico and Central America.* University of California Press, Berkeley.

Williams, Louis O., (1981), The Useful Plants of Central America. *Ceiba* 24(1/2/3/4):1-381.

Williams, Robert G., (1986), *Export Agriculture and the Crisis in Central America.* University of North Carolina Press, Chapel Hill.

Williams, Robert G., (1994), *States and Social Evolution: Coffee and the Rise of National Governments in Central America.* The University of North Carolina Press, Chapel Hill.

Wolf, Eric. R., (1966), Kinship, Friendship, and Patron-Client Relations in Complex Societies. In: Banton, (M.) (ed.), *The Social Anthropology of Complex Societies.* Tavistock Publications, London.

Wolf, Eric, (1972), Ownership and Political Ecology. *Anthropological Quaterly* 45(3):201-205.

Wolf, Eric R., (1982), *Europe and the People Without History.* University of California, Berkeley.

World Bank, (1983), *Honduras. An Inquiry into Rural Population, Small Farmers and Agrarian Reform.* Report No. 3963-HO. Country Programs Department I, Latin America and the Carribean.

Worster, Donald, (1993), *The Wealth of Nature. Environmental History and the Ecological Imagination.* Oxford U.P., Oxford.

Wrigley, Gordon, (1988), *Coffee.* Longman, Harlow.

Yearly, Steven, (1996), *Sociology, Environmentalism, Globalization: Reinventing the Globe.* Sage, London.

Zamora, Roy, (1994), Sistemas de Producción Campesina y Cambio Ecológico: Analysis de Suelos. Unpublished project document. POSCAE, Tegucigalpa.

Zimmerer, Karl S., (1993a), Soil Erosion and Labor Shortages in the Andes With Special Reference to Bolivia, 1953-1991: Implications for "Conservation-With-Development". *World Development* 21(10):1659-1675.

Zimmerer, Karl S., (1993b), Soil Erosion and Social (Dis)courses in Cochabamba, Bolivia: Perceiving the Nature of Environmental Degradation. *Economic Geography* 69(4):312-327.

Zúniga Andrade, Edgardo, (1990), *Las modalidades de la lluvia en Honduras.* Guaymuras, Tegucigalpa.

271

About the author

Kees (C.E.P.) Jansen (born in Bemmel, the Netherlands, in 1961) attended the 'Aloysius College' in Den Haag, and graduated at the Wageningen Agricultural University with majors in tropical agronomy and sociology of rural development. He was a research assistant at the department of Tropical Crop Husbandry and staff member at the department of *Studium Generale* (Wageningen Agricultural University, 1990-1992). Subsequently he completed research fellowships at the department of Sociology of Rural Development with grants from the European Union and the Netherlands Foundation for the Advancement of Tropical Research (WOTRO). He was visiting researcher at the 'Postgrado en Economía y Planificación del Desarrollo' (UNAH) in Tegucigalpa, Honduras. He co-organized the congress 'Agrarian Questions: the Politics of Farming anno 1995' in Wageningen in May 1995.

Kees carried out fieldwork in Peru (1984-1985) and Honduras (1992-1994, 1997). His publications in the fields of rural development, sociology of land use, ecological anthropology, and sociology of agricultural science include: (with E. Roquas) 'Modernizing Insecurity: the Land Titling Project in Honduras', *Development and Change*, 29:81-106, (1998); 'Ecological Dilemmas of Coffee Exports and Local Food Production in North-West Honduras', *European Review of Latin American and Caribbean Studies* 60:7-30, (1996); and (with R. Brouwer) 'Critical Introductory Notes on Farming Systems Research in Developing Third World Agriculture', *Systems Practice* 2(4):379-395, (1989).

He currently is a research fellow at the Department of Gender Studies in Agriculture and at the Working Group of Technology and Agrarian Development, both at the Wageningen Agricultural University. His research interests deal with risk and the political ecology of conversion to sustainable pest control methods, and comparative analysis of gender, livelihood, and labour process issues in Western and non-Western ecological agriculture.

Samenvatting

(Summary in Dutch)

Politieke Ecologie, Berglandbouw en Kennis in Honduras
Kees Jansen

In het dorpje El Zapote in Honduras wordt landbouw bedreven op erosiegevoelige hellingen. De boeren telen er maïs en bonen voor eigen consumptie. Een deel van hen verdient daarnaast een inkomen met de verbouw van koffie en tule. Van de tule maken vrouwen slaapmatten die op de nationale markt terecht komen. Op bijna de helft van het landbouwareaal graast vee. Veel boerenfamilies zijn arm, analfabeet, en de kinderen lijden aan ondervoeding. Sommige boeren daarentegen verdienen goed met hun landbouwbedrijf en kunnen het zich veroorloven om zelf niet meer op de velden te werken maar de benodigde arbeid in te huren. Verschillen in sociale positie dragen bij aan de diversiteit in de landbouw. De verschillende vormen van landbouw hebben op hun beurt weer uiteenlopende effecten op de natuurlijke hulpbronnen.

Dit boek opent met een serie uiteenlopende opvattingen van boeren over de oorzaken van milieudegradatie: een eerste indicatie voor het bestaan van contrasterende meningen over hoe en waarom degradatie blijft optreden. Ze wijzen op een verwevenheid van menselijke en natuurlijke factoren, van direct observeerbare fenomenen en achterliggende oorzaken, en van individueel menselijk handelen en sociale instituties. Deze interpretaties van boeren bevatten elementen die we terug kunnen vinden in verklaringen van milieudegradatie die worden gehanteerd in beleidskringen en wetenschappelijke studies. De volgende verklaringen komen in de loop van het boek aan de orde: de onwetendheid van boeren, overbevolking, gebrek aan economische groei, de specifieke vorm van kapitaalsaccumulatie, falende autoriteiten, onduidelijke eigendomsverhoudingen, gebrek aan wetenschappelijke kennis, en het niet serieus nemen van boerenkennis. Het doel van dit boek is om deze verschillende verklaringen te onderzoeken aan de hand van een gevalstudie.

Het onderzoek is gebaseerd op een tweejarig verblijf in El Zapote, een dorp met 450 huishoudens. Via kwalitatieve en kwantitatieve methoden werden de gegevens verkregen die zijn verwerkt in een analyse van de historie van landverdeling, de eigendomsverhoudingen, de natuurlijke omgeving, de belangrijkste productiesystemen, de verschillende percepties van milieudegradatie, de arbeidsverhoudingen en de relaties tussen lokale en externe kennis. Deze diepte-studie biedt niet alleen een beter inzicht in de specifieke relaties tussen agrarische verandering en milieudegradatie in de bergstreken van Honduras, maar leidt ook tot een heroverweging van sociale theorieën over milieudegradatie in de landbouw.

Een centraal theoretisch probleem is hoe we de relaties tussen landbouwproduktie, sociale verhoudingen, en natuurlijke hulpbronnen kunnen benaderen. Ik bespreek dit probleem door in te gaan op benaderingen die een zogenaamd 'functioneel dualisme' in de agrarische structuur waarnemen en hieruit de specifieke vormen van milieudegradatie afleiden. In dit model is er een kapitalistische sector die de betere gronden controleert en met behulp van intensieve landbouw snel hoge winsten genereert, met name door zich te richten op exportproducten. De vervuiling door bestrijdingsmiddelen zou het voornaamste effect op het milieu zijn in deze sector. De sector wordt in stand gehouden door een leger van zogenaamde 'semi-proletariërs'. Zij worden voorgesteld als kleine boeren die net genoeg toegang tot land hebben om niet dood te gaan, maar niet genoeg om behoorlijk van te kunnen leven. Doordat ze een deel van hun voedsel zelf produceren kunnen de lonen laag blijven. Daarom kunnen ze als goedkope arbeidskrachten fungeren op de kapitalistische bedrijven. Deze boerenfamilies bewerken meestal de marginale gronden, bijvoorbeeld de berghellingen, en hun teeltmethoden leiden noodgedwongen tot bodemdegradatie en erosie. Deze interpretatie van het functioneel dualisme gaat uit van een lineaire relatie tussen sociale structuren en milieudegradatie.

Bij nadere beschouwing blijkt dit model echter belangrijke tekortkomingen te vertonen. De landverdeling van El Zapote weerspiegelt niet eenduidig het beeld van grote bedrijven op de vruchtbare gronden en kleine bedrijven op de berghellingen. Het model relateert daarnaast op een te simpele wijze bedrijfsgrootte aan arbeidsrelaties. Kleinere bedrijven kunnen arbeidsintensief en op de export gericht zijn, terwijl grotere bedrijven soms alleen voor de consumptie in het huishouden produceren op basis van familiearbeid. Tevens is de relatie met het milieugebruik veel complexer. Semi-proletariërs kunnen er lustig op los spuiten met bestrijdingsmiddelen omdat ze geen tijd hebben om handmatig te wieden, terwijl grotere boeren over tijd en kapitaal beschikken om te investeren in meer milieuvriendelijke productiemethoden, of anderzijds juist over genoeg invloed beschikken om zonder repercussies te ontbossen rondom belangrijke drinkwaterbronnen om daar koffie aan te planten. De verschillende hoofdstukken tonen aan dat landverdeling, technologiegebruik en arbeidsrelaties niet te begrijpen zijn vanuit de dualistische categorieën van het functioneel dualisme model. In plaats van lineaire relaties vinden we diversiteit.

Desalniettemin beargumenteer ik dat de diversiteit van landbouwpraktijken niet enkel is terug te voeren op toevallige individuele handelingen van geïnformeerde en kundige actoren. Het feit dat er empirische diversiteit bestaat, betekent nog niet dat er geen sociale structuren zijn die het gedrag van actoren, buiten hun directe wil om, beperken of juist mogelijk maken. Het problematische karakter van het functioneel dualisme model ligt dan ook niet zozeer in het feit dat de empirie niet overeenstemt met de veronderstelde toestand, maar vooral hierin dat landbouwpraktijken en milieu-effecten worden gereduceerd tot *één enkele* structuur van productieverhoudingen tussen kapitalistische bedrijven en semi-proletariërs. In een alternatieve benadering onderzoek ik welke andere processen of structuren het landgebruik vorm geven.

De studie gaat uitvoerig in op de geschiedenis van landverdeling en constateert dat het zogenaamde *ejido* systeem tot halverwege deze eeuw de kleine boer van een relatief goedkope toegang tot land verzekerde. Gedurende deze eeuw nam de druk op land echter toe. De bevolkingsgroei speelt daarbij een rol, maar dient te worden gerelateerd aan de wijze van landverdeling. Vanaf de jaren vijftig versterkt de veeteeltsector zich en enkele personen weten zich grote stukken land toe te eigenen. De zogenaamde 'vrije gronden' verdwijnen en veel armere families zijn aangewezen op de laatste stukjes gemeenschapsgrond van slechte kwaliteit. De druk op land binnen de gemeentegrenzen varieert dan ook sterk. In dezelfde tijd veranderen ook allerlei productietechnieken: de braak in de maïsteelt wordt verkort of verdwijnt, vee loopt niet meer los rond maar op omheinde weilanden, rotatiesystemen veranderen, grasland wordt voortaan gezaaid, en sommige gewassen verdwijnen. Vanaf eind jaren zeventig zet zich een intensivering en uitbreiding van de koffieteelt in. Zowel in de maïsteelt als in de koffie komt het gebruik van bestrijdingsmiddelen in zwang.

De boeren in El Zapote signaleren een aantal belangrijke milieuproblemen. Ten eerste heeft het verdwijnen van de braak negatieve gevolgen opgeleverd. Naast bodemvruchtbaarheidsproblemen zorgt dit voor een toenemend onkruidprobleem, met name door nieuwe grassoorten die zijn geïntroduceerd voor de veeteelt. Boeren blijken hele andere oplossingen te zoeken dan de officiële benadering van dit probleem voorschrijft. Ten tweede zien boeren zich geconfronteerd met het probleem van branden. De veranderende omstandigheden nopen boeren tot het heroverwegen van het nut van deze techniek om het veld schoon te maken voor het zaaien. Ten derde constateren zij dat ontbossing het microklimaat beïnvloedt. Het gevolg is dat belangrijke drinkwaterbronnen opdrogen gedurende de droge tijd van het jaar. Ten vierde wijzen boeren en landarbeiders op de gezondheidsrisico's die het gebruik van bestrijdingsmiddelen met zich meebrengt.

Deze praktijken en percepties worden in hoofdstuk vier en vijf gerelateerd aan sociale relaties. De problemen die voortkomen uit een afnemende braak kunnen bijvoorbeeld worden opgevangen door kunstmest of land te kopen en de braak te herintroduceren in het rotatiesysteem. Hoe dit gebeurt hangt samen met processen van sociale differentiatie. Een andere voorbeeld vormen de risico's bij het gebruik van bestrijdingsmiddelen. Deze worden veelal afgewenteld op de arbeiders die boeren inhuren om, zonder enige bescherming van het lichaam, te spuiten. Hoofdstuk vijf behandelt de vaak subtiele maar cruciale verschillen tussen producenten en tussen producenten onderling en ingehuurde arbeiders.

Hoofdstuk zes bespreekt twee visies over kennis als veroorzaker van het milieuprobleem. Sommigen wijzen naar de onkunde van boeren en dragen nieuwe moderne kennis en technologie aan om een vermeend gebrek aan kennis op te vullen. Anderen vinden dat juist de moderne wetenschappelijke rationaliteit de niet-harmonieuze interactie met de natuur veroorzaakt. Hoofdstuk zes bespreekt verschillende argumenten om beide visies te kritiseren. De oorsprong van kennis is niet altijd te achterhalen. Via migratie of externe handel bijvoorbeeld is er altijd al kennis in het dorp geïntroduceerd. Het lokale of niet-lokale van kennis zegt weinig over de praktische bruikbaarheid van die kennis. Lokale kennis heeft niet altijd het antwoord op milieuproblemen en is niet per se goed voor het milieu. De 'lokale kennis'-benadering heeft in het algemeen te weinig oog voor de ongelijke verdeling van kennis en de strijd om kennis tussen producenten. De dichotomie tussen lokale en wetenschappelijke kennis leidt vaak tot 'overculturalisering'. De overlap tussen lokale en wetenschappelijke kennis en van de werelden waaraan beide soorten kennis refereren, wordt dan ontkend. Ondanks het belang ervan is kennis, of gebrek eraan, niet de hoofdoorzaak van milieudegradatie.

Het functioneel dualistisch model reduceert landbouwpraktijken en hun milieu-effecten tot één centrale oorzaak, namelijk de structuur van productieverhoudingen tussen kapitalistische bedrijven en semi-proletariërs. Dit boek pleit voor het loslaten van het mono-causale model. De actuele staat van het milieu wordt beïnvloed door een veelvoud van onderliggende structuren op verschillende niveaus, die specifieke mechanismen genereren in de vorm van noodzakelijke en contingente relaties. Politieke ecologie is een benadering die tracht te breken met het mono-causale model. De politiek-ecologische metafoor van de 'keten van verklaring' past echter niet bij het idee van veelvoudige structuren. Sommige auteurs stellen daarom een verbinding voor met het post-structuralisme. De nadruk komt dan te liggen op de percepties van verschillende actoren ten aanzien van hun sociale en natuurlijke omgeving. Doordat men echter stelt dat er geen waarheid is, geen 'juiste' verklaring, dreigt een relativistische positie, waarin het idee wordt verworpen dat kennis toetsbaar is omdat het is gerelateerd aan iets dat buiten die kennis ligt. Alleen daarom kan de mens praktisch handelen en anticiperen op nieuwe vormen van praktisch handelen.

Op basis van de gepresenteerde gevalstudie en met behulp van inzichten voortkomend uit het kritisch realisme wordt een alternatieve politiek-ecologisch benadering geformuleerd. De eerste uitdaging van zo'n benadering is om materialiteit te incorporeren in theorieën over het arbeidsproces. Hiervoor is een perspectief nodig waarin de combinatie van natuurlijke en sociale condities van de landbouwproductie haar plaats krijgt. Deze condities of beperkingen zijn niet altijd direct observeerbare entiteiten en komen voort uit de gestratificeerde en gedifferentieerde sociale en natuurlijke structuren. Een belangrijk uitgangspunt is om natuur niet te zien als een homogene categorie. De natuur bestaat uit vele dingen en elementen, biofysische processen, energie, enzovoorts. Niet alleen de samenleving maar ook de natuur is gedifferentieerd.

De tweede uitdaging voor een politiek-ecologisch benadering is om kennis over het milieu en contrasterende perspectieven ten aanzien van de milieucrisis helder te theoretiseren. In tegenstelling tot post-structuralistische benaderingen gaat deze studie er van uit dat het wel mogelijk is om op praktisch niveau verschillende verklaringen te testen en een *betere* kennis te ontwikkelen van concrete problemen en de onderliggende structuren van milieudegradatie en het bestaan. De gevalstudie trachtte de *best mogelijke* beschrijving en verklaring te geven over waarom producenten in een fragiel milieu doen wat zij doen, juist door een oordeel te vormen over de verschillende contrasterende percepties en verklaringen.

Ten derde is het de vraag hoe politieke ecologie zal kunnen bijdragen aan het verminderen van de kloof tussen natuurlijke en sociale wetenschappen. Het object van analyse, onze relatie tot de natuur en de oorzaken van milieudegradatie, vereist een methodologie waarin plaats is voor de analyse van de sociale en natuurlijke structuren die

276

ten grondslag liggen aan biofysische processen. Het vereist van sociale wetenschappers minder arrogantie en meer openheid naar het werk van de natuur- en technologische wetenschappen. Hun theorieën zijn niet te reduceren tot enkel culturele noties.

De vierde uitdaging van politieke ecologie ligt op het politieke vlak. De recente aandacht voor de ontwikkeling van de 'civil society' heeft de aandacht afgeleid van de centrale kwestie van de staatsmacht. De meeste huidige pleidooien voor 'ontwikkeling van onderop' via basisorganisaties en niet-gouvernementele organisaties zeggen weinig over het vraagstuk van de organisatie van de staat. Politieke ecologie zal het neoliberale project van decentralisering van de staat en de 'civil society'-benadering theoretisch en politiek van elkaar moeten scheiden. Dit vereist de oplossing van een paradox tussen de staat als deel van een onderdrukkend hegemonisch project en de noodzaak van democratische controle over de wetgevende, juridische en uitvoerende macht. Dit laatste is een vereiste voor elk politiek project dat verandering bepleit van sociale differentiatie en uitbuiting, slechte levensomstandigheden, armoede, ecologische crisis en etnische en gender-conflicten.